Edgar Cayce

A SEER
out of
SEASON

Edgar Cayce
A SEER
out of
SEASON

The Life of History's
Greatest Psychic

HARMON HARTZELL BRO, PH.D.

A.R.E. Press • Virginia Beach • Virginia

To my graduate students, who for nearly half a century have taught me so much with their questions and creations, and to those bold graduate students of the next half century who will try to figure out where seers and open vision belong in our culture.

And to my wife, June.

"The best (including most absorbing) account that has been written about history's best–documented psychic. William James would have liked this book."

Huston Smith,
author of *The World's Religions* and *Forgotten Truth*

Contents

PREFACE

Harmon Hartzell Bro, Ph.D. (1919-1997) was a psychotherapist, an educator, a writer, an ordained minister, and an inspirational lecturer. As a young man, he lived and worked in the Cayce home and witnessed several hundred readings. That experience enabled him to come to know Edgar Cayce better than most individuals who have written about the Cayce legacy. Eventually, Harmon wrote his doctoral dissertation on Cayce's life and work, as well as several books about the Cayce information, including this one, *Edgar Cayce—A Seer Out of Season*.

Harmon first came to Virginia Beach in 1943 as a young minister, just graduated from Divinity School at the University of Chicago. He came to meet Cayce first-hand, as he was both curious and troubled that his mother, Margueritte Harmon Bro, had become involved with Cayce's work. However, what Harmon witnessed in Virginia Beach was very different than anything he might have imagined. An October 1943 letter to his wife, June Avis Bro, expressed his enthusiasm for a work that would transform his own life. That letter stated, in part, the following:

> Thin tubercular women, crippled boys, cancerous workmen, arthritic grandmothers knotted in pain—they all find healing. But that's only the beginning—what really happens to them is what has happened to Mr. and Mrs. Cayce, Gladys Davis [Cayce's secretary] and some others—they find that "there is a river" of God's love flowing about us all, only waiting to be tapped by humble minds. The real miracles at Virginia Beach are the radiant, transformed lives, the people who go away realizing that they can actually find God and

know Jesus and live like it. They say, "I am my brother's keeper" and their lives show it. They say, "There is only one God" and all their friends feel it. Buddhist, Muslim, Jew, Catholic, Mennonite, Christian Scientist, Humanist, Presbyterian—it goes on like the "Ballad for Americans"—they all find what they are searching for in the work of the readings and Mr. Cayce . . .

Harmon and June Bro moved to Virginia Beach and became close friends with the Cayce family and worked as members of the Cayce office staff. At the time, there was a tremendous increase in requests for Cayce's readings as a result of the publication of Cayce's biography, *There Is a River*, by Thomas Sugrue, which was followed by Margueritte Harmon Bro's own article in *Coronet* magazine entitled "Miracle Man of Virginia Beach." Harmon and June listened to hundreds of readings. They had access to all correspondence, and they had the opportunity to repeatedly see how people's lives were changed by the Cayce work.

Harmon became interested in psychology and decided to continue graduate work. He went on to Harvard and then to the University of Chicago where he did a doctoral dissertation based on a study of the Edgar Cayce readings. For this dissertation, he coined the following phrase for Edgar Cayce: "a seer in a seerless culture."

Harmon called the story of Edgar Cayce's life "one of the most challenging and appealing adventure stories of modern times." He went on to explain that the story was about much more than a psychic—much more than he had ever expected when he first came to Virginia Beach as a young man:

. . . to call him a psychic is to call an opera star an athlete of the vocal cords. For Cayce's aid was not simply raw data dumped on frantic seekers, but carefully devised counsel as fraught with values as with information. He spoke not only of organs and tissues and interventions, but of justice and love, and of beauty and holiness, as the context for healing and wholeness. Only a time so impotent for personal and social goodness that it must seize on powers ahead of meaning would be satisfied with labeling him a clairvoyant. To find his visionary yet practical gift, one must remember Judaism's Baal Shem To combining healing with mystical vistas, Melville viewing the world from the bowels of whales, Blake painting fiery creation, Freud finding darkness and light through sexuality, and Jung glimpsing with Plato the starry heavens of archetypes within human deeps.

Cayce was not fascinated with his own prowess, though others often were. Nobody who knew him well could imagine that he went to bed at night and got up in the morning thinking about his trance skills and how to improve them—any more than he focused on his paranormal abilities outside of trance, such as seeing revealing colors (auras) around others, reading minds, conversing with the recently dead, or previewing the future. His concern was not first of all with powers but with relationships. On the one hand he sought to be deeply and helpfully related to the damaged persons that he served. And on the other hand he sought to be related to the divine, which he saw as the ultimate author of his gifts, within the kind of community and tradition that serves such a source. This was a man who lay down and arose with prayer, not as duty or accomplishment, but as a hunger reaching for companionship with God, seeking to be grasped more than to grasp, so that he might create usefully for those who wept with pain.

Harmon's book presents an eyewitness account of

Cayce at work. It draws upon Harmon's personal experiences, as well as upon hundreds of interviews with Cayce's relatives, associates, sufferers seeking aid, and even some disappointed detractors. It presents a story of a man with tremendous gifts, tremendous challenges, and tremendous love for God and the human creation.

When Edgar Cayce died on January 3, 1945, in Virginia Beach, Virginia, he left well over 14,000 documented stenographic records of the telepathic–clairvoyant statements he had given for thousands of people over a period of forty-three years. These documents are referred to as *readings*. In 1931, Cayce founded the Association for Research and Enlightenment (A.R.E.) to research, document, and disseminate his psychic information.

The readings constitute one of the largest and most impressive records of psychic perception ever to emanate from a single individual. Together with their relevant records, correspondence, and reports, they have been cross-indexed under thousands of subject headings and placed at the disposal of psychologists, students, writers, and investigators from around the world.

Today, Edgar Cayce's A.R.E. offers membership benefits and services, a magazine, newsletters, publications, conferences, international tours, an impressive volunteer network, the Cayce/Reilly® School of Massotherapy, a Health Center and Spa, a retreat–type camp for children and adults, prison and prayer outreach programs, and A.R.E. contacts around the world. A.R.E. also maintains an affiliation with Atlantic University, which was founded in 1930 by Cayce and some of his closest supporters (AtlanticUniv.edu).

For additional information about the Edgar Cayce work, contact A.R.E., 215 67th Street, Virginia Beach, VA 23451–2061; call (800) 333–4499; or visit the website EdgarCayce.org.

Kevin J. Todeschi
Executive Director *&* CEO
Edgar Cayce's A.R.E. / Atlantic University

INTRODUCTION
by June Avis Bro

In the spring of 1943, I had no idea that my life and career plans would soon change dramatically. In a few months, I would be married and would leave my master's program in music at the Chicago Musical College where I had a full scholarship. My future mother-in-law, Margueritte Harmon Bro, would be the change agent.

She had been asked to write a review of *There Is a River* by Thomas Sugrue. It was truly amazing that in 1943, this prominent Protestant magazine would ask for a review of Sugrue's book on the life and work of Edgar Cayce and that my future mother-in-law would write it. She was so intrigued that on her next lecture trip to the East Coast, she decided to visit the Cayces. She spent several days with Edgar and Gertrude Cayce and Gladys Davis, Cayce's secretary. I didn't know it then, but my future was hanging in the balance.

It turned out that Edgar Cayce was as intrigued by Margueritte Bro as she was by him. She told him that she and her husband had been educational missionaries in China, and that struck a deep chord in Edgar's soul. He had led youth groups in his church, and his deep desire was to prepare them for the medical missionary field. To add to the excitement, my future mother-in-law and Edgar Cayce discovered that they had grown up in the same church, the Disciples of Christ. You can be sure they had a lot to talk about.

At Edgar's request, my mother-in-law spoke to the missionary society in his church before he lay down in his modest study to give a reading for her. When he did, she was entranced. She had just returned from the Battle Creek Sanitarium in Michigan after a thorough checkup for various ailments. The physical reading Edgar provided was even more detailed than the hospital printout she had been given. She was so thoroughly impressed that she requested and received life readings for the whole family.

She came home all afire with what she had seen and heard. I was deep into studying the piano at the Chicago Musical College and didn't have much time to join in on the conversations. But my fiancé, Harmon, was mesmerized. He couldn't hear enough about Mr. Cayce and his work.

Harmon and I were married in June of 1943, and in the fall came an offer from Mr. Cayce asking Harmon if he would be interested in coming to work for him until his son Hugh Lynn returned from serving in the Army. Hugh Lynn had been managing the Association since the early 1930's and was sorely missed. Harmon decided to go to Virginia Beach for a week to talk with the Cayces about the work that needed to be done.

Harmon came home a changed man! Although he went to Virginia Beach wondering if the Cayces were self-deluded about Edgar's gift, he came home feeling sure that Edgar's gift was truly authentic and that his faith in God was deep and real. Harmon went to Virginia Beach a humanist, believing that the only God that existed was the highest good that humans could accomplish in the world. However, he came home believing that after all he had seen and heard in Edgar's study, there had to be a God Force out there somewhere: an Intelligence, a Transcendent Goodness far greater than the God he had been reducing to human kindness.

I had asked Harmon to write to me about his experiences with the Cayces, and he began on his train ride home. I want to include some of it here, because he mentions this change in his attitude toward God. As I reread this letter, I am amazed all over again that Harmon at the age of 24 could grasp in one week the essence of Cayce's work. This is part of what he wrote:

It's not complicated or difficult, this philosophy.

It's simple and all in the Bible just like that, without esoteric emendation ($.50 please!) Even an ignorant, self-centered fool like me can understand it when it's finally shown to me. I hadn't the faith that you had to believe anything that wasn't shoved right into my puss for observation. Cayce comes along and I can actually see God's will working in men's lives. When it's that plain, even I can at last believe!

But the trouble is that I have been such a sad apple in religion and sometimes vinegar in finances that you doubt my judgment. Then how can I ever persuade you that to work with the Cayces would be the most enriching thing we could possibly do? I can't I fear. But hearing Mr. Cayce give a reading, hearing him tell someone in pain to be kind, loving, patient in a voice of infinite tenderness and gentleness—his readings are so much like what it must have been like to hear Jesus talk, that I'm sort of expecting the Lord God himself to persuade you. If you and I really search for Him in the next few days, I think we'll find our answer, and our way.

We haven't mentioned the advantages to us in going out there. They are like the advantages the disciples had in going off to help Jesus. Nearly anyone on earth would trade places with them now, but at that time they were thought to be crazy. Some of them even lost their lives as well as their friends, family and security. I don't think we will! Mr. Cayce told me enough stories of prayer answered in the work there to convert even an addlepated horse to the idea that God takes care of those who forget themselves in service.

Now mind you, I'm not crazy enough to think that this is the only way, or even the best way, for us to serve God right now. I think we have to go right on in music, and especially you do. If we go out there with some determination, actually there is opportunity to grow a lot more in music than there is in our busy household in Chicago. For that growth has got to come from *within* and not from the dazzling cultural advantages of a big city— when you really get down to it.

Heigh ho, ain't this fun? Don't think this is all sober business. I've laughed till I ached during [these] last few days. These people who live so very sincerely seem just as near to the bubbling fountain of humor as they do to the well of eternal life. Mr. Cayce is just as much fun in his readings as he is out of them. I'll tell you about this when I see you.

I could go on, darling, but it gets me too excited, wondering whether you're going to knock me down or listen skeptically, or be annoyed, or thrilled, or all packed and ready to go—or what? I'll be seeing you in a couple of hours, my little blonde sweetheart. I love the hell out of you, Honey.

Your Hubby, Harm

Yes. I had already started packing!

Harmon had hoped that I would be willing to put aside work on my master's degree and join him on this new leg of our journey together. I loved my husband, and the more we talked, the more I could see this was an opportunity not to be missed. We talked about the changes that would have to be made in our lives.

We decided I could always get back into my master's program. Harmon would have to tell his small weekend pastorate that he would be leaving. He would have to talk to his draft board and ask whether a year researching the work of the Cayces would be acceptable as part of his ministerial training. In actuality, the board approved the research as an appropriate subject for a doctoral dissertation and subsequently deferred him.

Years later when Harmon entered his doctoral program, it was not easy for his professors at the University of Chicago's Divinity School to deal with the subject matter of Harmon's dissertation. His committee changed at least three times. One professor said, "I live in a world where I believe this kind of thing can happen, but I can't remain on this committee." He then walked out. To add to the problem, the university also required Harmon to take a year of post-doctoral work to ensure his methodology was sound. Despite their reservations, they couldn't find a single flaw in his reasoning. When the dissertation was finally completed and accepted, we celebrated and said a heartfelt prayer of thanks to God.

Hugh Lynn Cayce helped with the thesis in every way he could to move it toward completion. He filled in gaps in Harmon's understanding, he told him stories, and he briefed him about the people who had been instrumental in the Association's growth. No one encouraged Harmon more than Hugh Lynn, and no one was more excited at the final approval of the very first doctoral dissertation based on his father's work.

Although for a long time, the medical, theological, and educational arenas largely dismissed the authenticity and helpfulness of Cayce's work, during the forty-four years of our marriage, until Harmon's death in September of 1997, he and I saw a slow but growing acceptance of many of the ideas in the Cayce readings, and it gave us joy. Today there are even more people who are unafraid to look at the idea of reincarnation; grasp the importance of taking care of God's creation; see the human body as the temple of the Living God; and welcome the disciplines of meditation and prayer, especially in small groups. Today many acknowledge the value of a balanced diet for maximum physical and mental health, are willing to entertain the possibility that certain mythic cultures truly existed at some time earlier than recorded history, and even look seriously at some of Edgar's remedies for certain physical illnesses.

Edgar Cayce drew to him many interested in parapsy–chology, but he was far too talented and complex to carry only the label of "psychic." Harmon placed him in a long line of idealists who have changed the world for the better:

We think of a psychically gifted person as a whiz, a genius, a star at little-known powers of the mind. Given the history of our technological achievements, we view such a skill as a process to be mastered apart from our motives, like space travel, computer calculation, quick-freezing the dead, or designing laser weapons. But the adventure of Cayce's life sets his paranormal accomplishments in a much larger context of high-purposed caring and creativity.

Cayce belongs somewhere among the stumbling, surprised explorers of new terrain, only partly able to describe what they see, and tempted to doubt their own experiences: Pasteur trying to prevent ravaging disease; Schweitzer offering medical care in the African jungle; Gandhi cleaning toilets with the outcastes in India; King marching with throngs of left-out African Americans; Jane Addams creating settlement houses in the slums; Mother Teresa clasping the poor and dying.

His trances disclose penetrating views of good and evil, worship and ethics, community and disintegration, the earthy and the transcendent, gifts of insight from East and West, and a Christ who is everyone's destiny but nobody's captive. They create a cosmology and attendant ethics which resonate to the prophetic tradition in biblical faith, yet invite disciplined lives in small groups congruent with both mystical training and the wisdom of psychotherapy about layered minds and troubled wills.

This book is an invitation to learn about a man, unique in our culture, one who was faithful to his calling to be helpful to people. I remember him as a man who didn't take himself too seriously. His ability to laugh at himself suggests a truly large soul. He loved and enjoyed people, and was ready to share his stories and wisdom with anyone who was interested. Although many people put him on a pedestal for his kindness and generosity, he was an extremist who never did anything half way, and his temper could flare when he was tired or ill. But his devotion to God and Jesus Christ and to his holy calling was real and constant, and I often felt his deep commitment to God and the Christ as he led our morning and afternoon prayer times.

Edgar, Gertrude, and Gladys helped steer me in a helpful new direction when I was twenty-three by expanding my world view. In the winter of my ninetieth year—after being involved with the Cayce work for more than six decades—I know that my time as a member of the Cayce household forever changed me. My life reading, in which they all participated, revealed God's design for me in this incarnation: family life, not my dreamed-of life as a concert pianist. He said, "You should have a lot of little ones, for the home is the greatest career in the earth, and those who shun same will have much yet to answer for." The reading showed me the temptations I would face along the way, too. I am like Scrooge in Dickens' *A Christmas Carol*, forever grateful for having the opportunity to change my life's direction. Reflecting on my reading over the years, I have realized that while I might have had technical prowess at the piano along with a measure of fame as a performing artist, I would have been lonely traveling to engagements and performing alone on the stage. I would probably not have had a family of my own, nor would I have been able to grow in the deepening life experiences that family life provided. So how deep and expressive would my musical interpretations have been?

In this book, Harmon asks a pointed question: "Is

Edgar Cayce just a last flicker of the past, when shamans and seers told their visions around the tribal fires? Or is he a glimpse of the future, when preoccupation with technical mastery, private comfort, and deadly weapons will yield to a just and loving society, close to the earth and bursting with invention and playfulness?"

That last sentence is the way I understand Edgar Cayce's dream for the future of each of us and our world. His view of the individual soul and of the God that created it was huge! He saw the future bright with the magical love and wisdom of the Creative Forces. When we souls can get in step with the lovely design laid out for us and make the right choices, one step at a time, we can be made whole and help transform the world into something like the Hebrew prophet Isaiah's "peaceable kingdom." That is the promise within Edgar Cayce's life story.

Part I

The Gift:
Love Surprised by Wisdom

CHAPTER 1

I Don't Do Anything
You Can't Do

There was literally a loaded gun on my
hip when I began a journey into the
scarcely believable life of Edgar Cayce.
It was wartime in the mild June of 1943,
and I was a graduate student at the
University of Chicago, holding a night job as a civilian
guard under military command. Between my rounds
through the laboratories in a large wooden building
(given a deceptive exterior to mislead saboteurs or spies),
I perched on a stool under a naked light bulb and read
chapters from a biography published the year before,
There Is a River: The Story of Edgar Cayce.[1] Now and again I
glanced around and fingered my gun when there were
creaking sounds in the woodwork or the dogs barked
hoarsely in the animal lab down the hall. There was real
danger from enemy agents, according to the supervising
Army captain. Recent break-ins had threatened research
secrets and cost the life of one guard. Often I wondered,
while trudging hourly routes through the night, whether
I would hesitate for a critical second before firing to kill
a man who sprang from behind a table of chemical re-
torts or around the great humming transformers.

Such images of violence, making all too real the daily
reports of GIs meeting sudden death on European and
Pacific battle fronts, were utterly incongruous with the
images in the book before me. There the author, Thomas
Sugrue, a respected editor and critic for the *Saturday Review of Literature,* described how an elderly ex-photogra-

---

[1]Sugrue, Thomas. *There Is a River: The Story of Edgar Cayce,* 1942.

pher in the oceanfront resort of Virginia Beach, Virginia, regularly entered a quietly creative state so potent that it mocked all the university technology surrounding me. The gun on my hip and the book on my knees represented radically different approaches to power. One stood for the skilled violence we guarded in an advanced and top-secret weapons research project. The other reported valuable knowledge about a staggering array of targets, reached peacefully and swiftly in a calm trance state.

Had I known the full nature of the research in my care, the contrast with Cayce would have been even more stark. The intricate equipment was part of the Manhattan District or Manhattan Project of the U.S. Army Corps of Engineers. Of course, we guards tried discreetly to learn what was happening in our cluster of buildings across the rolling, grassy Midway from the main campus. We could not puzzle it out, because some rooms with flasks and bubbling tubes were clearly for chemical research, while others were crowded with electrical apparatus that suggested work in physics. And why did we have live animals, such as dogs, monkeys, and rats? What was the connection between living flesh and the technology we suspected was connected to the university's atomic accelerator across the campus? When I tried to question my friend and neighbor from boyhood, the distinguished physicist Arthur Compton, I got only pleasant generalities.

The well-hidden truth of the Project was known in 1943 only to a score or so of scientists such as Robert Oppenheimer (working at the level of Compton and his Chicago colleagues under Enrico Fermi), selected military chiefs, and President Roosevelt plus a few advisors. Just a few blocks from where I was reading through the night about Cayce, a team of researchers in quarters created under the west stadium grandstands of Stagg Field had achieved the first controlled atomic reaction, which they were now turning into an atom bomb. At the end of the same football field, where I had so often flung my javelin towards the sky and watched its distant puncture of the soft earth, they had created a new weapon that would make even warships and tanks seem as archaic as javelins. Just months ago, in the cold and blowy Chicago December, they had turned loose a power which in two years would create an agony of screaming in Japan— enough to drown out all the throaty roars of Saturday football fans that I had heard throughout my youth near Stagg Field. In the very playground of the University, these gifted scientists had fashioned an instrument to suddenly kill some ninety thousand human beings at Hiroshima, with an equal number maimed. Nobody would ever know the exact casualties there and at Nagasaki, because so many civilians would be vaporized and incinerated in the August days already destined at our gracious campus.

A Kind of University All by Himself

Power was in the air, in the whirring machines and humming electrical circuits of the laboratory in my keeping. It was our American genius, our gift for know-how which we hoped would win the war. We raised the banner of technique over university campuses and assembly lines alike. This was the Century of Progress celebrated at the World's Fair in Chicago a few short years ago, where I had viewed with awe the sparkling technical displays in the Hall of Science, with my father in charge of the University of Chicago exhibits and programs.

But power of a different sort was the theme of the strange Cayce story. If the facts reported of him were even partly accurate, he had an extraordinary capacity that made him a kind of university all by himself, without technology at all.

Twice a day for decades, he had entered a trance state for up to an hour or more. In that unconscious condition (so unlikely that it had never appeared in any of my

courses in psychology, religion, or the history of cultures)
he seemed able to examine and describe whatever was
posed to him by someone in genuine need. Most often
the unknown goal had been a sick body and the treatments to heal it. But under certain conditions the target
could also apparently be a virus, an ancient kingship, a
marital conflict, the movement of the stars, the ontologi-
cal foundations of human existence, the political affairs
of nations, or a teenager's heartbreak. His descriptions of
these many objectives came in discourses of uneven
rhetoric, for he was not educated beyond the eighth
grade. He appeared to observers to struggle as he described what he saw as fluid "forces" (to use his word) or
fields and flows in intricate dynamics, as structures his
listeners could recognize and use. But he was reported
to demonstrate stunning accuracy, typically using medical and technical terms not known to him. How could
one even begin to think about such skill?

The university employed precision hardware to un-
lock structures of reality, under the direction of trained
minds that formed themselves to secrets of nature and
history, supplying power on demand, from engineering
to medicine to politics. But Cayce had no tools. He had
methods and routines, such as not entering his trance
too soon after eating, and praying before he went unconscious. But what were these devices, compared with
the university's electron cloud chambers and huge libraries? Cayce's power came without equipment, in
quiet. He appeared to empty himself, to hollow out his
consciousness as a receptacle, a conduit. Yet in his seemingly artless art he produced flashes of useful knowledge that could leave behind not only unspeakably
potent weaponry but perhaps an entire civilization built
on tools and technique.

It was not easy to keep an open mind about the story
that occupied my June nights. Cayce was triply an af-
front to learning. First, the untutored Southerner's
knowledge was encyclopedic. He could describe and
analyze in dozens of fields what only advanced special-

ties should tell him. Second, he accomplished his reports by means that no professor would dare to claim. He did his analyses at a distance from his absent medical subjects and removed by continents or centuries from many other targets. Third, he had no mentors (of the sort that graduate students expect) to chronicle for his developing ideas or achievements. Either the reports about him were fraudulent or deluded, or—if his skills were stable and could be taught to others—he represented a breakthrough of staggering scope.

His own claim was forthright: "I don't do anything you can't do, if you are willing to pay the price.[2] Evidently he did not mean that others should go into trance twice a day, rather that they could find their own means for connecting with the same helpful sources he had found, in a process he saw as once natural for the human condition but long ago lost. If he were correct that others could do it even to small degree, that should be enough to open up entire continents of the mind and further reality for exploration. Any student of science knew that small phenomena could have large consequences, as Franklin's sparking kite showed.

Yet there were nagging questions, even if one could imagine that Cayce's feats actually happened and might in some measure be replicated. What was the "price" of which he spoke? He had learned that his ability was somehow tied to his character and purposes. He could not use it to exploit others, nor to help others gain advantage over their fellows. It deserted him if he tried. Instead, he had to use it for those with real needs, who would invest themselves and grow personally as they explored and applied his counsel. This predicament seemed out of line with the enterprise of objective, detached science. It suggested a cosmos going somewhere purposefully, with creative demands at its heart.

And what would be the personal costs of trying to

---

[2]Cayce, Edgar, *What I Believe*, 1976, p. 23.

duplicate Cayce? How tough would be the requirement to stand tall and be just? How lonely would such a gift make its possessor, if others envied it or worshipped it or feared it? How would one prevent its misuse for the kind of mindless hunger for power that in wartime seemed so frightening, not only in Hitler, Mussolini, and Tojo, but in the millions who ecstatically followed them? Cayce's ability might beggar technology. But it also might prove even more demanding than a costly Manhattan Project. Perhaps it was not surprising that Cayce's breed was so rare as not to be cited in any university courses.

It was reassuring to read that his skill had limits. Limits meant order and regularity, so that his ability might be placed somewhere in the vast system of nature, not consigned to vague supernatural realms. It appeared not to be a freakish miracle, a once–only comet or Grand Canyon of the mind. It could be investigated as a lawful process with relatively predictable variations, however little these were presently understood. Differences among seekers made his skill climb or drop in some degree, not only with respect to their nobility of purpose, but also in accord with their ability to act productively on what he supplied. A well–informed and large–spirited mind got advanced and even technical discourse from him, while the merely curious were put off. Then Cayce's own state of mind and health, as well as his motivation to serve the seeker, appeared to affect his unseen visioning. Similar influences were evident from the helpers in his family and his small uncommercial office. Evidently there were conditions that could make his power yield distorted data or outright mistakes, however rarely this had happened in the decades bringing him to his present age of sixty–five. As any scientist knew, failures could often teach more than successes. All in all, he could be studied.

A Noiseless Flame of Goodness

What were the stakes?

If the reports about Cayce were even partly true, his process might one day help to curb international warfare. Such a talent might undo the combative efforts of dictators, soldiers, and scientists alike, by inspecting and reporting on unseen technical developments and unknown military deployments, as well as unsuspected plans for aggression. Perhaps warfare among the nations, undercut by such relentless exposure, could one day become as extinct as gunfights on streets of the Old West. It was not clear from Cayce's biography whether his talent could be directed to overcome coercive power. Through most of his life it had been used for rescue and nurture, chiefly medical and psychological. It might be so designed for growth of individuals who used it that only those who had removed violence from their hearts could call upon its aid in peacemaking—and then only for information that would jointly empower others to new life.

But even if Cayce could not be enlisted for military or political ends, surely he could help remove the causes of war. He was reported to have located oil with his strange gift, and guided inventors of useful chemical products and mechanical devices. Why should he not be enlisted to fight want, that old tormentor of the human spirit which ran ahead of wars? What might he suggest as new crops for farmers, or uncover as energy resources, or show as food in the sea, or propose as innovative products to manufacture? Would it be too daring to think that he might even have solutions to the riddle of distributing goods and services, so that the hatred and fear between the haves and have-nots, the developed and undeveloped peoples, might be tamed?

These were not mere speculations for me. Like many reared in Depression years who remembered Chicago's breadlines, I was an activist and had been one all through high school, college, and graduate school. Peace, a just peace, was our passion. For years we had taken part in rallies, marches, and picket lines, as well as studied the issues and methods of political science. We could barely remember a world without Hitler, and burned with shame over American Nazi or Fascist brown shirts, black shirts, and silver shirts, as well as over noisy anti-Semites. Choosing my own undergraduate major with care, to make the required courses count as training for social reform, I had settled on labor economics, with my major professor the able Paul Douglas (later to become a distinguished U.S. Senator). At his encouragement I had taken a year of graduate courses in economics, with a career as a labor organizer a serious option, though I had finally chosen studies at the Divinity School, because they seemed to engage more deeply both human evil and human greatness. No one with this background, who had already published an article on poverty in the nearby steel town of Gary, could look at Cayce without asking what he might contribute to peace and social justice.

It did not occur to me yet that my approach to the entranced man in Virginia was shaped in part by the same ethic which had generated a civilization now torn open by a frightening world war: if you find a good thing, use it. Only confrontation with Cayce in action would prove, as it turned out, vivid enough to shift my perspective from simply using to more total responding: if you find something important, be open to transformation by it. Martin Buber's penetrating distinction between I-it and I-thou relationships in every area of life had not yet hit me with the revealing force it later brought—though my Chicago classmate and friend, Maurice Friedman, was beginning a lifetime of setting forth Buber's ideas.[3]

But on some of the June nights when I walked across the ample Midway to my post, gazing at the stars, I won-

[3]Friedman, Maurice. *Martin Buber: The Life of Dialogue*, 1955.

dered whether we might be seeing in Cayce much more than better methods of social engineering. He might be part of a noiseless flame of unguessed goodness, shooting out from the center of war-tortured humanity to answer the thudding bombs, the goose-stepping troops, the wailing of swiftly orphaned children. Under the eternal night skies patiently bearing their witness to order, it seemed possible that the collapse of my world into hate and conquest, concentration camps and strident slogans, might awaken some awesome answering current deep within us all. Cayce might belong to the future, when procedures as dazzlingly simple as his might free a great campus such as ours to give full attention to hunger, illness, bigotry, illiteracy, and urban blight. With such aid, even the lowliest among us might help to create music, inventions, or imaginative schools.

Chicago's Doubts, Yet Discipline

How could he be real?

Nobody on Chicago's faculty had knowledge or even interest to contribute about him, though a university was by definition committed to study of the universe. I went one day to the bachelor quarters of a professor who had just taught a brilliant course in the Gospel of Mark, gleaming with all the unsolved riddles about Jesus that modern scholarship had posed. What if, I asked him cautiously, we could directly inspect New Testament events of the far past through a trance state such as Cayce's? His response was withering, made more icy by his personal courtliness.

His colleague in the psychology department, for whom I had just written a research paper on creativity in music, had a comparably disparaging response. Cayce was doubtless a medium, and researchers had exploded that fraud. I knew the category he was using, having read some years before the proceedings of a symposium held at Clark University in Massachusetts (the same campus which first brought Freud and Jung to this country), entitled *The Case for and Against Psychical Belief.* At that meeting had been a young researcher named Gardner Murphy, destined years later to become the dean of American psychologists and the most respected spokesperson for psychical research.[4] Also with him were two biologists, Joseph and Louisa Rhine, who had graduated from our own Chicago campus. They were building a reputation for their research at Duke University in the field they renamed as parapsychology.[5] (Not until much later did I discover that by 1943 they had already sought experimental aid from Cayce for their daughter, and had been interested enough to send a psychologist, Lucien Warner, from their staff to interview and observe Cayce in action. Dr. Warner would report to me years afterward how he had been so impressed that he stayed not the day he planned but a week, getting Cayce's trance counsel for every member of his family.)

Cayce's biographer reported that he vigorously denied being a medium, refusing to entertain messages from the dead and insisting on following a procedure that essentially let him go out to inspect for himself what he needed to know, by a combination of clairvoyance and what seemed to him religious guidance or inspiration. There were in fact solid psychologists who had already investigated him, from Harvard and elsewhere, though none had written him up. If the biographer were correct, no qualified professional scientist had ever investigated Cayce and charged him with error, delusion, or fraud.

How could the proper authorities have missed studying him in depth? Part of modernity was the conviction that science would sooner or later explore every worthwhile lead in the major disciplines. Of course, science

---

[4]Murphy, Gardner, *Challenge of Psychical Research,* 1961.

[5]See Rhine, J.B., *The Reach of the Mind,* 1947. See also Rhine, Louisa, *Hidden Channels of the Mind,* 1961, as well as *Psi: What Is It?,* 1975.

was a social institution, subject to pressures of career, money, and respectability. But Cayce represented something, in biblical language, "not done in a corner," for over four decades. Only my years of banging away at social change helped me to look a little further. It was not difficult to picture responsible social leaders being wrong about political and economic issues. Why should not those of comparable stature in psychology or religion also make mistakes in judgment?

Where should one begin? What would provide entry to Cayce's world?

One possible avenue was the history of religions, the comparative study of traditions and practices of East and West, ancient and modern. There the rich array of oracles, sibyls, seers, healers, prophets, wonder-workers, and primitive shaman figures might well have types that resembled Cayce enough to help separate usable facts from hasty guesses about him. But my professor of World Religions dismissed them all as victims of "overbeliefs."

Cayce saw his gifts in the framework of those promised in the Bible, which he had read through once for every year of his life. By now he had almost entirely memorized it (an unheard-of accomplishment in my world of university biblical scholars), in part through his peculiar gift, and in part through teaching it in church school ever since his youth. For him it was the best ultimate background for grasping what was happening in his unusual state. Trying to imagine his viewpoint, I went more than once to the Oriental Institute, just a block from my graduate house, to stand surrounded by artifacts from the Near East. As I wandered through the cool halls with their mute but eloquent displays, ancient Israel, Assyria, Egypt, and Persia stood before me in full dignity, summoned by the stone carvings, the jewelry, the pots and amulets, the mummies, and the figures of the gods. Models of temples and dwellings were arrayed with figurines of horses and chariots. There were javelins like those I had thrown so long in track and field events. On each visit I asked myself whether the people of those times and places had known something which Cayce had discovered again but the rest of us had lost.

There was no reason to think so in my courses on the Bible, where unusual gifts of prophecy or healing were uniformly explained away as mistaken perceptions from a superstitious age when "the sky hung low."[6] There were no miracles or useful trances in the world of the University of Chicago Divinity School; the biblical legacy came without a parted Red, or Reed, Sea or fallen Jericho walls, and certainly without a virgin birth or an empty tomb. The only unusual perception was essentially moral and theological insight. Not arrogance but honest conviction and disciplined scholarship lay behind this position, seen in the writings of gifted theologians such as the existentialist Rudolf Bultmann (whom I came to know well in later years when I brought him to teach in the religion department at Syracuse University, where I held a chair).[7] But as though to make up for affronting tradition by discarding so much of scriptural content, the Chicago Divinity School turned intently to facts and empirical inquiry. Its building was next to that of the department of sociology on campus, and more than a few mused that the methods of the two were interchangeable. The model was to inquire, inspect, and analyze—not just to speculate. Surely, this was what the Cayce phenomenon required.

Chicago was the university which took on the discipline in every department of humbling itself before any reality to learn its secrets—even before the unseen atom. What it offered to study Cayce was most of all the attentive empiricism which made the university stand tall on the Midwestern prairies. The school had as yet no his-

---

[6]See Case, Shirley Jackson, exponent of this viewpoint, as in his *Jesus*, 1927.

[7]Bultmann, Rudolf, "New Testament and Mythology" in Bartsch, H.W., ed., *Kerygma and Myth*, 1961. See also Ogden, Schubert, *Christ without Myth*, 1961.

tory of great formative minds such as had graced European and New England campuses for centuries. John
Dewey was no Kant, and Thorstein Veblen no Max We-
ber. Nor was Chicago rich in literature and the arts, except in criticism. But it was carefully, even ruthlessly
determined to be taught by the data at hand, in every
field of academic life. That was the reason for the parade
of Nobel laureates in physics and chemistry, as well as in
economics, that had made (and would continue to make)
the university great.

Yet when I stood in the quiet halls of the Oriental
Institute, it was not at all clear how to reduce Cayce's
service to inspectable, manipulable circuits of his psyche.
In those corridors it seemed that Cayce might lead to
encounters with an active, loving Agent that could use
ordinary shepherds or fisherfolk, or tent makers (or even
photographers such as Cayce) to get wounds healed and
minds stretched, or to call entire peoples to new ways of
life.

First-Hand Reports

Still, Cayce's capacity seemed so outrageous, so utterly unlikely, that I might have dismissed it as impossible, but for firsthand reports from those who had
sought his strange counsel, called "readings." Among
these were friends of my family, such as the levelheaded
Myrtle Walgreen, who years before her present wealth
and community leadership had baked the first pies and
cooked the first soups in what was now an extensive
drugstore chain. She sought Cayce out. Another was
Lowell Hoit, the widely read and distinguished head of
Chicago's Board of Trade. A third was Sherwood Eddy,
the author and respected leader of the worldwide YMCA,
who had not only secured Cayce's counsel, but gone to
see him in action. Then there was my mother.

As a longtime contributor to the *Christian Century*, a liberal Protestant journal (some of whose editors were lead-

ing members of our innovative home church adjoining
the university), she had been sent a copy of Cayce's biography to review or discard. Perhaps her skillful handling of religious controversies in the past, which had
won her coverage in *Time*, prompted an editor to think
she could make a sensible evaluation of the hardly believable Cayce story. As someone who had written nearly
a dozen books of her own on religious subjects, and been
the editor of the Congregational periodical, *Social Action*,
she was a demanding reviewer.

In Cayce's life she found threads of her own, as she
traced his growing up in Kentucky, also once her home,
and his vigorous lay leadership in the mainline Protestant group called the Christian Church or Disciples of
Christ, which had been her family's heritage since shortly
after its beginnings in 1820. Further, she thought she saw
in Cayce some of the disciplined idealism of her generation which had led her and my father (now president of
Frances Shimer College in western Illinois) to spend a
number of years as educational missionaries in China,
my birthplace. And while she had no special interest or
knowledge in the psychic field, she was deeply drawn to
prayer and had published a widely used book of
devotions, *Every Day a Prayer*,[8] as well as learned how to
meditate from Gerald Heard, the pioneering British anthropologist and philosopher.[9] She concluded she had
useful perspectives with which to assess Cayce. So on a
lecture trip to New York she took a side journey by overnight train to Virginia, where she could meet Cayce,
watch him work, and test him thoroughly with a trance
evaluation of her health. Having recently been through
a complete workup at the noted medical center in Battle
Creek, Michigan, she had sufficient records of medical
laboratory work, together with reports by specialized
physicians, to measure Cayce's performance with care.

---

[8]Bro, Margueritte Harmon, *Every Day a Prayer*, 1943.
[9]Heard, Gerald, *Training for a Life of Growth*, 1959.

Since she was not in any critical medical need, she could simply ask Cayce for help but not demand a remarkable cure.

Her account to me of Cayce's work, like her review in the *Christian Century* entitled "Explain It As You Will," was careful but clearly favorable.[10] Cayce was apparently neither a fraud nor self-deluded. He scored bull's-eyes again and again on confirmable targets in her Battle Creek reports. He then suggested some cogent directions for treatments which her physicians had overlooked and subsequently found useful. Cayce was open and straightforward about his unritualized trance process. To her he seemed modest, with a sense of humor that kept his peculiar talent in perspective. He was committed to research on his work, about which he assured her he remained convinced that "I don't do anything you can't do, if you are willing to pay the price." And he had in fact amassed much helpful data about the ability, built on thousands of case files, for study by any interested specialists. He appeared to have a good, critical mind. His wife and the people drawn around his consulting work seemed genuine and unpretentious. They had the refined Southern dignity and graciousness which my mother knew well from that part of her life when her father had been president of Transylvania University in Kentucky.

Taking On Cayce in Person

If Cayce were not a crook and not a mental case, if he were not a promoter and not a self-appointed messiah, then his efforts might be a huge adventure to explore. When he wrote to my mother that he really needed help (now that both his sons were in the Army) and asked whether I might be interested in working with him for a

---

[10]Bro, Margueritte Harmon, *Christian Century*, June 2, 1943, pp. 664–665.

year, I thought carefully about it.

Would it be proper to go down this strange path in the midst of a brutal war that had already taken the lives of some of my classmates? My draft board had given me a 4-D rating of exemption for study in theology, and I took this privilege very seriously; already I had been to the Navy recruiting office to discover the requirements for the chaplaincy when I completed the needed years of graduate study. The draft authorities indicated that I could take a year for field research, so long as the effort was clearly tied to graduate studies. I outlined a plan to interview not only Cayce but dozens of his associates and those who sought his counsel, collecting data for a later doctoral dissertation. My father thought the design would be sound in his academic circles, and the university assured me that I would not lose my degree track.

It seemed unlikely that someone more authoritative than I, from Chicago or any other university, would get around to investigating Cayce soon. This was wartime. Posters cried out for victory from bulletin boards in gray academic buildings just as loudly as they did from store windows and subway platforms. Platoons of soldiers, airmen, and sailors in distinctive uniforms marched briskly between classes among the stately campus towers. They carried textbooks, not weapons, because this was the Midwest, and invasion was so far unlikely—unless England collapsed under the ceaseless airborne Blitz by the Germans. But the drilling groups swinging their wooden rifles to sharp commands shouted on the Midway made clear that combat was a universal destination. Small lines of troops stepped smartly past libraries that held the treasures of centuries, and past the subdued dark-wood classrooms with arched Gothic windows where Robert Maynard Hutchins as president (and my friend since high school) had led the movement to study classics he called Great Books in a thinking man's university. It was a time to bend wisdom to technique, to make learning serve conquest. The university did its part, even to opening the atomic husk that would one day release a blinding flash and a mushroom cloud.

My task would be to ask the right questions about Cayce, illuminating the productive potentials of his gift and suggesting how far it might be replicated. Otherwise I would be abandoning my post in a painful time of history, not only in the Manhattan Project, where I would scarcely be missed, but in the hard inner demand on our generation to unscramble a devastated world. I looked on the potential assignment with great seriousness. The gold stars that hung mutely on little cloth squares in windows on many a nearby block, signifying a military death in that family, demanded no less.

Friends posed tough questions, as graduate students should. If Cayce were real, why wasn't he rich and famous? Why wasn't he already being used in Washington for the war effort? Why had the Cayce Hospital failed, as did the fledgling but respectable Atlantic University built on his work, with such guidance at hand? How would such a gift—if truly there—ever make mistakes? Surely there was a catch in the story somewhere. Perhaps he had developed some sort of cult, to which the author of his biography belonged. Wouldn't it destroy one's perspective and balance to move into his orbit? Better, they said, just to read about him and wait for someone to expose him.

In particular they hammered at the one area where Cayce seemed most vulnerable. It was reincarnation. Midway in his adult life, after twenty-some years of winning increasing respect for his medical counsel, he had been stunned to hear his trusted trances present a view of human psychology and destiny that included being reborn on earth over and over. Many church friends had backed away from him. Physicians consulted him more guardedly.

One might suspend judgment about his capacity to retrieve verifiable information and make sound judgments about medical targets. But to consider that Cayce might be correct about reincarnation required challenging all the major thinkers of Western civilization—except

Plato and Origen. If Cayce were correct, then what of the
great parade of philosophers and theologians who had
given their lives to studying the human condition but
had not seen reincarnation as part of it? What of Augustine and Aquinas, Luther and Calvin, Spinoza and Kant,
not to mention Darwin, Marx, and Freud? To question all
these minds was like blowing up our campus. Only a
fanatical empiricist, it seemed, would start fresh in such
an investigation when there was so much else important
to study in a world at war. If Cayce were right, then large
portions of the Orient had been correct all along in their
Hindu and Buddhist perspectives. Who knows where
this might lead? Were we not at war with the Buddhist
country of Japan? Shouldn't that reveal something about
their understanding of ultimate reality? (That we were
also at war with Germany, the cradle of modern philosophy and theology, and the source of much of the
greatest in Western music and poetry, did not come up
as readily.) Surely if Cayce's work were tragically flawed
on reincarnation, it must be flawed in other areas. No
wonder it had not been more studied.

How Cayce Asked to Be Evaluated

So I put off the idea of working with Cayce, throwing
myself into courses and my new marriage. A faculty appointment came through for me at George Williams College, only blocks from the university. Preparing my
teaching while I kept up my graduate studies was demanding, and I was grateful to be able to give up the
night work in the Manhattan Project. On weekends I
preached at a little Disciple church on Chicago's far South
Side. We moved into a row house and delighted in fixing
it up, as young couples will. My wife, June, was a concert
pianist, a pupil of Percy Granger, who had already started
performing with orchestras. Now a graduate student at
Chicago Musical College, studying with Chicago's most
respected pianist, Rudolph Ganz, she had a bright future

in music. This was no time to move to an isolated summer resort in Virginia.

But now and again I pulled out the transcript of a counseling discourse that I had requested of Cayce and studied it to the accompaniment of June's sweeping passages from Liszt, Chopin, and Bach. There Cayce undertook to spell out my life purpose and talents in what he called a "life reading" that included several supposed past existences. What was in it to suggest that I should look further into his work?

The material was not exactly promising. He assigned me no prominent stature—which I noted with relief, since he had already given my parents roles within the circles around Jesus in a comparable reading for my mother. If he were passing out ego trips, he could forget my help. As seen in his trance vision, the past lives which most shaped my present existence were those as a sculptor of religious images in prehistoric times, a priest occupied with music and dance in an Egyptian temple, an aide and confidant to Joshua, and a preacher in the Early Church of the Hellenistic period. It did not comfort me to have him add that I had been his son in the latter period; this seemed to lay the groundwork for his manipulating me in some way.

Indeed, possible manipulation was my main concern about the entire essay. He warned against a career in church music, which increasingly beckoned to me as a part of ministry (though outrageous to my activist friends in the labor movement), and insisted I must, as he put it, "go the whole way!" in a vocation of psychological and theological scholarship and practice. The prospect was not appealing, because the small churches I had served as pastor often seemed stifling and I did not want to spend a lifetime as a scholar debunking Western and Eastern religious traditions. It seemed more than a little likely that Cayce had been influenced by his own church ties to push me in inappropriate directions. He included in the reading a lengthy and earnest discourse on theological issues, which seemed far too conservative and Christocentric for a Chicago theological student.

If I ever went to work with him, it seemed I should help him disabuse himself of the reincarnation material, so he could get back to good, solid medical service. Since he came from the same church background as that in which I was ordained, he might listen to me. Of course, it would be difficult for him to face up to a major and long-standing error in his work, because it would throw a shadow over other unknowns that emerged in his trances, such as making considerable use of osteopathy and linking many disease processes to poor attitudes and emotions. But he deserved my help, if he proved as sincere and modest as he was reported. Until then I could lay him aside.

Several developments changed my mind.

The first was studying a little twenty-page autobiographical booklet sent with the life reading. Not slick but straightforward, it was called *Edgar Cayce, His Life and Work*. At first I had only glanced through it, but now I looked at it carefully and liked its modest spirit, where in some passages he was rueful about mistakes he had made in handling his ability:

> Man's pageant must pass and fade, but God works in slower and more secret ways, His wondrous works to perform. He blows no trumpet, He rings no bell. He begins from within, seeking His ends by quiet growth. There is a strange power that men call weakness, a wisdom mistaken for folly. Man has one answer to every problem—power; but that is not God's way. Then why shouldn't I dread publicity?
>
> You ask, I am sure, "Have there been failures?" If there were not failures, friends, I would be afraid there was something super-natural about me. I am only human. Humanity is doomed to failure when it trusts in its own weak self, and most of us have that failing.[11]

---

[11]Cayce, Edgar, *Edgar Cayce, His Life and Work*, Association for Research and Enlightenment, 1943, p. 10.

At the end of the essay he suggested how people should evaluate his work for themselves before seeking his aid. Such issues of critical method were crucial for me, because they were at the heart of my graduate studies.

First, he said, those asking his assistance should become well informed on it, by studying readings and consulting others who asked his help. Evidently he was not cultivating the gullible, for he added, "Do not seek a reading to satisfy some emotional whim or idle curiosity." Second, he offered a pragmatic criterion as American as William James, and in line with his own Disciple church life: "Does the application of the information make individuals better husbands, wives, sons, daughters, citizens, friends?" This approach by itself could be merely moralistic, unless the concept of "better" were an ample one. But Cayce went right on to a third dimension, which gave the term size by firmly grounding it in the Bible and church history, as well as in reflective theology: "Do the principles expressed in the readings bear the stamp of divine approval in the light of His standards?"

Then he offered an existential criterion by inviting people to stick with the reading they got long enough to see how it reflected their real purposes: "That which an individual seeks, that he will find. Those that seek only that which is of the earth–earthy may only find such; they that seek to bring a whole, well–rounded life, may find it." Without the wrappings of biblical language, Cayce was recommending an empirical, rational approach to evaluating his work, balanced by the use of religious tradition in a self-critical, active spirit. A Chicago student could work within such a framework, because it allowed putting any one apparent finding of his up for grabs, including reincarnation and the high view of Christ seen in my reading.

He offered one more criterion. Familiar to those of deep faith in traditions of both East and West, though not stressed in Chicago theological studies, it was the test of the Spirit, to be joined to the others: "To be of real value, the information must strike a vibrant chord with

your inner being, ringing true with your spiritual desire."
This further test, added to the others, tipped the balance
until our Cayce year could not be put off longer.

One feature of his work that rang true as he suggested
appeared in a booklet I had ordered from the small nonprofit organization that sponsored Cayce's work, bearing
the oddly nineteenth-century name of the Association
for Research and Enlightenment. It was composed of
excerpts from readings given in recent years on public
affairs. Entitled *Am I My Brother's Keeper?*,[12] it set forth in
selection after selection an uncompromising insistence
on social justice, including the rights of workers, the dignity of minorities, the claims of the poor, and the imperative of peace. One shocking passage even affirmed
that the hope of the world would one day come out of
Russia as social responsibility in everyday life. For my
generation the task of separating the good from the bad
in Marx and other utopians, while joining it to prophetic
faith, had been central business, seen in Reinhold
Niebuhr just as truly as in the picket lines where I had
marched and been briefly jailed.[13] When Cayce warned
that America had to build social and racial justice or
experience rioting in the streets and terrible hardship,
with world leadership passing to the Orient, I knew that
I had to take him seriously. He spoke to my deepest sense
of the spirit of the prophets of Israel.

The other source of inner prompting to seek out Cayce
was the choral music I conducted in my new college
post. Music had always been my carrier of transcen-
dence, as Cayce had correctly noted in his trance counsel
for me. Theology was not. My sermons did not proclaim
that God was dead, but an objective listener might conclude that He was misunderstood or overrated, com-

---

[12]Cayce, Edgar, *Am I My Brother's Keeper?*, 1942. Reprinted as *Times of Crisis*, 1945.

[13]Niebuhr, Reinhold, *Moral Man and Immoral Society*, and *The Nature and Destiny of Man*, vols. 1, 2, 1943.

pared with our own responsibility to take hold of our lives and our troubled world. Prayer meant little to me, except as a poetic exercise in worship. But serious music picked up the sense of a nameless Beyond. I could keep busy in causes. I could lose myself in the puzzles of scholarship. But music, especially sacred choral music, spoke of an Other before which I too often felt a stranger.

As June and I talked about the puzzling Cayce trance, we suspected there were clues from heightened creativity in music to help us guess what he might be doing. Both of us knew from long experience that highly disciplined singers, holding a sustained chord in a Latin motet or reaching for a racy Bach figure, could sometimes transcend their usual skills. They could reach notes higher or lower than when they were practicing alone, and in moments of ecstatic absorption together they could phrase with unexpected genius, finding their way into experiences they had never encountered—death on a cross, the love of a mother for a holy child, flesh transformed and healed by spirit. They could even touch into far centuries of plainsong, or distant worlds of Russian or Spanish anthems as though they belonged there. Such singing, we thought, might enter a state similar in principle to Cayce's trance and only a breath apart from his attainment of distant or hidden knowledge.

So (after some further exchanges with Cayce) I left my courses at the university unfinished, as June did hers at the downtown graduate music school. My college classes went into the hands of a substitute, and another minister took the weekend church. We piled our belongings into boxes and barrels to move to Virginia Beach for the rest of the school year, answering Cayce's invitation to help him and to explore for ourselves his striking claim, "I don't do anything you can't do."

Most difficult to leave was the Navy choir that I had rehearsed and conducted daily at the college all through the summer and into the fall. The singers were students in a V12 program for technical specialists, who had grown skilled at their choral art, performing entire pro-

grams from memory. When I took them on short concert
trips and sent them tramping down the aisles of audito-
riums in their gleaming whites, voices ringing in male
harmony, they seemed to stand for all the heroism required of young men in wartime. Audiences caught up
in the spell of their marching songs or tunes from musical plays could move easily with them into the hushed
or elevated spell of a spiritual or a chorale or a motet.

Some of the strongest music we sang came from the
mystical tradition of Russian Orthodoxy. One anthem
that I arranged, by Tschesnokoff, started with low voices
in subdued harmony, reflecting in open fifths on the
claim, "Salvation is created." Then a bold melodic leap
in high voices opened up the rest of the thought:
"Salvation is created in midst of the earth. Alleluia!" The
full choir passages that followed required all the singers'
vigor, until the music bowed down to a deep-toned, so-
norous, and hushed resolution. When we spoke of the
text in rehearsal, I confessed that I knew little of what
salvation was, though I was sure it had in it freedom
from war, freedom from hunger, freedom from tyranny,
and freedom from discrimination. Beyond that I could
only guess. But there was reason to suspect (as I told the
men in stumbling phrases, explaining why we were leaving) that much more might be trying to unfold itself "in
midst of the earth" during bloody and trying times.
Cayce might be part of it, and we had to know. They
understood. All of them in the room grasped that this
was the season to reach for the farthest goals, the truest
visions. All of us knew it was a time for dying, when
some in our ensemble could soon meet violent death on
a far battlefield or beachhead. So at our last rehearsal
they stood and spontaneously sang to June and me,
without conductor but with wondrously sensitive phras-
ing, the Russian anthem as their blessing on our venture. The image of these earnest young men stayed with
me as a fierce demand to make every step of our Cayce
journey count—in part because word came within
months that two had already been killed.

CHAPTER 2

Mr. Cayce, I Am Dying

It was nighttime and raining when we arrived in Virginia, after traveling two long days in a train crowded with service personnel of many ranks. To get into Norfolk, the country's great naval port jammed with wartime shipping, where we could take a commuter train to nearby Virginia Beach on the exposed coast, our string of railroad cars had to be ferried across the large, unbridged port river that bordered the city. As we glided through the dark, our train appeared to be riding on the water. It seemed that we were leaving behind what was substantial and safe, breaking from the mainland of our lives, either for great discovery or great disappointment.

As a cab at Virginia Beach took us from the train station to a waterfront inn, we were stunned by the overwhelming darkness. Peering at the rainy streets, we could dimly see the outlines of a few closed shops and unlit buildings two or three stories high along the ocean. The scene was eerie, because a complete wartime blackout was enforced so that light from the shore would not silhouette great ships coming to the nearby entrance of Chesapeake Bay and the Norfolk port. The cabdriver told us that local people had watched more than one ship sunk by German submarines lined up right off this coast, after which bodies and debris had washed onto the sandy beach for days. To prevent further catastrophes, every window in the resort community was heavily curtained at night. There were no streetlights or store lights at all. Autos drove with headlights painted to allow only slits of beams for navigating. The feeling for us Midwesterners was that we had stepped straight into war. Directly ahead of us, across the surging ocean, was open combat. If there were to be an enemy invasion, we were told, this port and this very beach would be prime targets for streams of troops debarking in the artillery–lit night.

Despite the light rain, we walked in the dark down to the meeting of sand and surf, after checking into our room. The old mysterious ocean, source of all life forms on the planet, was moving rhythmically, rolling its waves against the continent which was our home. Sober questions kept our comments terse as we walked, sorting out thoughts and feelings. What was signaled to us by the endless moving waters? Were we staring at an emblem of the great expanse of the Spirit, flowing with helpful resources which Cayce had found how to tap? Or was this impersonal ocean with its cruel storms and great sea creatures a symbol of forces indifferent to humans, carrying submarines ready to smash out life? Help or threat, life or death, the sea reminded us of all we did not know about Cayce's efforts.

Standing on the margin of the land where it met the dark salt water, we felt sudden empathy for the many who turned to Cayce as a last medical resort, an outrageous possibility just on the edge of sanity. Most people approached him, by mail or phone, in grave illness or injury. They brought their pain–battered bodies before him for much more than a colorful reading in an exotic trance. He was often their last chance, after they had trudged down medical corridors to the brink of death, as near as we were to the ocean's drop–off from the beach. They sought his aid stripped of their defenses, like patients unashamed in plain hospital gowns. The cases reported in the biography and told to us by friends were mostly people writing to him at his seacoast town, at the far edge of reality, "Mr. Cayce, can you help me?"

Near the appointed hour we turned from the ocean and walked to the Cayce home, just blocks from our inn. In the dark, softened only by glimmers from passing cars, we found it across the street from the low and modest

Star of the Sea Catholic Church. What we could make out was an ample frame home with an enclosed side porch and shingled exterior. An attached annex had to be the office area for what a small sign identified as the association with the long name. The Cayces were waiting for us, together with Cayce's secretary for twenty years, Gladys Davis. They welcomed us cordially into their longish living room with a fireplace at one end. The furnishings around us were pleasant but not pretentious: a couch, a plain carpet, overstuffed chairs, a waist-high console radio, wooden floor lamps with large shades, and end tables joined by a magazine rack for *Collier's* and the *Saturday Evening Post.* These could have come from the home of almost any of our middle-class relatives—schoolteachers, a librarian, a real estate agent, a game warden, a produce distributor. As we settled down to talk in this unremarkable setting, I tried to assess the people we had traveled so far to see. These were to be our guides to a region of the mind and spirit which most of our friends and relatives thought did not even exist.

Cayce was tall, in the six-foot range, with a body that combined firmness with rounded contours. His figure was spare but not thin, and his shoulders slightly sloped. He seemed to move economically, as was fitting for a man in his mid-sixties, yet he carried himself with dignity and confidence. He was cordial, but he had a touch of reserve associated with Southern graces, familiar from a part of my boyhood spent in Kentucky. It was appropriate from this background for him to be addressed by all but his family—even by his secretary—as Mr. Cayce, just as he called her Miss Gladys. His large and full mouth smiled easily and commanded his face, with its slightly receding yet well-defined chin and his hairline yielding space to age. His gaze was level and steady behind his rimless glasses, and his hair combed flat gave him a composed and thoughtful appearance. I noticed how large his ears were and recalled that such ears were a mark of spirituality in Buddhist traditions. His gestures were not expansive, but he put us at ease by the relaxed way he smoked frequent cigarettes and leaned back in his chair, as well as by taking the lead in conversation. He did not appear to study us unduly nor try to impress us. There was a prompt responsiveness in his dignified facial expressions, and he held the center of attention when he spoke. Within his low-key manner there seemed to be a high-strung man who did not miss much, with an abundance of natural bearing and charm, sufficient to reassure even suspicious inquirers if he chose. His speech was measured, not hurried, and clearly Southern. Only a few colloquialisms suggested limits to his formal education, by contrast with his ample working vocabulary.

His wife, Gertrude, was petite and winsome, attractive even in her sixties. Her graceful features suggested refinement and natural beauty, as did her well-knit body and restrained but expressive movements. One lens of her glasses was frosted over, and I recalled that she had lost the vision of her right eye in a fall. But her face was so alert and focused, framed in her graying dark hair, that one promptly forgot the defect in the pleasure of her engaging smile and quick speech. She appeared to defer slightly to her husband, but not in lack of confidence—rather from what seemed a more self-contained and perhaps thoughtfully introverted temperament. Her teasing wit, which could be downright merry, and her judicious comments made her easy to talk with as we groped our way toward being natural with people doing something absurdly unconventional in such a conventional home. The care and fluency with which she expressed herself in a Southern accent, choosing her words and offering defined ideas, suggested an intellectual but also a person with feminine tact. She listened to others a bit more intently than her husband seemed to do. Cayce and his secretary occasionally called her Muddie, which I remembered was a family nickname that endured long after it had been invented by her infant second son as his way of saying Mother. The unusual name seemed to celebrate her individuality while still cherishing her evident nurturing qualities. Here was the proverbial able woman behind a gifted man.

Gladys Davis was larger of build and taller than Gertrude Cayce, with a body not stocky yet solid, and appealingly full and curved. She wore her honey blonde hair braided around her head, and her movements and gestures were thoroughly feminine. She seemed to be in her mid-thirties, and I recalled that she was unmarried, having put aside wedded life for single-minded devotion to the Cayces and their work. But nothing about her suggested a future as an old maid, and I wondered briefly how the three animated persons before us had avoided problems over her wholesome charm. She smiled and laughed as though inclined by nature to want to put us at ease. Her speech touched with Southern dialect came in bursts, as she seemed to grope for the right expression, giving the impression of breaking an inner barrier of shyness with the energy piled up behind what she wanted to say. Although the Cayces addressed her as Miss Gladys, the title was clearly just her name, for they related to her as a family member, not as an employee. She in turn gave them the lead in conversation, but she responded to stories and sallies with original comments, not merely conventional remarks, which showed an independent and able mind that made her a peer in the family circle. Evidently she had the best memory of any of them, for they consulted her without hesitation to supply needed details in our exchanges.

How Much Does He See?

During most of the conversation the topics we addressed absorbed me. But now and then I noticed a second train of thought in the back of my mind. What was Cayce seeing in us? Did he judge us adequate for the roles he had planned? His biography had noted that he could see auras, or patterns of color around people's

heads and bodies, and could evaluate character and conflicts from them, as well as directly read minds. There
was no hint that he might be using second sight to amplify or change his surface perceptions—no squints or
faltering exchanges to suggest he was consulting an inward vision. Still, the thought of being inspected in the
recesses of one's psyche was uncomfortable.

Would he pick up my systematic doubt, as part of my
determination to use my academic training in objectiv-
ity? I would be showing an affable side to him, as I did
in my teaching or weekend church work. But another
side would be watching closely for clues that might show
him misguided or self-deceived, or exaggerating his capacities. Would he notice my suspicion that he might be
self-important, pushed by a sense of divine mission?
Surely someone conducting an incredible activity in a
skeptical world, and able to think the unthinkable in
concepts of reincarnation, would have considerable self-
assertion in his makeup. I owed it to him, and certainly
to the larger university and church worlds, to expose
any messianism I found. And of course, if he turned out
to be greedy or flawed in character, commercializing his
ability, I would have to expose that, too.

Yet deeper than these concerns, which had to irritate
him if he read my mind, was another layer in my
thoughts: fears about my own adequacy. Would he pick
up trends in my personality which I either did not recognize or preferred not to think about? He might see in
my so-called aura a band of red for a strong temper. Or
perhaps there were flashes of color for sexuality, not exactly erased by my recent marriage to a curvaceous
blonde of Norwegian descent, whom I had courted with
fervor for several years. He might even conclude that my
activist resistance to arbitrary authority was colored by
personal rebelliousness. Worse, he might find that my
attempts to be objective about his capacities were partly
intellectual arrogance, meant to balance off great uncer-
tainty about my own spiritual maturity. I had not done
much business with God outside of moments in choral

music or in nature, though I had preached about him at some length. Cayce might find me tone-deaf to the inner notes of his work.

As we talked on, I felt a bit less vulnerable. It occurred to me that Cayce's reported intuition should often have shown him in others the kind of momentary hesitation and fear which shadowed my thoughts (as I later found they had June's). He must by now know well that people with varying needs to prove themselves would approach him with masked doubts and even strategies to unveil his delusions or flaws. Part of his strange vocation would be having to live with currents of unpleasant suspicion. He would also have learned to reassure others who approached him that he would not suddenly expose whatever he saw in them that was unworthy. His calling, if authentic, was not enviable. He had to be lonely at some level. Perhaps those who got to know him dropped not only their doubts, but their secret ambitions to use him. If they did not, or could not, then here was a man who could safely wrap around himself only his household. That limitation would be costly to his sense of identity and worth, already upended by the peculiarity of his gift.

The sense of his being stranded without peers or deep support outside the family would return often in the months ahead, when he seemed increasingly someone whose ability might have been welcomed in another time or culture, but a figure out of season in modern America. The implications were serious. If others who sought to duplicate his skills had also to stand awkwardly alone, even among well-meaning friends, who would try? What sort of person could meet the test of unending estrangement, created not only by doubt of unfamiliar capacities, but also by sudden fear of his or her penetrating accuracy?

His Sense of Global Violence

We made small talk about our trip on a train so crowded that soldiers and sailors stood in the aisles. Cayce spoke with such easy knowledge about Chicago and other cities on our route, as well as about porters and dining cars and berths, that it was soon clear he was a sophisticated traveler. Later I would learn, in part by journeying with him, how much he liked to take trips and how (as his family put it) he could pack a bag in five minutes. I would discover that he had been to most of the major urban centers of the country, often many times, as he responded to emergency pleas for aid and searched for how best to serve with his unusual gift. At the moment I could only note how the image of a well-traveled American collided with stereotypes of a help-less, unworldly ascetic which his Catholic biographer had faintly suggested in portraying him as the victim of a remarkable endowment.

Soon we turned our exchanges to the war, comment-ing on the strangeness of the total blackout. Cayce spoke with quiet pride of his two sons in military service, Hugh Lynn and Edgar Evans, one overseas and the other headed there. Yet as he described their assignments, his face showed for a moment the sharp-edged loss he felt from their absence. It seemed likely that family ties might be more important to him than Southern mores already made them. Being a man with a dubious calling would enhance his dependence on them and make their dis-tance under peril a persistent wound.

The gravity of the war engaged him deeply as he con-tinued to speak. He told of the servicemen who wrote him often from their overseas posts, telling their anxiety about the meaning and destiny of their lives and their nation. A few even asked how to face their own threat-ened dying, since they knew him well enough to credit his unusual abilities, including seeing past death. What would happen to them, they wanted to know, in the first hours after being killed, and how should they prepare?

Most were young men from the Sunday school classes he had taught for over fifty years or the sons of those in his classes from churches at Virginia Beach, at Selma, Alabama, or in Kentucky. He tried when he answered each letter, he said, to create a helpful perspective. And he prayed for those to whom he wrote. To him human-kind was going through a terrible trial and refinement by fire, having to learn to rely more on spiritual reality and on brother–sisterhood before God. Each individual caught in the conflict had to search for the same final realities. His observations did not sound like ritual sentiments from a Bible teacher, for he spoke haltingly, as though searching for images for the unthinkable destruction which crowded us all.

How deeply he felt a part of the times and responsible to affect its outcomes, rather than being a mental wonder-worker on the sidelines, became even clearer when Gladys referred briefly to a vision which had come to Cayce in 1936, telling him of the coming world conflict. Cayce had been working in his garden, where he loved to spend his hours out of his office, when he looked up to see a searing panorama of blood–red chariots riding across the sky above the ocean. Beside him there suddenly stood a man in tunic, helmet, armor, and leg guards of ancient times, saying, "The chariots of the Lord, and the horsemen thereof," before he abruptly disappeared. To Cayce the vision meant the coming of death and destruction on a tremendous scale, and he dropped his hoe and ran into the house. He shook so badly that his elder son thought he was having a heart attack. And Cayce was so affected by the tragedy he had seen that he was unable to speak of it for several days. Such an experience might be psychic. But it was a long way from giving mediumistic messages from the dead in a darkened room. It spoke of Cayce's profound concern for his fellows in an ominous and bloody age.

He Sent Himself to Unknown Territories

The phone rang several times, and Gladys reported calls from people seeking urgent medical aid. She had just been told, she added, that the phone company was limiting their incoming long-distance calls, because so many were being placed to Cayce that others in Virginia Beach could not get lines to call out, and wartime restrictions made extra lines impossible. How, we asked, did local people see Cayce, now that his recently published biography had made him a public figure? For example, how did the priest across the way at the little Catholic church view Cayce's efforts? Cayce grinned and suggested that we look tomorrow at the large twin candles in holders, each over three feet tall, which were placed to keep unlit vigil on either side of the outer door to his office. The priest had quietly brought them some time ago as a blessing and a protection. He had not stayed long, but his encouragement seemed heartfelt.

When we spoke of the Presbyterian Church, where Cayce had his membership (since there was no Disciple or Christian Church in the community), we turned to his Sunday morning adult Bible class there, and drew Cayce out on the passages he was currently teaching. My worst fear was that he might be a proof-texting pietist, citing Bible verses as inerrantly inspired and capable of predicting current events, as well as dictating arbitrary rules of behavior. After all, here was the first man I had met who had memorized most of the Bible.

But my fear was ungrounded. When Cayce likened the uprooting of millions in Europe and Asia to Israel's painful exile in its time of humbling and cleansing, and when he spoke of the worldwide hunger for leadership by referring to Moses leading a wayward people through the Exodus wilderness, I could see that he looked to the full scope and weight of the biblical drama. Sin and grace met in his comments. He offered neither shallow optimism nor Calvinist gloom but a steady realism about the human heart and will. He could evoke with a

photographer's acute perception the legendary individuals in biblical accounts. But he also saw the vista of an
entire people trying to serve God and failing as often as
they succeeded. Here was no arbitrary fundamentalist
demanding conformity to doctrinal touchstones but a
man for whom the Bible was home country, peopled
with ambiguous relatives of his, reported in sagas both
driven and noble. When he spoke of the responsibility
on all of us to use our abilities to help others, while our
destinies were being weighed and spirits stretched by
war, it was clear that for him biblical faith was not a
smug retreat from the world, but a prod to be found
worthy of that part of events entrusted to each of us.

As Cayce spoke, something familiar about him beckoned to me.

It was his resemblance to missionaries from my boyhood in China, where my parents had been educators.
Those I had known best were doers, not just evangelists;
they were teachers, nurses, engineers, and physicians,
determined to help train the native leadership among
those they served rather than make themselves indis-
pensable. Their faith had much practical worldliness, of
the sort that Cayce evinced. I could recall my father
bringing home to the kitchen baby girls he found abandoned on the walls of our Chinese city, where they had
been left to die because girls were so little valued; patiently he and my mother had brought them back to life.
And I could still see both my parents unbinding the feet
of young Chinese women, knowing that their newfound
freedom of healthy movement would be bought at the
price of alienation in their villages. Such missionaries
thought they could make a difference in some part of
the globe or in some human need which others considered hopeless. Their combination of prayer and unflagging action made them remarkably vital. Cayce seemed
to have some of their stubborn goodwill and confidence.
No wonder he had made it his business to recruit couples
to be medical missionaries in every church where he had
taught, sending them off to underdeveloped countries

in what would later be called the Third World. He sent himself in his odd trance into territories of the mind and heart just as little known but marked by similar human needs.

My mother's relish came to mind, as she told how Cayce had arranged for her to speak to the missionary society in his Presbyterian church on the occasion of her first visit. Her letters had mentioned her overseas background, and he had acted promptly. When she arrived, he announced that she was scheduled to speak to the missionary group that morning, and her protests that she had come to witness readings were useless. Cayce was quite clear on his priorities: she could hear his readings anytime, but addressing the group on overseas missions was really important.

He warmed to our exchanges, which gradually became a series of his stories, told with quietly dramatic skill and charm. Indeed, one tale followed the other so easily that he paused only briefly to draw us out. It was a pattern which (I later learned) he used deliberately, to keep himself from picking up unwanted psychic information about those before him. Sharp concentration too easily led him to read people's minds—and he thought these were none of his business. The problem was the same, I would discover, as that which blocked him from playing bridge, though he loved the game and was good at it. Players concentrated so hard that he could read their minds, and the fun went out of his play. Finally he had taken to inventing his own card games, one of which had been the noisy bidding contest of Pit or Corner the Market, which I had often played as a youngster, as had many in my generation.[14]

Our conversation turned naturally to Cayce's biography. Reporting on the strangeness of reading it in the setting of a weapons project, I studied Cayce's face for hints of self-importance. Evidently pleased with the

---

[14]Pit, or Corner the Market, manufactured by Parker Brothers.

book, he was not so fascinated to find himself in print that he could speak of nothing else. But now that he had considerable public respectability at last, it seemed reasonable for him to be tempted by grandiosity. We were catching him at the crest of his life. If success were as much a test of a person's mettle as failure, then we were there at the right time to discover his essential character. He would be less than human if he were not tempted to use his new position to make up for past disappointments.

Prayers at the Ear of God

But Cayce turned aside the talk of his fame by remarking with a smile, "Your mother has just about ruined us." He meant not only the effects of her favorable review in the *Christian Century*, limited to church readers, but the much larger impact of her later story about him in *Coronet* magazine[15] which was a widely read newsstand periodical—a sort of *Reader's Digest* with photos. The issue with her article had sold more copies than any other in the magazine's history; the editors had told her they had been forced to commandeer a whole wing of their floor in a downtown Chicago skyscraper just to answer letters and phone calls about Cayce. But we were not prepared for what we saw next in Cayce's home as a result of that article and the publication of his biography.

He took us all into the dining room, pleasantly conventional with its dark wood buffet and china closet framing the table and straight-backed chairs. There, stacked waist high along every empty wall space, were bundles of letters still in their envelopes, wrapped in rubber bands. And when we went through a small pantry-like room into the library which formed the center

---

[15]Bro, Margueritte Harmon, "Miracle Man of Virginia Beach," *Coronet*, September 1943.

of three offices that made up the addition to his home, more letters in envelopes, opened and unopened, were stacked three feet high along the walls. Airmail and special delivery letters, and even telegrams, were stuck indiscriminately among the bundles, frustrating their senders' hopes for urgent attention in a stupefying flood of mail. All of these piled-up communications represented thousands and thousands of persons. The packets seemed to stare reproachfully at us, and the effect was like the ringing of unanswered telephones, which violates the response patterns of a lifetime. June and I sat down in dismay.

Cayce explained that once before he had faced an outpouring of hundreds and even thousands of letters asking for help, when in 1910 *The New York Times* had run a piece about him after a report at a medical conference in Boston. But the inquiries then were as mild rain compared with this storm of response. We could see for ourselves the help he needed to take the place of his elder son, his chief helper before being drafted.

To start with, a great many of the letters contained money. There was cash in some, often a twenty-dollar bill but sometimes fifty or a hundred dollars or more. Others held checks, waiting uncashed while their senders tried to balance their accounts. There were money orders and telegraph drafts. Cayce was determined to send back all of the money, every cent. His policy was to offer his trance service only to those who understood exactly what they were getting. Each seeker had to be mailed a small booklet telling of Cayce's life and work, and explaining the modest but real research and educational program of the organization which sponsored his readings. Only if they agreed to the ideals and purposes of the effort, and signed up as members, could they then request a reading—all for twenty dollars. He wanted people to pay only what was required, and even this amount he found difficult to charge. As recently as a couple of decades before, he had still depended on a free-will offering for his aid—just what he had grown up with in churches where he belonged.

This was my first look at the honesty and generosity in handling money which I would see in Cayce during all the months ahead. Much later I would learn by inspecting his records that he not only gave his readings free to physicians and ministers, but did not charge as many as a fifth of those who sought his aid. Nor did he ever harass a delinquent who had promised to pay later. Evidently he placed his trust in something besides cautious business practices.

Here also was evidence of his disinclination to promote himself or to capitalize on the distresses of others. When in the months that followed I dug through all his files and clippings and queried his associates, I was able to find only one week when he had advertised his services, twenty years earlier in Alabama. He trusted that those who needed his aid would find him, as they were certainly doing now.

It was clear we would have to hire and supervise a number of typists if we were to process all this mail, together with the hundreds of letters which could be expected to continue arriving each day. In addition, there were letters to send to the many who had already written a second time, joining the Association and asking for a reading. These people had to be reminded that Cayce was booked ahead for months, except for the most severe emergencies. They each needed a time given for their appointment, and instructions to keep the period in a meditative state of asking for help from the divine. Not a few of them also needed encouragement just to go on coping with their personal traumas. Evidently Cayce would like to find a plan to allow him to write personally to each inquirer, feeling a responsibility to all those who reached out to him across the bounds of normal reality. But his was a hopeless hope. Even with a full platoon of stenographers taking down his words, he could never answer so many letters individually. Yet one could sympathize with his desire.

For these were not fan mail. They were not, except in

a few instances, notes from curiosity seekers. The bulk were accounts of genuine and sometimes desperate need. Each told of pain at the center of a life, whether of the writer or someone close, often a child or relative. Not a few of the envelopes were from overseas, including some in foreign languages but most on the thin, blue, folded V–Mail from military bases. One handwritten note I picked from the top of a pile began, "Mr. Cayce, I am dying."

Perhaps if one stood at the ear of God and heard the anguished prayers of a given night, one would discover just the kinds of cries that were scrawled and typed on these thousands of letters and wires. Cayce grew quiet as the rest of us pulled out letters at random and read portions of them aloud. It was clear that he knew where the responsibility fell for acting on all this need. When he spoke tersely, it was with strong, compressed feeling and addressed only one question: pain. His deepest promise, which he saw as the ground of his ability, had been to lift pain from sufferers. Here was pain beyond measure. How was he to keep his word?

I made notes, as I had been doing all evening. One letter was from a mother whose son was in prison, falsely accused, she said. Another was written in failing handwriting from someone with advanced multiple sclerosis, given no hope for recovery but only the prospect of slowly disintegrating as a human being. A teenager wrote that she was pregnant and asked what to tell her parents and whether to confront the young man soon to be a father. A man wrote about his wife's convulsions, slowly taking her away from him and their four children. An older person wrote that he was dying of cancer, asking how to make his remaining life count most, if Cayce were unable to prolong it. A mother enclosed a photograph of her son missing in action in the South Pacific, begging Cayce to locate him. A youngster, not knowing the modes of Cayce's aid, explained that her Scottie dog, the love of her life, was lost and that she needed Cayce's unusual help to find him. A woman wrote of her sister in a mental institution and hoped Cayce might find a cure to get her out and returned to her family. A retired mechanic scrawled in a shaky hand his greetings whose cordiality overleaped spelling, "Best whiches," as he asked for aid with his arthritis.

We had begun reading aloud from the letters in good spirits, to get a feel for their content. But as we read further, our voices began to trail off. It was too much. Who could bear all of this suffering?

To be sure, a few of the letters we read that first night made us chuckle. Someone wanted to know what to do for toes that "curl up when they are cold." A woman wanted advice on what color to dye her hair to go best with her eyes. Several sought guidance on choosing between lovers or possible mates, ready to consult Cayce without hesitation on such weighty decisions. But even the small requests, which brought relief by contrast with the heroic needs, were obviously important to the petitioners: bunions, bad breath, snoring, big feet, small breasts, and an unbearable employer. Surprisingly few people asked to be told of their past lives.

Many who wrote referred to Cayce's ability as a gift from God.

Some appeared merely pious, voicing stereotypes. But others did not. They seemed to be saying, "The universe ought to produce just what you are doing. As soon as I read your story, I knew it was right." I made a note to explore what made people assign different types of meaning to Cayce's gift (and later wrote my doctoral dissertation on this same theme).[16] Even if Cayce's counsel proved sometimes flawed, he had an unusual opportunity to help those who so clearly opened their hearts to him, pouring out in letters their renewed sense of the goodness and closeness of the divine.

---

[16]Bro, Harmon H., *The Charisma of the Seer: A Study in the Phenomenology of Religious Leadership*, unpublished doctoral dissertation, the University of Chicago Libraries, 1955.

A Small Dying

But his opportunity to serve was also his threat. Gertrude explained, when we asked how he could possibly schedule readings for so many people at the rate of two per day, that he had taken to squeezing several readings into each period. Now at the morning time of eleven and the afternoon time of three-thirty he was giving two or four or six—or even more, if they were short check-ups. This meant he was unconscious each time not for forty-five minutes but up to twice that length or even two hours. She was obviously concerned, citing trance counsel some time ago which indicated he could safely do two to five readings a day when in good health. Under our questioning she spelled out the danger to her husband's well-being, and perhaps even to his life, as he tried to respond to the pleas in so many letters. Cayce turned away and paced the floor, obviously determined not to be deterred.

She explained that from both physicians and their own readings they had discovered his state was not a simple hypnotic trance. It was a deep change in Edgar's entire body, as we would see. They were told it was near to a death coma, with most of his body functions greatly slowed or suspended. His daily work was a kind of small dying. They had to be careful to give him a precise suggestion at each session, just before he awakened, that all of his vital processes would be restored to normal, concluding, "Now, perfectly balanced and perfectly rested, you will wake up." Once, when Gertrude had hurried this suggestion a bit mechanically as she guided him out of the trance, a voice broke out of Cayce with the warning that he was like a window blind stretched to its absolute limits. A little more tension and the damage would be irreparable.

Indeed, there had been a few times that he gave readings while too tired or distraught, when they could not waken him with the usual hypnotic suggestion. Instead his breathing had grown slower and slower, his skin color ashen, and his body processes evidently weaker as they tried frantically to return him to consciousness. Twice the family had ended up on their knees beside his studio couch, where he lay barely breathing. They simply prayed aloud and wept, because they did not know anything else to do until he finally recovered.

Back in the Manhattan Project it had seemed a small matter for others to determine to pay the price to do what Cayce did. Now that was less clear, and I asked Cayce whether he thought successors could be found to share this load with him. He nodded, saying that his readings had promised this repeatedly. But, he added, he thought that many could be shown how to get their own answers to the problems on which they sought his aid. Part of my task (as it had been his son's) would be to study his trance for leads and to prepare materials for future researchers on this very question. That would begin the next day.

CHAPTER 3

When I Am Absent from the Body

What took place in the morning and afternoon trance sessions, in the months that followed when I heard and took notes on some six hundred of Cayce's readings, was a profound shock. Nothing could adequately prepare one for the amount of swift helpfulness that flowed from the unconscious man.

His outward procedures were simple enough. Cayce sat on his plain green studio couch in his cheerful windowed study, across the room from his desk and little portable typewriter. He prayed, then lay down and step by step went unconscious. He spoke in measured address about each person or need to which his wife, sitting beside him, quietly directed his attention. After an hour or more of discourse and questions which his secretary recorded in shorthand, he came swiftly back to consciousness, remembering nothing of what he had said, and got up to resume the activities of his busy correspondence and office. It was all done in broad daylight and simplicity, as naturally as if he were still taking portraits in a photographic studio. But the plainness of the process did not take away the jolt of seeing him accomplish day after day what our culture said was impossible.

House Calls on the Desperate

In some ways, watching him was a huge adventure. His body was in the room with us, but his consciousness appeared to be elsewhere. He seemed to go exactly where he was sent—to a California coastal city, a Maryland suburb, a Mississippi small town, or a factory city in England—wherever he was needed that day. Like a busy doctor making house calls and phoning back to his office, he often offered little asides on what he saw as he located his patients:

"It's raining here," or "Rooster in the yard," or "Right pretty pajamas," or "You can see the capital from here." Sometimes he made comments under his breath about the person he was about to counsel: "Quite a blade!" or "Has been a very lovely person," or "What a muddle-puddle, yet what a beautiful, talented soul!" or "Not much to be done here but help the soul to leave the body." His asides in a half voice, whose crisp accuracy had been verified hundreds and hundreds of times over the years (but which I promptly set about checking for myself, with letters and phone calls) set the stage for the high drama of the detailed formal counsel to follow. Often the small comments, as neatly accurate as they were impossible to explain by any normal means, assured seekers that he really was in touch with them. To be sure, a few of his observations were unverifiable, though they added to our sense of adventure by their matter-of-fact tone, such as "Not alone but accompanied by many besides those visible to the naked eye."

People from varied stations and walks of life streamed into his far-ranging vision, one at a time. In just the first few days he addressed a secretary, an Army officer, a housewife, a newspaper editor, an ice manufacturer, a factory supervisor, and a pianist. He also took on a tutor, a salesman, a retired mechanic, a bank president, an infant, a lay preacher, a film director, a diplomat, a student, a filling station attendant, and an asylum inmate. Where else might one find such startling contrasts? Given social stratification, they were unlikely at any one doctor's office. But many might show up at a marriage license bureau or an undertaker's parlor—some place where common human destiny calls us all.

At first I just took notes in amazement, stunned by
the unusual activity. But within a few days my attitude
began to change under the pressure of such severe needs.
Three died in days after getting their readings. Cayce recommended brain surgery for a six-year-old girl and surgery of the throat for a woman of fifty. He observed
quietly that the body and mind of an elderly woman
were just holding onto life, right while he spoke. And he
told a man of forty-six with hypertension and near
blindness that his condition could only be stayed but
not removed. One's feelings while listening moved from
awe to compassion, pushed by the evident pain of sufferers, until fascinated observation gave way to alert desire to be helpful. The intellect alone, I thought, wants its
labels, its constructs, its triumphs of understanding and
prediction. It wants to cut events down to manageable
size in order to group them with similar phenomena and
pronounce generalizations. This was all too raw, too
quick, too far-reaching to delight the mind. Being in the
room was like standing at the scene of an accident or at
the bedside of someone dangerously ill. What one asks
is how to be useful.

More common than terminal cases in the first dozen
or so days were those with chronic conditions which had
taxed sufferers to their limits. A man of fifty-eight shook
constantly with Parkinson's disease, a woman of forty
was a psychotic alcoholic, and an elderly woman of sev-
enty-three was senile and weak, while a young housewife of thirty-six was desperate with asthma. A man in
his thirties was dragging his leg from multiple sclerosis,
and a construction worker had a chronic anxiety neuro-
sis (whose origins Cayce surprisingly traced to an injury
to his spine from a baseball bat). The seriousness of these
conditions made abundantly clear how often people
turned to Cayce after all else had failed. A retired woman
suffered with uncontrollable sneezing, a severely retarded infant had been in and out of hospitals, a woman
of sixty was paranoid and thought Cayce was attacking
her telepathically, and a mid-life woman had progres-

sive arthritis (among Cayce's multiple treatment recommendations for her was cobra venom). While one case was a young student helpless to stop white blotches spreading on her skin, another was a military man in his forties who had endured migraine headaches for twenty years, and a third an older woman with tumors headed for malignancy. Still other medical extremes that emerged almost at once were deafness, blindness, paralysis from an auto accident, and epilepsy. It was a relief to have less threatening cases appear now and then among the others, although these often entailed their own hardships for persons with constricted lives: gall bladder infection, a chronic rash, neuritis, high blood pressure, and tilted pelvic organs.

Whatever the disability, the individual got a careful review of the health of his or her total body, organ system by organ system, focusing on the primary medical problem and followed by a thorough treatment regimen for rebuilding the total person—sweeping in its detail, balance, complexity, and tailoring to the individual. Alongside specific medications were massages, surgery, diets, packs and compresses, as well as electrical applications, exercises, osteopathy, and not infrequently prescribed work on attitudes and emotions, together with other interventions that ranged from ocean travel to prayer. Since most of Cayce's subjects were already under medical care, he took pains to evaluate the effectiveness of drugs and other treatments in use, explaining why modifications or substitutions might be required. Once in a while he specified an utterly unconventional treatment in these first readings I heard, as when he told a woman with cancer that it could only be retarded, but spelled out a procedure with a magnet "strong enough to raise a railroad spike." For a small number of those with chronic afflictions, he offered, along with treatment measures, the explanation that the causes of their suffering were partly karmic from their own previous lifetimes—meaning that ultimately a soul lesson of growth was to be sought in illness along with relief from symp-

toms (a perspective that he did not hesitate to use about
disabilities not connected to past lives, as well).

Time Travel for High Purpose

Amid the stream of physical suffering, the vocational
and psychological counsel, or life readings, offered some
breathing space. These had accounted for as many as
one in five formal requests for Cayce's aid since the publication of his biography. To be sure, those whom he
counseled in this mode were not without problems.
Loneliness and confusion were often represented in the
letters asking for help, alongside marital conflicts, sexual
indiscretions, mental illnesses, black moods, and business failures. Cayce himself provided the gravity in some
instances, as when he told the parents of a ten-month-
old baby to take special care lest the child drown again,
as it had in a prior life. Yet the same reading assured
them that the lad had talents for a career in chemical or
electrical engineering. His brother, aged three, was the
only individual I heard given a famous name from history, in the first months of my listening to such readings.
Cayce said he had been Gladstone of England and could
one day serve well as U.S. secretary of state, adding details of his past-life service as an imperial advisor in
Rome, a governor in Persia, and an emissary to ancient
Egypt from Indochina.

It was a relief to hear this latter reading tell the parents to bring the child back for further counsel at age
sixteen. Unless Cayce had in his entranced view successors we did not know about, he should still be giving
readings when he was nearing eighty. The same implication was in a reading for a child of three in New York
City, who surprisingly received no incarnations at all in
his life reading. His parents were told to bring the lad
back for further counsel in ten years, after making sure
they had not let the youngster dictate the terms for his
own life. Perhaps Cayce was destined to be around

longer than the pressures on him in his mid-sixties
might suggest.

The reincarnation material, spanning centuries and
touching every aspect of the personalities whom Cayce
counseled, was baffling to evaluate, though it often
seemed to fit well the person whose correspondence
could be compared with the reading. If in trance Cayce
were using the past-life material simply as a projective
framework to analyze and motivate people, he was doing it rather skillfully. But the scenes were demanding to
visualize. Just one morning session presented such contrasting extremes as the sands of a Bedouin caravan, the
forests of an early American trapper, the bloody combat
of the Crusades, the hushed halls of a Chinese temple,
and a weaver's cottage in Ireland.

Since these readings summarized many an incarnation of the past with the comment "Here the entity
gained," or "The entity lost in this experience," or noted
some combination of gaining and losing in soul growth,
it was reasonable to compare vocations and life-stations
in which the entranced Cayce saw people making major
progress. There were salutes to the wife of a colonial
American innkeeper, a trainer of future mothers in an
Egyptian temple, an emissary to Africa from Hellenistic
Greece, a nurse in an ancient Persian hospital, a helper
to Thomas Paine, a companion to an Inca leader, an early
monk, a decorator of Indochinese temples, and the
daughter of Cyrus "in love with the cupbearer to the
King, Nehemiah." Evidently there was no easy division
of secular and sacred callings, high and low station, male
or female, educated or ignorant, which marked the
growth of souls that Cayce reported. There was no caste
hierarchy from peasants up to Brahmins, such as India
had long conceived. Instead, the quality of each life,
whatever the circumstance, seemed to grasp his attention.

But interests, once developed, were often described as
surfacing in successive lives for a time, though Cayce
insisted that souls had free will to develop in many directions, like plants with varied shoots and blooms. A

woman now in her fifties, for example, was urged to become a physical education director for teenage girls. Previously, he said, she had lived during colonial times in
the same Mohawk Valley of New York where she was
born this time. There she had helped to develop "strong-
bodied, long-waisted mothers," while in an earlier Norse
incarnation she had focused on a different development
of her sex, as she "spread the gospel of woman choosing
the companion for herself."

Not all of Cayce's counsel in these life readings was
solemn. The reading for the Mohawk Valley woman was
full of high spirits, reminding her that when younger
she had played good tennis and that she should keep it
up, even at her age. And a young dictaphone operator
whose past lives he traced with care was told that when
the present war was over, she could sing herself to glory
with her talented voice, developed in other existences.
When she asked how much of the confusion in her
present life was attributable to a gynecological distur-
bance, the entranced man responded briskly with obvious mischief and a touch of a smile: "Forty-three and
seven-tenths percent!" He was evidently not about to
foster fatalism.

More difficult to conceptualize were past-life causes
that yielded present afflictions or distressing circumstances. How could the universe be organized to bring
these about? A woman now suspicious of her husband,
for example, was told that she had been swapped by
him for tobacco in an early American fort but that in a
yet earlier life she had been unfaithful to him. "We only
meet self," the reading insisted. Could we all dimly remember such betrayals at times? Which part of us would
do the remembering? Another woman, in her forties and
having difficulty finding a husband, was told that some
of the problem was having changed sexes often from life
to life, and having difficulty settling on a feminine identity this time. But the counsel added the cryptic encouragement that she had already met the right man and
had only to catch him. The recommendations were much

more serious when a leader in the publishing world,
from a distinguished family, was told that he had helped
bring on the collapse of an ancient civilization and once
again would have the opportunity to make "for success
or naught." The research task in following up these claims
seemed huge.

It was easier to picture the unfolding of talents across
supposed lifetimes, for here a model from nature seemed
to work. Something tended and used well in the garden
of one lifetime might be expected to bloom in another. A
Southern businessman nearing retirement was told he
had once interpreted for a high priest in Egypt and
should now get trained and ordained so that in his new
leisure he could plunge into the church work he enjoyed. A woman described as a deaconess in the Early
Church who had argued against Paul in favor of marriage was told to make up with a man she now loved
and build the home she had talked about. A young stenographer in New York was instructed that in an earlier
century she had come to French America of the South
and should now learn French. After the war she would
have exciting opportunities for a life and career in
France, "only don't be led by men!" as she had been then.
For an artist Cayce began his reading with the observation "Once a wonderful Cossack and rode a horse!" Then
he went on to show the man how to combine his many
talents with fabrics, buildings, and acting but warned
him that he had too much ego to take up hypnosis, currently tempting him. And in a beautiful reading which
stirred us as we heard it, a mid-life man in the service of
the British government, stationed in the U.S., was told he
had once helped William Penn bring refugees to this
country. Then he was described as having been often
with Jesus centuries ago, as one of the seventy sent out
by him. Today the man's essential kindness despite his
self-doubt would assure that he would again "meet Him
in the way." Tenderly the reading addressed the man in
closing as "my son," and urged him that in all his doings
he should be not only the statesman in his present call-

ing, but a "messenger of hope from the Master, even Jesus the Christ." Much later I would get a clue as to why the sending of the seventy might mean much to Cayce, from depiction of a past life of his own.

Were it not for the attention given to ultimate values, it would have been easy to view these life readings as colorful imagination. But Cayce used them to do serious business. Often he employed them to enunciate principles, such as "We only keep what we give away." At other times his counsel was boldly practical. A mother was encouraged to let her son go, because it was his own deep choice. A wife was told that she might well divorce her husband after her children agreed to stay with her but she should not judge him for his actions. A secretary to a bank president trying to make life decisions was reminded that Thursdays were usually her bad days and to avoid them for such reflection. Then a businesswoman in Ohio was abruptly refused any past-life information at all and sternly told to apply herself to charity. When she wrote to object that her reading was defective, Cayce promptly returned her membership fee. A young engineer was guided to seek a job in Bridgeport, Connecticut, and then given an essay on how General Electric at that time was a corporation "almost with a soul" (startling to one with my labor-organizing attitudes to large businesses). An editor interested in the psychic field was encouraged to proceed with his magazine on the mysteries of the mind but to stay away from Spiritualism. And a film director, considering how he might actively help the Association sponsoring Cayce's work, was told first to convince himself on its purposes and ideals; if these did not answer to him, he should have nothing to do with it. Cayce's counsel was evidently not interested in promoting itself.

To make sense of all this material, one would have to handle a huge array of unconscious variables. As it turned out, it would be twenty years before I found professional tools to begin exploring reincarnation in the setting of doing psychotherapy, using a Jungian perspective and such procedures as dream study, guided imagery to music, and projective tests, along with inventories of interests, attractions, and repulsions. But in the midst of war's extremes, the whole enterprise seemed daunting indeed.

First of All an Emergency Clinic

Besides, every hour given to such psychological archaeology was an hour taken from someone waiting as though in an invisible line outside Cayce's study, hurting with leukemia or polio, or sweating with fever, or coughing with tuberculosis. Cayce's work was decisively medical. All that lacked to make his home and office a clinical treatment center were the smell of antiseptics and some white jackets. Everything important was molded around the relief of pain: the mail, the phone calls, the small but growing research, the day's most earnest conversation, an unpublicized visit of a physician or nurse. Cayce's house might have been an emergency station set up near a catastrophe, taking in each one who came with a wound or hardship.

This was not forced on him by circumstance but came from his own choice and purpose. He was sure his gift was rooted in direct service of those in need. Were he to get too far away from that, it might soon distort or wither. To him the trances were not just his private prowess, but part of a circuit much larger than he which reached from an invisible and transcendent source of goodness directly to someone's scabs or cramps, tumors or aches, birthing or dying. If the lightning of helpfulness in our midst also lit up the far sky now and then, so that lifetimes and mysteries of the soul could be glimpsed, that was a bonus. But for him the central business was medical service. Listening to him, one wondered whether the urgent ministering to those in pain helped to keep him sane in a wholly unlikely vocation that had brought him extremes of both scorn and adulation.

Might his priorities be reversed after his death by those drawn to study the transcripts of his readings? He could be turned into a revealer of arcane truths, with his work of lifting physical suffering from others shoved into the background. There was plenty in the history of sects and movements, including the transformation of the work of the active young healer and teacher from Nazareth, to indicate how quickly and decisively such change could occur. As had happened in churches, future students of Cayce might find it too frustrating, taxing, and expensive to focus on failed organs, wrenching injuries, damaging childbirth, chronic fevers, convulsions, and schizophrenia. Where Cayce might want a hospital for the blind or deaf, others might prefer to remove the blindness or deafness of their fellows to metaphysical mysteries of rebirth. Power and wisdom were forever pushing themselves beyond their roots of caring, like mindless social climbers.

Watching Cayce at work was like staring into a flame, making the mind go momentarily numb. For despite the perplexing past-life claims, all too much of what he produced was reality that we and others could verify. The unending accurate medical data, the fitting details of individual history, personhood, talents, relationships, and choices were staggering. Had Cayce not asked me to make the trance sessions part of my job, I might well have absorbed myself in the backed-up correspondence, or editing the small monthly *Bulletin* of the Association, or adding to the booklets on specific diseases as his readings saw them. (We had collections on appendicitis, arthritis, the common cold, epilepsy, intestinal fever, scleroderma, streptococcus infection, and multiple sclerosis.) Then I could have attended the trance periods from time to time and settled for being amazed and stimulated. But Cayce beckoned me to his study at the appointed hours each day, and I put down my projects, preparing to be as calm and cheerful as I could before what was necessarily as shattering to my University of Chicago worldview, and therefore to my personal sense of identity, as it was adventurous.

Asking Questions of the Unseen

Cayce assigned me a task in the middle of the action, insuring that I knew more about each case as it came up for a reading than anyone else in the office. The job was to prepare the questions to be asked Cayce by his wife, at the end of each reading when the steady voice would indicate, "Ready for questions." By comparing the discourses with what was in letters already sent in by each person, often over a period of many months, and not infrequently supplemented by notes on phone calls, it would be possible to study with some care the strengths and weaknesses of his counsel. Making maps and models of the operation would also be natural, looking for what made it go better. For one reading had tersely warned, the norm for his aid was to be "informative, constructive, enlightening, yet practical."

Before long it became clear which kinds of questions would get helpful replies. The most useful to the inquirer elicited fresh information not supplied in the main body of the reading. Issues could be discarded which experience showed would be covered in any case, and the remaining queries carefully arranged, putting the most pressing first, for none of us could predict how many questions the unconscious man would answer before moving swiftly on to the next reading or terminating the session.

Usually there were appropriate questions about puzzling side issues in health, business affairs, or relationships. "Why have I had digestive upsets since I injured my back?" "Why do I have such difficulty with mathematics, when I am a good student?" "How can I guide my daughter, who seems to me so stubborn?" Such concerns, often urgent to the seeker, were likely to get patient replies of a few sentences, if the topic had not already been covered in the reading (as central concerns

typically were). Less likely to be answered were questions on the margin of real need. Once people got Cayce
on the line, so to speak, quite a few were tempted to get
all the information and guidance they could. They inquired about warts, about dreams, about real estate
holdings, about psychic experiences, or about marriage
prospects. Cayce was not likely to mix radically different
kinds of counsel, such as answering vocational questions
in a medical reading. "We haven't that" might be his
abrupt reply. His response meant that the opening suggestion given him for a particular kind of reading had
not put him in touch with some other area of the
individual's activity or relationships. Medical counsel
was not available in life readings, and vice-versa. Would
they seek at their bankers for tailoring aid, he asked?

Yet if he were feeling expansive in trance on a particular day, or if something touched him in the spirit of
the seeker (which could be noted in the tone of his voice),
he might offer at least a partial answer on any issue important to the person's welfare. So the challenge was to
phrase and rephrase the questions carefully, conveying
the best spirit in the letters. And it was necessary to keep
my own interests out of the exchange, not slanting questions to elicit explanations I wanted. Several blunt refusals taught me to try harder to be a detached channel of
aid.

It was reassuring that Gertrude would be scanning
the typed-up questions as she put them to her husband
in his strange state. She would skip those which had already been answered in the body of the reading and
sometimes make up clarifying questions of her own. Her
determination to subordinate her own able intellect was
impressive, as she sought to stay out of the way and be
the "passive" helper which the readings had indicated
should be her role. She set aside her emotions, too, so as
not to react to a particularly demanding or officious
seeker, represented by letter or occasionally present in
person for a reading. A deep dream which she told had
depicted her collecting unique shells on the beach, as

she loved to do. The reading taken on the dream interpreted it as she suspected: she was being encouraged to
see each seeker in appreciative wonder and respect as
she did shells. One could readily guess how crucial this
woman must have been in Cayce's life and work, and
why the readings had grown fuller and clearer after she
took on the work of "conductor," which had been handed
about to many in the years before their move to Virginia
Beach in the 1920s.

Nothing in my work on questions offered any warning of what tumbled from the lips of Cayce on a few
days when the pressure was heaviest to serve people in
rapid order. Usually Gertrude would read the questions
aloud to him, one at a time, and he would methodically
repeat each before answering it. But on these days Cayce
would come to the question period and simply go right
down the typed list, answering each query in order without waiting for his wife to pose it. Then he would instruct her to move on to the next reading, while we
would stare at each other in astonishment. There was no
way he could see the sheet of queries. His eyes were
covered, and the little stack of correspondence in his
wife's hands was clearly out of his line of vision in any
case. Part of his consciousness seemed to be present with
a person in Denver, or Bangor, or Miami, or Seattle, judging by his prompt and detailed reports. But part of his
mind was still in the room with us, running over unseen
papers in his wife's hand.

A second task assigned to me was to write out for the
entranced man precisely where he would find each individual. For medical aid this meant giving him the exact street address and sometimes an apartment or office
at that location. In the past he had shown that he would,
if directed to the wrong place, patiently describe it in full
and accurate detail—right down to paint on the walls
and stuffing in a mattress—while searching for the person. But when properly guided, he would repeat after
his wife the complete address and then seem to move as
though in narrowing orbits by citing out loud the state,

then the city, then the street and the building, concluding often with an aside on what he observed at the site
before firmly stating, "Yes, we have the body." For a life
reading he needed the time and place of birth, which he
followed down to the point of a not infrequent aside on
how it had been snowing in that locale on the day of the
birth, or how the delivery was complicated, or how big
the town was and what could be seen of the mountains
from there. Then he concluded, "Yes, we have the
records." For those who requested it, he would supply
the precise hospital and time of birth, providing one
more surprising item we could then verify.

There were colorful complications. An address I supplied for a man in Los Angeles was one we later found to
be incorrect. Cayce promptly commented that it was the
wrong address, and his wife hesitantly suggested that he
try to locate the person anyway. With something like a
groan he observed of Los Angeles, "Mighty big place!"
After a lengthy pause, he found the man in the huge
urban tangle and proceeded to give the reading, full of
accurate personal details.

By contrast, the instructions were a bit too specific on
highway directions to a farm in Minnesota, exactly as if
Cayce were to drive there from a nearby town and num-
bered highway. The last leg of a dirt road according to
the correspondence was "a mile and a half." Cayce found
the state, the town, and the highway, as usual, but then
corrected the final distance to a mile and two-fifths.
When we asked the family of the seeker about the discrepancy, they responded that Cayce was correct, since
they had rounded off the distance, as they said, "so he
would not be confused." From our perspective he was
not easily confused. For a man in New Orleans the unconscious Cayce pronounced the street name in what
sounded like French. Leaning toward Gertrude from
across the room at Cayce's desk, I hastily repeated twice
what I thought was the right pronunciation, which she
gave her husband. He stuck with the French version (one
we later found was correct for local New Orleans usage)

and asked the brisk question, "Who's giving this reading?" Despite his being in trance, we were evidently dealing with a process more than mechanical hypnosis. Some
sort of active agency, some wide-ranging intelligence,
seemed both to be following and leading us.

It Kept Us in Mind

Whatever it was, it kept close track of us.

Gladys was seated several feet from him, making her
notes on a steno pad at a little table. Cayce could not
even see her notebook without lifting himself from the
couch, much less read her rapid, cryptic inscriptions up-
side down. Besides, he knew nothing of shorthand. But
he did not hesitate, though the occasions were unusual,
to correct her spelling, her punctuation, her para-
graphing, or her medical terms. Her eyes would flash
with surprise and humor when part of his consciousness
monitored her careful work, after more than twenty
years of serving him. Perfection did not seem to be his
goal so much as care on important details. There were a
few words which the unconscious man habitually
mispronounced and she corrected for him, such as
"angrandizement" for "aggrandizement," and "obogdulla
mengata" for "medulla oblongata," or "morstle and petar"
for the pharmacist's "mortar and pestle." He did not
bother with these. But he did interrupt her when the use
of an *i* for an *e*, for example, might change the meaning
of a medical term, or a comma change the intent of a
sentence.

How he kept us in view also showed when he answered my own unspoken questions. After studying an
individual's correspondence, I often wanted to understand how a back injury had affected the person's vision, or why certain foods precipitated a young man's
fits, or why a mother and daughter were such strong
rivals for the husband/father's attentions. Sitting all the
way across the room from him, with my notebook open

and my pen scurrying along, I would be trying to abbre-
viate technical terms and to underline key factors in a
disease, a personality, or the structure of a reading. Now
and then my thoughts would shoot up with a spontaneous "Why?" when Cayce linked a cold spot on a child's
abdomen to epileptic seizures, or traced a woman's mental illness to a fall on the coccyx at the end of her spine,
or described a man's deafness as karmic consequences
from having "turned a deaf ear" to the pleas of others in
a previous lifetime. There were similar questions when a
reading suddenly became eloquent, after proceeding as
detached discourse. But I said nothing and did not stop
writing, only thinking my questions. Yet on occasion,
when the entranced man appeared to be in an expansive mood, he would pause, saying, "As to the question
being asked . . ." or noting my query in some other way.
He might even instruct his secretary to keep aside what
briefly followed, as he had done with unspoken questions of his elder son and others before me. Then he
would give a little essay on the theory, or explain a chain
of medical reactions, or suggest how we should investigate further the laws he had just implied. My breath
stopped a moment each time.

There was little to suggest the limits of his peripheral
awareness in trance. For example, how had he known
that a small boy cherished by Gladys, T.J., was out on a
fishing dock behind Cayce's house and in danger of falling into the little freshwater Lake Holly? What prompted
him to interrupt his speaking with a terse "Better go get
the boy from the dock" and then wait in silence until
Gladys returned?

More sobering were comments that might be made
about the attitudes and priorities of those of us in the
room. The voice we listened to was not unkind, but it
could be blunt. In the files were warnings to "Do something for yourself!" when people in his immediate circle
had grown too fond of getting guidance on everything
that came up. "Next thing," he added pungently in another transcript, "you'll be asking whether to blow your

nose with your right hand or your left!" And Cayce
showed me ruefully that the shortest reading in the files
was one given for him: a medical checkup which elicited
only the sharp comment that he hadn't done what was
given to him last time and promptly terminated. None
of us wanted a brush with the shining blade of this counsel.

Love As Quenched Wrath

The Cayces spoke of his readings as an active agent,
which they called "the information," though it provided
as much judgment as data, as much values as facts. They
appeared to do this in humility, not wanting to claim
overmuch for the presence in their midst. It was indeed
a presence for them, almost another character in the
drama of their lives, and often the protagonist. Dependable yet never fully predictable, compassionate yet never
indulgent, and lawful yet not to be manipulated for private gain—it was familiar, but it was always awesome.
For it showed flashes of such purity, goodness, and staggering helpfulness as to leave all of us uncertain of our
worthiness to be there. Its spirit many times recalled for
me Rudolf Otto's description of the holy as numinous,
partaking of a *mysterium tremendum et fascinosum*,[17] and his
observation that God's love was only his quenched
wrath.

Some of our sense of humility and awe, of course,
came from the awareness that "the information" would
be accurate on items we could verify. We had the sense
of staring over Cayce's shoulder into an abyss of final
reality, where being and non-being were divided and
apportioned. If he said someone would soon die, then
we could expect it to happen. If he promised that careful
treatment would produce relief or even a cure for a

_____

[17]Otto, Rudolf, *The Idea of the Holy*, 1923.

seemingly hopeless condition, then odds were that the treatment would work, if it were fully carried out. If he rebuked someone for a corrosive temper that spoiled a marriage, then that temper would prove to be the problem, although it had never been mentioned in the correspondence. If he ascribed to a youth a talent as a pianist which could stand out in his generation, then that talent would prove to be there, though the youth might choose not to cultivate it far. If (on rare occasions) he counseled someone in such detail as to specify that the best companion to marry would appear in a certain year, then such a person could be expected to show up, with the qualities he described. And if he commented, as he did, that the war would end suddenly and by unexpected means in the Orient, we had reason to think it would, though none of us knew at the time what was being prepared in the Manhattan Project.

Were we brainwashed, hearing more accuracy than was actually there? On one of the first days I went into the study for readings, he advised a twenty-year-old Army Air Corps cadet in Texas to use an Elliott machine every other day for three to four weeks as part of the treatment for a debilitating catarrh. When Gertrude Cayce asked where the young man could have access to one, her husband responded instantly that there were three near to him in San Antonio. I set out to verify this small item and discovered that in fact there were three, and only three, of the colonic irrigation machines in that area, since the prescribed model was newly available. One was in a civilian hospital and two at military bases; none of the institutions knew of the other locations' use. This was impossible. This was unthinkable. My professors at Chicago would deny it, and who could blame them? Centuries of Western science and philosophy would back up their denials, as well as their own manifest experience. But Cayce was doing it anyway.

Here he was in a deep trance, stretched out on his back. He had the deliberate breathing and some of the restrained movements of subjects hypnotized to a deep

level. Yet his speech and thought patterns were far from
jerky or mechanical muttering. He was not less but more
alert than in his waking consciousness, as his readings
pointed out. Indeed, he seemed to have his whole psyche
concentrated for action, not dissociated for mumbling
response to a conductor. This hypnosis, as a small dying
into larger consciousness, was different from classroom
exhibitions.

His eyelids fluttered over unseeing eyes until covered.
He spoke in phrases paced by his breathing, using a formal and sometimes elevated but not pretentious mode
of discourse. Evidently he was working hard, for his expression mirrored concentration, and his lips were
lightly pursed. Yet he spoke in firm composure, as
though quite sure of what he said. His voice was clearly
his own, but with little notes of stateliness that heightened its dignity, and with a resonance that gave it authority while not sounding preachy or oracular.

The manner in which he addressed those who sought
his aid added gravity to the encounter. He spoke to or
about each one only by name, never using a title, no
matter what degrees or positions distinguished the inquirer in daily life. There was a Quaker-like simplicity in
this usage. He flattered none and he belittled none,
though he challenged many. He did not exaggerate,
though he used irony and wit. Such unaffected discourse
was at first unsettling to hear and then reassuring, as he
seemed to plant himself before the absent person called
to his attention with a forthrightness which invited more
than it accosted. His speech was not sententious or
pompous, just serious. In later years, when I sought out
mediums and studied them in trances, I would find their
speech dramatic or chatty, as the case might be, but
rarely so unadorned and direct as here.

Beyond Safe Limits

Was this the same man as the one with whom we had

been talking in the office, or running an errand to buy supplies, or having coffee with guests just a short time ago? He spoke in trance as someone on important business and typically used an editorial "we" instead of "I." These were times when his face and speech outside of trance were close to the even discourse of his altered state. The man awake looked and sounded similar when teaching the Bible, whether on Sunday mornings at church or on Tuesday evenings at home. There serenity and depth marked his face so that he was immensely appealing. Some of that same self, so like the person giving readings, came to the fore when he prayed aloud at table graces or at the break every afternoon at two when the entire office stopped for fifteen minutes of Bible reading aloud, prayer, and quiet sharing. And just after he emerged from taking some troubled visitor into his office for an hour of counseling while wide awake, his face was as peaceful and shining as during readings.

How much continuity existed between Cayce's trance self and his waking self seemed important to discover. For if he were taken over by a strange intelligence, however benign, then what he did was of little relevance to the rest of us who did not become unconscious for a living. But if, as his own counsel suggested, he put himself by prayer into a state which for him extended easily into trance, and there stepped into relation with what he called "universal" currents which lifted up and used all that was best in him, then we were looking at a process which might in some way apply to any of us.

Cayce rarely spoke of himself as a psychic, preferring instead to refer to "the thing I do." In later years, when I would investigate many professional psychics, that distinction would become sharper. He was not focused on his own skill but upon a relationship, which he would describe as one with his Lord. In that respect he differed from many strongly endowed mediums, healers, and clairvoyants. He saw his ability as gift, in a double sense. It was a talent, to be sure, in the familiar sense of a gift as ability. But it was a talent exercised in cooperation with an active reality much larger and wiser than he, making his skill a gift from out of that relationship. As a result, the whole enterprise of getting readings was seen by him as stepping into a cherished Presence, not as a high-jump leap by his psyche alone.

He would gesture to us to come into his study, and one of us would cover the noisy parrot, a gift from a sea captain, that whistled and expostulated at one end of the library. We shut the door behind us as we entered. There were necessary procedures. For example, we were warned that sudden interruptions could cut off the flow, or even catapult him convulsively from his couch to his feet, leaving him upset in mind and body. Were a hand or a piece of paper to be passed across his solar plexus, or sometimes his head, he could awaken with a violent start. Readings explained that it was important not to interfere with a delicate invisible connection like a cord, connecting Cayce's body to his consciousness, off in-specting someone ill. And on the few occasions when they had tried successfully, years ago, to get Cayce to locate murderers, he had sometimes wakened shouting, "He's killing her! He's killing her!" as though he had wit-nessed the very event. The distress stayed with him for days. An additional health hazard in years past had been violent, persistent headaches after giving readings, which he had traced to occasions in which a conductor sent his mind off for business and financial counsel when Cayce thought he was giving medical aid. Whatever he was entering with his trances, it involved his whole being and could threaten his health, his sanity, and even his life, since in the process, as one reading put it, "the soul is near to leaving the body." The danger was greatest to him when he was overtired or ill, and that was just what threatened us as he tried to match his efforts to the stacks of unanswered letters.

As a result, we entered his study with soberness in the backs of our minds, even though we often joked and teased a bit to achieve the relaxed atmosphere which experience showed was optimal for the best readings.

We were like those sending a diver to unknown depths, whose equipment was not designed to assure his safety at such far reaches but somehow continued to function. Adding to the seriousness of our effort was another possibility which Cayce had been forced to face. It was the chance, however small, that his counsel might prescribe a powerful medication in error and cause an injury or a fatality. Back in the Cayce Hospital days, when he had worn himself out not only by giving readings but taking on the administration, a full medical reading had been given for someone already dead, not noted in the counsel. Each day, each session, then, was the one in which his gift might prove lethal. Only the sense that he was bound to One who would protect him and others, Cayce observed with no little feeling, allowed him to go on taking this risk.

To start his journey into another kind of awareness, Cayce would sit down on his studio couch and loosen his tie and shirt collar, belt and shoestrings, while his wife seated herself beside him to give instructions. After we had talked enough to create a mood of unforced expectancy, Cayce grew silent and we all joined him in inward prayer. This was, it seemed, the decisive act. It expressed a desire for connection, not private attainment. Essentially it defined the trance which followed as an extension of the prayer process—exactly as Cayce saw it. Many who visited and wrote to us sought to understand his feats by using patterns from hypnosis, which was certainly involved. And in later years Cayce would be studied by me and others in the context of research on altered states of consciousness,[18] not only those drug-induced, but those derived from intense concentration, sensory deprivation, sensory invariance (white noise), as well as states initiated by pain, sex, or dying. But the model that always seemed to me closest to reality was

---

[18]See Tart, Charles, *Altered States of Consciousness*, 1969, and *States of Consciousness*, 1975.

prayer, with which he started the entire process.[19]

Next Cayce stretched out on his back on the couch and pulled an afghan cover to his waist. He put his hands together, palms up, on his forehead, and kept them there while breathing regularly and perhaps a little deeper than usual. Then with a bit of a sigh he lowered his hands, taking a few moments as he crossed them at his waist. This was the point at which suggestion to do his counseling had to be given to him. Otherwise he would drift off into a deep sleep from which he could not be awakened for hours, even for a day or longer, if he were tired.

He told us what was going on in his mind, which often gave him the cue to lower his hands and enter more deeply into trance. The experience varied but usually involved following a small dot of light. Particularly vivid was the process of avoiding entanglement with the dead, who seemed to be ready to press into his consciousness in the fashion reported and used by mediums. Here was yet another threat to his effort and one he felt more severely than most outsiders realized. This danger became even greater if a seeker actively hoped for a message from some dead relative. There had been times (relatively few, to be sure) when someone had broken in and spoken through him. Avoiding this outcome was, in part, the intent of asking seekers to be in a prayerful, meditative state, asking for help from the highest source, or the divine, not from discarnate entities. It was also the intent of his own prayer, where he sought to serve God, not to plunder hidden realms. One description he dictated gave an account of going for the records he needed to give a life reading.

As he described to me his inner signal to proceed, it was a flash of brilliant white light, sometimes tending toward a golden color. Without this, he knew he could not give a reading that day. There were also times when

---

[19]See Bro, Harmon H., *Dreams in the Life of Prayer*, 1970.

he went to what seemed to him a hall of records, following that same light and aware that he must not stop, so that he could secure the counsel for life readings. On the journey he passed through what appeared to be several planes, which he experienced as realms of experience after death. First there was a level of humanoid forms which were like exaggerated expressions of particular human desires. Then came a level with individuals in forms familiar on the earth, satisfied with their condition and having even homes and cities. As the light grew stronger and he followed it onward, he came to a realm where all was like springtime; some desired to stay here while others pressed on for greater understanding, more light. Finally he came to an ethereal, lovely place where records of earth lives were kept. Here he picked out what seemed to be volumes or scrolls of information, or—for what proved to be specially developed souls—he was handed the material he needed.

On a Narrow Ridge

Cayce's eyes in trance at first stared sightlessly until his wife gently covered them, as she spoke words become familiar in their decades of journeying together into invisible regions and bonds: "Now the body is assuming its normal forces, and will be able, and will give, such information as is desired of it at the present time." The term "the body" simply meant the person, in the language of the readings. But what was meant by "normal forces" was not so clear. The phrase demanded attention. If Cayce's readings were given by normal means, as implied by these instructions approved by his readings, then what of the rest of us? How normal were we? What was our true nature and destiny? How ought we to be related to the source or sources of Cayce's extraordinary aid?

His working vocabulary in the trance (apart from technical terms), as well as many of his figures of speech and illustrations, were similar to his usages while teaching or dictating letters. At times in his counseling, especially as he neared the end of a period, his typical colloquialisms or homey aphorisms popped into the discourse. But, as though to foster the relationship into which he sought to enter, he leaned part of the time toward relatively archaic usages of King James English so familiar to him from the Bible. The impression was that to his deeper mind nothing would have sufficient dignity, grace, or amplitude of spirit for the task at hand or for the Source whose help he sought. "Ye" and "thee" crept into the readings, with associated verb forms not always perfectly matched. Often he spoke elliptically, as most of us do in conversation, leaving out modifiers and referents which the inflections of his voice implied. All in all, he seemed to be the man we knew outside of trance but on a serious errand. Yet there remained puzzling bits of his unconscious word usages, where he used roundabout phrases such as "those of" for "the," creating an effect like transliterated German.

His speech was spare, never loquacious, and grew more terse as the reading period came toward its end. The mood was that of a man traveling a narrow ridge with no time or effort to waste in showing off. Getting technical or factual information seemed no problem, provided that it served the autonomy and well-being of the seeker. It was there instantly as needed. But sometimes he groped to find the right words—not so much stumbling as having a concentrated expression, nearly a frown. Often he used synonyms piled on top of each other to make a point, as though he could only reach us by the intersection of related terms. And he obviously chose images to awaken and fire each petitioner as needed, not just to deliver information.

At times one would wonder whether he saw reality in visions like that of the poet/artist William Blake. His frequent use of the term "forces" suggested that he viewed directly the dance and swirl of molecules, the flow of bright blood and nerve impulses, the pushes and blocks of psychological and spiritual thrusts, the tides of history, all moving in their courses through time and space, yet all related to an indescribable Center. Those of us listening had to think in terms of solid chunks, while he may have been trying to show us naked reality, shimmering and bouncing and transforming. The riddle of his actual vision came closer to being solved two decades later, when Aldous Huxley[20] and many others described their experiences of familiar structures when viewed in a psychedelic state. But the pattern was already there in the experience of Moses before a bush that seemed to burn yet was not consumed.

The entranced man set the pace for each counseling session.

When he felt he had said enough to an individual, he concluded, "We are through with this reading," or he closed an entire session with "We are through for the present." After the latter his wife would give him an extended suggestion to enhance his well–being and balance, then direct him to wake up. Cayce's body would jerk slightly as he opened his eyes and stretched a bit. Then he often asked, "Did you get anything?" His question was reasonable, for sometimes fatigue, emotional upset, or some less understood cause would block his activity. But the question was outrageous to the rest of us in the room, who had been listening intently to a stream of original material. His query only underscored the fact that he remembered nothing of what he had said. We would be sitting there wondering or bemused, sometimes eagerly starting to talk, and sometimes lost in thought. About us were stacked invisible remnants from vital organs, the garments of ancient times, or traces of tangled lines connecting psyches and relationships.

Cayce would patiently rouse himself to get a snack of milk and crackers from the kitchen. When he returned, we might have left the study. But often we were still

---

[20]Huxley, Aldous, *The Doors of Perception*, 1954.

there, discussing what we had just heard. It did not take him long to join in. He knew intimately, of course, the structure and conceptual thrusts of the readings. Other parts of the counsel just given he seemed to pick from the air or from his own blocked memory of the trance. Perhaps this capacity explained why he never appeared to study a transcript of a reading for any length of time. When he held one or just scanned it, he seemed in touch with its contents, much as when he startled secretaries taking his dictation by offering thoughtful observations about the strangers to whom he was dictating. Though the detailed personal data he cited were not in these letters, they were often verified in later phone calls or visits from the senders.

He Never Heard a Reading

Was Cayce the waking man in competition with Cayce the entranced man? It did seem now and then that he delayed the move from the larger library to his study, especially when there were interesting visitors. Even though it was time for him to go unconscious and the conversation stumbled into awkward pauses (when those present manifestly wanted him to begin his unique process), he might extend a story as though to say, "Look, I matter as a conscious person, you know." But when the conversation lagged further, he took the demand in good grace, laying aside his consciousness and putting his life on the line by entering a pressure chamber which none of us fully understood nor could guarantee that he would leave unharmed.

He was the only one among us who never heard a reading. He alone must take his gift on faith. The rest of us were daily reinforced in our reliance on it. The doubt he had to conquer showed all too clearly in a dream he told from some years earlier. In it he held an infant girl in his arms. (Other dreams showed her as a mummified Egyptian girl who had to be brought back to life, since the young female was often his dream emblem for his unusual talent, as what Jung called the creative anima.)[21] She spoke precociously and was being examined by authorities to discover whether she were in fact a midget and doing nothing unusual. Inspection proved, to his relief, that she was an authentic prodigy. The reading taken on this dream confirmed that the infant stood for an ability which seemed to him at times small, of little account in the world affairs. Yet it would grow, he was admonished, to bring joy and aid to many. "Good dream!" "the information" concluded.

More poignant and revealing was a dream he shared with me which had come at one of the many times when he was out of money, facing the nagging doubt which would confront any modern American: "If you're so smart, why aren't you rich?" The dream took place in a courtroom, where his wife—ever the bearer of rational judgment in his life—had him arraigned on lunacy charges and brought in their forlorn-looking children to show how incompetent he was to take care of them. Somehow in the trial he managed to affirm his adequacy and ended up giving what amounted to a mini-reading for each prominent figure in the courtroom, starting with the judge. He cited details of their past lives with him which none could deny, and convinced his hearers that he was mentally sound. The reading taken on this dream recognized his financial distress but urged him to be faithful. Then it added that getting in touch with the one man who had vouched for him in the dream would bring him requests for readings and needed income—as it did when he followed up the lead. Obviously in such dreams, Cayce's unconscious during the night mirrored his fears over the sanity of having to rely on a process he only partly understood, never saw or heard for himself,

---

[21]On the anima, see Jung's most systematic statement of his theories in *Two Essays in Analytical Psychology*, Collected Works, vol. 7. Also, Jung, Emma, *Animus and Anima*, 1957.

and found brought him only as much money as he required for everyday needs.

But a very different, visionary dream he related set his trance efforts in a larger context. He saw himself preparing to give a reading ("fixing" to give one, was his Southern expression) and observed his consciousness as a tiny speck at the base of a great funnel or spiral which reached upward and outward toward the heavens. Between the rings encircling the funnel at different levels were located sources of the information and aid he sought in order to help others. Even the resources of whole cities were available to him, according to their quality depicted as rates of vibration. The tiny dot of his consciousness was tugged by someone's need to whatever points on the vast spiral he should reach for aid. The dream with its cosmic, mystical scope affected him strongly, and he sought a reading on it. There he was told that his little consciousness was indeed as nothing in the great vortex or spiral of the universe. Yet by its purpose of service it could be lifted to whatever heights and specific resources were needed, "even unto the Thrones themselves," the ultimate thrones of divine grace. The spiral he had seen was like a great trumpet of the universe, resounding with whatever was required for one who would for a time empty himself of all self-seeking.

Given the soaring imagery of such a dream, Cayce's response was understandable when I asked him what he felt essentially transpired in his trance. He chose an image from a letter of Paul's to the Corinthian church, and spoke of being absent in the body but present in the spirit with those who needed him.[22] His image often returned to me in later years when I worked intensively with parapsychologists and gifted subjects trying to replicate some of Cayce's doings. Typically our emphasis was on states and circuits in the psyche and in the body. Not

---

[22] I Corinthians 5:3.

often was the model stretched as far as his dream of the
spiral suggested it might be.

Where Power and Love Meet

Slowly it became clear that Cayce's readings were a
joining of power with love.

Cayce's power was his distinction. In a technical culture, his skill with facts stood out as the hallmark of his
gift. To most of those who learned of his story he was (if
real at all) a psychic, a supplier of unknown data, a purveyor of useful facts, a trafficker in unusual power. Yet
we were hearing more than facts. We were hearing engagement and encounter, call and sending, of one person at a time. We were dealing with power, to be sure,
but it was power infused and shaped by love. Or it was
love surprised by wisdom.

We were watching a consciousness instantly form itself into the person being counseled. Comparing the tone
of voice and the choice of words given in readings at the
same session showed that we were not dealing with a
grand Western Union of the mind, hunting up psychic
data to drop on listeners. This counsel was far more personal, more individual. It was bent on engaging each
seeker in terms appropriate for just that person's growth.

To one the counsel might be demanding, brusque, and
businesslike, to another supportive, gentle, or even tender. The factual information was firmly knit to the effort
to reach and quicken the person. Caring formed, paced,
and sharpened each reading, both in content and in
style. The counsel to a somewhat officious Army colonel
startled us when Cayce made a rare departure from his
usual impersonal address to admonish, after answering
a question, "Take that and think it over, sonny boy!" By
contrast, for a little old lady in her eighties who only
wanted to know in the question period, "How am I doing?", he capped a reading of warm praise for her generous life with the words, "Who can tell the sun how to

shine, who can tell the wind how to blow? Who can tell a rose to be beautiful, who can tell a baby how to smile?" She needed, he said, no evaluation from him.

The entranced Cayce took his own measure of each counselee, not judging by appearances. Often he impressed us with his patience. An alcoholic who insisted on several checkup readings, but kept up drinking (to his wife's dismay), received not the rebuke one might expect but firm and supportive counsel. We were surely dealing with power. It was skill, knowledge, and judgment in superb measure. But its quality or essence was active love. We were seeing not just a general spirit of goodwill, but a specific, original engagement of each person. To be sure, the counsel often took up the same series of issues in a given type of reading. But within this framework were the flashes and angles, the embraces and the stiff challenges which lifted the aid above mere information.

Getting clear on the union of power with love in this effort seemed important when we asked "How can such an ability be developed and nurtured in others?" Visitors steeped in the American ethos of know-how tended to focus on such manageable techniques as hypnosis and yogic concentration when the question arose of how to duplicate Cayce. But this narrow, engineering perspective, which gave maximum attention to mastery of a new power, tended to miss the element of caring and compassion which seemed the heart of Cayce's gift.

Further, when some of Cayce's friends and associates, outside his intimate circle, quoted "the information" on subjects as varied as nutrition and ethics, they did so as one might quote the Bible in comparable church circles. Lifted out of individual engagements and made into abstract admonitions or general principles, these quotes could be impressive. But they produced an oracular mind-set about Cayce's work which easily lost the element of concern to free and empower the listener. Such an approach, it seemed, could easily produce a cult. Pronouncing rather than serving, explaining rather than

eliciting, informing rather than inviting—these were classic temptations in viewing Cayce as a purveyor of unusual data or teachings rather than as a channel of active
love, deftly and incisively varying his aid from person to
person.

Cayce told a dream which contained a succinct warning on just this score. In it he had found through the aid
of his readings that his dead grandmother had come
back to life. He had located her resting body, breathing
and capable of being wakened, in a thicket far away. In
the dream he was eager to leave and tell others of the
remarkable discovery he had made with his unusual
trance skills. But he found to his horror that dogs nearby
might damage the body before he could get help to bring
it fully back to life. When he awakened, it was with the
thought that he was letting his real work go to the dogs.
The reading he sought on the dream did not encourage
him to feature the prowess he wanted to exhibit for others in the dream. It emphasized instead the grandmother's return to life—the symbolic process of
resurrection. The "information" urged him to keep clear
on just this purpose in every reading he gave. To him
this counsel meant he was to call people to fuller life
who were, in some part of their beings, dead or dead-
ened. He was not to call them to another existence, or to
a spiritual existence floating in the air, but to their
present existence, awake and potent.

The dream motif of resurrection seemed fitting. The
people he served were indeed being summoned one at a
time from death to new life and given aid to make the
change. Whether the death process was a disintegrating
body, a troubled and defensive mind, or a flagging spirit
turned back on itself in doubt and self-condemnation,
Cayce's counsel was undoing the burial wrappings. He
did his own dying from waking consciousness so that
his hearers would walk, grin, plan, and build. For those
of us listening to his measured speech, the revivifying
brought awe and delight side by side. Tears would come
to our eyes when some young mother was told that her

desperately ill baby could be treated and would live. Laughter burst out of us when a too spiritual couple asking for a propitious site on which to build a house were told it had best be done "on the ground."

It was not difficult to think of death around us, waiting to yield to resurrection. Actual death threatened in many of the pleading letters. It was also in the very air, rattling the windowpanes of Cayce's study while he spoke his unhurried readings. (Big artillery guns practiced their booming volleys at a base just down the coast from us.) And daily we could hear fighter planes from the nearby Naval Air Base at Oceana, droning over the house like angered hornets, intent on some offshore target. Sometimes we could not catch Cayce's words, so loud were the planes carrying a load heavier than bombs—a reminder that most of mankind was caught up in an effort to kill. All of the mind-wrenching contrasts from the Manhattan Project laboratories, when flickering dials and buzzing machines could be weighed against Cayce's simple trances, came back in those moments.

What seemed important was that our civilization's struggles for ever greater power over nature, over the psyche, over institutions, and over competing nations must one day be taken up in a commitment to love. Not just vague goodwill, but passionate commitment to the hungry, the poor, the ignorant, the ill, the discriminated against, and the lonely. And the love would need to stretch to the earth itself, whose face we smashed so easily with our bombs. If we could not love the land and the lowly creatures, how could we love each other?

The way in which Cayce's readings joined power with love, wisdom with caring could be seen clearly in what he chose *not* to say. When the life of an individual seemed to lie bare before his vision, he could be pungent, even confrontational in his trances. But the steady voice refused to shame people. It would not reveal humiliating personal secrets, except in cryptic references that only the recipient would understand. There was a record of an instance in which Cayce had given part of a reading in German (of which he knew nothing) so that severe points could be made without exposing the person. In the same spirit, he refused to take away crucial choices. "This must be answered within self" was the frequent response to an ethical dilemma in a marriage or a career, in a sexual tangle, or in deciding about conscientious objection to military service. The reading might spell out the issues involved in such deep choices and even point to overlooked consequences or to dubious motivations. It would formulate principles and evoke biblical or historical figures faced with similar choices. Still the thrust, demanded by love, was to turn the responsibility back to the individual. Sometimes it seemed that the most important readings to understand might be the ones he did not give, because love restrained his speech. When he insisted "I don't do anything you can't do," the price was ultimately both simple and difficult—love itself.

In later years when people studied his readings in the form of typed transcripts, or even downloaded computer excerpts, they all too easily skipped over the element of caring which so deeply shaped each encounter differently from those readings given just before and after it. The result was not just missing nuances, but perhaps missing the key to the entire operation.

Especially revealing were a series of readings he had given for a man depressed by business failures. A husband and father, he had deserted his family, who were frantic that he might have killed himself. Coming to Cayce, they were told in the trance that the person they sought was alive in another city but that the location could not be given because the fleeing businessman did not wish it. However, Cayce added, if they would come back each week, "we will be with him." They came back, week upon week, and the entire hour-long reading went by each time in utter silence, supported by the family's prayers. One day Cayce said, "He's ready now, and will call home soon." That was exactly what happened. Both the man and his family credited his recovery of perspective and motivation in part to the quiet, holy presence he felt again and again, alone in his hotel room. Nothing in the usual definition of psychic would fit such a wordless activity, representative of Cayce's process at its core.

Could power and love be brought together on a large scale, as the basis for a whole civilization? Or were we seeing in Cayce a fluke, a geyser that appears from a crack in the earth and then is gone for a thousand years? The answer seemed most clear when one turned from watching Cayce to glance at another face in the room. There he was on the couch, supplying fresh data yet also analyzing, evoking, inviting, and calling forth the person in the same sentences which plucked resources from nowhere visible. Then one might look across the room to someone else, perhaps his grave wife, his earnestly inscribing secretary, or just a puzzled visitor on hand for the day. Repeatedly would follow the surging surmise: "It's got to be in all of us! We are made for such consciousness, as birthright and destiny." Of course, the thought was not provable. But again and again it seemed as we listened that each of us could well be appointed to grow toward a love so strong, so steady, so clean that we could become channels of resources from beyond ourselves, where love would be surprised by wisdom.

As visitors came (often to hear their own readings), I asked them what they made of the process as they left the room. Two themes dominated their responses. One was best put by a thoughtful student: "We are known, all the way. And not just by Cayce." As did others, he felt the astonishing certitude, almost alarming in its force, that he was known to the smallest details of his bodily organs and the deepest recesses of his thoughts. Who did the knowing and supplied the helpful responses to it? He answered that no sparrow falls without that same knowing.

The other response which I heard in varying words was this: "How we are loved!" Here even the fact of intimate knowledge was absorbed in the sense of being cared for and called by name. Something greater than Cayce seemed present to these people in the peculiar trances at the edge of the ocean, during a shattering time of history.

The next task was to see the larger outlines of Cayce's work. What was he essentially called to be and do in his resurrection process? But as the days slid into weeks in that rainy fall in a blacked-out resort town, it was evident that a portrait of the unschooled but immensely creative Cayce would require painting on a very large canvas indeed.

CHAPTER 4

No Disease without a Cure

One rainy afternoon a car pulled up at the foot of the walk that curved to the Cayce home and offices. A woman in her thirties climbed out, hoisted herself onto crutches, tugged her crippled legs to the steps, and entered the door to the library, where half a dozen of us were working. She had stopped by before to see a volunteer on our small staff who was giving her daily massages at her home for her poliomyelitis handicap. "Watch!" she commanded us. Laying down her crutches, she slowly walked the length of the room unaided, then back again while we shouted and applauded. There were tears in the room. Her achievement had climaxed two years of intensive daily work in a taxing, multiform regimen specified by readings. We all knew how rarely, anywhere in the country, limbs were restored after damage by this frightening disease. She had more rebuilding of her body to do but left using her crutches jauntily, delighted with her small but triumphant excursion.

Soon after came another case just as forceful. A naval officer in uniform arrived with his wife and infant from the Chicago area for a reading which seemed their last hope. The child was crying, and I offered to hold it while the parents went into the study. It never stopped crying. The little boy had been in and out of hospitals, suffering with cancer of the head and eyes, which had made him blind. His pain was continuous. When the parents emerged from the reading an hour later, it was bewildering to see them smiling and energetic, for the case had seemed impossible to cure. According to "the information," they could expect a full recovery. They must undertake without deviation a complex treatment under the care of a Philadelphia physician. (I followed the boy's dramatic case all the way to complete cure and restoration of his vision, keeping the doctor as a colleague and friend for thirty years.)

We had to be mindful of spontaneous remissions. And there were faith cures; how the mind could influence the body had been shown in studies of what was called the "subliminal" region by William James[23] and F.W.H. Myers[24] and so brilliantly elaborated by Freud[25] and others as the unconscious. Such influences could not and should not be ruled out in remarkable cases of healing. But one could not overlook, either, Cayce's specific clinical procedures, used under medical supervision. Months or years of tedious effort were often required. To be sure, the demanding nature of this effort sometimes seemed part of the cure because it taxed and fired the faith and active love of all those involved.

The faces of the cripple and the tormented baby stayed with me as I interviewed scores of other subjects and talked with their family members. Especially compelling were children whom Cayce had guided through threatened births or rescued from life-imperiling illnesses. Even while I played and teased with them after interrogating their parents, I weighed the thought: this youngster might not be here at all but for a photographer who took better pictures than our culture thought possible.

---

[23]James, William, *The Varieties of Religious Experience*, 1902.

[24]Myers, F.W.H., *Human Personality and Its Survival of Bodily Death*, vols. I and II, 1903.

[25]Freud, Sigmund, A., *A General Introduction to Psychoanalysis*, 1924. Note his essays in *Studies in Parapsychology*, from 1919-1923, reprinted in 1963.

I Never Read One of Cayce's Readings

A few doctors in the Virginia Beach and Norfolk area took referrals from Cayce seriously and were willing to talk with me. Most were osteopaths. But there was also an M.D. who would on occasion write prescriptions that Cayce recommended. He insisted that Cayce's transcripts be read aloud to him so that he could affirm to any suspicious colleagues that "I never read one of Cayce's readings." There was the local pharmacist, a college classmate of Cayce's eldest son, who had for years filled Cayce's prescriptions, even those that seemed to his training to be dubious, hopeless, or dangerous. So far he had never regretted it. He reported case after case to me in which an unorthodox chemical resource from Cayce's readings had produced surprisingly effective results.

Suppose Cayce's process could one day supplement medical care? How would it work? Would there be one or more gifted figures attached to clinics or hospitals, busy with baffling cases? Though it seemed unlikely, we had already processed a request to Cayce from the dean of a Harvard graduate school and had discovered that Still-Hildreth osteopathic hospital in Missouri found Cayce's aid so valuable that they routinely sent him reports on patients he referred. Decades later I would witness the unobtrusive use of psychic specialists by multi-staff clinics run by medical doctors. But the prospect seemed dim in the mid-1940s.

Would medical education include courses and supervision in heightened perception, equipping physicians to use their intuition and prayer guidance? I could not guess then that within two years I would be meeting with a medical faculty in Chicago to explore just such options, and in later years be invited to medical centers (several times to the Mayo Clinic) to conduct workshops and consultations on maximizing such resources for physicians. Would patients be pressed to use self-help intuitive guidance, with nightly dreams checking their daytime impressions? This, too, was difficult to conceive, though in fact I would later lecture for national medical groups on just this process and watch it gain surprisingly wide momentum. It was more reasonable to picture researchers providing the decisive parallel to Cayce, working in teams to follow leads from him and other gifted figures on particular illnesses. Given the perilously small number of researchers interested in Cayce during wartime, it seemed unlikely. But later I would meet with faculty from Johns Hopkins and a whole cluster of Philadelphia medical schools to work on just such projects.

In the years that followed, the potent impact of observing and studying Cayce's medical service would lead me into my own second vocation of health care alongside my teaching in psychology of religion. As a professional counselor and psychotherapist, I would labor for decades with Cayce's concepts of health and treatment, not only in private practice in Chicago, Boston, and elsewhere, but serving several years apiece as a consultant and staff member in teaching hospitals. In due time I would teach psychotherapy in graduate schools and institutes, supervise graduate counselors, design a major Veterans Administration hospital program for substance abuse, serve in a residential farm community for young psychotics, run a multi-unit hospital research program, and even find myself cited in *American Men of Science*.[26] June would also get her doctorate and do Jung-oriented counseling. But at twenty-three in the boarded-up resort town of Virginia Beach, all of this was yet to unfold, while I struggled with the enormous puzzle of evaluating Cayce's medical aid.

The place to start seemed to be outlining Cayce's view of normal health maintenance, upon which his specific treatment programs could be mounted for examination. Reviewing the daily entries in my black leather notebook and comparing them with sample transcripts in his thousands of case files led to summarizing the Cayce

---

[26]1962 edition.

model of health care with four plain words: Out, In, Push, and Circuits. Each represented a process for keeping healthy, as well as for treating impairment, with variations that ranged from common sense cures to weighty interventions.[27] Each process could be tracked not only in bodily health, but in mental and spiritual dimensions to produce well-being and productive wholeness with others (a perspective which would much later be called "holistic health").[28]

Out, Or Elimination in Health

The word *out* went alongside portions of my notes on each day's readings, standing for elimination as a basic health process. Here the principle seemed to be, "We are what we release" and how we do it, whether grudgingly, patiently, or sporadically, as well as what we deeply mean in the process, by acting in a spirit of trust or of hoarding.

By promptly attending to elimination of wastes and toxins in the ailments that came before his far-seeing vision, Cayce affirmed the body as a self-maintaining, self-restoring system. If alien or stress-producing substances or drosses could be removed, the body would begin to set itself in order—provided that vital processes were not critically damaged and needed nutrients and stimulants were supplied. This was one reason he turned first, in the sequence of examinations in his medical counsel, to circulation, just as physicians routinely got blood workups. For the circulation carried off much of what needed eliminating, whether through kidneys, res-

---

[27]On Cayce treatments, see McGarey, William, *The Edgar Cayce Remedies*, 1983,

[28]The contributions of C. Norman Shealy to the holistic health movement (like those of Dr. McGarey, above) cannot be overstated. See for example his foreword to *The Holistic Health Lifebook*, 1981.

piration, or perspiration. Cayce placed more emphasis than many physicians, however, on circulation of the lymphatic system, seeing it as a complete delivery operation for servicing organs and tissues. To foster healthy discharges through circulation, he often recommended massage and sometimes baths or sweats, as well as manipulative therapy to realign skeletal–muscular structures and release cramped or knotted muscles. Readings exhibited a whole array of exercises for parts of the body, as well as for circulation, tonus, and organ support. (The time would come, decades later, when several million Cayce readers contributed to the interest in jogging that would change the shape of American daily routines.)

Cayce in trance attended to actual wastes and poisons just as carefully as he attended to the carriers of what must be eliminated. There were special compounds to stimulate and cleanse the liver and other organs, including the use of fumes from brandy in a charred oak keg for cleansing lungs. There were special cleansing diets, such as eating nothing but apples for three days, followed by a small portion of olive oil. More basically, he counseled that everyone should drink six to eight glasses of water each day, facilitating kidney and bladder elimination processes. One procedure that applied especially to elimination and lymphatic circulation was used in a number of ways: castor oil applied externally in flannel packs under heat for an hour. Later research would show the impact of this unusual substance, with a centuries-old reputation as the *Palma Christi*, or palm of Christ,[29] on the complex chemistry of the immune system.

Among the substances which the readings frequently singled out to be eliminated were residues of medications which had turned into burdens on the body—as even excessive vitamins could do. But often, of course, the gastrointestinal tract required central attention as an avenue for elimination not only for obvious constipa-

---

[29]McGarey, William, *Palma Christi*, 1970.

tion or colitis, but for lesser studied effects of caked fecal matter adhering in patches to the sides of the colon. To Cayce's vision this material could generate poisons in the bloodstream that resulted in a range of deleterious effects, including migraine headaches. He counseled laxatives in dosages and periods tailored to individual needs, advising alternating mineral and vegetable types so that the body would not become dependent on one or the other. Fasts and special diets aimed at improving gastrointestinal operation were not uncommon, and the use of high colonic irrigations to thoroughly cleanse the bowel from time to time were almost a Cayce trademark.

The general pattern in the readings was careful and slow action, however, not violent purgings, as the campaign for elimination was interfaced with restoring natural capacities of the body to fight disease and rebuild tissue. Fletcher's Castoria, for example, often appeared as a recommended laxative, but in surprisingly small, "broken" doses given frequently over several hours or a day. This was a compound (one of several) on which readings had shown instant keeping-up with the manufacture, since the trance noted at once when the makers changed the formula slightly, and insisted on adding supplements to restore the needed properties. Yet other compounds were abruptly dropped when changed.

Cleansing and Freeing the Mind

The entranced Cayce set about helping his counselees eliminate poisons or blocks in their minds and emotions as well, where I also wrote *out* in my little notebook. He did not refer to Freud's anal type of character structure, meant to describe the person overly committed to holding back or hoarding in order to have power over others through what was withheld, supplemented by excessive order, control, and tightness. But he operated as though this were an important set of psychological patterns. Those who were secretive with their thoughts, feelings, and belongings, and who failed to give themselves fully to relationships, were pushed by Cayce in his medical readings to more free traffic with both persons and things. A banker, for example, was asked how long since he had played with children, or gotten his hands dirty, and was urged to new ventures. Anyone who overly stressed order and control, or who wrongly eliminated either natural drives or natural conscience, might be challenged. Cayce's constant emphasis on service meant that life was fullest in terms of what was given out rather than what was held back.

Grudges and resentments needed flushing out as truly as poison–making material in colons. He traced how holding onto these negative patterns not only troubled the mind but upset the tissues. In similar fashion he out-lined how withholding affection and honest feeling in the effort to impress or control others, or even suppos-edly to please God, could upset the physical system just as much as indulging in exaggerated emotions. ("One without a temper isn't worth much, though one who doesn't control it is worth less.") In the physical readings, just as in the more psychological and spiritual life read-ings, he took account of not only what must be cleansed from the psyche, but also what was being wrongly elimi-nated, denied, repressed, ignored, overcontrolled, or held in. Here he pointed to what Jung described as response to the overdeveloped persona or social mask in a dis-turbing inner shadow.

Cayce also gave special attention to vows which indi-viduals had made, whether named by them or not. In his view, such strong commitments (for example, a vow not to get hurt again in intimate relationships) could be surprisingly effective for long periods, requiring disci-plined cleaning. Indeed, vows could last for several life-times, creating severe health–and–wholeness problems. Yet in general Cayce was not an advocate of dumping feelings. Just as in handling the body, he gave priority to measured and repeated small steps rather than drastic catharses or excisions.

Cleansing and Freeing the Spirit

When the term *out* appeared in my notes beside Cayce's references to the spiritual dimensions of healing and health maintenance, his suggestions developed the theme of "emptying self to be filled." Of course, the idea was not to cleanse one's house and let seven demons rush in from the unconscious or the culture. The intent was a particular kind of disciplined emptying which would enable one's habitual will to conform more closely to the will of God, and one's mind to be transformed by the renewing action of larger Reality.

One form of this emptying, or elimination in the spiritual mode, was forgiveness. Repeatedly the counseling man struggled to soften the self-condemnation in those he advised. He warned that while sin and guilt before God were real and universal, there was danger in arrogating to oneself the function of divinely authorized judge, whether over oneself or others. Humans, in this view, were not well equipped with the wisdom, justice, and mercy to serve as their own final judges; too often they usurped the place of divinity, even taking secret pride in the condemning process. While attacking themselves or attacking others, they were belittling a part of creation dear to the Creator: a soul, a unique person, brought into being for God's own companionship.

Of course, those who failed to examine themselves, just as those who repressed deserved guilt (and therefore dodged seeking forgiveness), were urged by Cayce to "step aside and watch self go by," for ultimately each soul "must give account of itself" for its actions and inactions. Some were asked where they would be if God treated them as they treated themselves and others, and the pungent answer might be "oblivion unthinkable." So the quiet voice of the entranced Cayce pleaded with his hearers to be responsible but not to condemn, turning for mercy to their Source while they turned toward their fellows with the compassion which they themselves required. Always, Cayce insisted, "As ye do it unto your fellows, ye do it unto your God."

What, then, could free one of all that must be eliminated as regret, guilt, and condemnation? Once the vio-
lation of deep values had been stopped and the
renewing mercy of God called upon, then forgiveness
and release or elimination of spiritual poisons would be
found by generous giving to others. Here Cayce could be
explicit as he was with medication. For he might name
the precise relationships in one's family or business associates where forgiving must begin in order to free up
the individual's clogged life force.

Yet the entranced man was careful not to humiliate or
frighten. He protected the privacy and final self-respect
of his counselees in the loving spirit already noted. Not
amputation but cleansing and washing, so well emblematized by immersion baptism in Cayce's church tradition, was the general spirit of counsel on elimination,
whether physical or spiritual. He did not advocate fierce
asceticism and penance for most, though there were
some self-indulgent persons for whom he advised regimes of ascetic simplicity and sacrifice. Surgery in the
spiritual realm was reserved for the divine, unless it were
clear that the individual already sensed it was time to
pluck out a corrosive temper, a business fraud, or a destructive extramarital affair. In such instances Cayce
spoke to further the person's own resolve.

The motif of "emptying self to be filled" also appeared
as part of the spiritual dimension when Cayce urged
meditation for everyone.[30] He was not dogmatic in his
urging, nor did he offer colorful benefits of mind or body
control, yet he saw meditation as part of total health.
When the subject came up, he spoke clearly and persua-
sively about it, decades before meditation became a
countercultural theme in American society and slowly
crept into organized religious practice. In prayer, which

---

[30]Puryear, Herbert B., and Thurston, Mark A., *Meditation and the Mind of Man*, 1975.

he suggested was the foundation of meditation, one properly filled the consciousness with thought, speech, and emblems until turning to God overflowed with thanksgiving, praise, and commitment, within which petitions might have their rightful place. Such activity was the heart of public worship and private devotions alike. By contrast, meditation meant emptying one's consciousness so that a deeper movement of thought and being might develop, which could be called listening to God, not so much by pursuing thought and symbols as by receiving the divine into one's stilled being.

In Cayce's trance view, the psyche had level upon level below surface consciousness, with innate dynamics as powerful as those which enabled a tiny plant to move a boulder as it reached for the sunlight. Meditation, which emptied and cleansed surface consciousness by a peaceful fasting from discursive thought, could set free a potent inward movement towards full and healthy humanness. He encouraged the use of focalizing phrases to start the process, whether bits of scripture or sayings familiar to the person, or more formal "affirmations" (his versions were actually as much prayer as assertions) on which individuals could model their own words. These small phrases functioned like the mantras from Eastern religions or like tuning from the texts and tones of anthems in choirs.

In his view, what was released in meditation was much deeper than the mere action of suggestion. It was the true and natural bent of the soul as the self held up its best chosen ideal. For what was "on the mind" at primary levels of the psyche would surface and bring accompanying energies in meditation. If the ancient art were practiced daily in concert with prayer, intercession, and service, and embedded in covenant community, the inner noble form of the person would assert itself, just as the plant grows from the seed or the embryo from the meeting of two cells. The process of pushing "out" whatever was not essential for stilled and hushed turning to God in prayer–based meditation was a prized kind of

elimination, not just for soul growth but ultimately also
for bodily health and wholeness.

In passages dealing with meditation, he employed the
language of kundalini yoga[51] from India and Tibet, right
alongside material from the Psalms about meditating on
God's law. For the entranced Cayce, the concept of *chakras*,
or spiritual centers, at seven key points in the body was
helpful to understand being "filled with the Spirit," since
all creativity used the same circuits in the body. What
had to be emptied to allow the fiery life force to rise
secretly within the person and be met by invisible
tongues of flame from Beyond was self–will and self–
aggrandizement—not self–identity. Here Cayce departed
from some forms of Hindu thought and practice that
emphasized dissolution of the ego and individuality into
the larger whole. In his view, identity was precious to
the Creator; else why the creation? But self–dictated autonomy needed purging, as truly as a clogged bowel.

In, Or Assimilation in Health

The little word *in* appeared in my notebook when
Cayce counseled ingestion, absorption, and assimilation
for healing. Here the focus was not emptying, but re-
plenishing and nurture and absorption of whatever was
taken into the person. The principle might be "We are
what we eat" or drink, breathe, swallow, rub in, soak in,
and sniff. The process was also affected by how we did
the intake, whether indulgently, absently, or anxiously.
And it was also important to consider what we deeply
meant in the process, whether to save or to serve, to
dominate or cooperate, in trust or in fear.

It was rare that a medical reading for a severe illness
did not spell out a regimen or diet for feeding and sup-

---

[51]For one exposition, see Keen, Sam, *The Passionate Life*, 1983, Appendix A. For Cayce's view, see Cayce, Hugh Lynn, *Venture Inward*, 1964,
p. 209.

plying the body. As poisons and drosses were removed, the struggling tissues had to be given the needed resources to restore natural function. Aiding assimilation might, of course, be as simple as providing more oxygen through exercise or time out-of-doors. But even then the circulation had to be in shape to carry the blood's freight to be assimilated, perhaps requiring massages, osteopathy, special packs, or baths. Sluggish organs charged with handling input by respiration or digestion might require stimulus or tempering, whether through osteopathic or massage action, to free and quicken nerve impulses, or through chemical or even surgical intervention, where poisons had collected or were strangling an organ or tissue. But once the body were set free to take in and use what was offered, then the game was to supply its needs soundly—and in balance. The two processes went on together, for elimination and assimilation continued unceasingly and could not be suspended for a few weeks to overhaul the plumbing and wiring or the girders and stewpots of the flesh.

Most of the diet suggestions seemed so sensible that people acted on them more readily than other aspects of his treatment regimes, even more than exercise and relaxation. To be sure, the special intervention diets or nutriments to provide substances for very sick bodies were difficult to evaluate: Jerusalem artichoke for diabetes, plantain weed poultice for certain cancers, carefully prepared beef juice for badly weakened bodies, a product called Kaldak for calcium deficiency, and much more. Preventive foods were easier to follow, not only the three almonds a day for cancer, but the lowly cabbage for pinworms.

But it was the normal diet which Cayce repeatedly outlined that appealed not only to nutrition experts but to thoughtful laypersons. Alternating eggs and cereals for breakfast, featuring salads for lunch, choosing fish, fowl, or lamb for dinner more often than the unchanging beef which Americans prize, two vegetables above the ground to one below, balancing yellow and green vegetables, eating foods grown in one's immediate environment, adding gelatin as a catalyst to assure vitamin absorption—the list was full and varied, but sensible, and in later years would generate a number of widely read books[32] as well as research.

Cayce was not fanatical in advising food distributions, and counseled moderation rather than rigidity. He was quite ready to spell out the chains of digestive responses and nutrient actions which he saw from his trance state. As in all his readings, he appeared more interested in developing independent grown-ups making their own decisions than in getting results on particular tissues, except where serious illness was present. Cigarettes (those made from pure tobacco—not easy to find) he allowed in moderation, as he did limited amounts of caffeine and alcohol, indicating that the body was equipped to turn these into foods or useful stimuli. He was less charitable about carbonated beverages, described as "slops" for one nutrition seeker (though pure Coca-Cola syrup he sometimes prescribed as medication). Many were startled, however, at his unyielding admonition over the years not to combine coffee and cream, or citrus juices and cereals, since these were on the breakfast menus of so many Americans. But the entranced Cayce insisted that careful research would show these combinations to be stressful to digestion.

Assimilation was presented, of course, as a wider process than digesting food and drink. There was taking "in" through breathing and through the skin. Fumes, special baths, and nutrient massages all had a place in the Cayce array of remedies. Peanut oil, he insisted, could in many cases prevent or alleviate arthritis when rubbed into irritated areas, especially in combination with soaking in Epsom salts and colonic irrigations, where needed. Other kinds of salves, rubs, and packs added to the assimilation process, including a compound originating with

---

[32]On the Cayce diet recommendations, see Bolton, Brett, *Edgar Cayce Speaks*, 1969, and the works of McGarey, William A.

Cayce which his files showed had been remarkably effective in reducing or preventing development of scar
tissue. He prescribed what to rub on or around breasts
to enlarge or shrink them, and what to apply for loss of
hair (part of it derived from another external covering,
the peelings of potatoes). Sunlight, so widely used by
Americans for tanning, he recommended only before ten
or after two o'clock standard time—hours when burning
was minimal.

The most sophisticated of the nutrient interventions
required reinjecting the leukemia patient's own blood
after treating it, or using electrical circuits to transfer gold
chloride to the body for rebuilding nerves, or applying
mercury-vapor light through green quartz glass for certain kinds of cancer. Even the body's own resources
could be used to bring it special aid, he explained, as he
directed the construction of a battery-like appliance to
take tiny natural electrical impulses from one portion of
the body and circulate them to others. In much of this
unusual counsel we were surrounded by riddles, many
of which would not in fact receive research attention
until well after the war. But overall it was clear that in
assimilation, as in elimination, Cayce was seeking to
maximize natural body function rather than practice
gross intervention. He insisted that the body could create, when not too damaged, all the chemicals it needed
from familiar, balanced supplies.

But of course bodies brought to Cayce's vision were
often grossly upset or impaired. So he supplied the
chemicals he saw as needed. His original compound to
prevent seasickness and other motion sickness was
widely used by those who knew about it. Other effective
original prescriptions dealt with the morning sickness of
pregnant women, in addition to his cough syrups and
laxatives. He dictated a formula for salve to place on
infected gums, which was modestly marketed by a friend
as Ipsab and another for hemorrhoids called Tim. A leading toothpaste which featured prevention of gum irritation, he told me, had used a derivative of Ipsab from his

readings, though I could not verify this. Further, a Hindu
scientist named Dr. Bisey had come to Cayce with a plan
to develop a form of iodine which released I-one molecules along with the usual I-two. A series of readings
produced Atomidine, which Cayce in trance suggested
in very small amounts for cleansing and regulating endocrine gland function. The range of what he saw or
created to add to the body through assimilation was
evidently as wide as it was cautiously handled.

Feeding the Mind

What did the readings feature to place "in" the mind?
That choice appeared to be more important to Cayce in
trance than to most of us, who thought in terms of stimulating and equipping the mind, but not usually in terms
of feeding it. Yet to him the mind was the great fashioner
not only of bodily health but of human destiny, when
used wisely with the will (which he saw as a primal given
in the human makeup). In this view we became not only
what we ate and drank, but also—in one lifetime or another—whatever we fed the mind upon, by what we
thought and cared about. Cayce paid more
attention to the daily working of the unconscious or
subconscious than most people not engaged in psychotherapy. Often he stressed the mind's ultimate suggestibility. The deeper levels of the psyche would build up,
magnify, and manifest what they were centered on, by
the remarkable creativity which was the mind's nature.
Like Paul he saw an important distinction between living
"to" the flesh and "with" the flesh, because in his view,
humans could be shaped to become virtual animals if
they chose. Choosing reading and companionship, then,
as well as play and devotions, employment and travel,
arts and artifacts, was not merely an issue of coping and
being pleasantly distracted. Choices set directions that
would bear results in the months and years—or centuries—of personal growth and health which followed.

The unconscious Cayce did not refer to the oral-character type from Freud, which represents a lifestyle of dependency and incorporation from others. But he seemed well aware that there were both positive and negative trends in the mind's ingesting process. There were gullibility, copying, and uncritical swallowing of people and ideas, just as there was biting or tearing at what came before the supercritical intellect. Cayce followed the Bible in counting the tongue a mighty member, and speech such a molder of reality and relationships that the Word became a symbol of God's own creative action. He agreed with Jesus that what came out of the mouth in speech was more important than what went into it, as he stressed what the mind fed upon through the mouth's chatter, with respect to fantasies, hopes, memories, gossip, or blessings. These would determine what later came out of that mouth as command, creation, and call. Hundreds of times he developed in his readings the theme "Mind is the builder," connecting it to the second person of the Trinity, the Logos with whom all things were made. Yet the mind alone, as in biblical thought, could trip itself with imagination and had to be correlated with a disciplined will. In his perspective, passions were not the central human predicament so much as the directing mind and will.

Cayce assigned to the mind a remarkable degree of autonomy, rather than determinism. While he took account of influences on the psyche from parents, teachers, and other molders of upbringing (not to mention influences from past lives or experiences between these), he seemed to assign even greater weight to the individual's capacity to feed himself or herself on prized values. Here he appeared to depart from orthodox psychoanalytic emphasis on childhood's definitive shaping. The key to using adult autonomy, in his view, was setting ideals, to be brought before the individual's consciousness again and again, both in coded symbolism (what would later be called right-brain activity) and in rational decision-making and planning (left brain

activity.)[33] Such self–chosen feeding would operate not
only on one's loving and productivity but upon health
itself. He meant by "ideal" not an arbitrary goal or what
he called an "idea" as part of a governing ideology, but a
thoughtfully weighed construct to which one would give
unreserved commitment in a major area of life. Such an
ideal embodied a direction to which one answered with
the depths of one's being, not an arbitrary, self–serving
aspiration.[34] Vocation, in the religious sense of being
called to live by chosen ideals, was a process not reserved for monastics or religious leaders, but meant for
everyone.

"Draw two lines upon a piece of paper," he often counseled, "and put into columns labeled as spiritual, mental,
and physical what you would enter as 'My ideal.'" The
entries in the columns, he warned, would often need to
be changed and correlated so that they supported and
implemented each other. And often they would require
erasing for restating or enlarging. Ultimately, he said, the
person would develop formulations not only practical,
but translucent to the divine. For those who found it
helpful, the ideal could be weighed against the person
and the prayer–sought presence of the Christ. In quiet
times and in turbulent times, one could well ask, "What
would He have me do?" A useful answer would come
more quickly to those who fed upon a chosen ideal than
to those who merely drifted or lived reactively upon the
pressures and demands of others.

Cayce never wearied of explaining that the care and
feeding of the mind required caution about projecting
its contents. What we saw in others that distressed or
commanded us with too prompt emotion, he explained,
was often perceived because it was actually within ourselves and ready for attention. Here he took account of
one of the classic Freudian defenses, as he also did of

---

[33]Ornstein, Robert, *The Psychology of Consciousness*, 1972.
[34]See Bro, Harmon H., *Begin a New Life*, 1971, ch. 4.

rationalization, repression, reaction–formation, and others. But he also paralleled Jung in noting that what is worthwhile and developing in us is often first discovered by projection upon others. His intent was not so much to call others to studied self-awareness at all times as to get them periodically to assess and modify what they were feeding their minds. What held their interest, what did they allow to fascinate or compel them? If they fed upon revenge, upon narrow ambition, upon sensual prowess, or upon the failings of their fellows, they would find several kinds of results in their lives: pronounced reactions to these concerns, temptations drawn their way, and ultimately physical illness or dysfunction.

The better way to feed the mind was to plunge into creating for others whatever one truly valued for oneself. "If ye would have friends, be friendly; if ye would have love, be loving." Here Cayce gave expression to a principle which he insisted was one of the great laws of the universe: "Like attracts like." The law was not about conjuring by sympathetic magic, or occult manipulation of correspondences, but similar to the thought of Carl Jung, where activation of an archetype within the psyche could lead to resonation with comparable archetypes elsewhere, drawing persons, objects, and events into meaningful orbit by "a causal synchronicity."[35] In such a view we could be seen as surrounded not only by chains of cause and effect, but by something like great meridians of force that girdled our world unseen, which drew like towards like (as Progoff and Koestler have suggested). Cayce's outlook seemed to embody such a perspective when he explained that what the mind feeds on is not simply a matter of gardening one's private corner of reality. By our thoughts we each act to "redeem the times," or to trivialize and perhaps demonize what is

---

[35]Jung, Carl G. and Pauli W., *The Interpretation of Nature and the Psyche*, 1955. See also Koestler, Arthur, *The Roots of Coincidence*, 1972, and Progoff, Ira, *Jung, Synchronicity, and Human Destiny*, 1973.

going on around us. From our minds would also be spun forth trends for our bodies, much as our faces as we get older reflect more and more of our essential character.

Feeding the Spirit

In the dimensions of the spiritual or the ultimate, my notebook entries of *in* showed Cayce also describing assimilation as a health process. Two images in the medical readings drew attention: breathing and communion.

Cayce made the same linkage of breath with prayer as had India, not unlike the biblical linkage of breath and wind with the Spirit. He even spoke of the quality of one's life as being "a sweet odor unto the Lord." His imagery on respiration as a spiritual emblem was vivid when he spoke of the breathing which occurs while absorbed in meditation or a worthwhile task, when one might rest lightly on the breath in the hush of focused attention. Such breathing was not technology, yet it had definite consequences for healing currents in the body, by affecting the kundalini centers and associated glandular function as one carried on exchanges with the ambient air. In using breathing as spiritual imagery Cayce appeared to counsel responsive trafficking with the universe, by allowing oneself to be met, accosted, and surprised, rather than everlastingly grabbing, grasping, and gobbling whatever could be of advantage. To be full one had to be filled, accepting gifts as gifts. Whether dancing, playing, puffing through a task, sighing, or singing, it made a difference to health to recognize that life came like breathing from invisible sources as blessing, not merely as goodies to be plucked and consumed. The unceasing traffic with the invisible air could be a model for a way of life that flowed rather than manipulated, which the ancients of my native China had long before described (and a reading cited) as the Tao.

The image of communing together also appeared in the medical counsel to signify the spiritual dimension of assimilation. "Until you can see in each person that you meet, though in error he or she may be, that which you would worship in your Lord, you haven't begun to live aright" was Cayce's demanding counsel. What he intended apparently was not a narrowing of focus to the other's abstract essence, or a psychic trick of connecting with the other's interior psyche, but a heartfelt effort to attend to the other person as a whole, unique being before God, which commanded one's unreserved attention. Here he offered a direct parallel to Buber's I-thou relationship, not as a posture to sustain at all times, but as an essential not to be left out of daily life.

Cayce made no effort to press on his listeners the rite of communion so prominent in his frontier-born denomination that formed part of each Sunday's services as what he called "the Lord's Supper." Certainly he had presided at this ritual table as an elder or deacon many hundreds of times in the communities where he lived. The ceremony was dear to him, but in his readings he spoke of it only to make a point, for what might be called sacramental living: so engaging in everyday actions as never to be far from communing with the Source of life itself. In one reading he spoke of the Spirit as being "in, with, and under" all our lives—an ancient formula for communion as "an outward and visible symbol of an inward and spiritual grace."

Traditionally the communion meal used a very small amount of food and drink to feed the person upon the life-renewing body and blood of Christ. In the medical readings theological language was not often pushed, but the point was made that whatever we fed upon with others, in our hearts, would take on form in proportion to its nobility. As breathing reminded us of our unseen Origin, moment to moment, so eating and drinking could remind us of incarnating our finest potential, won in commitment to others and not apart from them. In earlier centuries Christians had called the food and drink of communion or the Eucharist the medicine of immortality. Perhaps it was not too strange that Cayce should speak of feeding daily on spiritual reality, in the spirit of One who said, "Other food have I that ye know not of."

Cayce seemed here to affirm something profoundly optimistic. Human beings could change. They needed help, even divine help from beyond themselves. But they were built on a large plan. The defeats, the failures, even the sins and monstrous evils, were not the last word about embodiment or about illness. Feeding on "what-soever is lovely" could in patience (a cardinal concept here) transform even a broken body, a desperate heart, or a bewildered soul. By acting "line upon line, precept upon precept" in the spirit of communing with the Eternal, anyone might grow toward health. As truly as we could choose what to place in our mouths and to rub on our limbs, we could choose what to emphasize in our strivings. "Magnify the agreements and minimize the differences" was the counsel which put communing to the fore. The full outcome would be gift, as is each gulp of free air. But it would be found through that whole-souled attentiveness and receptiveness to others which might be called communing.

Push, Or Investment for Health

The word *push*, scribbled beside entries in my notes on each day's readings, tagged what Cayce's counsel saw as health from how we invest ourselves. The principle here appeared to be "We are what we seek to create." The approach also embodied how we do it, whether too little, too much, or the wrong way, as well as what we deeply mean or intend as we do it, such as gratification or service, freedom or control, knowledge or love.

It was clear that Cayce did not view the body as a set of interacting tubes and organs, whose physical health came only from what was taken out of it or put into it. The body might better be described as a vessel, shaped and marked by the blows and polishing in its use. This concept appeared, for example, when observers were told to watch closely at the end of one reading session, when Cayce might be seen reentering "the vault" of his body. But even that would be too mechanical an image. The emblem which Cayce preferred, drawing on biblical sources, was of the body as a temple. Like any temple, it could be ignored, it could be used for idolatry and indulgence, or it could help to lift the spirit soaring beyond itself toward others. The issue lay in where and how one would "push" the effort.

The term that Cayce most often used to describe the functioning of organs and systems of the body was "forces." Apparently he saw tissues and energies in dynamic terms, as thrust and "push" which could be underdone and overdone. One might cleanse and feed the body well, but if it went relatively unused, it could not be expected to stay healthy. The flesh was an instrument for going somewhere, getting things done, building worlds, loving people, creating beauty, truth, and holiness. Not to use it fully was to betray it, so that the very forces in the nerves and glands which fired up passion and direction would strike inward to make the flesh sick. Such illness might be manifest in symbolic form, as seen in what one could not "stomach" or could not bear on "my aching back," or how one could not "stand" a person or activity. Indeed, just such metaphoric illness was the basis of part of what Cayce called karma in the physical dimension. One reading told a man that his asthma (which almost suffocated him) was set up by his squeezing the life out of others in a prior existence. The implication was that how we pressed ourselves and others, or how we invested ourselves, shaped our health as truly as what we discharged or ate.

Since one dimension of "push" was failure to push enough in useful directions, Cayce in trance spoke firmly about health consequences to those who drifted or indulged themselves, not using the treasures of their talents or experience. He often asked people who sought his aid why they wanted to get well, daring them to set a better life direction. One could see the pattern he addressed in questions from correspondence that betrayed narcissism, hypochondria, or other over-absorption in self. In the view of the readings, bodies were made to be used, love was for creating, and life was for spending. Not infrequently someone given medical counsel might hear a burning citation of the needs of the poor, lonely, or downtrodden, alongside drugs, rubs, and enemas.

But failure to push was no more destructive to health than the opposite pattern—pushing too hard or in the wrong directions. This problem was prominent among Cayce's counselees, since he tended to draw for counsel independent thinkers who drove or dominated themselves and others. So he offered relaxation procedures, with places and times for getting reflective and refreshed, along with admonitions about balanced lives in which work and play were intertwined under the star of high purpose. Changes of pace were presented not simply for stimulus or distraction, but for survival, since the body could not sustain the compulsive ways so often visited upon it by strong-minded people. Even Cayce himself was sternly warned in his own readings to take breaks, seek contrasts, go on trips, play and go fishing, lest he grow ill and fail to serve the very people for whom he drove himself.

To relieve pressure and stress, there was massage given by someone loving, just as setting out to massage another would help to awaken one's own sense of un-forced vital energies. Exercises were spelled out for each region of the body, and for internal needs of various organs, to implement the proper, unhurried use of "push."

There were exercises to prepare pregnant women for delivery, exercises to reduce or eliminate the need for glasses, and exercises helpful to meditation. Walking was enjoined on everyone, and swimming often encouraged. A healthy body had to be used physically, but rest and relaxation were a necessary counterpoint to the effort. A period of rest after lunch was often advised, a thrust that might delight those from cultures featuring siesta. Travel, vacations, and sport all got their due. Cayce took prompt account in his readings of limits from injuries and congenital impairments, or exposure hazards to chronic body weaknesses. But a fundamental note was sounded. Like a fine musical instrument, the body would perform best and keep its health if it were used in balance to bring joy into the world.

Investing the Mind

In the mental dimension of health, *push* also appeared. How an individual used the conscience or control systems of his or her life would be reflected in tissues. Self-indulgence under faulty controls would lead not only to flaccid muscles and poor circulation, but to organ impairment, depending on whether the indulgence were food, sex, alcohol, self-importance, or some other. Cayce pressed those whose life circles had collapsed inward to reach out to others in need, to take up new hobbies, to take on new friends, to read, to risk. Yet by contrast he warned those who allowed their mental controls and expectations to press them too hard that they would have their own health problems. They would find effects on tissues in congestion, inflammation, and other destructive consequences of too much adrenaline in the system. Correcting either excess required sorting ideals to discover what was really worthwhile and then changing what was not truly and wisely self-chosen.

The entranced Cayce did not use Freud's concept of phallic character structure to represent personality trends toward exhibitionism or overly competitive striving against others. But such processes seemed well represented. For example, the first law of growth in the sequence of tasks that made up the spiritual manual developed anonymously by Cayce and his friends, called *A Search for God*,[36] was not assertive self-improvement but cooperation. Such an emphasis was useful for those of

---

[36]Anon., *A Search for God*, Books I and II, 1942, 1946.

his counselees who were perfectionists caught in their self-appointed striving, or so gripped by ambition as to eviscerate their humanness. Yet the other pole of behavior—not being sufficiently self-assertive—also caught Cayce's attention because of the self-pity and self-damaging anger which it so often generated, as well as lonely lives. "Every tub must sit on its own bottom," he urged, and added for some, "So live that you may look anyone in the eye and tell him to go to hell." For those who had sold out to a symbiotic relationship with parent, spouse, or some other guarantor, Cayce stipulated a self-inventory to take full responsibility for one's own life, lest illness mirror the protesting spirit of the person, through the rebellion of cancer cells, the irritation of an ulcer, or the throb of headaches.

Cayce did not offer an ascetic model as the optimal means for balancing push and relaxation in the body, though he did not condemn it for those who chose it wisely. Like the Buddha he offered a middle path, which brought together ecstasy and responsibility. Joy should be the spirit of a vital life at all levels, including the sexual as well as the intellectual when these were responsibly chosen. Bodies were viscera as truly as muscles and nerves.

A special trap to the mind, as one sought to give effective "push" to one's life, lay in excessive fear and doubt. Over and over the readings pointed out that these normal processes could, if exaggerated, produce dismay, consternation, depression, and even disintegration of personhood. Fear and doubt were the primary sources (other than organ impairment) of mental illness, both in their corrosive action on self-respect and judgment, and in their debilitating effects on nerve circuits and body organs flooded with anxiety. Those caught in the twin mires of fear and doubt might well need to be rescued by others. Yet such persons must not be left in dependency but encouraged to formulate their own governing ideals and values and to begin acting on them (precisely as modern psychotherapy so often attempts). To tame fear and doubt, each person could well inquire about the difference between what Cayce called one's "personality" and "individuality," where the former stood for the self necessarily set before others to be seen, appreciated, and engaged in workaday affairs, while the latter stood for the true nature of the unique being. (The distinction was a solid match for Jung's contrast of persona and self.)[37] Both structures, in Cayce's view, had to be brought into alignment, until the outer person expressed the patterns of the inner person and one could affirm self-worth without exaggerated fear or doubt. Cayce's formula for both self-appraisal and the appraisal of others was "What ye measure in others will be inwardly measured in you." While biblical in origin, it was congruent with the perspectives of psychotherapy.

Investing the Spirit

For my entries of *push* in the spiritual dimension of health, the first question was who did the pushing: the ultimate author of an individual's life and opportunities. Self-responsibility was a strong, recurrent theme in the readings. It was prominent, for example, in the treatment of reincarnation and karma, where both suffering and creative talents were frequently presented as fruits of choices and deeds undertaken long ago. But self-responsibility and trying to author oneself were not the same. In Cayce's view the biblical metaphor of call and response was most often used to address the question of destiny. Each soul had been called into being with certain unique possibilities, talents, and gifts. It was not finally self-invented. Being responsible, then, meant responding to that original call of the Creator, however dimly or clearly heard, in activities which plucked the

---

[37]On persona see Jung, Carl G. *Two Essays on Analytical Psychology,* Collected Works, vol. 7.

vibrating string of central purpose set within each person by the Maker. At times Cayce drew on Isaiah 6:8, urging, "When the call comes, 'Here am I; send me; use me!'" to suggest how the individual's pushing might best be shaped in relationship to God. Such an approach could forestall the cramp and rebellion of a self-contrived life, sure to manifest itself in disorders of the body.

The spiritual issue of sacrifice came up inevitably in notes on the "push" or investment character of health. When might one expect to push, or be pushed, so far as to threaten self-interest or self-development? For all of the entranced Cayce's concern with health as wholeness and balance, he did not try to go around sacrifice. Instead he affirmed that for everyone the fires of self-will and self-indulgence must someday, in some lifetime, be extinguished on the altar of love. Each person could expect what amounted to an ultimate crucifixion, not as punishment but as fulfillment of the very nature of existence, where self-centeredness had finally to yield to God-centeredness. Each could discover in the temple of the body, by turning within to meet the Author of life, when such sacrifice was appointed and could be met without fear. It would not be a call to extinction, though it might involve humiliation and suffering. For Cayce quoted often the biblical promises as sure: "God hath not willed that any soul should perish, but hath with every temptation provided a means of escape."[38]

The entranced man did not counsel self-mortification or needless martyrdom. It was not identity that required sacrificing, but only those preoccupations that were outworn, to be left behind. There might be a different kind of sacrifice, too, of privilege, in order to learn through the soul's choice of hardship, pain, or lowly estate just what others were in fact enduring and how to be filled with longing to be helpful. As Cayce spoke about the suffering and crucifixion of Christ, he affirmed that it

---

[38]II Peter 3:4; I Corinthians 10:13.

had entailed real pain, not sham. But he also disclosed (in what seemed a daring extension of his counseling vision) what was the spirit of Jesus that enabled him to choose faithfulness, even to the cross. Cayce reported as the inner prayer often in the Galilean's thoughts: "Others, Lord, others." Choosing to live by the same spirit, none could expect to avoid the crucifying of self-will.

Circuits, Or Connections in Health

The final area of basic health processes jotted beside entries in my notebook was *circuits*. It was the need for belonging, for giving and receiving in commitments, flowing in larger channels than self's orbits, which might keep not only the blood moving, but the life force itself. Here the principle seemed to be "We are whom we are *for*," in our chosen connections and accountability. Just how we gave ourselves to larger circuits also mattered in whether we merely identified with others or undertook risks of being exposed and ultimately changed. In the same way, what we deeply meant in our circuits shaped their impact, as we might embody or miss out on mutual caring in the round of life.

When the unconscious man described the life of cells and tissues, he reported no strictly private state of health. Just as a cell could not make its way alone in the liver, brain, or biceps but must function in consort with other cells throughout the body, so the total person could not find and keep health without entering into larger circuits than personal comfort and survival. The body was made for covenants, made to share and relate, made to give. Holding in the vital energy, sealing off the vital flame, could damage the temple from within as truly as attack in battle or microscopic invaders could damage it from without. In one way or another, Cayce asked sufferers to whom they belonged, for whom they lived, with whom they claimed health in the three realms of work, love, and faith. His was a social, contextual view of health in sharp contrast to that medical perspective which treats ailments and syndromes as if individuals were monads wrapped in skin.[39]

In the Cayce view one could be sick in vocation, in daily work, and in political life. The problem would be lack of creating, fashioning, and building as "a workman not ashamed," to use a favorite New Testament phrase in the readings. Whether for the youth without a calling, the older person mired in doubtful retirement, or the parent looking for a career before or after, instead of, or with the very special career of homemaking, Cayce's treatment regimen did not hesitate to call an individual to rethink daily work, both for the right employment challenge and for new work attitudes, freed from resentment, unreal fantasy, or ruthless ambition. At the same time, health required commitment to building the communal, political, and economic structures in which work could proceed justly for others and for oneself. No private health could be maintained, because its appointed circuits would fail.

One could be sick, too, in loving. Close relationships required healthy covenants. Courtship, marriage, conception, parenting, caring for the elderly, choosing and carrying friends, reaching out to strangers—all of these came under the scrutiny of the entranced man when he probed individuals for the ultimate causes of their illnesses. He offered no categorical judgment against the single life, pointing out that Jesus had been single, and strengthening those who chose this walk of life as an authentic ideal. But he offered as the norm for most the life embedded in family relationships as the nearest experience on earth to what he called "the shadow of the heavenly home." In the unmediated intimacy of the family the challenge to self-transcending love was as close as any relationship on "earth to the venture of the soul's

---

[39]For a larger view of health and faith, see Kelsey, Morton, *Healing and Christianity*, 1973.

ultimate comradeship with God, and "those who avoid same continually will have much to answer for." It was startling to hear Cayce affirm that anyone who truly wanted a life companion would be led to one. His counsel showed no fear of normal sexuality, or any hint that the truly spiritual life would be one without passions. The challenge was not to amputate drives but to direct them. Too little or too private loving could wound a body as badly as auto accidents or poor nutrition.

Parenting was described in many readings as the noblest kind of circuit. Cayce warned that choking off the life force at the primal level of creating new life in children could choke off the growth and restorative flows in the body, working on the glandular network to unbalance and even profoundly upset the economy of the flesh. Yet disorders could come not only from love withheld, but from love misdirected in the family circle, by a spirit of domination, identification, manipulation, or squeezing attention from others. Illness might then follow as a demand from one's soul to stop the destructive behavior in the right theater of loving but the wrong roles.

Because circuits of work and love required constant stretching and cleansing, Cayce spoke of a third kind of circuitry, that in ultimacy or faith. In his view, human beings needed serious religious activity which was not undertaken as self-righteousness or idolatry of narrow values nor expressed in bigoted teachings and rituals. Not surprisingly, he picked out the family and even the clan as central carriers of religious tradition and commitment, often prodding individuals to work harder on valued family ties. Yet church and synagogue life were categorically encouraged, as I often heard, partly because they were required to temper the idolatries that so often distort family life. Cayce told his counselees not to seek the perfect religious vehicle in which to practice their faith. Instead they were to take on some fallible organization and work to make it better. Pointing to yet deeper circuits in the life of faith, he encouraged those serious

about health and wholeness to enter into small disciplined sharing groups for spiritual growth.

Connections for the Mind

At the mental level of circuits, Cayce did not use the
pungent Freudian image of genital character structure
to suggest those who could freely give and freely receive in the exchanges of mature adult life. But his intent seemed similar when he pushed people to find
health not solely by tinkering with their chemistry and
posture, but by their placement in the streaming circulation of daily existence pledged to their fellows. He
urged many to take up new interests, new reading, new
associates. Some he counseled to go serve overseas,
where encountering a radically new culture would bring
to life their hidden talents and flagging vitality—if their
motives were larger than self-interest. Some he steered
toward the dirt of gardening, as though sure they
needed to open their minds to the cycles and irrepress-
ible growth dynamics of nature, while others he challenged to spend time with pets or wild creatures. Indeed,
he made it clear that being a soul "in the earth" was an
opportunity wasted if one did not learn from the other
creatures who manifested many patterns in more pure
form than humans.

He pressed the ill or handicapped to take on others
even less fortunate, whether younger, older, poorer, lone-
lier, or discriminated against. Helping others, he insisted,
was a crucial way to get relief from one's own troubles.
Like Alcoholics Anonymous, he gave special prominence
to the healing which could come from espousing those
with problems like one's own, often in one-to-one sponsorship. In his view there was always a way to "turn
stumbling blocks into stepping-stones" by using the energy and sensitizing of pain to redirect oneself to the
bitter needs of others. In the mental dimension, too,
there was no lasting private health, for the wholesome

mind partook of the larger Logos itself, always creating fresh expressions.

Connections for the Spirit

Finally, in the spiritual dimension Cayce saw the imperative to develop full "circuits" in two juxtaposed images of "law" and "light." He described the large laws of human existence as governing health just as truly as they did nature or history. "Judge not that ye be not judged" was such a law. So was the process implied in the question he often quoted, taken from Psalm 103: "Who healeth all thy diseases?" In his view all healing required turning to the divine and attuning even individual cells and atoms to their Source. Ministrations and treatments were needed, but the goal in all interventions was setting the very atoms of the flesh humming in attunement to what he called "the Creative Forces." And since healing had this nature, then so did illness, injury, and disease as distortions of the process. "All sickness is sin," not necessarily of the moment or even of this lifetime, was a phrase in the readings which shocked many. Yet in the Cayce view only someone's alienation (not always the sufferer's alone), however long ago, could finally produce the blocking, the weakening, the lack of coordination which seemed so central to his view of illness.

In making this affirmation, he did not scold, nor did he substitute accusations for informed love to those who sought his aid. He merely stated what to him seemed fact. The universe was lawful, and the body and mind reflected this in natural health, until something twisted the process by excess, by withholding, by attack, or by denial. The sin which he meant was not naughtiness, but something far deeper—rebellion of the spirit—ultimately selfishness. He espoused selfhood in the name of a God who sought uniquely developed companions. But self-centeredness he saw as betrayal of destiny, often eventually found as illness, whether a cold brought on by anger at an in-law, or a chronic handicap brought on by misusing others somewhere in the soul's journey. He did not counsel ignoring the pain of others because they somehow had a hand in it. Illness and suffering were typically partly social, in ways that demanded response from everyone. Neglecting to aid those who hurt only wounded one's own soul.

But the cosmos he described as filled with dependable laws was not mechanical, not merely a puzzle to be unraveled or a set of principles to be mastered. It was formed out of "Light" in a more-than-machine universe. His evocation of shimmering and dancing rays and vibrations, varied in intensity, color, and combinations, suggested a universe whose nature was like music, using harmonies of freedom within design, and answering to love and to hope as truly as to medical skill. At times Cayce urged childless women who longed for offspring to be mindful of grace from beyond themselves, as had even Sarah and Hannah of old when their age or condition made childbearing seem hopeless for them. At the heart of the universe there were not blind laws set in hierarchies. There was pure love, expressed in power to transcend all manner of obstacles to purposeful health and wholeness. For such a love the metaphor of light completed and corrected the image of law, inviting intercessory prayer alongside the surgeon's scalpel, the nutritionist's diet, and the analyst's dream interpretation.

No Disease Without a Cure

Viewing the total picture of health in the four processes of out, in, push, and circuits led me back again and again to the striking claim in the readings that "there is no disease without a cure." There were no disease processes in this view, no microbes or viruses, loose in the universe as alien forces outside the governance and providence of the divine. What bodies needed was to be found in the Body of the divine, one of Cayce's favored

pictures of the relation of the soul to its Maker. There
was no dualism here, no story of matter and flesh at war
with the spirit, which must transcend them to upper hierarchies and levels of existence. Matter and flesh expressed spirit under the impulse of the Creator, but given
shape by free human choice. Health in such a view was
not a convenience, or a mechanical freedom from symptoms, but a kind of radiance shining through all the dimensions of the individual's existence, from its Source.
All who were and wore bodies were parts finally of one
Body, destined to be joint heirs with their fellows. To the
Lord of all flesh it was not impossible to call any type of
diseased tissue back to normal function—or even stand
off death—using medical techniques or nonmedical interventions. No disease was without a cure, although
many illnesses had progressed too far in individuals to
be reversed. But even this outcome was never final. The
quiet voice of the entranced Cayce observed without res-
ervation that the claim of One risen from the tomb was
factual. Here cells had bowed to their Author in the ultimate healing, and flesh had stepped forward in new ca-
dences and harmonies to present a reality which had
surprised faith.

Pretty Good Pattern to Follow!

The entire scheme of health care contained puzzles
upon puzzles. There were physiological processes, based
in turn on physics and chemistry, but also psychological
processes, social and even cosmic dimensions. Yet all of
these systems were not the ultimate challenge in Cayce's
medical work. He was not, first of all, a system builder, or
a teacher, inventor, or researcher. He was a practitioner
of health care, engaged in helping individuals one at a
time.

Why? Was it some carryover of his photographer vocation, portraying individuals? Was it an accident of the
culture and the times, in which he served individuals

simply because they were brought to him, in an age when people used "psychics" for "readings"? Or was this dogged focus on individuals revelatory of the heart of the process that worked through him, combining facts and values in transformative encounters?

For me as a social activist, individuals were important, of course. No social order could expect to thrive which did not assure development of their potentials free of want, war, ignorance, and abuse. But what had most occupied me, as June and so many of my generation, were institutions and movements. We wanted to change government, change business and labor, change education, change the arts, and change religion. Primal reality seemed to lie in these structures which shaped history; only by their transformation would individuals be given, it seemed, their rightful opportunities. Having Cayce invest so much in one person at a time seemed downright wasteful, especially when his experience and files showed how few followed his counsel fully. Many were put off by such strange categories as colonics or karma, laying their readings aside. Others could not find physicians to guide and administer the treatments. Few could find religious leaders or communities who talked Cayce's full language. He might be throwing away his efforts in many cases.

We had plenty for him to work on if he shifted his focus to diseases, injuries, and disabilities, giving generic readings on the causes of ailments and their cures rather than laboriously taking up case after case, where he often repeated himself. Once he had described a particular disease entity, researchers and practitioners could follow his guidelines for themselves. It was easy to identify in my own notebook over two hundred and fifty medical conditions examined in his readings, and ready for such concentrated trance study. They ranged from the most intractable (of which there were many, since people so often came to Cayce as a last resort), such as severe burns, multiple sclerosis, epilepsy, tuberculosis, poliomyelitis, heart disease, chronic depression, alcoholism, schizophrenia, and cancer, to such familiar hazards of life as tonsillitis, sterility, obesity, measles, hypertension, varicose veins, and gallstones, as well as the annoying problems of colds, athlete's foot, baldness, fractures, poison ivy, and constipation. Why not focus on such entities one at a time?

Getting the aid of a skilled nurse, Phyllis Goodall, who was also a medical librarian and willing to make frequent unpaid trips from Washington, D.C., to help me organize the medical files and histories, I began making collections on particular disabilities, supplementing those already available in mimeographed form. It was a laborious task even to develop an index. Each reading had to be studied together with the correspondence to discover what clinical entities Cayce described. Often there were several ailments for each person because the seekers had been gravely ill for months or years and complications were common. Further, Cayce was cautious about labels, preferring to treat persons rather than diseases or collections of symptoms. He typically went right to the causes and cures, and a trained person was often required to recognize the ailment he described. In addition, his treatment regimens were so thorough, typically involving the entire body and not uncommonly the person's whole lifestyle, that they generated multiple index entries. Still, it was possible even for me to begin to recognize the patterns of causation and treatment he described in arthritis, Parkinson's disease, ulcerative colitis, dysmenorrhea, skin cancer, and a score of other disabilities which came swirling past in each week's readings.

As it turned out later, I would spend six months on an intensive project shortly after Cayce's death, laboring with a long-suffering and skillful colleague at preparing a handbook of health and dietary hints and guidelines from the medical readings. Not at once published, it became the core of a collection eventually given to thousands upon thousands of persons as the "Individual Reference File" when they joined the Association in years that followed. Later on I would help to persuade a gifted colleague and fellow alumnus from Harvard, Walter Pahnke (who held an M.D. from the medical school and a Ph.D. from the divinity school), to go to Virginia Beach in the summers, starting in 1960, when he began the laborious task of writing up and evaluating the diagnostic, etiologic, and treatment patterns in hundreds of types of diseases and injuries. These would lay the foundations for extensive clinical and laboratory research in subsequent decades.

With Cayce before us, it seemed we should begin at once to refocus him on diseases and traumas as such, rather than take him through week after week of a practice that could occupy an entire clinic. So I asked him to secure a reading on the subject. He seemed hesitant but finally agreed. My mother and the nurse both came, June joined in, and we mapped out a plan to present, as part of a larger reading on the conduct of Cayce's work.

First we asked how many readings per session Cayce could safely give. We were firmly told that it was none of our business but something between Cayce and his Lord. Then we asked about shifting his focus to processes and principles rather than individual seekers. The reply was laconic but pungent. "What did Jesus do? He took them as they came. Pretty good pattern to follow!"

Abruptly, the reading soon ended. In the perspective of "the information," individuals were as precious now as they had been to the Master. Each deserved a chance not only at health but at the "resurrection" process symbolized in Cayce's dream. The point shook me out of my engineering mindset and stirred me deeply.

Cayce's patient focus on one individual at a time shone in his swift and accurate locator service. He used it to find unusual medical products, even naming exactly where they might be placed on a distant pharmacist's shelf or specifying the precise formula of a discontinued compound. He called on it to tell sufferers where to track down unusual or rare equipment or specialized facilities. Above all he used it to locate physicians. Since he had performed this kind of instant service for years, his family took it for granted. But it left June and me speechless.

He would be spelling out a treatment pattern, then pause calmly to cite the best physician in that person's geographical area to carry out the procedure. Indeed, he might name the few best in the country when top experts were needed. It all sounded so easy when he ran through the names. But how did he know? What sort of universal file, what kind of computer (to use a later term) was activated by his absorbed engagement of the unique individual he saw before him? Over and over his accuracy and alert helpfulness were verified, even when a distant physician he named had just moved into his office and not yet hung out his shingle. There were instances when two or three of the specialists he cited were figures of national reputation, but the fourth was unknown—only to be proven their equal in later performance. Somehow this skill of Cayce's was as stirring as any he exhibited. It was so precise, quick, and helpful. He seemed to pluck, as a busy physician might ask for a scalpel or sponge, whatever was required from anywhere, and *that* suggested his access to a transpersonal Source in our midst, pouring upon us such care as to be unbounded grace. There was no way to verify his claim that the universe was so designed as to have no disease without a cure—somewhere. But hearing the locator operation in action, as an expression of profound attention to one person at a time, led one to suspect that whatever was available or ever had been available for a given medical need might be found by such an approach.

There were railroad tracks running through the trees and sand from near our home in the woods to Cayce's home and office. On days when we had to hurry to work, it was quickest to stride along these tracks, passing by little Lake Holly that boldly offered its freshwater depths only blocks from the salted ocean. In sunlit mornings when the birds sang in the trees, before the snarling planes got going or the big guns set up their chattering and booming down the coast, we walked with eager steps along the ties and remembered the Navy choir, singing words I could not interpret for them: "Salvation is created in midst of the earth." Now we could grasp a bit better how "salvation" was drawn from *salus*, meaning health and wholeness, not only for individuals but perhaps for a war–spent world. And we could more than half believe the old mystical image of the infinite emptying itself into the finite for just such a purpose.

What indeed was Cayce's vocation, and where were the others like him?

CHAPTER 5

In Those Days There Was No Open Vision

We needed to know who else had done all this in the past not only to make sense of it for an expanded worldview, but to gain perspective on helping Cayce. He was tired. Some days he was gloomy and discouraged, telling us the war would drag on and he would never see his sons again. There were now ten people on the staff of our little office, including a full-time bookkeeper. I had a secretary, and June was working there, as well. To speed up the transcription of the many readings given at each session, even Gladys had a secretary, who typed up transcripts as Gladys read from her notes. Cayce kept several stenographers, mostly Navy wives, busy with his constant swift dictating. As I wrote up a report for the monthly *Bulletin*[40] in my charge, I noted that we now had some forty-five hundred appointments scheduled ahead for the next two years, excluding spots that Cayce saved in each week's calendar for readings on emergency medical cases. Not infrequently he gave readings on Saturdays, once in a while in the evenings, and occasionally on Sunday afternoons after church services.

It had been just such a time of pressure in the days of his hospital over a decade ago that his "information" had frightened him and others with mistakes. We knew we had to act with care and as wisely as possible. But we had precious few analogues for what was going on in our midst, like something from a bump in history, a warp

---

[40]January, 1944.

in time, or outer space. We might liken the reading process to a meteor from a far-off star cooling in the yard
beside the house, laden with secrets to be found before
it hardened. Or perhaps it was like a huge prehistoric
creature from the ocean a few blocks away, which had
plodded up to eat our bushes and garden, carrying patterns of lost times but needing to be kept safe while we
learned its needs and habits. Or, better, we could use
Cayce's dream image of resurrection. We were like people
confronted with someone from the grave. How had the
friends of Lazarus approached him when he unwound
his burial cloths and sat down to lunch in his second life
with them?

Nothing from the University of Chicago allowed me
to think that Cayce could be the only phenomenon of
his kind. There had to be parallels and precedents. But
where were they? The readings insisted that what we
were seeing was entirely lawful and that the process was
open in varying measure to all. Where could we find
helpful models?

Reviewers of Cayce's recent biography provided little
aid, because they disagreed sharply and had so few in-
terpretive categories and comparisons. *The New York Times*
called it an "utterly bewildering biography" of "one of
the most remarkable men in America,"[41] while the *New
York Herald Tribune* observed, "Surely no fiction could be
stranger than this biography of a living man. No novel-
ist would have dared to delineate an imaginary character such as Thomas Sugrue here describes on the basis of
fifteen years intimate knowledge of Edgar Cayce . . . In
outward terms . . . the biography of an American who
has lived a simple and hardworking life of unusual devotion to his family and friends, his community and his
Christian faith." The reviewer concluded, "For any but a
dogged and ironclad skeptic, to read *There Is a River* can-

---

[41]March 5, 1943.

not help but be an adventure . . . "[42] The Washington *Times-Herald* described it simply as "an astounding story of a man who tried hard to lead the accepted kind of life, despite his being endowed with the gift of clairvoyance,"[43] but the reviewer in the Buffalo *Courier-Express* wrote, "Personally, as a rank materialist, if we may be permitted to turn in a vote, we turn in an agnostic blank,"[44] and his counterpart in the Trenton, New Jersey, *Sunday Times-Advertiser* took a similar position: "The book is easy to read, but we feel a bit sorry to see such unlimited approbation accorded to so microcosmic a manifestation of oracularity."[45] The *Chicago Sun* piece spoke of "much that is baffling and contradictory and even confusing,"[46] while the *San Francisco Chronicle* reviewer concluded, "Frankly, I don't know whether this volume is a guidepost to new knowledge or a monument to self-delusion. It is at least a unique document of the life of an extraordinary man, and a singularly stimulating book."[47] Closer to Cayce's home, the University of Virginia *College Topics* reviewer observed, "It seems unfortunate that a man of his apparent wisdom should have waited so long for recognition, and that his work should have remained hidden until so late in his life. Clearly, if Sugrue has not over-emphasized his powers, he might have changed much of the world's history, in fact, may yet."[48]

The reviewer in the *Catholic World* objected, "We still remain one of the 'indurated' skeptics,"[49] while the writer

---

[42] March 14, 1943.

[43] March 7, 1943.

[44] February 28, 1943.

[45] May 2, 1943.

[46] April 4, 1943.

[47] March 7, 1943.

[48] February 24, 1943.

[49] April, 1943.

in the *Boston Herald* spoke of "the man who has caused a national controversy" and advised on the book, "It is amazing, bewildering, and much of it seems incontrovertible. You'd better read it and see how it affects you."[50] In the Washington *Star* the piece noted that "the story of Edgar Cayce sounds far more like the life of a medieval saint than like that of a modern American man of the middle class,"[51] but the *Library Journal* called the book "not of sufficient interest to warrant purchase by the average library,"[52] and the *Hartford Times* observed, "In these war times even such a labor of love seems scarcely worth 447 pages."[53] The author of the review in the *Providence Journal* took a more practical approach to investigating Cayce even during global war: "The first thing that ought to be said is that there is no evidence of fraud. Subject, writer and publisher seem wholly sincere. There may be vast error, but nowhere, one feels, is there deceit . . . The safest thing for a reviewer to do with a book of this kind is to laugh it off or denounce it, it is so fantastic; but the truth is that there is probably nobody in the world with authority enough to laugh it all off or denounce it. It would be a lot more to the point if some foundation were to squander a thousand or two experimenting with Mr. Cayce."[54]

Not a Shaman or Oracle, Diviner or Medium

It was time to look afresh at the history of religions. But this time I was not so confident as my professors had been that the record of religious practices and leaders was the record of superstition and error. What Cayce

---

[50]March 10, 1943.

[51]March 21, 1943.

[52]March 1, 1943.

[53]March 27, 1943.

[54]March 21, 1943.

was doing day after day called into question the almost universal assumptions of critical university scholarship of my time, that accurate visions and healings and comparable wonder-workings were impossible and therefore errors of judgment or transmission in the biblical legacy, not to mention in other traditions.

There was the shaman, the medicine man of a primitive or preliterate tribe. Such figures entered into trances of their own, often by dancing or drumbeats or by taking potent herbs or drink. In their special states they claimed to be possessed by spirits which told them where to locate game to hunt or how to avoid attacks by enemy warriors. They were also widely supposed by their fellows to have diagnostic and healing power over the sick and dying of the tribe, not unlike Cayce's main business. They gave names to the newborn and assigned roles to leaders, reminiscent of Cayce's life readings. But they were also reputed to influence the weather and the behavior of animals, not in Cayce's repertoire.[55]

Yet Cayce gave no evidence of being taken over by spirits, and spoke in no strange voice, nor did he claim to be taught by great shamans of the tribal past. He used no rattles, masks, dances, or contortions, such as I had studied so often at the Field Museum of Natural History in Chicago, where shaman figures—often life-size—were vividly depicted near frozen Eskimo igloos and steamy African huts, as well as beside Tibetan tents, South Pacific pole buildings, and American Indian tepees. A decade later I would be comparing Cayce's trance very carefully with that of the shaman, using Eliade's exhaustive work[56] together with field studies of the Papago Indians and Australian aborigines, and especially noting that Cayce had entered his strange career through a prolonged illness or disability that had cost him his voice. But at this time, with no libraries in the closed-down

[55]See Neihardt, John C., *Black Elk Speaks,* 1932.

[56]Eliade, Mircea, Shamanism, 1964.

and blacked-out resort, I had to look elsewhere for models.

There were figures of the ancient Near East, to whom both rulers and ruled turned for guidance given in trance, such as the famed oracle of Apollo at Delphi, where a votary gave cryptic counsel as she sat over a crack in the rocks, apparently carried by vapors into a visionary trancelike state. There were the Sibylline oracles, again mostly women, some of whose ambiguous sayings and advice had been collected by contemporaries.[57] I had looked up references to them, back at Chicago's Oriental Institute. But Cayce's counsel was not cryptic like that of the oracles and sibyls, which often required interpretation by priests. He spoke directly and clearly as had Israel's prophets, though he categorically refused to affirm in his counsel, "Thus saith the Lord."

He was not a diviner. These augurs and soothsayers were reported not only from the Near East, India, and my native China (where I could remember Taoist functionaries casting fortunes in the streets), but from nearly every culture. Typically diviners used an apparatus: cracks in the shoulder blades of sheep, lines in freshly removed animal livers, sticks fallen into odd clusters, patterns in palms, the direction of flights of birds, as well as dice, cards, coins, tea leaves, and designs of planet and star trajectories. Usually they were limited to putting yes and no questions to their inner vision, given structure by the objects at which they stared. They were expected to "read" signs and omens from the designs in the unusual equipment laid out before them just as Cayce's work was called "reading," for lack of a better term in his small-town America.

But the concept of reading by divination was wrong for describing Cayce, and one would hope his counsel would someday be renamed. For he used no token objects, inspected no constellations of cracks or stars, and

---

[57]Bevan, Edwyn, *Sybils and Seers*, 1929.

watched no wheeling flight of birds. And he certainly offered more than yes or no answers to his questioners. Not a passive scrutinizer of signs, he spoke as directly as had the biblical prophets. And unlike diviners, Cayce addressed some of his counsel not only to individuals, but to his entire people in the light of history (more often than his biography had reported) when he took up the issues of peace and social justice seen in the collection *Am I My Brother's Keeper?*

He was not a medium calling on the dead for counsel, like the biblical witch of Endor, who had been pressed by Saul to raise the shade of Samuel. Although there had been times when someone deceased had seemed to intrude into readings, usually with advice or harmless generalities and encouragement, against Cayce's explicit wishes, and at least two occasions when he seemed to converse animatedly at the end of a reading with dead relatives (the others typically heard his side of the exchange), we had no reason yet to doubt the claim of his "information" that it did not rely on discarnates such as those he deliberately bypassed when he followed his white dot of light to start a session. His lack of a guide or control had been reported in an unusual exchange of trance sessions with the much studied modern medium, Eileen Garrett,[58] which she confirmed for me many years later. Her guide, Uvani, had watched Cayce at work and reported that Cayce would do better if he had one like himself. Cayce in trance observed Uvani but declined the opportunity to acquire a guide or control, affirming that he would continue to seek to attune directly to the divine or the universal. A dozen years later, when I began observing and recording scores of trance sessions of the noted American medium Arthur Ford,[59] his control,

---

[58]Garrett, Eileen J., *Adventures in the Supernormal*, 1948. See Cayce reading number 507-1, 1934.

[59]Ford, Arthur, with Margueritte Harmon Bro, *Nothing So Strange*, 1958.

Fletcher, would also report that Cayce had used no guide, and I would see for myself how profoundly different these mediumistic trances were from Cayce's, in both form and content.

Neither did Cayce call upon some angelic being or entity from a supposed far galaxy in a way that would become fashionable four decades later in the New Age movement, when many claimed to be "channels" for transmitting both lofty teachings and practical advice from such sources. He was offered the opportunity by a supposedly angelic source, after it broke into his counsel, but he turned down the aid. Unlike most such supposedly exalted beings (of whom I studied many in later years), Cayce's readings refused the authority of any special role, advising listeners to accept only what they could test for themselves in daily life.

Not a Prophet

Was he then a prophet, like those of the Hebraic tradition? In the popular sense of one who sees the future and the hidden, he would be called *The Sleeping Prophet* in a widely read book by the journalist Jess Stearn in 1966.[60] In the more careful sense of one who speaks to his times with elevated vision and systematic wisdom, cutting to the heart of contemporary religious and social issues, he would be called "a twentieth-century prophet" by the distinguished Presbyterian theologian and scholar of the history of religions Richard Drummond, who would in 1978 group him in this category with Karl Barth, Karl Rahner, Dietrich Bonhoeffer, Sundar Singh, and Toyohiko Kagawa in the theological journal *Religion in Life*[61] (responding to a public query on Cayce by the scholar Seward Hiltner). The article was

---

[60]Stearn, Jess, *The Sleeping Prophet*, 1966.

[61]Drummond, Richard, "Edgar Cayce, Twentieth Century Prophet," *Religion in Life*, Spring, 1974.

reprinted in Drummond's *Unto the Churches*.[62]

But while faced with the man at work, it seemed best to withhold the designation of prophet, taking account of Cayce's limitations and honoring the modesty which both he and his reading showed on the subject of his ultimate stature. To be sure, just as Isaiah had done in counseling the dying King Hezekiah where to place a Cayce-like poultice remedy so that the king might not expire, Cayce diagnosed, prescribed, and (as needed) rebuked persons of any walk of life. But Cayce had no direct healing ability, as seen for example in Elisha. Cayce interpreted dreams, as was reported of Joseph and Daniel, but he did not enact signs for his people through his personal behavior, as did Ezekiel. And he could not directly work physical wonders, causing objects to move, springs to gush forth, individuals to rise from the dead, battles to fail, or walls to fall—whatever the exact truth in the storied legends of Israel's prophets and judges. He was limited to speech. Even here, in the skill that marked all of Israel's great prophets, he was only periodically eloquent and impassioned in his readings, though there were times both in his trance and in his wide-awake teaching when he could stir his listeners to tears of awe and joy. In a culture where none was thought able to provide unknown facts, his gift for data obscured his moments of eloquence as a preacher and poet in his unusual calling.

Like the major prophets, he was a teacher, both in trance and out, but he presented his ideas as interpretation of the great tradition of his faith, rather than as revelation of a new doctrine or way. Viewed historically, he was not a founder, a disciple, an apostle, or a reformer. Unlike a number of the prophets, he was neither a leader nor a counselor to political figures (though I was later to learn that he had been called to give readings at the White House), nor was he a skilled organizer and ad-

---

[62]Drummond, Richard, *Unto the Churches*, 1978.

ministrator, though he had struggled to direct a petroleum company, a hospital, a campus, and a small research–oriented association. Moses, reputed to command
both nature and peoples while receiving his transcendent guidance and power, was not Cayce's prototype.

An Unseasonable Seer

All in all, he seemed to belong among those who
could manifest only one or two of the prophet's typically many–sided gifts. Where some figures in the long
history of religions, including the tribal medicine man
or magician, appeared to specialize in direct healing,
Cayce's was essentially a cognitive gift, dependent on
the activity of others to change bodies or human affairs.
The category of seer seemed most fitting for one with
authentic visions and a genuine relation to the divine
yet in effect a stunted prophet. Several years later I would
find the right description of him at the University of
Chicago, where a Swiss scholar of worldwide reputation
and encyclopedic knowledge in the history of religions,
Joachim Wach, described in his definitive *Sociology of Religion* a type differentiated from the diviner and the
prophet alike. Although Wach knew nothing of Cayce
when he wrote, he correctly caught the ultimately tragic
loneliness apparent at the core of Cayce's life story. It
was a loneliness which would, in a little over a year, play
a decisive part in Cayce's death:

> In many respects the seer can be regarded as a
> precursor of the prophet. His authority is less pro-
> nounced, although the prestige which seers en-
> joyed in many societies has been considerable.
> That can be explained by the fact that whereas
> the prophet is an extremely active figure, the seer
> is usually an individual of a more passive type.
> His charisma, like that of the prophet, is derived
> from a genuine but less creative religious experi-

ence. The seer is granted communion with the deity and is credited with knowing intimately the spirits or gods and with being acquainted with their will and intention. He is able to interpret their tangible and intangible manifestations. In contradistinction to the augur, the seer accomplishes this by intuition rather than by methodical and systematic interpretation of certain specified phenomena. The seer draws more from his inner experience than the augur, who observes exterior objects. His attitude is different from that of the prophet in that, according to the passive character of his state, he is less concerned with developing norms of judgment and rules of action than the prophet. Furthermore, the seer deals usually with individual situations and rarely commits himself to general statements and judgments as does the prophet. The charisma of the seer is by definition personal, and an official seer would be a contradiction in terms. Since there is such a thing as a tradition and a rudimentary technique for seers, the seer may begin as a disciple before becoming a master and have himself disciples whom he introduces into his world and who "follow" and serve him. Nevertheless, the seer, like the prophet, is a lonely figure, set apart by the nature of his experience and the awe which he inspires by his presence. The seer is held in great reverence and honor, part of which may be due to his age or psychological peculiarities. Like the prophet, this type of *homo religiosus* may be visited by ecstatic states, visions, auditions, and even cataleptic trances. There have been few young seers; the experience of a long life seems to be necessary. Moreover, the seer is credited with a particularly close connection with the past which enhances his prestige and is often regarded

as the keeper and guardian of tradition. Whereas
the bard and scribe hand down the literal content
of the oral and written lore, the seer guarantees in
his person and message the spirit of this heritage.
Like the magician and pronouncer of charms, the
seer speaks solemnly, and emphasis is placed on
each of his words and utterances. The audience of
the seer are drawn to him by various motives.
People approach the magician to obtain a favor,
but the seer often takes the initiative himself and
challenges others by his sayings. The tragic un-
dertone in the existence of the seer is due to the
overpowering burden of his insight which may
anticipate some future catastrophe. At the same
time, he is aware of the difficulty, danger, or
impossibility of imparting his knowledge without causing fear, sorrow, or despair to others.
Cassandra symbolizes this aspect of the seer's
existence . . .

Now the seer has not always been rightly recognized and identified as such by historians and
students of religion. Some of those personalities
who commonly are regarded and described as seers
will have to be placed in another category . . . The
seer is well known in the history of Hebrew religion. With Balaam and Deborah, the prophetic
element outweighs that of the seer. Samuel, mani-
fold as his activities were, clearly represents the
seer. Characteristically enough both terms *ro'eh*
and *chozeh*, the former applied to Samuel and the
latter to Gad have the meaning "to see," "to look,"
or "to gaze" which differentiates their charisma
from that of the prophet, *nabi*. There is, however,
much that is characteristic of the seer in the great
prophets, particularly the earlier ones, in Amos,
Isaiah, Micah, Jeremiah, Habakkuk, and others.
That fact is recognized in the Old Testament itself

("for he that is now called a prophet was before-
time called a seer," I Samuel 9:9). When they are
called "men of God," "messengers of Yahweh,"
and "watchmen," the nature of their commission
is clearly indicated. The seer (*mantis*) was well
known in Greece and enjoyed high authority
there. Frequently he appears connected with a
sanctuary; if Apollo himself was regarded as the
mantis of Delphi, according to a recent study
(Fascher), the Pythia was the *promantis*. The Greek
prophetes or *hypophetes* was more a seer than a
prophet, as we can infer from the "impersonal"
character of his utterances and the absence of historical reference which latter characterizes the
Hebrew prophet.[63]

Working under Wach's guidance, I would in time find
parallels to important features of Cayce in such seers as
the Moslem *kahin*, the Hindu *rishi*, the Sumerian *baru*, the
Japanese *urandi*, the Egyptian *honu*, the Buddhist *arhat*,
the Peruvian *piage*, and figures from Roman and Celtic
history. Especially helpful would be the aid of the British
scholar Guillaume, who carefully linked clairvoyance
with prophetic gifts in his *Prophecy and Divination among
the Hebrews and Other Semites*.[64] But Cayce in modern
America, with no recognizable tradition for his gift and
work, and no community of faith to support him, was a
seer out of cultural time or season. For decades he had
been improvising his way in a culture more attentive—if
it noticed him at all—to his exotic capacity for information than to the ultimate values which he both advo-
cated and represented in the act of his readings. His work
might be love surprised by wisdom, but his times saw it
only as a new power.

---

[63]Wach, Joachim, *Sociology of Religion*, 1945, pp. 351–353.
[64]Guillaume, Alfred, 1938.

No Open Vision

In spite of the pressure of daily activities, reminiscent of a busy clinic, Cayce and I found time to talk of the nature of his unusual work. Inevitably, given our common footing in biblical thought, we turned to Samuel, called there a seer, whose story began in I Samuel 3:1, "And the word of the Lord was precious [my Bible said "rare"] in those days; there was no open vision." I asked Cayce on one of our all-day drives to Norfolk to buy office supplies if he thought our present time was one of no open vision, such as the prophets had possessed and perhaps the figures in the Early Church when "filled with the Spirit." He refused to liken himself to Samuel, whom he saw as a towering figure. But he thought our times might be similar to Samuel's, with some of the same problems as when the sons of Eli, the priest, were greedy and unrighteous. The present war was a time of winnowing and cleansing for the sons and daughters of many a house.

Then he told a dream which had come to him repeatedly in various versions. He felt it was symbolic, not literal, but that it pointed to ours as a time of no open vision, when God would have to take fresh initiatives to rescue us all. In the dream a messenger came to take him ("fetch" him, he said) to a meeting held somewhere that seemed high over the open ocean. As they walked, Cayce recognized all they joined as now dead, most of them ministers and evangelists whom he had known personally, including Dwight L. Moody. The mood was sober and anticipatory. They reached their destination, a great hall, and a hush fell on the throng assembled there. Finally a voice spoke, which seemed in the dream the awesome voice of God. "Who will go again to my people?" it asked. The answer came firmly from one whom Cayce recognized as Jesus: "I will." Then the voice asked, "Who will prepare the way?" In the exchange which followed, someone spoke and said, "Send Cayce; he's already there. After his efforts may come one to prepare the way." Others chimed in, "And we will all help."

I studied Cayce intently as he spoke, looking for signs of self-importance or messianism. But he spoke with diffidence, as always, about his own role and emphasized the deprecating "he's already there," whose spirit was not unlike the briskly impersonal and sometimes unflattering references to him in his own readings. He saw in the dream not a unique divine commission, but a call to be true to what he was able to perform for the coming of the Christ to earth again, this time not by birth, as others must also use their gifts. His job was no different from that of the many respected ministers who had gone before him, as seen in the dream.

What was clear to him in the dream, however, was the urgency in human affairs. Ours, as a period of worldwide slaughter, was again a time of no open vision, when ways must be found for many to see the reality of their direct access to God and His guidance and strength. This was not a time to find the Cayces of this world, he told me, but to find the process itself.

How to Study Open Vision

How might Cayce's work best be studied to illuminate such vision as a possibility for all? By itself it could not establish much, even if we followed the dictum of the French pioneer in psychical research, Richet, that evidence of the paranormal should be collected as carefully as for a murder trial. Science proceeded by widely repeated experiments built upon hypotheses, predicting results, and then verifying or disverifying them. Ultimately we would need to replicate elements of Cayce's process with diverse subjects until we knew what were the preconditions, triggers, modifiers, modes, stages, aftereffects, and side effects. In the meantime we needed to identify what appeared to be major variables and create some models, such as the four-part health scheme that had already become apparent. Where could we best begin?

J.B. Rhine at Duke University had proposed bringing Cayce into a laboratory for long runs of guessing dull target cards. But Cayce's counsel had refused, insisting that to get stable results with such a fragile process Cayce should operate at home in familiar surroundings and gear his efforts to a task of maximum meaningfulness: serving the ill. Careful and patient observers could see there, his readings advised, all the processes they wished to study. Rhine needed at that time to gain scientific acceptance by establishing simple repeated phenomena with such targets as cards and dice used on unselected subjects, so he settled for sending his associate, Lucien Warner. Only in later years, it developed, after parapsychology had exhibited over and over in laboratories around the world its basic phenomena of telepathy, clairvoyance, precognition, and psychokineses, would researchers be ready for just the conditions Cayce prescribed, not any longer to prove ESP but to learn its laws.[65] Meanwhile, we were stuck with a task that seemed like catching Niagara in a cup.

Needing all the help I could get to sharpen the investigation, I wrote to friends who were established professionals and faculty members, as well as graduate students, all around the country; my years of social causes in the American Student Union and elsewhere had yielded many contacts. Cautiously I explained what I was doing in Virginia and invited them to visit if their wartime journeys (most were in the service) brought them to Norfolk or Washington. A number came, sometimes staying several days longer than they had planned, in order to hear as many readings as they could and to offer their suggestions to June and me. They came from the Midwest, New England, and as far away as San Diego, staying up long hours of the night to talk with us in our little duplex in the woods. Several had vivid stories

[65]Rhine, J.B. and Pratt, G., *Parapsychology*, 1957; also Thouless, Robert H., *From Anecdote to Experiment in Psychical Research*, 1972.

to tell from life-threatening battle duty or air clashes in England, North Africa, the South Pacific, or China, to which we listened intently. Yet they found the country of the mind and soul which we were exploring with Cayce to be as strange and compelling to them as the distant places of their awesome combat were to us.

We went over and over the range of Cayce's activity, trying to specify the most promising leads for study. One senior colleague and longtime family friend from the University of Chicago's sociology department (now an Army captain) complained with rich profanity when he realized he had no adequate explanation for what he heard coming out of Cayce. But he was determined to be objective, and he tried to get us a newly developed wire recorder to use in Cayce's daily sessions, though he found them all commandeered by the military. Especially helpful was an extended visit from my father, busy as the president of an Illinois women's college already becoming a laboratory for Hutchins-type Chicago education. He read my letters, talked with my mother about her impressions of Cayce, and took the train to Virginia. Listening quietly to readings for several days, he drew Cayce out at length and then sat down to talk through the issues with me. Whatever the odds of getting specialists to attend to Cayce in wartime, he concluded, June and I should give the effort our best, and he would help me later to recruit advisers and consultants for my doctoral studies on the Cayce process.

All of us were in general agreement that four features of the open vision that Cayce seemed to exhibit should be studied at the same time. We took to calling them its *potential*, the necessary *personhood*, the *process*, and its *price*.

We needed to estimate the range and depth of potential in such aid for areas as diverse as medicine, archaeology, and political action, as well as for philosophic and religious issues. Five categories of readings in Cayce's files seemed to bear on this question. We needed also to learn about the kind of person Cayce was, to consider who else might exercise open vision, whether they were gifted or ordinary, alone or in groups or communities. Then we needed theory or models of the process itself, with attendant disciplines. Three more categories of readings in the files appeared to bear directly on these issues. Finally we needed to discover, using Cayce and his own readings on himself, the personal and social price involved, in one lifetime or many.

My next venture had to be into the musty cement vault off of Gladys's study, where thousands of transcripts and associated correspondence and reports were stored in some sixteen filing cabinets alphabetized by names of seekers. Many of the folders I found there were fat with readings, though the majority contained only a few. One testimony to Cayce's apparent reliability jumped out at once: family trees of cases. One person would get a reading, or several, and then almost at once folders would appear in the file for spouse, children, parents, in-laws, and relatives of relatives, not to mention friends, neighbors, and business associates, who often started their own family trees. But this pattern was only suggestive of Cayce's value. What mattered for real research was careful reports, and these were too often missing or incomplete. Those who became Cayce's personal friends wrote him back, sometimes keeping the correspondence going for years, and even enclosing copies of medical records. A few physicians sent reports on patients referred to them by Cayce. But most people simply went on with their lives, although some answered questionnaires occasionally sent out by Cayce's son, Hugh Lynn. After all, patients visit a doctor to get well; who reports back if the treatment works?

Concerned over the lack of follow-up to the readings, in which we might learn Cayce's accuracy and helpfulness or limits and lacks, I set about designing a thorough form for a medical history, with the help of my experienced nurse volunteer. It took a couple of weeks of overtime and hours borrowed from other activities, but I thought it would serve us well if many of Cayce's future clients would give us thorough information before the reading and then complete the same form within a few months afterward. Finally I mimeographed five hundred copies and showed them with some pride to Cayce.

Three lessons followed at once: one about the strain he was under, one about his methods of relating to clients, and one about his telepathy. For after he glanced through the form, he promptly picked up the stack and dropped it all in the wastebasket, then turned to leave, evidently irritated that I had not checked out the project with him. His abrupt response was not untypical of his brusque manner when he was overtired: "Anybody who knew all that wouldn't have to be psychic." I was outraged but too shocked to say anything. I only thought "You're a sonofabitch." As he reached the door, he turned and retorted, exactly as if he had heard me, "So are you!", and marched out. Others in the office had warned me that he could read minds, but this was my first vivid experience.

Later, after cooling off, I realized that his chances of deeply engaging someone seeking his help, and therefore his chances of getting them to follow his complex treatments, would indeed drop if people thought he were feeding them data from their advance forms. He continued to make it clear to me that he was committed to research as long as the process did not threaten the fundamental health-bringing task.

There were evident gaps of several kinds in the data. Cayce had given readings since 1901, but only about five hundred out of many thousands of early trances had been recorded and kept in his files prior to Gladys's advent in 1923. This meant that about half of his active work, in terms of years, was lost. In addition, we frequently had only a first medical or life reading but none of the follow-up type which he called "check readings." As a result we could usefully sample his typical first counsel to seekers but not develop as adequate a picture of what might have appeared in later detail. The lack was especially important in the case of life readings, in which material on karma and past-life talents was spelled out best in follow-up readings.

Not gaps but a different kind of problem emerged when an accidental error appeared in the numbering of transcripts. So I began the laborious process of tabulating files by hand, comparing them with Gladys's date-book records. Cayce's biographer had reported in *There Is a River* that thirty thousand transcripts were in the files, but eventually I verified that there were in fact only a few hundred over thirteen thousand, although we were adding to the total daily.

Whenever possible I spent hour upon hour bending over file drawers, pulling up cases to scan and peering at the carbons on yellow paper. In the evenings I took home folders or notebooks containing batches of excerpts on the same topics, some of them typed on the backs of old stationery, where Gladys and Cayce's elder son had started helpful collections on particular diseases, historical periods, or the sources of Cayce's "information." Sometimes I got unexpected dramatic accompaniment to my discoveries as June took breaks from studying the collections of excerpts with me to practice on the grand piano we had rented. Her crashing chords or lyrical melodies underscored my encounters with this astonishing material. I wondered how records kept by priests at the Delphi oracle might compare and how the first oral traditions about Samuel might have looked, if typed up for study.

In each category of readings, of which the medical was only the largest, there were four questions to address. First was the obvious issue of *accuracy*, when it could be verified. Second was the issue of *scope* of both information and judgment in each type of reading. Cayce's accuracy on particular targets might be admirable, but if he were producing too many vague generalities, overlooked in the halo effect of his hits, then his counsel was of limited value. We needed to assess the range, depth, and usability of his counsel. Third was the issue of *perspective*. We had to evaluate the comprehensive adequacy, as best we could, in the overall picture of reality and the principles presented, for any given area where he turned his attention. Fourth was the question of *engagement*. Here the issue was not technical skill and depth, but person-building sensitivity and concern—how fruitfully Cayce took on individuals and equipped them to think for themselves rather than simply dumping his data or opinions on them.

In years to come June and I would think back gratefully to those long hours spent weighing Cayce's files by the four criteria.[66] For in the course of research and teaching we would investigate scores of psychics of various types, at times studying them for months or years in dozens or even hundreds of sessions apiece. None would be seers or prophets, but a few would be at the top of their unusual callings. In addition to the medium Arthur Ford,[67] who was a minister from our own denomination, there would be Ambrose Worrall,[68] the church-based healer who was also an executive of the Martin Aircraft Company, and Peter Hurkos,[69] the psychometrizing Dutchman who was part showman and part sleuth for both the police and the military, as well as surprisingly effective in medical diagnosis and even in direct-treatment interventions.

---

[66]See Bro, Harmon H., "Where is the Truth?" *Venture Inward*, March/April 1985, p. 50.

[67]Ford, Arthur and Bro, Margueritte Harmon, *Nothing So Strange*, 1958.

[68]Worrall, Ambrose, *The Gift of Healing*, 1965; Worrall, Ambrose, and Worrall, Olga, *Explore Your Psychic World*, 1970.

[69]Hurkos, Peter, *Psychic*, 1961; also Browning, Norma Lee, *The Psychic World of Peter Hurkos*, 1970.

CHAPTER 6

Friends, I Have Nothing to Sell

First, for any systematic view were the medical readings, about nine thousand of them, constituting roughly two-thirds of the transcripts. Here was where Cayce felt the fire of his gift burned; all the other kinds of readings were brands ignited from this central flame.[70] Patients in hospitals, cripples in their wheelchairs, infants in cribs, distraught parents, relatives wistfully hoping against hope for rescue of the psychotic[71]—all of these beckoned from the silent files, each of which began with the same instructions:

> You will go over the body carefully, examine it thoroughly, and tell me the conditions you find at the present time, giving the causes of the existing conditions, also suggestions for help and relief of this body, answering the questions as I ask them.

In the booklet on his life which Cayce sent to all who wrote to him, he recounted a brief speech he had made to a gathering of many he had helped, after the heartbreaking loss of his hospital in the Depression years. It began, "Friends, I have nothing to sell." The question he posed was, "Do you, as a group, as individuals, want to see a study of the phenomena, or the information, con-

---

[70]An overview of the Edgar Cayce health database can be found at www.EdgarCayce.org.

[71]See Bro, Harmon H., "Healing the Mind," *Venture Inward,* September/October, 1987, p. 53.

tinue?" They wanted the study done, but few knew how to proceed, and none had research funds. Cayce went on quietly serving individuals, and the records piled up. Now, over a decade later, we needed to survey the actual potential of open vision in various types of readings, as his elder son had already begun to do. Cayce needed no selling. But the remarkable process he exhibited deserved an informed evaluation, if we were to discover its promise for duplication by the rest of us.

How *accurate* were these readings? A full answer would require complete case records and the judgment of competent physicians and medical researchers. Although I was learning every day more about particular disease entities and the Cayce approach to each, I had to look for medical targets I could promptly verify in files or by interviewing those who came for their own readings. So I checked in drawer after drawer of cases whether someone distant had broken the left leg or the right, what Cayce said a blood count would show, at what time of day the individual felt dizzy, how near to death the person was; how an organ or limb would show up on an X-ray when surgery had been done or how a fall had occurred years before. In the first weeks of study, only a handful of cases appeared in which any question of accuracy of this sort had been raised. Although seekers not infrequently reported that their physicians disagreed with Cayce's larger analyses of their problem, they just as often reported medical confirmation. The total effect of Cayce's steady accuracy on such immediately verifiable material was so numbing that it seemed best to look for errors, just to keep alert. No serious person, it seemed, could brush all this aside.

Accuracy in treatment prescriptions, usually multimodal, was much more difficult to determine, especially on procedures such as castor oil packs or low-voltage appliances, about which physicians would disagree. Even more uncertain were natural remedies which Cayce either invented on the spot or found in some far corner of the globe or history. There was no way to validate or invalidate all these treatments and interventions, and it was unclear who could. But there was a rough pattern that did emerge from the hundreds upon hundreds of medical case files. When someone had reported using Cayce's treatments exactly as he prescribed (which he could easily confirm in a checkup reading), then improvement usually followed. By no means was there always complete recovery, though there were hundreds of instances of seemingly impossible recovery that left one in awe. But real and lasting changes toward health would follow whenever Cayce did not specify that the individual's body was already too devastated by illness. There seemed no instances in which he simply reported that no cure or ailment was available for a particular disability. Except in the gravest of terminal cases, he always had something to offer. The result, in genuinely impressive degree, was that those losing sight could see better, those crippled could get around, those insane were quieted—the list was long, but the point about the accuracy and *scope* of useful treatments was inescapable.

On his overall medical *perspective* or theoretical system only an expert could offer a final judgment. What was initially evident was that it appeared consistent in its physiological, psychological, and theological principles across decades of aid. Also consistent was that part of his *engagement* of sufferers which assured them that he never forgot them. Some part of his "information" apparently kept case records. At the start of a medical reading, he would often observe of the body before him, "This we have had before." Over the years those who had worked with him had learned two things about such comments: they were never omitted when the files or memories showed that a person had sought a prior reading, and they were never wrongly specified, even when recipients denied it at first (as when a parent had sought a reading, unknown to them, in their infancy). This little feature was only a part of the larger process of engagement of seekers which made Cayce's medical aid appealing.

He seemed to use what would later be called a feed-back loop, monitoring how his aid would strike the recipient and suggesting which one should be pushed, which admonished, which nurtured, or which invited. Few aspects of his work were as dependable as this dimension of taking on not just the illness but the whole person in a social context. Part of his engagement, which appeared in all sorts of readings, was encouraging people to think for themselves, to try courses of action and study the results. He gave their bodies back to them, after standard medical care had seemed to reserve these for physicians. And he did not hesitate to employ varied means to motivate them in the search for well-being, from revealing their innermost thoughts to quoting their loved passages from the Bible or using images of lyrical beauty and even detailing how they would one day laugh and play and dance. This was the dimension which required viewing his work as power exercised in love, or love given form in power.

Why were there not more interested physicians than the handful of those who regularly worked with Cayce referrals or sought him out for counsel on intractable cases? The potential of open vision in the Cayce medical records was compelling. The few doctors who came to visit offered their answers.

Medicine, they explained, was necessarily a conservative profession. Practitioners had to follow safe tracks most of the time or be subject to professional censure, lawsuits, withdrawal of patient support, and their own anxious consciences as to whether they were experimenting on human subjects. Besides, medicine was a technical art, drawing many (though by no means all) whose temperaments inclined them to skilled engineering, at home with equipment, substances, and laboratory findings but not with elusive trance states. Further, Cayce was not a promising candidate for clinical investigation. Even apart from his peculiar trance means, which could bring prompt ridicule to a cooperating physician, his language was often stilted and complex, while his

caution in labeling clinical entities—in favor of diagnosing and treating the whole person—made his work annoying to classify. It was also natural to worry that
scientific attention given to Cayce might foster a cult or
tempt others to copy him who might be far less talented
(as subsequent decades would in fact see). Perhaps most
threatening of all, Cayce looked like the very morass
from which science had only dug itself out in recent centuries—mixing medicine with theology and the occult,
and staining it with such views as reincarnation.

But, they reminded me, medicine was finally driven
by the actual suffering of patients. If Cayce's form of vision were understood and in some degree manageable,
then responsible practitioners would increasingly be
drawn to it, just as patients would. There would be evidences of Cayce showing up in research, in consultation,
and in medical education, as well as in the rest of the
social complex called health care (they were right, as the
decades-later movement to holistic health would show,
developing under leadership of practitioners deeply influenced by Cayce). And because of the ground he had
broken, we might well see fresh inquiry into little-known
processes of treatment which Cayce himself could not
exhibit yet claimed were valid, such as healing by laying
on of hands.[72]

The Potential of Open Vision in the Life Readings

The next largest category of readings in which to explore the promise of open vision from the Cayce history
was the life readings, making up something over half of
the remaining four thousand in the files.[73]

Strongly psychological and vocational, including cen-

---

[72]Krippner, Stanley, and Villoldo, Alberto, *The Realms of Healing*, 1976.

[73]A sample life reading, with comments, may be found in Appendix B, of Cayce, Hugh Lynn, *Faces of Fear*, 1980.

tral themes of spiritual counsel, these were supplemented by two small batches of related aid. One was
readings for couples struggling over their marriages.
Here the available reports suggested that Cayce's "information" was impartial but penetrating, usually putting
both parties on notice of work to do and encouraging
them to solve the riddle of their relationship now, lest
they come back in another life to do it the hard way.

Very different were a group of readings given in response to requests by a few for artistic designs of personal "aura charts," which were actually not studies of
auras, but depictions of archetypes in color, intended to
help the individual focus on the best legacies from journeys through past lifetimes. These were difficult to evaluate, but their personal heraldic symbolism seemed
helpful to recipients. Such readings suggested parallels
to the paintings which Carl Jung urged his patients to
create from decisive dream symbols,[74] and to the later
specification of "life seals" by such sensitives or psychics
as the biblically based Norwegian in Washington state,
Aron Abrahamsen.[75]

The life readings exhibited the same broad *scope* in
taking up present issues which appeared elsewhere in
Cayce's trance counsel. They addressed themes central
to any adult life: what line of work to undertake, how to
understand and improve particular relationships, where
to strengthen faith by study, worship, or service, how to
approach mental and physical health, who were the
types of people and communities most valuable to engage, when to play and to celebrate, and how to work
with unique patterns of urges, temperament, attitudes,
and emotions, so as to live vitally but not trapped in
ego-centeredness. In scope they were veritable charters
for each person and richly different in their *engagement*,

[74]Jung, C.G., *Modern Man in Search of a Soul*, 1933, ch. 3.

[75]Harmon Bro's personal files contain examples of many of Aron
Abrahamsen's seals.

sometimes inspiring, sometimes warning, sometimes teasing, sometimes prayerful, but always offering clues for the individual personally to investigate and verify. Specifying particular past lives was in a sense a mere framework for all this engrossing business.

What did this type of reading mean to the Cayces and Gladys in each day's reading sessions? Life readings were sometimes a welcome relief to them in the midst of sad and urgent medical cases. But they also took note of individuals assigned to periods when they felt that they themselves had been active, according to both their own readings and their dreams, as well as their hunches. Especially certain periods in Egypt, Persia, the Early Church epoch, and the American frontier caught their attention, for reasons I would later learn. But they did not handle reincarnation as a cause to be promoted nor gave any preference to these unusual readings. A dream of Cayce's showed him giving a reading and surrounded by people who were green frogs. The trance interpretation told him that any effort to pressure others into accepting reincarnation would reverse the usual fairy tale sequence—turning princes back into frogs. Cayce consequently refused to put such readings into the emergency slots on his calendar, despite urgent requests. Past lives were evidently not for the Cayces a doctrinal issue or a saving mystery. They were just the way things went, like the workings of the liver, in a thoroughly remarkable universe. What they did draw helpfully from a life reading, from time to time, was a lift in spirits, as the measured voice on the couch spelled out the soul's growth in the person before his far-ranging vision. All of us were quieted and centered when shown a lovely person glorifying God in daily life through these extraordinary portraits.

Studying the life readings in the files produced mixed feelings. Here were not only variables that seemed hopeless to trace, but perhaps the single largest barrier to wider study and use of the kind of open vision in Cayce's medical counsel. Reincarnation seemed manifestly wrong to most of Cayce's contemporaries and to mine. If he could be so mistaken on such a major issue, how could he be trusted with bodies, even though he scored many successes? None of us guessed that by the 1980s the Princeton Religious Research Center, related to the Gallup polling organization, would report in *Emerging Trends*[76] that one American in four accepted reincarnation as a fact of their existence. This was to be an incredible social change, given that no major religious group or leading philosopher, theologian, or psychologist had espoused it in the interim (though both Jung[77] and Horney[78] quietly included it in their worldviews).

Still, when caught up in the details of an individual profile in the case folders, with its vivid accounts of influences from supposed past-life deeds and choices, we were into sweeping adventure. If all of this were only fiction, it was beautifully worked out, consistently emphasizing what the person might constructively use now, as well as try to validate from inner impressions and nightly dreams. If by any chance it were true, then there were huge implications for the conduct of education and the arts, in which past talents and balanced wisdom needed to be evoked without past regrets, prejudices, or pettiness, and for vocational placement, in which clues to the right calling, work style, and even neglected inventions could be found. Cayce suggested that eighty percent of children could be guided into the lines of work best for them by study of some of the kinds of dynamics exhibited in these readings.

There were new tracks to explore in medicine by discovering what made a person especially vulnerable in a body system and by probing the preconditions of depression, addiction, or other mental illness, as well as by

---

[76]*Emerging Trends*, Princeton Religion Research Center.

[77]Van der Post, Laurens, *Jung and the Story of Our Time*, 1977.

[78]Reference to this viewpoint was made in her eulogy by Rollo May, after her death. Her system is in Horney, Karen, *New Ways in Psychoanalysis*, 1939.

illuminating sexual and gender problems. (Later decades would see psychotherapy first make systematic professional use of reincarnation perspectives, ahead of other professions.) Religious leaders might find grounds for fresh approaches to self-sanctioning morality and to the amplitude of souls seeking to glorify God, while social and political issues might need reframing in the light of the possible collapses of whole civilizations as Cayce indicated had happened. The potential or promise for the use of open vision, as embodied in these life readings, was stirring to contemplate, making even the accomplishments underway in a Manhattan Project seem limited to an extension of familiar technical prowess, rather than offering radical new vistas in human affairs.

Verifying the Life Readings

But how much in these readings was *accurate*? Often the entranced Cayce offered individuals crisply verifiable items of character, conflict, or endowment—from temper to perfectionism to sensuality—and even chronic bed-wetting (derived in one case, he said, from dunking accused witches in early America!). When his items could be checked out simply as personality features in the present, he was apparently as accurate as on medical data, judging by letters in scores of folders, and by my interviews of recipients.

Yet what could be verified about claims of specific past lives? Scattered throughout hundreds of transcripts were scores of suggestions to individuals on how to explore for themselves the factuality and relevance of past existences. They were encouraged to study their choices, interests, fears and phobias, as well as their unexpected fascinations and attractions, and any surprising talents. They should note ethnic foods they liked to eat, the countries where they wanted to travel, the historical periods they chose in novels, the clothing they favored, the museum displays they sought out, the languages which came easily to them, the artistic forms they savored, the romantic ties that lured them, or the articles of faith which compelled their hearts. All of these and more were shafts of ore from which they might mine bits of useful recall of past lives.[79]

There were reports in the files that some of his counselees had gone to history books and courthouse records, occasionally with Cayce's trance aid, to prove for themselves the correctness of details he offered about their supposed past. Others, while on trips, had looked up their own tombstones and stared wonderingly at them. A few had deliberately gone to far countries which Cayce specified had once been theirs, finding artifacts of the sort he said they had handled before, and stepping into haunting reveries that seemed to recall other days. None was led by readings to expect blinding revelations of total recall but rather to trust that steady effort would increasingly bring useful memories of far-off existences still at work beneath the surfaces of their lives.

But Cayce's counsel did not ask his hearers to reconstruct the past solely by inference, enriched by sensitive introspection. It offered direct aid essentially the equivalent of Cayce's trance state—dreams. In these nightly dramas Cayce's "information" insisted that consciousness could slip into awareness of formative themes from past lives carried into the present, and even view scenes from other existences. To be sure, the readings assigned to dreams more reference to everyday psychological conflicts, and even physiological health concerns, than they did to reincarnation material. Yet over and over, in the interpretations of more than fifteen hundred dreams which began in Dayton and stretched across the next twenty years, the trance counsel noted themes and scenes derived from past existences and suggested how to recognize and use them as such.

---

[79]See the questionnaire developed by Hugh Lynn Cayce in *Faces of Fear*, 1980, Appendix C.

There were dreams in the files which incorporated actual flashbacks of memory, with the tents, pyramids, ships, or battles of past times. And there were other nighttime dramas, introduced by emblems of the ancient or antique, or by maps and scrolls, which traced karmic themes from past existences, in dreams where literal recall of scenes was subordinated to the unfolding of motifs in character. Such conflicts as love and wisdom, authority and freedom, or individuality and group life could well be enacted in dreams today because they reflected the struggle of a soul growing into its own truths through centuries of time. Cayce and his family and close associates could all cite dreams of past experiences which to them had been helpful in defining their present lives.[80]

The trance counsel also identified waking states, along with dreams, which might yield heightened awareness of the past living on in the present. Hypnosis might aid a few, as it had Cayce in his trance, but the readings did not generally recommend it because it threatened integration of the psyche. More commonly, states of deep reverie, inner absorption in creative tasks, and prayer were encouraged as doorways to recall, whether in association with nature, Bible study, or daily labors. Meditation was offered first of all as an activity worthwhile in itself, of listening to the divine. But the trance counsel also noted that meditation worked to clear the troubled waters of the psyche, through which vistas, relationships, skills, and themes might more easily come to consciousness from hidden past existences. Suffering and pain had their own capacity to alter consciousness toward heightened perception of the past, whether in childbirth, illness, or dying, though the readings did not urge the ascetic cultivation of pain, preferring to reach the same ends through taxing labor for worthwhile projects. In letters in the files, as well as in the reports of those whom I interviewed, were many occasions on which individu-

---

[80]See Bro, Harmon H., *Edgar Cayce on Dreams*, 1968.

als had slipped into special states containing past–life material, not infrequently validated by readings. The stimuli for such perception ranged from chemistry, such as the anesthetic for surgery or childbirth or the bio-chemistry of fasting, all the way to mystical states in which the initiative seemed to lie wholly with the di-vine, yielding visions of the great panorama of the soul's journey Godward, such as Boehme had reported long before Cayce.

Since there were several dozen persons in the Vir-ginia Beach and Norfolk areas who had sought life read-ings (and in some cases follow–ups on particular incarnations), I interviewed those who were available and willing, sometimes repeatedly, including most of the extended Gimbert clan in nearby Oceana (now Virginia Beach).[81] To be sure, I did not use the psychological tests, projective instruments, and dream analyses which would years later become everyday tools for my work as a psy-chotherapist. But my theological training, backed up by sociology and psychology courses, had included some supervised pastoral counseling skills useful for collect-ing case histories. So I devised a one–hundred–item questionnaire to secure data for a later doctoral disser-tation on the Cayce phenomenon. What my interviews produced about the present temperaments, abilities, in-terests, preferences, conflicts, values, and sometimes crip-pling problems of those whom Cayce counseled suggested that he was a masterful photographer of the inner world, while he mounted his portraits upon what seemed to him montages of past lives.

Verifying Historical Data in the Life Readings

More promising for getting bearings on the accuracy

---

[81]The Gimbert family story is contained within the chapter "The Family of Anna Campbell" (pseudonym) in Todeschi, Kevin, *Edgar Cayce on the Akashic Records*, 1998.

of the past–life material was examining Cayce's account
of historical periods, which formed the backdrop of the
little vignettes of past lives, usually four to six in each
reading, selected as most relevant to the individual's
present. Day after day I pulled back into mind what I
could recall about Egypt from reading and hearing
Breasted at Chicago, or identify about the Hellenistic
world from Case and Goodspeed and Colwell at Chicago,
or recall about Mongolia from studying Roy Chapman
Andrews, or reconstruct about the French or American
revolutions from college courses. Some of Cayce's accounts seemed fanciful, such as his ascribing technologi-
cally advanced civilizations to ancient Egypt and even to
a sunken continent of Atlantis (despite Plato's affirmation that such a land had indeed once existed).

In one historical area Cayce was manifestly wrong. He
insisted that the Essenes had been a group of considerable importance at the time of Jesus. He saw Jesus linked
with the movement by his family but breaking away
from its perfectionism and separatism. Life readings described Essene settlements in some detail, with the clothing and occupations of adherents, as well as ritual
practices and teachings. In particular, they insisted that
women had been part of the group, with significant leadership roles. I knew I could show that responsible scholars all over the world denied any serious stature to the
Essenes within Judiasm of the period and that they
agreed emphatically that the movement had not included women. So I was stuck with Cayce's surprising
failure for over a decade until, of course, the Dead Sea
Scrolls were discovered, proving Cayce correct on point
after point, including the place of women and an actual
location near the Dead Sea which he had identified.[82]

In other historical areas, more easily verified than the
far past, Cayce's material appeared surprisingly accurate,
as he provided names and dates, places and movements,

---

[82]Kittler, Glen D., *Edgar Cayce and the Dead Sea Scrolls*, 1970.

or customs and issues which were easily recognized, although he also included plenty of material not so simple to certify. The data from history which he offered were so wide-ranging and careful that one might suspect he had memorized, book by book, not simply the Bible but an exhaustive encyclopedia, except that he showed no evidence awake of such knowledge, as he did of the Bible and a complete book sales catalog he had once memorized. And when and how might he have learned so many languages of the past from which to draw crucial terms and proper names so casually?

Whatever his sources and methods, he had a remarkable facility for keeping straight what he saw as interlocking lives from the same periods in history. Whether reporting individuals from the French Crusades, the Ming dynasty, Galileo's Italy, or settlers in American colonies, he did not contradict himself or repeat (except in a few puzzling instances) among four or five or more incarnations apiece for some two thousand persons. His memory for details of relationships and positions he assigned in other times seemed virtually flawless, as he linked individuals in readings given as many as twenty years apart. His own readings said that in such counsel he was inspecting and interpreting objective "records written on time and space," or "Akashic records," like delicate impressions still left on the ether. Visualizing such a process was difficult for me. But so was imagining a memory that kept all this outpouring about centuries, cultures, and individuals neatly stored and interwoven so that he did not fall over himself.

The Purpose of Life Readings

The "information" kept the *engagement* dimension to the forefront in the life readings and in some unusual instances refused to give past lives to those considered not well served by such reports, substituting character analysis and recommendations for disciplines in the

present. Evidently this source thought that seeing the
unremembered past could be destructive for some by
tempting their egos to undue importance, by swaying
them to escape into fantasies, or by burdening them with
guilt from opportunities lost and damage done. That the
visionary counsel could prove corrosive in some instances would later become clear when June and I
watched a gifted young lad (close to our family circle)
grow up under what seemed a heavy burden of vocational and personal choices after Cayce had affirmed to
his parents (in a highly unusual reading) that he had
been both Thomas Jefferson and Alexander the Great.

For each lifetime chosen from what the entranced
Cayce reported could be hundreds before his gaze, a soul
purpose was suggested: some secret, lovely seed of humanness waiting to uncoil its hidden opposites through
experience and choices. To us who were listening each
day, the challenge of finding chosen purposes in one
another began to look like one of the great opportunities of human existence together. Some individuals he
saw as needing to stretch to new stature, like the fairy
tale frog waiting to become a prince. Others he saw as
requiring a self–chosen discipline or privation to
straighten out some bend or kink in the soul. But he
spoke to all with respect. In this view there were no
cheap souls, no shallow entities drifting aimlessly
through time. All were on a purposeful journey, whether
they recognized and honored this fact or not. All were
precious to their Source, who had created each one at
the beginning of time, bearing an original promise which
no other soul could replace.

In the *perspective* of the readings, each soul started a
given lifetime with a special focus, since "no soul enters
by chance." The focus for each reappearance was some
lesson, some prize of human value, which the soul chose
to encounter when it picked parents and birth circumstances, in the light of the general overview of the lifetime and choices to follow. These unique purposes were
not spiritual in the narrow sense of religious propriety,

but better fitted with the themes celebrated by novelists, poets, and playwrights, as well as by discerning psychologists and biographers. Not only the classic motifs of the beautiful, the true, the good, and the holy, but the great components of character were there: patience, courage, integrity, openness, willpower, imagination, generosity, and more. The Cayce source was working with a large canvas of human destiny in picturing the soul's journey across the sweep of centuries and the parade of cultures, now a man and now a woman, in vastly differing circumstances, until it had made its own chalice out of lived experience to present brimming with energy to the Creator who would also be Companion.

What was gained, we asked, by viewing the unconscious as peopled with past personalities rather than as a portrait done with the bright colors of childhood? The answer seemed to be clues to hidden potentials. If each of us had lived numbers of lives, then each of us had learned precious lessons about human existence, and so we ought not to settle for mediocrity in each other. Here again was reason for Cayce to give his readings for individuals, fishing for the treasures in the waters of each. He was quite capable of discourses to map out illnesses, discuss cultures, and explain inventions. But who would make use of these, and how? Who would make sure that such wisdom was not misused? Ultimately the human race advanced on signal and sweat of those who cared, those who endured. Character could often be more crucial to worthwhile social change than blueprints and manifestos. Cayce was seeking the nucleus of the cell of society: the unknown person, the pilgrim in progress.

If the reincarnation perspective of the readings were true, our human efforts should be marked less by pounding sense into each other and more by drawing forth. The politics of our lives should consist of setting meaningful choices before each other, and less of slamming each other into cages of conformity. This was the spirit in which Cayce summed up the challenge he placed before each individual at the end of the main body of the life reading. Some were saluted, some supported, some questioned. None was belittled, though many were warned.

Weighing the reincarnation hypothesis required remembering that each age reworked its sense of heredity and environment in the light of fresh data and intuitions. For the West, a many-life view would be but the latest in a series of such challenges. People from the Middle Ages would find our world barren and deceiving because it had no angels and demons. Thoughtful persons of just a couple of centuries ago would be amazed to see us manage our illnesses around the fortunes of invisible microbes. Wise leaders of but a few decades past would find incomprehensible our casual claim of simian ancestry, though they might find poetic truth in our endless chatter and our unlimited simian sexuality. Those who were quite certain in times gone by that the mentally ill should be locked up as demented or distorted subhumans would be astonished to see our physicians place them on couches for talking cures. And our immediate ancestors in the American South would be bewildered to face our doubt that some races were biologically destined for slavery. To the people of each of these ages, the changeover to modern views of heredity and environment would have been as difficult as a changeover to reincarnation seemed now.

One way to view reincarnation was to approach it as an extension of the realm of the unconscious. The working contents of the psyche which Cayce described were in many respects the same as Freud, Jung, Adler, and their associates had reported. There were in the readings phobias, dependencies, roles for each sex, self-images, defenses, vows made, anxieties, guiding fictions, accident proneness, psychosomatic illness, irrational fears, and sexual fixations. The list was long and vivid. Most of these operated with the same invisible force as psychoanalysis had ascribed to childhood traumas or repressed material (in which the readings also assigned the origins of some behaviors).

What would be added if we knew for certain that some of these unconscious dynamics came from previous lives, awakened by stimuli in this one? In many respects little was added. The task of unfolding and integrating the potentials in a given individual, while transcending hardened defenses or outworn postures, might be conducted under the perspective of childhood causation, Oedipal or otherwise, as truly as under the perspective of past-life causation. As long as some imaginative canvas or myth was spread before the mind's eye to contrast with the present, easing guilts and suggesting new values and adaptations, much growth could be accomplished.[83] Yet there were interesting directions or *scope* suggested by the reincarnation hypothesis which might be missed if one worked with a view of the unconscious in which everything of importance began in infancy or later.

Temperament in the Life Readings

Temperament, for example, was presented here more carefully in every life reading than in mainstream American psychology. Researchers and my professors tended to look down upon studies of body types and temperaments, from the medieval preoccupation with sanguine and choleric humors to Kretchsmer's first efforts at body patterns, and the sophisticated melding of panels of body tissues which Sheldon[84] had developed as the basis for temperament contrasts, as well as the eightfold divisions of temperament (including introversion and extraversion) which Jung[85] had invented and made famous. By

---

[83]See the myths in Neumann, Erich, *Amor and Psyche*, 1956, and *The Origin and History of Consciousness*, 1954. Also Haas, William, *The Destiny of the Mind, East and West*, 1956.

[84] Sheldon, William, *The Varieties of Human Temperament*, 1942.

[85]Jung, C.G., *Psychological Types*, Parts I, II, Collected Works, vol. 6. See also Quenk, Alex T. and Naomi L., "The Use of Psychological Typology in Analysis," in *Jungian Analysis*, edited by Stein, Murray, 1982. See further, Kelsey, Morton, *Encounter with God*, 1972, pp. 229–231.

contrast, Cayce's readings suggested that temperament offered valuable clues to understanding not only an individual's habitual perceptions and responses, but even inner conflicts. Innate trends of disposition might clash, or the person be forced to choose between a natural behavior pattern and the pressures of family or ambition to present a different style.

The basic framework of the "information" for describing temperament was strange indeed. It was presented as the effects of existences between earth lives, when the soul had immersed itself in particular spheres of interest. There were no ready precedents for such origins of individual diversities. Nothing I had read in Hindu or Buddhist thought or in Platonic and Neoplatonic speculation offered exactly this approach to temperament. (It would be years before I discovered precisely the same outlook as Cayce's among some of the Greek Stoics, who also employed the names of planets to suggest realms of experience between earth lives, as did the Austrian Rudolph Steiner [1861–1925] in his modern clairvoyant visions.)

The readings insisted that the planets linked with temperament were symbols, not actual locations where the soul would incarnate as on earth. Each stood only for a dimension of consciousness, a kind of awareness and preoccupation in which the soul was steeped for a time by its own choice before returning to earth. Mercury represented the realm of the mental, the intellectual. Venus stood for a sphere of beauty and harmony, both in objects and relationships. By contrast, Mars symbolized a realm of action and energy, as well as anger and aggression. These regions of consciousness were like primary colors, which the journeying soul combined into unique hues of temperament, depending on the recency and frequency of its saturation and the uses of the impulses made in earth lives.

In some respects there was a parallel to the three great temperament paths of the soul to God, represented in the *Bhagavad Gita:* the way of knowledge, the way of devotion, and the way of action.[86] India's other great alternative path to God, sometimes seen as the magnifier of the first three, was the way of intuitive realization through disciplines of yoga. For the Cayce readings this latter emphasis was symbolized by Neptune and Pluto, designated as realms of mysteries, the psychic, and the unusual, including altered states of consciousness.

However, there was no familiar Indian tradition to parallel the Cayce realm of Uranus. Here the readings spoke about the soul's learning extremes, gaining capacity for excesses but also the capacity for selfless sacrifice—a climactic theme in the *Gita* as in the Gospels. What determined the qualitative weight of Uranus, as well as the aspirations from other realms, was a period of immersion in Jupiter. This could produce a universal and benevolent outlook, the most beneficent influence for the soul, leading to concern with the underdog, the unfortunate, and all the social structures and norms of justice and compassion. In sharp contrast with Jupiter was the realm of Saturn, described by the readings as the dimension of purging and change, where the soul undertook a cleansing of all that was unworthy in its makeup and learned the art of renewal and repentance. A thoughtful observer might find in this description of Saturn some kernel of the Western notion of hell, just as the Jupiterian largeness of outlook might be the kernel of the Western notion of heaven. In essence Cayce was saying what prior centuries of Western faith had affirmed: we "go" somewhere appropriate after earthly life to a realm which is more consciousness than spatial.

But the affirmation in the readings of a measure of truth in astrology was difficult to relate to modern thought. In Cayce's view it was possible to discern the mix of influences in an individual's temperament by using the positions of the heavens at birth. Only in later

---

[86]*Bhagavad Gita*, 1962.

years when I explored Jung's studies of astrology[87] and
found there his concept of archetypes helping to shape
both humans and the stars, as well as the rest of creation, would I have a mediating term for thinking about
correlations between the heavens and the psyche.

Even in what seemed to be a sensitive, if perhaps
mythological, depiction of trends in temperament, Cayce
also offered hints about talents. Obviously one who had
recently sojourned in a Mercury consciousness was a
better candidate for a professor than one who had ma-
jored in the "martial" arts of Mars, though the combination might make a quarrelsome or combative dean. But
the issue of fatalism arose at once about the astrological
material, since it had been a problem in the Hellenistic
world[88] and elsewhere, when credence was given to influences of stars and planets. It was a relief to find Cayce's
trance source insisting in almost every life reading that
no influences of temperament or disposition, correlated
with distant spheres, could ever surpass the human will.
Often the entranced Cayce noted that the individual had
made choices which already rendered ineffectual the astrological part of the soul's inheritance. But he was just
as quick to comment when the individual had claimed
well the heritage of between-lives existences.

The Long Journey of the Christ

Cited in many life readings were the person and work
of the Christ, evidently not seen by readings as simply a
blessed memory or a legacy immolated in the ceremonies and teachings of the church. He was described as a
radiant presence, alive now to all who truly sought his

---

[87]Redd, Ry, *Toward a New Astrology: The Approach of Edgar Cayce*, 1985.
For verbatim Cayce excerpts see *Library Series*, vols. 18 and 19,
Astrology, parts I and II, 1985.
[88]Bultmann, Rudolf, *Primitive Christianity*, 1956.

aid—ever offered but never forced on any. Whenever love flagged and courage failed, when suffering broke the spirit and depression clouded the mind, when illness knotted up the body or death blocked further growth, there was always available the refreshing stream of assistance and love from the Son sent from the Father.

This one whom the readings often called the "Elder Brother" would not take from the individual soul its own choices, nor did he offer to remove all burdens and struggles. But he would, if responsibly asked, take away the soul's dimness of vision, as the person acted in Christlike spirit on opportunities at hand. He would also remove the terrible sense of distance from God which guilt and failure created. The Cayce picture of reincarnation was not a drama of lonely climbing to the heights of spiritual perfection. It was a lighted pilgrimage, full of opportunities to give away to others whatever one found of value along the way, with the help of this Christ. It was a journey in which anyone could take bearings from the unseen but genuine presence of the Brother who had gone the whole way, even to crucifixion of the old enemy—selfishness.

Yet the view of the Christ in the readings offered a twist which was not in any modern theology. The trance counsel described past lives for Jesus just as it did for others. In this unusual account, the one called the Son had grown in grace by becoming flesh, learning obedience through suffering, not once but many times, and remaining faithful to the end. To be sure, the gospel of John and some other Christian materials had asserted the preexistence of the Logos, identified with the Christ. But the readings gave this old claim a new dimension by reporting that the Son had experienced all the earthly predicaments and temptations known by others.

He had incarnated in the biblical drama as Adam (it was not immediately apparent to me how far this was literal and how far poetic, any more than it was clear how he had been Amilius before Adam, when souls first began to enter the earth's sphere). Then he had been

Enoch not long after Adam. Next he was the priest Melchizidek at the time of Abraham, author of the core of the Book of Job. After that came a series of incarnations with similar themes of growth (except for one as a poet–singer named Asaph, in Solomon's temple). He had been Joseph in Egypt, counsel to Pharaoh, and afterward Joshua, aide to Moses. He was Jeshua the scribe in the return from the Exile, collecting and transcribing the books of the Torah. Then he was Yeshua or Jesus of Nazareth, who completed the long journey as the Way by being crucified and risen from the tomb. At a time yet to come, the readings indicated, he would reappear to those who were ready for him in the same body as in Galilee.[89]

Such an unheard–of portrait might not be unexpected in a reincarnation perspective, in which the central saving figure lived out the same journey as did others. But the readings stretched the work of the Christ even further beyond traditional formulations. This same soul, the trance counsel indicated, had played some part in each of the great monotheistic traditions of the human family. It had not always incarnated, but sometimes influenced the religious leadership from a higher plane of consciousness. As a consequence none of the great spiritual legacies of mankind was without some direction from the Christ, even though his central gift and pilgrimage had been among the small people of Israel. He had, for example, been Zend, one of the early developers of the Zoroastrian traditions, as he had long before been Thoth or Hermes in Egypt, and he had been a non–incarnate influence on Mohammed.

What would be the consequences for the faith of Christians if they considered such a cosmic portrait? For

---

[89] Drummond, Richard, *Unto the Churches*, 1978, deals well with the supposed prior lives of Jesus and the New Testament period. John Cobb, *Christ in a Pluralistic Age*, 1975, deals with a Christ not exclusively Christian. For Cayce verbatim excerpts see *Library Series*, vol. 10, *Jesus the Pattern*, 1980, and vol. 11, *Christ Consciousness*, 1980.

those who did not find the evidence for reincarnation convincing, a claim that Christ had been a pilgrim in earthly existences might seem to rob him of his authority. That he might have had to grow into a stature when his humanity and divinity were expressed with equal force would cast doubts on his ability to work salvation for his followers. This doubt was already raised by the prospect of souls of the faithful having to return to earth, rather than leaping over such purgatorial routes into a blessed state.

Yet for others it might provide no offense that the Son should be Lord of history that included his own past. For these it would still be his lifetime as Jesus which made him definitive of God's plan of redemption. The readings were quietly emphatic in repeating the scriptural claim "He who climbs up by any other way is a thief and a robber." In this view Christ was the only figure in all human history and experience in the earth plane who had fully embodied obedience in love of the Father, becoming (as they put it) "one with" the Father and uniquely able to help others. Discussing this material with Cayce, I found that it did not reduce for him the majesty or mission of the Christ to think of him as having known power and poverty, love and betrayal, intimacy and parenting, through the full human stations of the lifespan in many ages and cultures. But it certainly might for others.

The Potential of Business Readings

Next in the records of this latter-day seer—given no cloak to wear or staff to carry in a modern age whose convictions made him invisible—were about seven hundred business readings, supplemented by a limited number on real estate, oil wells, and mines.

It was a surprise to learn that such transcripts existed, for this type of counsel was not even offered to those who joined the little Association by mail each day, ask-

ing for readings. Although some form of business aid
had been given as early as 1910 (for Cayce's father), it
was evidently not a type of assistance important to Cayce
now. He did not want to tempt people to reach for shortcuts to wealth, not out of unworldly asceticism, because
his biblical faith was thoroughly at home in everyday
living, but because his special task was aid to the suffering, and challenging others with resurrection from narrow values. Each business reading would clutter up his
calendar at periods that might crowd out the sick. Besides, his own counsel warned him that too much time
given to readings in which power and money concerns
predominated could leave him upset and irritable, with
a residue of impulses to control and possess which were
not in his best interest. In any case, experience had
taught Cayce and his family that business counsel offered no magical solutions, though the readings were
often strikingly accurate. Explicit guidance to actual inventions, sales, or stocks would only be offered in proportion to the self-investment, discipline, and worthy
purposes of the seeker.

To grasp how Cayce felt about his business readings, I
turned to a dream he shared. It had come after he had
been approached to coach two young stockbrokers to
use their dreams for business ends. He had been hesitant, remembering how once he had lost his ability for a
year by giving gambling information. But he believed
the two brothers would use their gains to help others,
and he prayed about it for several days. There came a
dream in which he saw as though by X-ray the bones of
a body for which he was giving a medical reading, the
kind of aid at the heart of his vocation. Upon each of the
bones was printed a quotation for a separate stock,
which turned out to be accurate. He got the point, confirmed in a reading: business aid given and received with
the same helpful motives and attention to individual
growth as his medical aid could be worthwhile.

What were the *accuracy* and *scope* of open vision in the
areas of business, mining, and oil, as well as inventions

of useful products? In the files was the record of one of Cayce's friends who had dreamt of a can with a nose. Under coaching of a reading the man had devised a container for putting oil into auto engines, which had made him wealthy. Also in the files were noted precise details on the future development of Virginia Beach as a major resort city—details which in later years would prove astonishingly correct but which nobody took seriously enough to act on, although they would have led to great wealth. The business readings carefully threaded their way through ethical and strategic tangles, giving practical guidance but refusing to help any individual take advantage of another. The case files and correspondence, together with telegrams requesting follow-up data, made it abundantly clear that Cayce could instantly tap details about markets, products, movements in the financial community, price changes, labor demands, agricultural forecasts, underground deposits, and government policies affecting business, as well as patterns and conflicts in international relations. Not a few persons had moved into entirely new and rewarding careers based on Cayce's coaching, partly with leads from past-life talents. Money had indeed been made and large services rendered.

But the *engagement* dimension of the business readings appeared more restrained than in the medical and life readings, perhaps reflecting what seekers wanted from Cayce. The many repeaters among those who sought business counsel (sometimes getting scores of these readings through their careers) made it clear in their excited correspondence that they often found the entranced Cayce dazzlingly correct and precise in scope when he assessed sales prospects, proposed corporations, commented on hirings, evaluated mergers, recommended loan sources, coached management skills, and took up other business affairs. But the resurrection thrust to change recipients seemed infrequent, although it could flare out in either encouragement or rebuke.

Might there come a day when vision such as Cayce's would be widely used in business and industry? The

answer was not clear, although Cayce's longtime friend
David Kahn (president of a large manufacturing company) told me with abundant enthusiasm how he had
used Cayce's guidance through two wars—both to serve
the government and to build his own fortune, as well as
to back the Cayce Hospital.[90] However, if other readings
given on social issues were correct, there might have to
be major changes in American society, as well as in individuals leading its economy and political life, in order to
have access to open vision for these ends. As the prophets of Israel had warned, grinding the faces of the poor
would not be allowed, nor would racial or gender discrimination. New kinds of cities would have to be built,
with decentralization leading to life styles much closer
to the land (a point on which the readings were insistent) and cooperatives more prominent. The Great Plains,
Cayce predicted, would one day feed much of mankind,
but there were hints it would have to occur in a new
kind of civilization not so divided by national interests
or threatened by war. Otherwise what was coming would
be gloomy indeed, with hunger everywhere, until a spirit
was finally abroad to be one another's keepers and helpers, accountable to the divine.

Only in later years would I find how penetrating and
valuable the principles and practices from Cayce's business readings could be, when my psychotherapy practice led into more than twenty years of business
consulting, usually starting from a Jungian perspective.
Working with firms as large as I.B.M. and as small as an
attorney's office, as well as with hospitals, campuses, a
prison system, and even a political campaign, I would
repeatedly encounter alert executives and managers who
sought larger *perspectives* that combined both sophisticated psychology and mature religious dimensions. But
all of that was hidden in the folds of the future while I

---

[90]Kahn, David, *op. cit.* See also Bro, Harmon H., "Engaging the Spirit
in Business," *Venture Inward,* July/August, 1987, p. 53.

studied Cayce's surprising transcripts in a small cement room.

Approaching institutions from a different yet complementary perspective was a considerable group of readings, over a hundred, which Cayce and his associates called "work" readings simply because they were about his work.

The Cayces and Gladys referred to this type of reading with respect, for here was where they themselves were put on the spot. This was Cayce on Cayce, readings on readings, and counsel on counseling in a culture with no place for seers. Although only a few readings of this type were given during the months of my stay, these few suggested why there were not more. Usually the guidance was presented in the patient manner of engagement that marked Cayce's other trance efforts. But it could also be abrupt, sharply challenging listeners to better cooperation, deeper trust in God, or more sunny dispositions in the busy daily labor. Nowhere was the *engagement* dimension of the readings more to the fore. Those who had chosen to help in Cayce's efforts were held to high standards, without indulgence or favoritism. On the few occasions in the past when new associates had tried to use this type of reading for self–glorification (for example, asking if they could present the readings as coming directly from God the Father), they were severely rebuked and told that they could make of themselves what the readings termed "a laughingstock," proclaiming processes they did not understand.

Also in this collection were readings that dealt with developing the little nonprofit Association which sponsored Cayce's work. Insofar as Cayce and his close associates were not only presenting and protecting Cayce in an orderly process of service delivery, research, and publication, but inevitably building wider understanding of his kind of work and the open vision it exhibited, then the *scope* of these readings applied to all kinds of social change: the peace movement, the cause of labor, better housing, the care of migrant workers, erasing racial dis-

crimination or anti-Semitism, strengthening consumer
cooperatives, or electing great-spirited public officials.
Even questions of how to develop pioneering models of
education at Chicago and elsewhere or how to refocus
church life on contemporary themes instead of too narrow recital of Bible tales seemed implicitly taken up in
the work readings.

All of the practical and policy issues of developing
and managing a worthwhile project were there, scattered
through readings on specific opportunities or crises in
Cayce's labors. How to build on explicit ideals, how to
organize and define roles, whom to recruit and when,
how to raise money, what to charge for services, what to
publish and where, when to hold conferences, how to
evaluate progress, how to face failures, how to be businesslike and still be a faith-centered community—they
were all in these readings. There was even a pregnant
formula in the *perspective* on social change which was evidently Cayce's answer to Marxism or any other authoritarian route, as well as his answer to Madison Avenue
selling by packaging: "First to the individual, then to the
group, then to the classes, then to the masses." When
spelled out in practical stages and strategies, this slow
but steady process seemed a huge adventure indeed.

The *accuracy* of the readings showed up here, as elsewhere, in precise assessments of unknown publishing
markets, funding options, or new personnel. But it was
judgment, not data, that counted most in the depth and
scope of this material, which was as theologically and
sociologically sophisticated as it was competent on day-
to-day management skills. In later years I would find this
part of the Cayce legacy often ignored by a larger public
more interested in novelties of altered consciousness and
extrasensory awareness, not to mention past lives and
buried cultures. But I would never lose the impression
from studying files in Cayce's concrete vault that these
particular readings and this particular kind of open vision provided resources on social change which might
hold a promise as great as his remarkable medical work.

Complementing this collection was another and smaller category of readings given explicitly on public policy and world affairs and on particular historical periods of the past, especially Atlantis and the time of Jesus. Since the "information" generally refused to give historical reports to any but those who could constructively use them, it was often necessary to wait for a specialist or author to get such readings, as the distinguished leader of the worldwide YMCA, Sherwood Eddy,[91] had done in securing what seemed an extraordinarily promising reading in *accuracy* and *scope* on authorship of books of the New Testament (the Gospel of John, for example, was assigned multiple and late authorship, but passages in chapters 14–17 were described as very nearly the words of Jesus). By contrast, when someone less qualified asked in another reading a sweeping question about how to handle Hitler, the sharp response came back: "When do you expect to see him?" Cayce's responses were like the pungent refusals of the Buddha to allow speculation on questions "that do not profit." Here again, the quality of *engagement* defined these readings as truly as the securing of data: ultimately the encounter was shaped by love, though the love could be tough and demanding.

Most of the historical reports in Cayce's files were embedded in accounts of particular past lives given to individuals—as might be expected of a seer. But he did supply for a small annual congress of members of the Association accounts of particular historical occasions (most recently, the presence of my mother's past life at the wedding in Cana, where Jesus began his ministry), provided that he could tie it to the present challenges of those who were listening. It was impossible to verify with any ease his offerings on Atlantis or ancient Egypt, of course, but his discourses on first–century times in Pal-

---

[91]Eddy, Sherwood, *You Will Survive After Death*, 1950. See reading no. 1598-2, in the files of the A.R.E., or online at www.EdgarCayce.org.

estine were surprisingly informed. On similar occasions he gave rare readings on public policy and international relations, with glimpses of the future, although he warned that the exercise of free will could change the future.

The Message in the Priorities

These five major categories of readings had provided some sense of the full potential that lay in open vision, exemplified in the seerlike photographer and Sunday school teacher. What remained to fill out the picture were largely individual readings, or small sets, on a wide variety of subjects. One series of readings, truly abstruse, was on the nature of sleep, while another equally dense was on the "Oneness of All Force." More quickly verifiable was his tracing step–by–step the kidnappers of the Lindbergh baby, seemingly accurate on provable details, but not used quickly enough to save the baby. Colorful in a different way was his specifying the location and angle of the sunken ocean liner, *Lusitania*, which enabled divers to find and enter it, locating even the preserved bodies he had noted. There were several film scripts, developed swiftly and with some skill by the man in trance. One of the numerous collaborations with inventors, on the camber of aircraft wings, seemed so promising that I sent the reading to an Army officer in Washington, D.C. He had it checked out by experts and reported that it showed such a striking grasp of this technical subject that further readings would be useful. But having been warned about following the priorities of Jesus, there seemed no chance of squeezing in further aid on aircraft, even in wartime when American planes were considered pivotal to ultimate victory, while so many stood or lay waiting for Cayce's aid with burning fevers, malignant sores, or retarded gaits.

One question sometimes jumped out at me from the rows of drab olive filing cabinets jammed with evidence of Cayce's decades of achievement. How differently might these same files have developed, had Cayce been plugged into the work of experts in various professions, rather than queried by adventurous or curious lay persons who heard of his story and sought him out for their personal needs? Had we missed precious chances to secure leads for research and invention in physics, biology, astronomy, or psychology? Had we lost priceless opportunities to clarify themes in history or archeology, political and economic theory, philosophy or religion? Should we try yet more strenuously to locate and interest specialists for task forces whose gains might outstrip even the Manhattan Projects of our times?

The actual distribution of readings in file cabinets might be answering those questions. Two out of three in these thousands of transcripts were readings given to lift the burden of medical pain. Here they were overwhelmingly accurate, comprehensive in scope, rich in perspective, and shaped to engage the growth of each seeker. Cayce's skill was rooted in active compassion. If our society were to learn how to duplicate and extend his remarkable work into a time when open vision were not so rare as in the day when young Samuel came to the sad old priest Eli, the price might be committing ourselves as never before to lifting the burdens of human misery. We would have to take on not only illness but poverty, hunger, ignorance, oppression, and the bitter fallouts of war. As individuals, and as a people, we might have to conquer dragons indeed.

CHAPTER 7

Such a Life Is Not Easy

Looking back over his work from the perspective of his later years, Cayce wrote in a brief, published account, "My friends, the life of a person endowed with such powers is not easy."[92] Yet he was convinced that the good which flowed through him was worth the struggle and, in some measure, within reach of everyone to accomplish.

What sort of man was this American seer, practicing his ungainly art far from the storied settings of the Orient or the ancient Near East? I began to put together all I was seeing from his daily behavior and judgments, matched by observations from those close to him and enriched by passages from hundreds upon hundreds of letters he had written, which I skimmed or studied as I worked my way through the files of various types of readings. My portrait task was unexpectedly speeded up when he dropped on my desk one day the booklet, *Edgar Cayce, His Life and Work*, which we mailed to all inquirers. "Revise it! Improve it!" were his instructions. He had been delighted with the form and content of a booklet I had written for seekers of medical counsel, entitled *Physical Readings: A Study of Their Source, Contents, and Purposes as a Personal Preparation for Their Use*. Aware that his autobiographical statement was uneven in its development, having often been revised over the years, he wanted me to edit it, fill it out, and smooth its discourse.

---

[92]Cayce, Edgar, *Edgar Cayce, His Life and Work*, 1943, p. 11.

For my part, I considered the relatively artless prose of his reflections on his life to be appealing, because its unaffected discourse testified to its authenticity. And I was more than a little hesitant to put words in his mouth, even when I knew he would review them and feel free to change them. But I promised to try, or at least to sketch out a more balanced version, and I set about gathering and reviewing all the relevant documents. There were three memoirs, two by himself and one by his father; one version he had dictated in 1932, and another more subjective account he had largely typed out himself. In addition, he had collected in a notebook many of his dreams and personal mystical experiences over a twenty-year period; for some of these he had sought the comments and interpretations of readings. Further, there were verbatim transcripts of lectures he had given on Sunday afternoons during the period of the Cayce hospital; these were eloquent enough to be reprinted, in many cases, in the local newspaper. Finally, there were the sometimes pedestrian and sometimes lyrical (and occasionally pungent) readings given on himself, with penetrating and revealing further references to him in readings given for his family and associates or for the Association.

The material was so illuminating that I sought permission at once to copy some of it for use in my graduate studies, including a doctoral dissertation on him. Since his life reading for me had advised me unexpectedly to continue my theological work at Princeton, Harvard, or Yale (not Chicago), we both joked and reflected seriously on the intent of this cryptic advice, and he was happy to have me use whatever materials I needed for my studies. In addition, he asked me to consider writing in later months an extended essay from the same resources in the form of long booklet or a book, on how best to approach his work as a whole. My perspectives of biblical faith were so close to his own, enriched by our common background in the same denominational tradition, that he wanted me to tackle his story as a scholar.[93]

I wrote up sections of his autobiographical mail-out booklet as asked but was so uncertain of what to include or omit, in summarizing more than sixty years of an astonishing life, that I hoped he would delay the revision until his elder son returned from military service. He finally agreed, and I was able, free of a deadline, to step back and view his personhood as it emerged from so much material.

His own readings defined him centrally by his hunger for the divine, citing a theme that ran through all his past lives as the "urge to be drawn nearer to spiritual elements of every force," even though that urge had been sidetracked at times. In the present life the covenant needed strengthening often "through the great amount of waters," which would have constructive effects on him "spiritually, mentally, and financially." For he had "first manifest on earth through the waters." This was the reason for the injunction, so often given, that he should live by the ocean at Virginia Beach. He had lived there long before, to be sure, but the important element was not recalling geography. It was waters as reminder of the everlasting Spirit. Close to the unchanging sea, the endless, indescribable deeps, he could find his way to the Eternal. By the Atlantic waters he could discover again and again that his "best forces come from assistance to others in understanding their ills." In a moving final passage of a reading given him in 1923, he had been urged to "keep the physical fit," not simply for the pleasure of good health or relief from personal pain, but in order to continue with his awkward trance labors, "that the world may know that through this individual the manifestations are of the Prince of Peace."

However deeply his ultimate spirituality marked him, it was his talent or "manifestations" that made him one

---

[93]A letter he wrote me in July of 1944 reaffirmed his desire to have me write about his life and work, and suggested that the same material might well serve in my doctoral dissertation.

of a kind. All of his life he had been somebody unusual. Not everyone agreed that his specialness was desirable or admirable. To some he was merely an irritating freak, a problem not worth the trouble to solve. At the other pole were those, beginning with his mother, who felt he was chosen by God for an important service. But all responded to him as a unique case, a notable phenomenon. There was no way he could think himself for long as just another father, just another photographer, just another Sunday school teacher.

Was he then to see himself as just another psychic, though a talented one? Cayce drew, as his files showed, many who were professional or amateur psychics, whether mediums, healers, or those who saw auras, read minds, and gained impressions from holding token objects. The psychic world was natural for him. But unlike many of these others, he gave little attention to his own prowess. Cayce's biggest interest was not Cayce. To be sure, he had been examined often on his skills. Houdini, the magician who had built a reputation on exposing psychics, once exchanged private demonstrations with Cayce. Houdini had himself thrown in the water, when they met in a Southern coastal city, while he was hand-cuffed and locked in a trunk from which he of course escaped. Cayce in trance obligingly gave a medical reading. Houdini's conclusion was reportedly that Cayce's gift was authentic but worked on different principles than the mediumship which had so engrossed Houdini. And Cayce's son, Hugh Lynn, had once presented a report on his father to a panel of medical experts in the American Society for Psychical Research in New York. The panel fell to wrangling over Cayce's use of osteopathy and gave up the inquiry. There had been other investigators in universities and medical schools. Some likened him to Swedenborg, the Swedish engineer with strange visions of the afterlife.[94] But in many ways he seemed one of a kind.

---

[94]Toksvig, Signe, *Emmanuel Swedenborg: Scientist and Mystic,* 1948.

He Knew His Size

His full stature was a surprise. Through his biography
I had been prepared for the trance, learning some of its
development, limits, and variety. But I had not been prepared for the actual size of the man. It had seemed likely
to me that he might be a kind of bumbling, simple person—a sort of country doctor, an affable small-town photographer, a pious Southern churchman. He could well
be the innocent and naive victim of a remarkable talent,
chosen or endowed for his role because his simplicity
would not obscure his gift. Because he had to be unconscious to do his work, it seemed reasonable that he
would be severely limited in other talents and interests.
Perhaps he would have a sterling quality or so, such as
faithfulness and honesty. But the rest of full personhood
would prove beyond him.

Though in later years I got to know well Cayce's biographer, Thomas Sugrue, I never asked him about the
slant of the book, fashioned consciously or not in a manner that nearly treated Cayce as a saint, in line with
Sugrue's Roman Catholic background, in which saints
can be people of great spirituality but not with much
wits or drive. The explanation given by Hugh Lynn Cayce
made sense, that his father may have rather enjoyed being briefly depicted in that way, not challenging overmuch the image Sugrue drew while he lived with the
Cayce family.

The real Edgar Cayce was in a sense ten feet tall, as
strong-willed and capable of risks as Captain Ahab in
Moby Dick. Though he chose to live simply, he embodied
complex, conflicting currents that gave him size and
depth sufficient to mark everyone he touched. A reading
given on him in the 1920s had observed that everyone
who met this "old soul" could benefit by association with
him. He put on no airs, but his charisma was enormous.
On meeting him one started out studying him, wanting
to grasp the puzzle of his unusual life. But before long
one was examining oneself, wondering what Cayce saw.

For this was a mountain of a person, despite his customary soft speech.

He knew his full size. He bowed to none, deferred to
none. When a phone call came from the actress Joan
Crawford, asking him to come at once to Hollywood and
give readings, I saw that he took it calmly and graciously,
indicating that he was busy but could schedule a reading for her by mail—a year or two hence. When Lionel
Barrymore phoned soon after, just to ask whether Cayce
remembered having breakfast with him some years ago,
Cayce acknowledged the event pleasantly and turned
back to his work without pause. His sense of his own
weight had shown awhile back in New York, when he
had been invited for an interview by a respected journalist, a woman with a national radio program of com-
mentary and criticism. When she began the interview
by asking with a bit of condescension what she might do
for him, he observed, "Nothing," and promptly got up
and left. He was not pompous, but he knew he cast a
long shadow.

His size was not made of otherworldliness. This was a
sophisticated man, used to commanding attention and
getting it. He had traveled widely and dealt directly with
American centers of power, from oil wells to the stock
market and Washington, D.C., as well as hospitals and
campuses. He was very much a man of his times, who
read the paper daily and knew both the social ladder
and social conflict. There was authority in him, despite
his plain suit and rimless glasses. Once when lecturing
in Washington, he had swept up his hands toward the
ceiling of the large hall to indicate the source of his abilities. The audience of hundreds, misunderstanding the
gesture, rose swiftly to its feet. Unruffled, Cayce brought
his arms down and returned his listeners to their seats,
never interrupting the flow of his speech. His evident
bearing not only appealed to audiences, it captured
them.

It puzzled me to note how little deference his readings gave him. Typically they referred to him merely as

"this channel," though they supplied him with the same full personal guidance they gave others. In early weeks it seemed he might after all be the humble, helpless victim or vehicle, a person of not much account apart from his gift. But this view had soon to be revised. Instead he emerged as a man of substance who already knew quite well his unique stature and needed no ego temptations from his readings. To be sure, there had been times of well-founded despair in the past, when his projects collapsed or he found himself in jail for his readings. Then his counsel had warned everyone around him to speak gently and appreciatively to him.

Framing his sense of his own mission of helpfulness through readings was his conviction that others with talents equal to or greater than his would appear before too long. The assurance came from his readings but also from his prayer times. Such individuals would offer, unless blocked by their own choices and choices of others, the kinds of guidance he gave in readings, and probably more, not requiring an unconscious trance. From promises in "the information," he expected that Paul or John or Peter, or all of them, might reincarnate somewhere and step vigorously into service of the one he called "the Master." The presumption seemed daring. But for Cayce it was just reality, as part of the demand on many to "make passable" the way of the Lord among his people.

His sense of personal companionship with Jesus, humbling and yet enlivening, was evident in a charming dream that came to him at one of the many times when he was out of money and troubled by it. Jesus and he and the Duke and Duchess of Windsor (whom he admired for acting on principle, even at the expense of a kingdom) sat down together for refreshment at a Paris sidewalk cafe. They ordered drinks and consumed them, after which the couple departed. Embarrassed as he and Jesus stood up, Cayce confessed that he had in his trousers only a couple of pennies. Throwing back his head in laughter, Jesus asked, "Will I have to send you after loaves and fishes, too?" The dream was one of many that shone with the same presence, including a delightful one about Jesus in a top hat.

Cayce's stature showed in the people he drew to him. Typically they were strong persons, both men and women. His closest associates over the years, whose files bulged with so many letters back and forth, were not the idle rich bemused by his powers. They were often able executives in national firms such as Western Union and railroads, printing and paint manufacturing, as well as bankers and attorneys and judges. There were also plenty of professional persons, such as reporters, authors, physicians, lecturers, artists, teachers, ministers, engineers, and public servants. Not a few of his friends were self-made in their busy walks of life. A small number were from the ranks of wealthy custodians of culture, in whose mansions he stayed at Long Island and elsewhere with unselfconscious ease. The greater the real stature of the persons, it seemed, the larger the likelihood that they would be drawn to him, once they got to know him well. Those who visited him did not patronize him, and except for his longtime associate David Kahn of New York, they did not count on special favors from him. Through their eyes, as through the vision of Baynes, his black part-time gardener and handyman, or Mr. Dozier the eggman, I saw a Cayce who was not a freak but a man of ample personhood and spirit.

Yet when the question was his inner resources for the tasks at hand, the answer seemed mixed. Weighing the degree of his collectedness, toughness, resiliency, and centeredness yielded a complex man still in search of his full identity in an age without seers.

A Wounded Healer

Despite his strength of character, intellectual vigor, and sometimes compelling eloquence, he appeared to be, as his life readings on himself suggested, a wounded healer, an exiled priest, a failed leader. He had a passion

to set many things right, which led him to undertake
with energy any task which commanded his attention.
The pools of pain which might fleetingly be glimpsed in
him served him well, since they led him directly to the
pain of others who needed him. But part of the time he
lived and acted out of inner deficit, not surplus. He worried. He was anxious. He made plans for the worst. He
stewed. He pushed himself and others further and faster
than necessary, as though to stave off some threatening
inner starvation. He spent money when he had it (which
had not been often in his life), as though it had to be
circulated or it would evaporate. Once he had ordered
by mail a hundred bed sheets, telling his wife he never
wanted to hear again about lack of sheets. He did not
simply live his extraordinary life; he sought to overtake
it. He could be confident and sunny. When he was, his
radiance melted all the troubles about him. Yet there
seemed to be flames of doubt in him that had periodically to be quenched, like peat-bog fires that pop up
erratically from the ground.

Was there something he needed to prove to himself,
whether from past lives or this one? It could not be the
scope of his psychic abilities outside of trance. Here he
was a confident master, diffident about his skills. One
had to prod him to show the range of his paranormal
abilities, or just wait until he was playful or expansive.
Then he might tick off the colors in an aura, or read a
palm, or describe the contents of an unread book by
merely picking it up, or tell an unknown waitress at our
table that she was about to marry again for the wrong
reasons. It was his trance skills, not his waking clairvoyance and telepathy, which jarred and worried him. Since
alone among us he had never heard a reading, his vocation always came to him secondhand, as though he were
a sculptor making his figures unseen behind a screen, or
an architect whose houses were built only far from him
in a foreign land, or a surgeon operating blind. His calling was preposterous, and he needed frequent reassur-
ance of its value. It was small wonder that he had taken

years to trust his ability enough to use it on members of his own family. Even now he pledged never to give another reading if just one person were injured by his trance counsel. All in all, his lot would have been easier had he not been given the keen mind which his readings described, capable of questioning his gift even as he trusted it. Sometimes I wished for him that he were the simple person his biography had led me to expect.

The demand to yield authority to his trance was not his only threat to secure identity. For his capacious psyche contained strong currents that assaulted his ego from the unconscious side. His conscience nagged at him, asking whether talents as great and good as his should have brought his family recognition and at least modest wealth. Had he betrayed the trust given him? Cayce knew his Bible well enough to understand with Job that hardship or privation was not to be correlated neatly with fidelity to Yahweh, or Jehovah. Still, the failures of his hospital days evidently left a sting and a smart that could grow into anxiety if he were not careful.

The extremism cited by his readings on himself was another kind of threat to his selfhood. When he went to the movies, he might go every night for a week. When he canned fruit in jars, he did it in huge batches, using so much sugar that he had once been investigated as a possible moonshiner. When he bought office supplies with me in Norfolk, he filled the trunk and backseat of the car with carton on carton of goldenrod, canary yellow, forest green, sunrise pink, and wedgewood blue mimeograph paper. People who knew him in one of his extremes were puzzled by him in another. When he taught the Bible, he made it sound utterly convincing as a guide to healing for any person of faith. Later that same day he might plunge into a bout of digestive trouble as though it would carry him away. Yet his capacity for extremes served him well, insofar as it enabled him to stretch out on his couch for readings as one nearly dead.

Strong emotions were natural to him, buffeting his ego. Anger, self-pity, fear, sex, compassion, tenderness, indignation—he was an orchestra waiting to play the next work. His body offered just the right combination of nervous energy and feeling-toned tissue to make emotions sing for him. In William Sheldon's terminology,[95] Cayce combined the high-strung cerebrotonic with the gut-oriented viscerotonic, while the power-wielding element of a muscular body was subdued. His mouth was full, his lips ample, his face expressive if he chose. As with many intuitives, he found sensate pleasure larger than life, both appealing and daunting. He was not an athlete, yet he loved fishing and gardening and bowling. He relished eating, as he did smoking his cigarettes. He loved sexuality, if the account of his readings and family (given me after his death) were correct. The compelling, many-colored world of the emotions, dotted with glades and gardens of the senses, provided so much energy and meaning in his life that it could sidetrack his genuine intellectual gifts, evident from transcripts of his lectures, as well as from his long, thoughtful letters[96] whose contents were not readily distinguishable from his readings. But unless he put himself under firm discipline, he could become a prisoner of his moods.

Some of his moods could be dark, depressed, and angry. He paid a price for his church-tutored idealism, with a conscience that could be perfectionist or even ruthless. When it attacked him, he could not always keep from attacking or criticizing others, as though he must dislodge the demon by saddling it on someone else. Harsh criticism of those close to him, infrequent as it was, brought evidence of a shadowed part that tore at him, whether from past lives or from more recent dynamics. Hearing him tell his doggedly devoted secretary

---

[95]Sheldon, William, *An Atlas of Men*, 1954. Cayce may have been a 345 in this terminology.

[96]See Cayce, Edgar, *The Work of Edgar Cayce As Seen Through His Letters*, edited by Cayce, Charles Thomas and Thomas, Jeanette, 2000. See also the letter in Cayce, Edgar Evans and Cayce, Hugh Lynn, *The Outer Limits of Edgar Cayce's Power*, 1971, p. 12.

to take some papers and "shove them you know where" seemed to us outrageous. And when he spoke severely to his wife, however infrequently, it was upsetting indeed.

Masculine and Feminine Currents

Earliest among the masculine influences and models in his search for a firm, stable identity and healthy, commanding ego was of course his father. Reading his father's journal suggested that he had tried to live through his son, robbing Edgar of a strong male model (as Edgar's youngest sister, Sarah, confirmed to me). A similar developer and promoter, Cayce's longtime friend who was almost a devoted younger brother, David Kahn, gave him unflagging admiration and loyalty. As a highly successful businessman, he seemed to touch the nerve of Cayce's desire to be not only solvent financially, but a capable leader in the world of practical affairs.

Evidently Cayce often drew to himself businesspersons. Having developed his own business in three cities as a photographer, he may have felt more kinship with those who risked capital and energy to market products and services than he did with those of extensive education. That side of manhood which is represented by wisdom and special skills Cayce already had. He stood on the staff side of work organization as a genius in his particular service. It was the line side of manhood, embodied in power and authority, which seemed to tug him toward friendships with men who embodied qualities less developed in himself.

To the men of influence and position around him he might have become a quasi-feminine bearer of inner mysteries, as is often seen when males of the arts and ideas and religion move among men of the marketplace. But he seemed to avoid this stereotype, perhaps because his intuition enabled him to assess his companions so well that he appeared their peer or coach. What he offered these businessmen in return for their friendship was benevolence as an ideal: doing good for mankind.

But the ultimate male figure for Cayce was apparently his son, Hugh Lynn, with whom he had often clashed swords. From what I could learn, the son was as strong–willed as the father, and as independent, with an equal temper which he generally controlled better, and with a more orderly mind. He also had enough of the intuitive and the psychic in his makeup to sample for himself most of his father's unusual experiences. Although in college he had played the role of Southern gentleman and nearly lost his way in heavy drinking, he had a spiritual ideal as strong as his father's, without the temptation to extremes. When a life reading quietly but firmly identified the son as having been close to Jesus, Cayce was deeply impressed, more so as the years seemed to bear out the characterization. Hugh Lynn became Cayce's conscience, as well as his primary aid. Now in his mid-thirties and off to the wars, this son already combined wisdom and the handling of authority in ways that won his father's respect as nobody else did. Yet Hugh Lynn evidently kept his distance so that his father could not dominate him, even though they had worked closely together.

Although I did not realize it until later, I came into Cayce's life not only to do his elder son's work in his absence, but as the unacknowledged bearer of his son's image in Cayce's busy unconscious. Often I could feel a measure of tension when he approached me with orders to give, as though he had to assert in large ways and small that he was in charge, in no uncertain fashion. When power was at issue, Cayce seemed almost to assume that he had to subdue me rather than teach or guide me as in so much else. Within months this kind of exchange would lead to conflict between us. I would learn, as others had before me, that when Cayce came into one's life, bearing his prophetic or seerlike mantle, he would predictably draw forth both one's best and worst.

Relating to the feminine within himself and in the women close to him presented him with a challenge often celebrated in heroes of myth and legend, as well as in biographies. His life work was open traffic with the unconscious, so often symbolized by the face, form, and force of the other sex—as poets, artists, mystics, and intuitive leaders before him had reported.[97] Cayce had ever to wait upon an inner partner, whether for trances, impressions, inspired letter-writing, premonitions, intuitions, or teaching and lecturing without notes. His struggling consciousness paid the price in vulnerability to the women who drew close to him. He was immensely sensitive to them, though not obsessed by them, starting with his strong and far-seeing mother, who became his first confidant and sponsor. Inevitably he was prompted toward subduing or conquering the feminine in others that exacted such tribute within him. Only by repeated choice could he keep from acting out his impulses, clearly depicted in occasional dreams of conquest and seduction.

His letters to adoring women showed a touching tenderness and sometimes verged on intimacy. But he also knew he must rely on the well-defined feminine to keep him in balance. Chief among these was his vivacious and thoughtful wife, whose sharpness of insight and strength of will made her both appealing and daunting to him. Though she was sometimes shoved into the background by his admirers, who did not grasp the richness of her makeup under her quiet manner, she was a diamond formed under years of self-discipline and pressure from his unusual calling and their evolving relationship. As his alter ego and his staying power, she was as devoted to principle as she could be saucily humorous or humbly devout. By contrast, his secretary gave him unstint-

---

[97]Jung, Emma, *Animus and Anima*, 1957. See also Whitmont, Edward, *The Symbolic Quest*, 1969 for a useful amplification of Jung. See Olds, Linda E., *Fully Human*, 1981.

ing devotion touched with romantic identification which
his readings explicitly recognized. He drew upon her
energetic, open-hearted attention as so many have
drawn confidence from those of the opposite sex who
personally served them.

Around Cayce's intimate feminine ring there gathered
others, though they did not outstrip the men drawn to
him in numbers or influence. Some of the women
thought he would do his work better if only they were
beside him as beneficent influences. A few were convinced that they should bear his child as a gift to a needy
world. There were even those so ardent that they thought
just touching him, when they pressed toward him after a
lecture in New York or Washington, might help them
conceive such an offspring. Some considered him secretly lonely and added to his actual guardedness and
loneliness by pushing their attentions on him with im-
moderate handwritten notes, perfumed cards, books of
poetry, and trinkets.

Serving in his office, where his human limitations
were apparent, had not always prevented admirers from
falling in love with him. But a few had managed the
difficult feat of balancing absorbed delight in him with
keeping their distance. Given this rich feminine presence, on top of his own inner dependence on the feminine unconscious, it seemed appropriate that upon the
filing cabinet in his office Cayce kept a nearly lifesize
carved head of the Egyptian queen Nefertiti. Her classic
features, caught in a timeless gaze, seemed to cast a spell
over the trance activities in his study, where he went
daily into darkened consciousness in search of light.

The riddle of relating constructively to the feminine,
which his life readings traced as a major theme in most
of his incarnations, had emerged early in his youth on
the farm, when he had a beautiful dream that would
repeat nearly fifty times before his death. Each time he
would be walking hand in hand with a girl or woman
unknown to him, whose face was hidden from him by a
veil and whom he deeply loved. They would meet an

unusual, winged, Mercury-like figure who threw a cloth of gold over their clasped hands and told them, "Together you can accomplish anything; apart you can do little." In various versions of the dream they crossed a stream and a muddy road, coming to a steep cliff whose top stretched out of sight. He found a knife and cut places for them to place their hands and feet as they climbed the cliff. They were still climbing when he awoke, without reaching the top or seeing his companion's face. He never saw that face, in all the years that followed. Nothing in his worldview suggested what Jung would later insist of such dreams and visions: that the woman was actually part of himself and the carrier of his soul—the anima or guiding and creating source within him, keeping guard over the deeper unconscious and not to be simply projected onto the opposite sex. His reading of the Song of Songs as a Hebrew love poem in the Bible might have given him hints, but biblical commentators had long since allegorized it into the love of Christ for his church. Besides, he had been reared since his youth in the traditions of courtly love so strong in the American South, where women were often to be idealized and adored, as they had been in patterns reaching back to twelfth-century troubadours and knights.

Disruption by Veneration and the Paranormal

Beyond the array of masculine and feminine currents, Cayce had to deal with another hazard to his defined identity: the burden of veneration in nearly idolatrous images, larger than life-size, projected on him by admirers. As I would later write in my doctoral dissertation on him, he became the "numinous as complement"[98] to many by filling out whatever side of their lives needed balancing with a Godlike image. To those lacking the

---

[98]Bro, Harmon H., *The Charisma of the Seer,* 1955.

potency of learning, he was a fountain of answers, some
of which they might collect and display before their fellows. To those of uncertain faith, he was the finger of
God, a biblical figure born outside of biblical times. One-
sided persons saw in him a large-scale archetypal bearer
of whatever they were missing; he was psychopomp, or
keeper of mysteries, for some, and for others the trum-
peter of a new age. For Cayce the task of fighting off all
these infectious projections of what Jung has called mana
archetypes,[99] each capable of overwhelming his ego with
inflated importance, was no small challenge. He met it
partly by a self-deprecating manner which was at first
puzzling. He grasped his talent and stature; why be coy?

But slowly it became clear that his modesty and humility (seen, for example, in his claim, "I don't do anything you can't do") were a determined effort to stay
life-size. To make the additional self-affirmations that
might have supported his best identity, he would have
needed the aid of peers who understood his full size
better than I or most others around him. Instead he
found men and women alike turning to him with relief
after testing his sanity and honesty, as one might end a
long search for a noble parent, a worthy political leader,
a wise spiritual teacher. To be sure, he could be tempted,
as when he clung just a little too long to admiring
phrases or glances. But then he would shake these off,
taking up determined simplicity with a shrug and strid-
ing another mile in the search for the person he truly
was and might be, for whom no models were at hand.

Yet another process hindered Cayce's search for an
integrating and commanding consciousness: his difficulty in calling his mind his own. The problem was
strange to contemplate, but there were plenty of signs
that he had constantly to guard his mind against intru-
sion by the thoughts and feelings of others because of

---

[99]Jung, Carl G., *Two Essays in Analytical Psychology*, Collected Works,
vol. 7.

his psychic gifts. Being master in his own house was not easy when others could run through it unbidden. His own complexity gave him plenty to deal with, so that there was only added stress in discerning a dinner companion's lust, or someone's secret intent to capture an investor, or a parent's habitual living through a child. All of this information could aid him when he needed it to counsel troubled visitors or friends outside of trance. But uninvited, it gave him clutter. His personality, as his readings had dramatized it in past lives, was already a kingdom of competing princes and princesses, with a few lurking ruffians, requiring monarchical tact and command to hold it all together. When he was tired or worried, intruders too easily distracted him from the business of ruling himself.

Equally challenging to the texture of his personhood were unusual happenings. Evidently he had lived for years with experiences which might disorient a weaker head and heart. He knew, for example, that he could waken others at a distance by concentrating on them; sometimes he did it as a favor, as he did for June and me. And years ago he had found that he could make people come to him by firmly willing it, a feat which he chose not to continue. He knew at once when certain individuals were writing or phoning him before their message. And he had what appeared to be unbidden traffic with the dead.

Sometimes after church he would describe the discarnates whom he had seen sitting in empty rows of his Sunday school class, listening. Others came to his home, as his family told me in accounts that corroborated his own. He might, for example, go to the front door to greet someone while the rest of his family were upstairs in bed. For an hour or more he could be heard talking, without an answering voice. The visitor, he reported, was typically someone he knew who had recently died, coming to him for directions in a new state and realm. I was relieved that he could joke about these encounters. One Sunday afternoon while sitting alone with him, I watched the door of the library open and close, though nobody came in. Cayce laughed at me for not perceiving the dead person who had entered, and my worries about my wits were only a little relieved when his wife called down to ask who had entered, since she had heard footsteps on the walk. Experiences of the not-so-dead did not help him define his unique identity. Nor did his encounters with what he called "the little people," whom he saw as sprites or nature spirits around plants that he tended so lovingly in his garden. Often he teased June and me for not being able to pick them out in a color photograph on his library shelf.

Disorienting in a different way were some of his experiences with money. On a trip to the Southwest to sort out his emotional tangles after the loss of his hospital, he had been absorbed with thoughts of his dead mother while out-of-doors on a camping trip. Suddenly a silver dollar that he associated with her appeared before him lying on a log. He told the story with delight and showed me the dollar. More practical had been the time when he was out of money and worried about it, as so often in his life. A reading taken had told him as usual to be faithful and he would find his needs met; this time there came an added instruction to watch the mail for thirty days. At once money began to arrive in every letter. Some were gifts, some were settlements of old debts, some were offerings from strangers; there were coins, bills, checks, even postage stamps. No piece of mail lacked the enclosure; people who did not know each other sent money from all over the country. At the end of the thirty days the flow stopped, its point made: "The silver and the gold are mine, saith the Lord, the cattle on a thousand hills."[100] Cayce was to draw assurance that he was working, as all should seek to do, with the Creative Force that held the whole world in its hands.

Given such an array of distracting impulses, was this

---

[100]Psalm 50:10.

a man whose judgments were to be trusted in the fullness of his years?

Longing to Be a Take-Charge Person

He was not a rebel, so often the first level of a developing mature ego. He was not a kite able only to fly
against opposing winds, who flaunted his skills and experiences to baffle authority figures. Neither was he a
cause bearer, frequently the second level of a developing
ego. He had plenty to espouse if he chose, from ESP to
medical remedies, and from reincarnation to the imma-
nence of a transcendent God. But he turned toward individuals, not causes and movements; he marched under
no banners. He had convictions, but he was not obsessed
or defined by them. His world was bigger than his own
life, his God greater than his own perceptions. Cayce was
not a Cayce-ite.

His selfhood came more clearly into focus at the third
level of a developing ego, the rescue of others. Like Joseph in Egypt or Moses called to his people, he stood
taller when those around him sought his emergency aid.
When that direct need for his rescuing assistance flagged,
as it had after some of his relocations to new cities or
when he was sidetracked into power struggles, then the
trolls and angels inside him got loose and tangled with
each other.

Some part of him seemed to yearn for a yet higher
level of integration and ego strength as a take-charge
person, captain of himself and others in good times and
bad, not dependent on dire need to be his best.[101] A core
piece of his psyche seemed determined to be able to give
the right orders, develop plans and strategies, hire and

---

[101]Cayce may be seen as aspiring to "transformational" rather than
"transactional" leadership, as these are developed in the definitive
work by Burns, James MacGregor, *Leadership*, 1978. He had gone the
transaction route in his oil well and hospital days.

supervise staff, husband and dispense money in projects which would entail whole campaigns, not just rescuing individuals. It was evident when he took over his classes and expounded with passion, rather than drawing others out, as it was evident in peremptory commands to his little office staff. The urge did not seem to be blind ambition but something deeper. He was a specialist in the wisdom side of the Logos, but the power side baffled and lured him. "Perhaps," he wrote hesitantly to his elder son while I was with him, "I am not a good manager." He was a man longing to lead but lacking troops, without the authority which his readings said had been his in other lives. For the present his leadership lay in disappearing from view in a trance state which submerged his manhood, his individuality, his ego. Yet he did it well. What made it possible for him?

The Gifts of Fishing

The answer had to lie in his biography, as he often said, at the points where his talents and texture met with opportunities and roused in him decisive covenants with his God. I could see that I must explore before long those promises of which his readings often spoke. Yet I did not really understand that such promises are more than a contract, but a pact made with a Surpriser who transcends all arrangements. So I interpreted our situation as one in which we must do everything right the first time. There seemed too much good to be done in each day's bustle to stop and ask, "Where does all this potential actually come from? Whose is it that we should try so hard to run it?"

Seeking to learn the laws of the trance process and soul growth, I did not perceive (as well as did my musician wife) the difference between mastering skills and pulling a gift as though from the waters. So of course I did not encourage Cayce to pull fish from the dock on Lake Holly behind his house, though he seemed to need the activity. The lake held simple fish. But they offered the same challenges, the same play of hidden forces, the same teasing surprises and happy gifts that fish offer to anglers everywhere. Cayce did not always keep the fish he caught; those he kept for the family to eat, he cleaned himself. In the creativity which was becoming ever more evident as the hallmark of his life and perhaps the greatest clue to his gifts, he had planted a tree in a wooden keg which he had caulked and pitched, then partly filled with earth, setting it afloat so that he could pull welcome shade to him at any time of day, where he sat on the dock.

It was not easy to grasp how this ritual of fishing with several poles in the water at once, giving him privacy and quiet harmony with the universe and balancing his efforts with forces beyond his own, might be important to him and to all of us. This was wartime, and grown men crouched behind bushes and under trees to survive gunfire, not to catch fish. National destiny was the prize, not wiggling creatures; fate was on civil patrol. It seemed reasonable for Cayce to keep busy when naval planes spun by with an unmistakable message: these are stark times. So Cayce let his fishing go. He took no walks. He worked less and less in his garden. He played no games and neglected to go to movies. I thought we were making progress, in the fashion of university experts such as those who work on a weapons project. But of course we were not.

CHAPTER 8

If This Is True, Why Haven't I Heard of It?

Having examined the *potential* of open vision for our times, and initially considered the *personhood* of Cayce as an example of what sort of individual might bear the full force of it, we had now to take up the riddle of the *process* in such seeing. Only then could we finally weigh the cost in one lifetime or many, which Cayce suggested when he affirmed that anyone could do what he did "if you are willing to pay the price."

Inevitably, each person who visited to receive or just observe readings turned to the mystery of the process itself, asking us and asking themselves how it might possibly work. Those who were comfortable only with anthropomorphic imagery insisted that somebody else spoke through Cayce in trance, despite his denials. A few of these went away insisting that they had heard a voice from the dead, because mediumship was the only model they could imagine. Others, of more traditional bent yet focused on personal agency, saw in Cayce a trance mouthpiece for angelic presences, or perhaps even for God addressing his people as he once had Moses and the prophets. In contrast were those whose temperaments inclined them towards venerating universal laws that arched rainbow–like against the heavens. For them, Cayce was a modern initiate who had been taught arcane principles in his trance excursions. And the more laboratory–inclined put forth theories of the vast suggestibility of the unconscious, able to do whatever it was told when relieved of fear and doubt by hypnosis.

Recognizing the inevitable questions about his process, Cayce noted in his introductory booklet how often he had heard, "If this is true, why haven't I heard of it long ago?" For him, the answer was insufficient study of such phenomena in our culture, partly because they were often clouded by extravagant claims and power-seeking.

Clues from Each Day's Readings

It seemed reasonable to me to begin exploring the open-vision process itself (as contrasted with its outcomes) by considering leads from the readings. These typically described the trance counsel as a kind of collaboration in a high order of creativity. If we looked carefully, we were told, we could see for ourselves key variables at work.

Each day's readings did in fact vary in small ways, suggesting multiple contributing forces. A given day's counsel, and even an individual reading within a morning or afternoon session, had its own clarity, precision, poetic force, and depth of development. Some were so sharply crafted in form that they could be scanned as unrhymed verse, paced in phrases by Cayce's regular breathing. Others rambled, leaving thoughts unfinished and references unclear, with run-on sentences and changes of voice, as well as sudden shifts of focus by association of ideas. Construction of even the poorer readings rarely damaged the content, for it seemed that the trance counsel had a kind of governor at work, checking to make sure that essential thoughts came across. It might even pause to tell us when we thought we understood something just spoken but in fact did not. Yet that same governor could leave the clarity and force of discourse at a minimum, provided the factual information were adequate. One might wonder whether the priests at the oracle of Delphi struggled as we did when her reportedly cryptic counsel became even less clear on a bad day.

Diversity of content was just as evident. Some seekers got the bare data and recommendations. Others got an explanation of an entire disease process or perhaps an essay on the nature of life after death. Perhaps someone's reading was shaped more than usual to the individual's memories and vocabulary. Within the first few moments after a given session began, we could often guess with reasonable accuracy how rich in verifiable detail, wide in scope, and sensitive in engagement would be that day's counsel, and whether we were likely to get bonus material which opened up Cayce's larger perspectives. The bonuses could be exciting, because they might extend to the destinies of nations, or give us mini-essays in physiology or psychology, or predict events to come in the lives of seekers or even those of us on the staff. Or they might be challenging formulations that started, "And this would be well for all to know." Naturally we tried to maximize the quality of both form and content in each day's productions because we were mindful of recipients waiting to use their transcripts in far-off homes and shops, as well as in hospitals or even aboard Navy ships. But we were also trying to learn and use the laws of creativity in the trance process.

It seemed reasonable to seek independent variables that affected Cayce's strange art, because conducting choral singers had shown June and me how small procedures could have large consequences for creating together. In days that they were "on," tenors or basses might, for example, answer a figure from the altos or sopranos with consummate originality, which made an entire work fresh on the spot. On other days singers merely produced their notes. Conductor and singer alike strove to influence the subtle skills we engaged. Sometimes just a sudden change of pace in rehearsal would throw us into a kind of overdrive, firing our creative impulse; or an intense, unrelenting performance of one short passage over and over would ignite the singers. Often, stopping to discuss the import of the text would free the fashioning spirit within us.

Cayce in trance also appeared to be creating as he spoke, not merely inspecting, and certainly not played upon mechanically. Like an athlete on a high wire, a swimmer under deep water, a dancer making every turn count, a surgeon intervening in live tissue, he showed in face and voice both concentration and discipline. By contrast, when he was fatigued or ill, he seemed to drift toward normal consciousness, in which he wearily slipped into colloquialisms and laconic first-person speech (instead of his customary editorial "we") mingled with his formal style.

What factors caused or shaped his variations? Cayce's trance "information" suggested three immediate sources of influential variables: *seekers*, those of us who were *helpers*, and *Cayce*. What we heard in the counsel was not one man's prowess, we were told, but a co-creation, a kind of string trio or ensemble making the helpful music of his aid, while vibrating to the winds of the Eternal.

The Role of Seekers in Open Vision

For those who sought readings, the first issue was their ideal or purpose in getting assistance. Often they were asked by the voice of the man on the couch, "Why would you get well?" or "What exactly would you do if you felt better?" It was not a taunt. It was a call to marshal the best, the noblest purposes in those who sought his aid. Without the force of such larger intent, the resulting counsel might be adequate, yet subtly flag, becoming skimpy in content or opaque in form. Comparing the correspondence with what was given to individuals, as I did, suggested that such a correlation was real.

The second need for seekers who wanted the best readings was to spend the time of their appointment with Cayce's far-seeing vision in quiet meditation. They were asked to keep the period in silence, using whatever means they knew to still their minds from worry and stress by hushed waiting upon the divine. It was especially important that they stretch themselves beyond the common American view that the only source of invisible aid in a reading must be discarnates, the spirits of the dead. Those who had any feeling for the Bible were encouraged to read it in preparation for their readings, letting its climate of devotion awaken their trust in the Most High. Any invisible messengers or helpers for Cayce could then be sent solely as "Christ's Spirit" directed. Some indeed, who later wrote us they had not kept their appointment periods as asked, appeared to receive readings less than the best. Perhaps this was why the unconscious Cayce muttered, "Come back here and sit down!" to a man in faraway Alaska at the time of his reading. This applicant had, we later discovered, gone out to push a car in the snow just as Cayce in Virginia was starting his inspection of him. Notes on each day's counsel suggested that the authors of letters who pleaded in their own way, "Help mine unbelief!" often got bits of detail or engagement that added to the weight of their readings. "The seeker answers" was the terse explanation of joint creation in this process, which appeared in a transcript.

The Role of Helpers in Open Vision

The next contributors or co-creators for the consulting process were those of us helping Cayce. Our attitudes and actions, we were told, affected the quality of the connection and expression each day. Again, the issue of ideal or purpose came to the fore: desire for genuine service was to be our key. Not blind succor, indiscriminately throwing medicines or portents at people in distress, but person-respecting love was to be our intent as we reached toward "the weak, the discouraged, the disconsolate." We were not to make them dependent on us or Cayce but act in a fashion that "God may be glorified among his children." The spirit should be "that all may know the face of God," not that all might know about Cayce and comparable phenomena.

Apparently our role was to be like that of Gertrude Cayce: restrained but helpfully cooperative. Cayce and the seeker were to be the chief active agents with what the readings saw as expressions of the outgoing love of God. Often the period of prayer just before Cayce lay down to go unconscious proved useful to us. A kind of vibrant yet peaceful stillness began and continued through the entire reading session, leaving us loathe to leave the room at the end, so that we made happy small talk just to stay in the ambient spirit.

Months later, a scorching rebuke in a reading would disclose how the behavior of all of us in the office could drag down the whole process. More immediately evident was the effect of humor among us on form and content of the readings. If we could get Cayce to laugh before he started in, by sharing something outrageous or ridiculous with him, then it seemed that a sense of proportion could free the channel of the readings for optimums. So we deliberately brought into the reading room preposterous items from the mail, or reports of weird phone calls, or observations of our own stupidity. Gertrude, with her swiftly darting mind that enabled her to turn back instantly on whatever she had done or said at the grocery, was especially good at this spontaneous fun. We told our tales. June spoke of Cayce's parrot, who had just shocked a staid woman visitor with a wolf whistle and an abrupt "Whatchawant?" There was the soprano in our local Methodist church choir whose inferior wartime hose had dropped to her ankles under her robe during the processional. I recounted a story of two drunks which I had recently heard: one exclaimed to the other, "You'd better put down your glass; your face is getting awfully blurry!'" Gladys read from a letter in which a spinster wanted to know whether her prowling tomcat was possessed by alien beings.

The impact of our assistance seemed even more evident, though there were many factors to consider, when seekers came for their own readings. We were all stirred when we had before us a deformed limb, an unsightly

tumor, a depressed mien, or a recently divorced person
floundering toward a new identity. Some of the readings
on such occasions jumped ahead in quality.

Cayce's Own Role in Open Vision

But Cayce's own contribution was the crucial creative
process to understand. It was natural to wonder why he
needed to be entranced at all when he was so sensitive
to people when wide awake. His readings observed that
because of his past-life excesses he was too vulnerable
to the emotions of those who sought his help. Perhaps in
a future life, when he had "regenerated" himself, he
might do counseling without trance. Whatever the large
dynamics, it was not difficult to observe that when he
was grumpy, or enduring a digestive upset—a problem
to him for decades—or put out with someone in the office for not doing what he told them (or thought he told
them, for we occasionally complained to ourselves that
he expected of others the telepathy which was natural
for him), the day's readings might suffer in small ways.

However, visitors affected his state of mind constructively at once. He wanted to talk with each one, no matter how unexpectedly they arrived. He loved people as
others might love flowers or music or the cause of justice. He collected people, delighted in people, savoring
them one by one. It became evident why there were
pinned to the wall over and beside his studio couch
scores of snapshots given him by friends from his Bible
classes or by recipients of readings. These photos were in
a way his icons. Though they were often unposed and
artless snapshots, including glimpses of bathing suits,
fishing scenes, and an old Hupmobile, his face shone
when he spoke of them. Among the prints were even the
faces of some who had turned away from him in the
painful dissolution of the Cayce Hospital; he was not
sentimental about them, but neither was he unapprecia-
tive of all they had given to him. At first all these pic-

tures suggested to me adulation, tempting him. But later they seemed less tribute and more demand. These people kept him on center so that he could continue twice a day in the foolish-looking act of going unconscious. They, too, became more distant participants by their effects on him in the co-creating reading process.

Correlated with the quality of each day's readings seemed to be Cayce's prayer, especially keeping regular his early morning hour, when it crowned his Bible reading. On those days we found he had skipped it, we thought we could see the consequences in readings. To be sure, this was not all of his daily prayer. He did not hesitate to offer to pray for those who wrote him in desperate need, since he not uncommonly asked others of evident goodwill to pray for him. As far as could be judged from his public prayers at the daily afternoon devotional times for the staff, his inner life with his Lord was not a ritual process but a free conversation carried on in that biblical humility which reminds that the fear of the Lord is the start of wisdom. So closely tied were the depth of some of his spoken prayers with the depth of the day's readings that it seemed once more his trance state was an extension of his prayer rather than a separate process for which prayer simply prepared him, as a musician might tune an instrument.

Sometimes less evident factors engaging Cayce the man affected the depth and clarity of his trance production. He might be methodically covering the details of an illness or some other target when suddenly his perception became enlarged and his discourse elevated. He would spread before us a vista of the soul glorifying God by small, generous acts in daily life, or of a nation now occupied but destined to rise after the war, or the essence of a past culture. Two stimuli seemed to trigger these welcome shifts. One was the quality of the person seeking aid. He appeared in trance to sense the texture of someone's individuality, as a skilled weaver might discern a fine fabric merely by touching it. A dimension of kindness, patience, sacrifice, or passionate principle fired his address as he reached out to the person, old or young. But in the same way he could be shifted to eloquence and wider focus by passages and biographies from the Bible. Illustrating a point from the great drama of scripture, he would build a growing resonance with something he apparently found at the core of the person he addressed. His tempo would increase slightly, his imagery grow vivid, his data more ample. We learned from this effect that his morning devotions, where Bible reading was central, were more than pious good works for him. They appeared to keep a flow of archetypal biblical images and motifs charged for him,[102] as did his weekly teaching of Bible classes, providing a value-laden thematic woof to the warp of his factual counsel.

Of course, his personal health and balance affected his readings. The counsel often warned him to moderate his diet or sternly advised a cleansing fast or periods of rest and vacation to keep the delicate instrument of his consciousness at optimums. He was not always careful to heed these admonitions, particularly when they might involve a taxing routine. Instead he fell back on his fierce determination to "get on with it," as he put it, in readings for which people begged. How far this doggedness was his great strength and how far a serious weakness, or both, was a puzzle not easy to solve.

There seemed to be small effects on his readings from his efforts at outreach service. The quality was up after he had engaged a lively Bible class or counseled a troubled visitor. Even his taking the youngster T.J. with him on errands seemed to have small quieting and freeing effects on his consciousness. He did not attempt in these months another kind of outreach that had often engaged him in the past: visiting prisoners in the local

---

[102]See the excellent study of Bible archetypes in Rollins, Wayne, *Jung and the Bible*, 1983. Also Jung, Carl G., *The Archetypes of the Collective Unconscious*, Collected Works, vol. 9. Tillich treats revelation with archetypes as "the depth of reason" in his *Systematic Theology*, vol. 1, 1951.

jail. Under pressure of war's priorities, these Sunday trips were pushed aside, and their absence may have affected his reading process. His hunger to do this work was evident in the story he told with strong feelings about a young convict whom he had taught to read, finding that the man wanted next to learn how to pray. Cayce had to leave before taking up the new direction, but when he returned the next week, he found the prisoner on his knees in the cell, saying softly, "A–B–C" and so on. He explained to Cayce that he was using his new skill at the alphabet to communicate with God, whom he felt could make the letters into an acceptable prayer.

On some days more than others Cayce let himself be affected by the spirits of the rest of us in the office, and the consequences showed up in readings. Certainly he was not as temperamental as an opera diva or movie star, yet he was sensitive, suggestible, and at times irritable. We appeared to have an impact on him, even at nonverbal levels, if he were not careful. He did not show off his mind–reading capacities, for he was an athlete who does not need to prance or a mathematical genius who does not need to add grocery slips just to exhibit skill. But his behavior disclosed that the rest of us were in his mind and feelings to a startling degree. He seemed to pull from our auras or thoughts details of our health and illness, talents and interests, moods and ideas, even events of past and future, so that we never quite knew what private facts he might be discerning about us, even though much suggested that he tried not to do this. One afternoon he commented to my secretary that she was pregnant just after she had been to the doctor for verification but told nobody, and it so shook her up that she asked for the rest of the day off.

He seemed to pick up our moods all too easily and magnify them with his own. On a down day for him (and he was an extremist in moods as in everything else, though within limits which his self–discipline could set for him), he could turn someone's curtness or indifference in the office into a storm of bad feelings that ran through our crowded circle. A painful phrase could be transformed by him into a bullet in a steel tank, ricocheting from all the walls until everyone in reach had been torn by it. Yet his smile, his forgiving glance, his cheery encouragement—each of these could, when he let them, lift him and the rest of us out of a stressful day into sunshine. There was no way we could avoid responding to him. This was a man of stature and force, a charismatic man. We took account of him. And he in turn, unless he had himself firmly in hand, responded to us on the general principle that anything worth doing is worth overdoing. The consequences seemed mirrored in small ways by the quality of the day's readings.

What was at his core to which others related when they affected him so invisibly? Though he could be instantly outgoing, and even described as an extrovert, he was also immensely private. In the midst of a conversation he could go away, shutting up his castle and pulling up his drawbridge. His elder son later told me he had never known someone who could be so suddenly absent while in the same room. Cayce's correspondence and visits of old friends made clear that there were a score or more people across the country who felt they knew him intimately. Many affirmed that he had a special niche just for them and that they understood him where others did not. Women could be deeply stirred by him, and some who visited suggested a sense of a private bower about their meetings with him in his office. Yet it was not evident who really knew him, and I noted the subject as one to explore in life readings earlier given on him.

He needed more than visitors and those of us in the office to create at his best. Those who chose to attend his weekly Bible classes on Sunday mornings at church and on Tuesday evenings at home gave him his lifeblood. They authorized him to do his impossible service. They were his troops, his medical support team, since they came just for his teaching and his friendship without cries of pain or asking for an edge on life from a trance.

They were fellow citizens of a biblical country, a home-
land he had claimed long ago in his boyhood. At the
same time, their loyalty had in it notes of hesitation, just
as did the loyalty of those of us in the office. For none of
us knew what Cayce might see in us, which we would
prefer to leave unseen. The gifts of a seer that drew
people to him also separated them from him. His vision
worked to dissolve the very covenant it created and to
leave him in some sense alone in his awkward calling.

Larger Processes in Open Vision

To amplify my notes on daily collaboration or distortion that seemed to affect the quality of readings, it was
necessary to put them in context with statements in the
files about the nature and development of such gifts as
his, through one lifetime or many. The range of counsel
on psychic phenomena or inspired guidance was exhaustive. I found two notebooks of selections that his
elder son had already assembled from passages in many
types of readings. There were analyses and recommendations about auras, impressions, premonitions, telepathy, far-seeing dreams, healing, visions, gifted leadership,
mediumship, wizardry, raising the dead, tongues, prophecy, unusual childbirth, inspirational or automatic writing, dowsing, hearing ethereal music, perceiving odors,
causing objects to move, and much more. Evidently
many who had such experiences, or thought they did,
had sought Cayce out for his specialized aid. The same
collected excerpts showed the entranced Cayce discoursing on independent variables that influenced such
modes of expression: health factors, past lives, spirits of
the dead, specific injuries, astrological influences, sexual
patterns, emotional stresses, the Christ and the Holy
Spirit, thoughts of associates, gems, prayer and meditation, studying scripture, ideals, service projects, haunts,
fears, and others. Everything observable for the three
categories of seekers, helpers, and Cayce himself was rep-

resented, with much more. Several large patterns emerged.[103]

First of all, the picture of final reality offered in the readings was not that of daily sensory experience. As a result, the problem understanding psychic experience was not "How do we get something we want from sources distant in time and space?" but "How do we get oriented to a dimension of reality in which time and space are relativized?" For the constant affirmation in the readings was "Oneness, oneness, oneness." All reality had not only one original source in the divine, but also one presence. Events were far more connected than we realized, resonating to each other so intimately that they could instantly be found by a consciousness with the right perspective. The practical issue became not "How in the world does Cayce get so much unknown information?" but "What keeps the rest of us from having more?" Cayce appeared to be suggesting, as had William James, that the mind and senses provided screening of what would otherwise be overwhelming awareness of all sorts of data and events and structures. That viewpoint would later be intensely explored when mind–altering drugs became widely used and individuals from all walks of life reported moments of altered consciousness in which reality was more unified than the senses report, with large segments directly available for inspection.[104] I would later find Whiteheadian colleagues at Chicago developing related views and find competent parapsychologists theorizing in the same direction.[105]

Second, Cayce in–trance described the mind as a dy-

[103]See Bro, Harmon H., *Edgar Cayce on Religion and Psychic Experience,* 1970. Also Thurston, Mark A, *How to Understand and Use Your ESP,* 1977, and Reed, Henry, *Awakening Your Psychic Powers,* 1988, and the excellent study by Cayce, Hugh Lynn, *Venture Inward,* 1964. For verbatim Cayce excerpts, see *Library Series,* vol. 8, *Psychic Development,* 1978, and vol. 9, *Psychic Awareness,* 1979.

[104]Cohen, Sidney, *The Beyond Within,* 1965.

[105]Tart, Charles, *Psi, Scientific Studies of the Psychic Realm,* 1977.

namic, layered structure capable of engaging this larger reality, but in lawful ways. He used imagery of fields of force to describe a person or "entity." We were not just static chunks of flesh mounted on feet, answering to drives, traumas, and conditionings. We were first of all souls: invisible, unique vortices of energy and consciousness, beckoned into life by the divine and shaped by chosen and remembered values and actions. Because of our essential identity as spirit, we were in principle able to relate to the divine and its larger awareness. At the same time, we were most assuredly finite physical bodies, with all the chemical, mechanical, and electrical features which engaged his medical counsel. These two poles in our fundamental makeup, spirit and matter, each had their own natures forming a dynamic tension that required our creative living to reconcile. Mediating and fashioning in this tension was the field of the mind, partaking of the other two yet having its own unique capacities to set values, shape thought, make plans, recognize the soul's imperatives, and direct the will into action. For the readings the three human spheres or dimensions of soul, flesh, and mind were definite enough to be called at times three "bodies" of the person.

In this view the mental realm had crucial responsibilities, in which "mind is the builder" and "thoughts are things" with their own invisible yet not inconsiderable vibrations of subtle energy. Cayce saw thought itself as the best depiction possible of a fourth dimension affecting the better-known three. The mind was not merely conscious intellect. It had strata and currents outside of consciousness rich enough to compare with the models in psychoanalysis. Many of the springs of thought and behavior had to be traced to their source in the subliminal realm of the subconscious. And some came from a realm of more universal awareness, or the superconscious, analogous to Jung's objective unconscious or collective unconscious as the matrix of archetypes and the governing self.

In this layered picture of the mind, where did psychic

phenomena occur, and how did they develop across lifetimes? Although they had to impinge on consciousness
in order to be recognized or controlled, they were medi-
ated by the subconscious, constantly in touch with more
than consciousness. This accounted for the complexity
and delicacy of such perception, subject to dynamics and
symbolism of the inner realm, as well as for the difficulty in mobilizing energy to affect targets beyond one's
own body, in psychokinesis or mind–over–matter phenomena. Whatever troubled or twisted, infused or inspired the subconscious also worked to affect psychic
awareness and action. But here Cayce made a startling
claim. The subconscious of the individual as he saw it
was not an isolated field, but capable under the proper
conditions of meeting or (as he put it) "communing with"
the subconscious of another person, living or dead, to
provide effects of knowledge or influence. This was how,
his readings insisted, the diagnoses in his medical readings were achieved, where he consulted the deeper mind
of each patient. Medical counsel, like much of the rest of
his readings, was a joint creation.

This same subconscious could be attuned to the
superconscious realm of the psyche, in which much wider
reaches of reality were accessible to the person, according to what had been "applied" in the life (Jung would
say according to the archetypes constellated in the life of
the person)[106] and according to the individual's need,
purpose, and capacity safely to use what was engaged.
Here the psyche drew upon its innate connection with its
divine source for a much more sweeping joint creation.
William James in his *Varieties of Religious Experience* had
grouped together as subliminal both the action of the
subconscious and the engagement of the divine in religious experience; Cayce was using a similar model to represent currents nearer to and farther from consciousness.

---

[106]See the impressive work of Stevens, Anthony, *Archetypes: A Natural History of the Self,* 1982.

But the readings added a dimension of personhood active in psychic experience that James had not posited. It was a "finer physical body" glimpsed in the aura as an invisible field which corresponded to the flesh and governed its development, healing, and some of its transactions. Within this inclusive realm of flowing force were what the readings called seven delicate "centers"[107] (what kundalini yoga in India and Tibet called *chakras*, Ezekiel had seen as wheels within wheels, and the Book of Revelation had named as churches) that swirled and pulsed like miniature galaxies in a line from the base of the spine to the head, arching over it. Each of these centers, in the account of the readings, interacted directly with a major endocrine gland of the physiological, visible human body, from the gonads and the adrenals to the master gland of the pituitary. This connection gave the currents in the "finer body" instant impact not only on moods and emotions, but on states of vigilance and readiness, as well as on longer-term processes of growth and health, and (most important for open vision) on chemical triggers of imagery and altered consciousness in the bloodstream. Further, it was these same centers through which the work of the Spirit took place.

In this system, Cayce's counsel insisted, psychic or inspired experiences were not freakish wonders of the mind, or whims of a capricious deity, but a natural consequence of the way human beings were constructed. One did not have to force and coax the psyche to produce unusual information and impacts, although careful attention and training were appropriate. Instead the soul was ever reaching out to express as much helpful activity as the person could handle in a body created to be "the temple of the living God." And the universe was so designed that the divine was ever ready to answer, a little more all the time, the efforts of an individual to

---

[107]See Keen, Sam, *The Passionate Life*, 1983, and Cayce, Hugh Lynn, *Venture Inward*, 1964.

love, to build, to worship, to serve in one lifetime and in many. The biblical promise of a Comforter to "bring all things to remembrance" was cited as a real process in which the superconscious might receive from the larger, universal realm whatever was needed for consciousness, provided that the person could handle it constructively and safely.

The keys to growth in psychic capacities or in spiritual gifts, not only for the seer but for the housewife suddenly prompted to look for her absent child in peril, were not engineering of the mind, but existential. Total personal stature and relationship to the divine were the issue, however many lifetimes were required. Ultimately we could see and affect as much as we were and as we took on. Procedures of hypnosis or incantations and breathing were not the crucial variables, although these and many processes might affect the finer body and related circuits used for psychic activities. But there were, of course, disciplines and procedures to be learned, as there were for any skill, for example (a reading noted) in boxing.

The book of Acts began to look interesting from this perspective. It could be read as merely chronicling slogans and unlikely feats when the new Christian movement pushed for converts in a superstitious time. But the Cayce approach raised the question of whether the principal figures, from crusty Paul and ambivalent Peter to raw recruits, were not describing some such process as he reported, when they spoke of being "filled with the Spirit" or "in the Spirit"[108] for unlikely knowledge or improbable healings, not to mention the ability to stand fast under persecution.

---

[108]Gerald Heard fruitfully links prayer and psychic experience in his excellent study, *A Preface to Prayer*, 1944.

Disciplines of Open Vision: Purpose

Three distinct types of readings, each represented by scores, sometimes hundreds, of cases, remained for me to explore in the packed file drawers of the vault off of Gladys' office. Each featured a process so helpful to the operation of open vision that it appeared to be a requisite discipline. First was the "mental and spiritual" reading.

The forms which we mailed out with Cayce's life story to thousands of inquirers about his services offered to new members of the Association this interesting third type, along with medical counsel and life readings. There were nearly four hundred of them in the files together with especially appealing correspondence about them. Those who sought this aid did not ask for medical wonders or for intriguing past lives. They simply wanted to hear what Cayce thought was their primary soul purpose or lesson in this lifetime[109] and how he thought they were addressing it. The Cayces seemed to welcome the spirit of humility in these requests, in which the resultant counsel was strongly biblical in tone and developed themes not too different from those treated by spiritual advisers for centuries: the adequacy of the individual's ideals, the vitality of their personal relationship to God, where they might undertake adventures in prayer and worship or in selfless service, what attitudes to change and emotions to transform, as well as which relationships to work on next. In an earnest and usually gentle manner, reflecting the spirit of the seekers, the entranced Cayce held up in these readings the essential purpose of one life at a time brought before the face of the divine.

The thrust of these particular readings was not unlike that in a practice of rural churches on the American frontier, which had been carried over into Old Liberty Church

---

[109]See Thurston, Mark A., *Discovering Your Soul's Purpose*, 1984.

in Hopkinsville, where Cayce had grown up. When it came time to present Bibles to young persons at the time of their baptism by solemn immersion, some wise and Spirit-led elder had been asked to inscribe each Bible with a unique scriptural verse that would illuminate the strengths and weaknesses of this one life for the years ahead. The task was done with great care and prayer. (I had talked to those from churches in Nebraska, Minnesota, and Texas who cherished such pregnant, inscribed verses.) Cayce's counsel in these plain but appealing readings served much the same purpose. The intent was not so much new information as direction and motivation, in prose that read at times like a personal litany. Clues here to *accuracy* and *scope*, which were subordinated to issues of *perspective* and *engagement*, came from interviewing those who had received such readings. Some recipients were disappointed, feeling they got less to work with than they had from their life readings (usually secured first). But others had tested for themselves the validity of this counsel by introspection, dreams, prayer, and Bible study. Their faces shone with appreciation of Cayce's efforts. In a time long ago a seer would have been asked for just such appraisal and direction of soul purpose by those who sought him out. But in a time of mail-order convenience, the transactions seemed strange, stripped of the awed personal encounter in another age.

How did this kind of counsel, a combination of psychological analysis and blessings like those from a tribal elder, illuminate the actual process of open vision which Cayce himself used?[110]

Readings insisted that psychic ability was not a feat of the mind, entering a marvelous altered state by hypnosis or yogic concentration, but a natural accompaniment of soul growth: "psychic is ever of the soul." As the indi-

---

[110]See Bro, Harmon H., "Was Edgar Cayce Really a Psychic?", *Venture Inward*, March/April, 1986, p. 33.

vidual grew in stature and in grace, bringing the personal will ever more into alignment with the Father's will and developing the talents it had earned in its long journey of earth sojourns, the personal evidence would mount for the promise in Romans 8:16: "My Spirit beareth witness with thy spirit." In small things and in great, from knowing who would answer the phone to knowing when to mount a political campaign, the promptings of the inner voice or awareness would grow stronger and clearer. The way to open vision was the way of the ancient prophet: "to do justly, to love mercy, and to walk humbly with thy God." To be sure, developing capacities such as Cayce's could take years. And how would one know whether progress were being made in such a murky area as soul growth?

Fortunately, two other categories of readings addressed just this question. One type (with well over a hundred readings) presented soul growth in group settings, undertaken step by step with like-minded seekers. The other was on dreams as a major path (Freud had called them a "royal road" to the unconscious) for guidance and self-evaluation on the way toward unfolding stature with God for service of one's fellows. More than seven hundred were in this category.

Disciplines of Open Vision: Small Groups

Over a decade before I came, a number of Cayce's churchgoing friends in Norfolk (from such ordinary walks of life as teaching and nursing and homemaking) had approached him to give them readings on how to become psychic. The idea had occurred to them after hearing of lessons offered by William Dudley Pelley, an occultist with a national following, who also sponsored Fascist-leaning troops of Silver Shirts. They thought Cayce might do better. He agreed to try. What followed involved them in years of demanding work, writing up two small anonymous manuals for spiritual growth, called *A Search for God*.[111]

Whether or not these people could be called spiritual geniuses after so many years of disciplined living, I found them a delight to know. Once a month on a Sunday afternoon, they came to the Cayce home for a group reading, followed by a work session on their manual and, at times, a high-spirited potluck supper. Their aspiration to become psychic had been realized as far as could be discovered from their absorbing personal accounts of guidance, telepathy, healing, and precognition, as well as visionary mystical experiences. Fortunately, several of them tossed me offhand counsel on diet, dreams, and prayer in the course of our growing friendships so that I learned for myself how swiftly intuitive they had become. Even more interesting was that they seemed to have long since grown beyond preoccupation with extrasensory feats and were now just sturdy pilgrims on a long road Godward, who found psychic happenings as natural as bird song on their way. The very first reading had set the tone with a lesson in growth. It was not on breathing or visioning or concentration, but on the much more mundane process of cooperation. Subsequent themes for their daily training effort were just as existential, not equipping them to manipulate their minds but to flex their souls, such as "What Is My Ideal?" and "Know Thyself" or "Patience," reaching all the way to "Love" after years of self-discipline, prayer, and sharing.

A second lasting group developed out of Cayce's seekers for soul lessons. This one, stimulated by a vivid dream, worked with healing by prayer, meditation, and laying-on of hands. The readings given for this activity appeared careful and detailed, though I could not evaluate them until years later. Then I would view them as some of the deepest and most helpful material I had ever studied on the little-understood process of faith healing, when I wrote a reference article for the *Encyclopedia*

---

[111]Anon., *A Search for God*, Books I and II, 1943, 1946.

Britannica,[112] citing Cayce's work along with that of others.

Cayce's insistence on setting disciplined spiritual growth within covenanting group fields made sense to me as an active church person, but again it would be years before I would see how crucial this aspect of the growth process really was. By then I had taught seven years in a college that offered graduate degrees in group-work education, and immersed myself in the literature on small groups, as well as led a variety of types myself. Small search-and-support groups offered not only fellowship in high measure, but nurture which was as prone to humor as to prayer, and no-nonsense guards against spiritual inflation, though groups poorly disciplined could become narcissistic and shallowly pious. Further, the best of such groups could learn to engage the stages in the movement of the Spirit, linked to the centers, or *chakras*, which Cayce patiently described. Decades later I would write a book on this vertical dimension of group life in Cayce's readings, called *High Play.*[113]

Disciplines of Open Vision: Dream Study

The files of readings contained interpretations for over fifteen hundred dreams of some seventy persons, across the decades since 1923, when Cayce was prodded into this kind of study by a reading that encouraged him to record his own dreams.[114] Such counsel had not been offered for several years to new members of the

---

[112]Bro, Harmon H., "Faith Healing," 1962 edition.

[113]Bro, Harmon H., *High Play,* 1970.

[114]Bro, Harmon H., *Edgar Cayce on Dreams,* 1968. See also Thurston, Mark A., *How to Understand and Interpret Your Dreams,* 1978, and *Dreams: Tonight's Answers to Tomorrow's Questions,* 1988. See further Sechrist, Elsie, *Dreams: Your Magic Mirror,* 1968. For Cayce verbatim excerpts, see *Library Series,* vols. 4 and 5, *Dreams and Dreaming,* Parts I and II, 1976.

Association partly because Cayce felt it had been misused by those tempted to depend on it too heavily in
the past.

The *scope* of what his trance counsel could accomplish
with dreams was breathtaking. When dreams were submitted for interpretation, it could promptly specify the
time of night when they had occurred. More commonly,
when asked for parts of a dream the dreamer had forgotten or even entire dreams, a reading would supply
the missing material for the dreamer's "Oh, yes!" (Of
course, some of the material retrieved in this fashion was
unflattering to the dreamer, which was why it had been
forgotten in the first place.) Together with dreams, the
"information" often specified what had been so significantly on the dreamer's mind the day before that the
concern emerged in the night. On rare occasions readings went so far as to predict the date, time, and content
of specific dreams yet to be dreamt correctly.

Although all of this was startling, the major task was,
of course, interpreting the meaning of dreams, which the
unconscious Cayce did so well that dream study became
one of the first areas to win his work wider recognition
after his death. His approach was in many ways similar
to that of Jung,[115] in distinguishing various types of symbols and correlating them with levels of the psyche
where they originated, as well as with stages in episodes
of growth and change. He distinguished nonsense content, in dreams stimulated by food, fever, or physical dis-
comfort which had, as he said, "no heads or tails," no
dramatic structure, from three other kinds of content.
Some dream material he described as literal representa-
tion of past, future, or distant events, picking up an old
motif in dream interpretation which had been largely

---

[115]A useful overview is in Jung, C.G., ed., *Man and His Symbols*, 1964,
in which Jung writes the long opening chapter, "Approaching the
Unconscious." See also Jung, *Memories, Dreams and Reflections*, 1961.
The best Jungian work on dreams is Hall, James A., *Clinical Uses of
Dreams*, 1983.

ignored since Freud. A dream of flying, for example, could be about a plane trip and not necessarily about the ecstasy of intercourse or some other elevated emotion. After the advent of laboratory research on dreams, starting with the epochal work of Kleitman and Dement[116] at my alma mater of Chicago, Cayce's insistence on external reference in some dreams would receive considerable support, as in the work of the British Gestaltist, Ann Faraday.[117]

However, the major part of most dreams was assigned by readings to symbols which were called (in this language) "emblems," meaning metaphors and other images to suggest particular activities and attitudes, as well as structures and dynamics of the psyche, in relation to external events. In addition, readings used the category of "visionary" for dream contents that were archetypal in cosmic, mythological, or mystical form. Like Jung, the entranced Cayce assigned dreams a function of being self-regulatory for the psyche and body, with the essential process each night being one of comparing the person's waking behavior with inner norms of health, total growth, and chosen ideals.

His wide-ranging vision allowed him to correlate dream contents with a mind-tumbling array of referents, reaching from childhood influences and past traumas to present activities and relationships, then on into the future and the distant. He gave careful attention to important dream themes or dream memories from past lives. Further, he showed how spouses or other family members might dream for each other, able to take up themes too threatening for the other person, and how dreamers close to each other might engage the same material on a given night, though physically far apart (two sisters separated by half a continent, for example, dreamt simultaneously of conception by one of

---

[116]Dement, William C., *Some Must Watch While Some Must Sleep*, 1972.

[117]Faraday, Ann, *The Dream Game*, 1974.

them early in her marriage).

For identifying the processes of open vision, the most important claim of these readings seemed to be that the dreams of all of us afforded the closest parallel readily available to Cayce's own trance activities. Systematic study of one's dreams, the "information" urged, would show that nothing important ever happens to us without first being previewed in dreams—not necessarily by psychic means, although that would often be found, but also by depiction of trends already set in motion in time to provide a warning, an alerting of opportunity, or a lesson on a principle. This view of the psyche showed dreams functioning at times in a teaching mode (appropriately set in classrooms) and not simply reacting to current or coming events. Further, all the psychic connections which Cayce demonstrated in trances could be paralleled in the dreams of ordinary people. Hundreds of dream analyses showed how the body monitored its own health and illness and prevention of injury or infection in dreams. It was this natural awareness in everyone which Cayce tapped in trance to do medical diagnoses of others. Of course, supplying treatments required drawing on a much wider array of resources, as his own dream of a great trumpet of the universe had shown. But how these resources were available to all dreamers, not just to him, was pointed out in dream-prescribed remedies of a number of persons, even including actual chemicals to be compounded. In this work on dreams about the body Cayce was truly a pioneer, and only recently has medical research followed him, although Jung[118] also was pointing in this direction at about the same time as Cayce.

Processes of inspired or psychic awareness, the entranced man reported, were often embedded in dreams stimulated by the dreamer's meaningful activities: work,

---

[118]See dreams in Jung, C.G., *Modern Man in Search of a Soul*, 1933, Harvest, Harcourt Brace Jovanovich Edition, especially pp. 24 ff.

study, loving, community building, inventions, political action. His careful tutoring on dream use in business had made millionaires out of stockbrokers, and led others to considerable wealth, although his own dreams did not bring him more than infrequent answers to current financial needs (because, he said, he had misused this kind of aid in a prior life and narrowed its availability in his psyche). Reaching far beyond the work world, he showed dreamers how their nighttime ventures could take them into realms beyond death for contact with loved ones, or review whole civilizations they cared about, as well as bring them the most elevated of religious experience (just as Jung[119] was saying).

It would be years before I could fully grasp and work with all these dream processes. By then I would be teaching psychology of religion and practicing psychotherapy with the regular use of dreams. In time I would publish articles and books on Cayce's dream counsel,[120] and include his materials in graduate courses. But right then, seeking to understand the process of open vision in Cayce's quiet discourses and how others might enact it, the most important clue was the claim that everyone had available a process for replicating what he did in the night, when habits of perception did not so quickly rule out the improbable and the mind could range to distant targets as readily as to those near.

But there were, of course, prerequisites for all this dream aid. One had first to learn to recall them. Cayce's instructions on training for recall were substantially the same as those of later sleep and dream researchers, who have shown in laboratories that everyone dreams four to five times every night about a wide range of subjects

---

[119]Jung, C.G., *Psychology and Religion*, Collected Works, vol. 11, analyzes religious dreams in his lectures at Yale.

[120]See Bro, Harmon H., *Dreams in the Life of Prayer and Meditation*, 1985, especially chapter 8, "The Adventure: Systematic Dream Interpretation."

and can usually learn to recall dreams of more than transitory significance (something I would see demonstrated again and again by hundreds of students in the courses I taught in psychology departments over more than twenty years). Such recall was more than techniques. It required a genuine interest in the inner world, supported by meaningful exchanges with others, just as did the development of skill in interpreting and applying dream leads. Not all of us might be inclined to this, whether by temperament or just the busy rounds of our lives, although Cayce warned that those who continually ignored their dreams and comparable visionary material would eventually rob themselves of their own natural stature, becoming busy nonentities. Again and again he showed his dreamers that patient attention to their nightly dramas and reflections (for he noted some dreams that were only that, in what today's research would call NREM [non-rapid eye movement] material) would improve the actual quality of dreams, sharpening their clarity, suggesting their own interpretation, and making them at least partially available to coding or programming for solving particular problems.

But getting serious dream aid required more. One had to deal with the psyche's own life-renewing agenda, whether it be the natural demands of growth beyond childish preoccupations and adult obsessions or demands for attention to inner currents of cruelty, escapism, exploitation, repression, denial, or some other distortion of the human condition. Dreams would give priority over psychic pickup or intuitive judgment to the larger tasks of building a healthy psyche and relating the soul to the divine. The ultimate requirement for open vision in dreams as elsewhere was wholeness in productive relation to others and to the universe.

It was time for us to consider that full *price*, by taking up the panorama of soul growth in reincarnation. There would be displayed the sweep of Cayce's own development that had led him to this ocean town in mid-century America, where the services of an untimely seer offered by a bespectacled ex-photographer seemed as unlikely as placing long-distance phone calls directly to the past or the future.

Part II

The Roots:
Cayce Before Cayce

CHAPTER 9

We Are Living Several Lives at Once

I stared in the mirror while shaving, and tried saying to myself, "You were many other people and you still are." Stepping back and squinting to get a hazy view, I tried to imagine how I might have been the persons Cayce had described in life readings for June and me. If that report were accurate, I was looking at the present manifestation of a soldier, a priest, a healer, a judge, a sculptor, a preacher, a musician. And these individuals were only the few of me chosen by Cayce because they bore on my present existence.

The view of reincarnation in the readings, I knew, was not that of lives completed and left behind like beads on a string. Instead, the major values and dynamics from each life carried right into the present, in sub–personalities which could step forward or backward on the stage of consciousness according to growth needs and choices. In this view, no life was finished. We were living all our lives at once, with several to the fore, as I found Hugh Lynn Cayce had written in an unpublished lecture. The human throb of each one pulsed on across centuries. I was right now living out the central promise and peril of definite people all essentially myself who had walked the earth and loved and labored and died in earlier cultures. I was their destiny. I was making choices, taking risks, dodging conflicts, which had troubled their dreams and quickened their prayers. I was loving or avoiding some of the same people who had been their spouses, their children, their colleagues, their enemies. June would have an identity just as complex. Looking in the mirror, I found, didn't help me much. The whole concept was unsettling to my sense of identity.

Just as peculiar was the claim that I was to become a whole series of other persons in future times and places. Indeed, in this view I was already a part of the nucleus of each of them. What I did now, as a young man in wartime America, could help bring pain and darkness to these individuals yet unborn, or help bring adventure and achievement into their lives, for they would all be me. I had in essence been my own parent, and I would in essence be my own offspring. The whole notion was unnerving. Yet in principle it did not differ from linking our adult existence in one lifetime to forgotten episodes of childhood and youth, which might be as decisively formative as they were long buried.

How would we feel about other people if we soberly considered that each person who went by, neatly wrapped in skin, were the surface expression of a personal archeological dig thousands of years old and part of many civilizations? Perhaps we would stare at others in awe if we felt sure that each individual were such a vast enterprise, so at home in the classic human ventures of childhood, courtship, illness, creation, sacrifice, and dying. We might want to seize our most promising fellows and wring from them soul treasures, whether these be art works, noble causes, prized skills, or authentic holiness.

The sheer strangeness of the reincarnation view did not reveal much about its truth.[121] One could not dispose of the challenge by falling back on ancient screening devices: scriptural authority, philosophical reasonableness, or immediate luminosity to the imagination. Our modern age was too conscious of pious persons in the past who had foolishly decided empirical questions on

---

[121]Gerald Heard was one of the few intellectuals of the time who fitted reincarnation into a responsible version of Western faith. See his Ayer lecture at Colgate Rochester Divinity School, published in 1946 as *The Eternal Gospel.*

criteria overweighted with tradition. Bible and eminent reasonableness had been fused to dismiss Galileo and Copernicus when they described the earth's place in the solar system. Comparable authority had opposed Darwin, just as it had drawn back in outrage from Marx's theory of class interests in history and from Freud's ascription of sexuality to infants. The same mind-set only decades before would have judged anyone intemperate if not ridiculous, who claimed that huge amounts of energy could be released from a few atoms—though in fact the Manhattan Project had already done it.

Two steps were needed to begin an empirical approach to Cayce's view of reincarnation, which might illuminate the ultimate price of open vision. First, one had to get clear on the point and method of the venture. What was the universe, or the divine, presented here as trying to do with us, and how? The other was studying a particular case as it developed toward that end. Edgar Cayce himself would be the obvious example to investigate, by following the course of soul growth that his readings tracked in him across several lifetimes and into the present.

Putting together patterns in the life readings yielded three themes to explore: a *co-creating spirituality*, grounded in *covenanting with God* and in *training of selfhood*.[122] These appeared to be what was important above all else for the reincarnation drama and thus for the kind of inspired capacity seen in open vision and psychic gifts which were, as the readings insisted, "of the soul."

The Intent of Reincarnating, I: Co-Creating

In the view of "the information," the act of choice was central to being human. All souls had been created to-

---

[122]See Bro, Harmon H., *Begin a New Life*, 1971, *High Play*, 1970, and *Edgar Cayce on Religion, Spirituality and Psychic Experience*, 2008.

gether in the beginning by God, whose nature was love
and who therefore sought companions. Their birthright
was free will, which they would use in little and large
choices until they learned enough to become conscious
co-creators and fitting comrades with the divine. Their
destiny was "to have that estate with Him which was in
the beginning, and be conscious of same." The pregnant
little phrase, "be conscious of same," said much about
the importance of the choices through all the experiences and achievements and trials, in the journey of
souls through time and space. Few Bible passages were
as often quoted and paraphrased by the readings as the
challenge of Moses to his people when he sent them on
without him into the Promised Land: "Choose thou
whom ye will serve!"

Although the freedom of souls was vast and the patience of God incredible, the cosmos and souls were designed to nurture certain choices, certain priorities,
certain directions. That was why it was critical for each
soul to establish and refine definite ideals and purposes
again and again. They would discover that in the long
run they would get out of any lifetime only what they
put into it.

The primal process to be learned through the many
choices was this: "The Spirit is the life, mind is the builder,
and the physical is the result."[123] To be sure, souls would
be delighted by such proximate values as power, position, learning, possessions, or self-indulgence. But they
would find each of these failing them unless the energy
and intent were of the Spirit, which meant committed to
ever unfolding creative outcomes for themselves and
others. The test of choices would be contributing to what
a reading called "the continuity of life" in whatever they
undertook, not merely by perpetuating the past, but by
facilitating those outcomes in which persons and nature

---

[123]This is the major theme in Puryear, Herbert B., *The Edgar Cayce
Primer*, 1982.

and beings from other realms—indeed, all creation—moved toward their fullest potentials together.

The means for souls to discern wise and productive choices was ultimately to "put on the mind of Christ" by using patterns and resources given them at the start. Every soul had three interacting constituents of its nature: spirit or coded energy, mind, and will.[124] Choices made by the mind and put into action by the will would prosper, insofar as they embodied the living spirit. To facilitate the best choices, a central archetype of Christ consciousness (not unlike the governing Self posited by Jung),[125] working to join the best interests of self and others in the sight of God, was given as a potential for each soul, waiting to be awakened or constellated by choices and by consequent experiences.

In this view, co-creating with God and others was not a far destiny in an exalted, perfected state, but an activity for each day, each hour, each relationship. Only what was faithfully and wisely undertaken now would be found enduring and active as the soul completed its multi-life journey to mystical union of purpose and consciousness with the divine. So the art or lifestyle of co-creating in all things became the hallmark of effective choices. By such a way of life the evil in human experience could be overcome and its energy ultimately transformed and freed, though not without failures and pain. Suffering would be part of the journey, but no soul would be tested or burdened, in the mercies of God, beyond what it could bear.

The essential choice process in co-creating down through the centuries would be reconciling opposed but complementary values, whose individual richness and

---

[124]See the thoughtful treatment of the will in Thurston, Mark A., *Paradox of Power*, 1987. Compare Peck, M. Scott, *The Road Less Traveled*, 1978.

[125]See, for example, Jung, Carl G., *Two Essays in Analytical Psychology*, Collected Works, vol. 7.

fitting proportions would require testing and plumbing
in many settings, until the soul found its way home
through many lifetimes, "conscious of same."

A co-creating lifestyle or spirituality would strive in
all the encounters of labor and loving to be mutually
empowering yet would constantly evaluate outcomes for
refinement of the effort. It would be generous, liberat-
ing, helpful, long-suffering, as one sought to be "a channel of blessings to others" (the most frequently suggested
phrase in the readings for aspiration). At the same time,
such a lifestyle should have limits, demanding the best
in self and others, not afraid to be different on principle.
No sentimental goodwill but engagement both passionate and sensitive shone in this counsel.

Radical and daring expectancy would be balanced
with heartfelt gratitude in such a lifestyle. One could
approach even the gravest of circumstances in lively
hope, convinced that God knew something productive
to do and wanted to do it (as we were told to observe in
so many readings). Yet such expectancy could never be
commanding God, nor plundering the Kingdom, for our
times and ways were not necessarily God's. Gratitude
must shape and temper hope. Those who understood
and accepted all of life as gifts were best fitted for the
wildness, the unspeakable richness in the farthest
reaches of expectancy which radical co-creating engaged.
Simplicity of manner, of address, of engagement would
be found flowing naturally from such gratitude.

Bold risking would need to be matched by patience
for true daily co-creating. "Be not fainthearted," the readings counseled as they urged many to bet their lives and
health, even their souls, on chosen courses of action that
befitted their noblest ideals. "Know that the try is
counted for righteousness" was a familiar phrase, not
meant to imply divine bookkeeping but the muscling of
the soul. Doing something wrong, if sincerely chosen,
was not as dangerous as doing nothing, for God would
help to correct a misguided course but could hardly aid
a soul that sat out the dance. Yet risking needed recon-

ciling with the steady enduring, the faithful patience, which kept stouthearted striving from excess. Often the readings spoke of "time, space, and patience" as the ultimate dimensions of human experience, lifting the third from a virtue to a law. "Be not overanxious" was the counsel. Those ventures truly committed to God would find their fruition in seasons not always evident. "Be persistent and consistent" was the encouragement offered to many, even in drastically threatening circumstances.

Co-creating required stretching the imagination. One could not ask for and build toward what was not even conceived. So this spirituality, in existence after existence, meant choosing to be playful, innovative, curious, inventive, open-minded, and not afraid to be startlingly original. We were seeing in Cayce, we were told, a gift that did not manifest as often as it should in others partly because the creative imagination required to depict many patterns was not sufficiently developed in others. Yet imagination functioned best when it was directional, tutored by aspirations that rightly mirrored human destiny. Better than imagining freedom from symptoms was imagining wholeness; better than wholeness was fulfillment found jointly with others, even through a trying cross.

No life pattern would suffice in the strategies of choices in daily life which did not embody a spirit of gentleness and kindness; achievements did not outweigh their means: "We only get into heaven leaning on the arms of those we have helped." In the same vein, the readings counseled, "Be affectionate to one another," not depending on attraction but on deeper caring and mutual attentiveness. But kindness and goodwill required discriminating insight, lest they become mindless parenting and indulgence of each other. So love needed wisdom, and was completed in habits of truthfulness, especially with oneself.

Recognizing and building on virtues in oneself and others was also part of a co-creating spirituality. This was a process we were invited to observe in readings. Whatsoever was honorable, just, lovely, or noble required tending in our gardens of selfhood and culture. Celebrating soul quality as it grew was in its way as important as aspiring to it. But making heraldry out of each other's unique "fruits of the spirit" did not mean leaping to condemn their lack. Few themes were as frequently sounded in the readings as not condemning self or others; instead, forgiveness was counseled, seventy times seven and more. No ornaments of the soul would suffice if they were won in harshness and subject to punitive review. In the view of the readings, we did not need to be perfect in order to be useful and beautiful. Humility and lowliness would take us further than self-righteousness, for the soul would exact of itself what it demanded of others. "Judge not, that ye be not judged" many were admonished as they were encouraged to glorify God, not to placate Him with standards that secretly usurped His place.

Lest all this counsel on co-creating in the soul's evolution seem too burdensome, the readings insisted, "Start with what you have in hand, and the next will be given to you." The next might be talents, it might be opportunities, it might be resources, and it would surely be character. But the way was to "Begin! Dig in! Use your will!" Only by application, by steady effort, would archetypes, or what Cayce specifically called "patterns," come to life in the psyche which would transform perception of what was already at hand but overlooked, or would draw new resources, since like attracts like, a major law of the universe. No amount of study would suffice for those soul lessons and insights which had to be found by spending oneself with others. But starting where one was did not mean accepting unworthy surroundings or unjust institutions. With each beginning needed to go ever unfolding aspirations. "Change the environs!" was the counsel when people ran up against poverty or ignorance or tyranny. Starting with what was at hand did not mean fatalism or narcissistic self-improvement, but rather the necessary energizing which would activate ample vision and rebuilding of one's world.

Finally, the readings summarized a co-creating spirituality, for one incarnation or many, with two words
which embodied "all the Law and the prophets." These
again were conflicting opposites which needed to be rec-
onciled in daily living: attunement and service. The first
meant "Thou shalt love the Lord thy God with all thy
heart, mind, soul, and strength," while the second meant
"And thy neighbor as thyself." The two were in tension,
for every step aside or back to view things or persons or
forms in attunement with God meant time not given to
worthwhile building or reforming or healing. Yet making without musing, reacting without reflecting, fashioning without being affected, were dangerous temptations
to play God. Here the readings came remarkably close to
Buber's distinction between I–Thou relations and I–It relations, which must alternate in a life lived before the
Eternal Thou.[126]

Given the extroverted nature of American popular
culture, the readings often emphasized for attunement
the necessity of turning within to meet the God within
who "has promised to meet thee, in thy flesh, in the
temple of thy body" through intuitive promptings that
combined perception with judgment, even paranormal
perception such as Cayce showed in readings and awake.
Such attunement required "waiting on the Lord" and in-
cubating problems for dream or other inner solution.
Solitude was helpful for such attunement, as were its
natural outcomes of prayer and meditation. But just as
earnestly, readings spoke of turning to "the God without," by attending to the wonders of nature and creatures, where the divine was constantly reflected, and by
stepping into the beauty of music, dance, painting, poetry, and the rest of the arts, which could become powerful agents for attunement when joined to a spirit of
reverence and the practice of worship. And attunement

---

[126] Buber, Martin, *I and Thou*, 1937; note also his *Between Man and
Man*, 1955, and *Pointing the Way*, 1957.

crucially required openhearted attention to one's fellows: "Inasmuch as ye do it unto the least of these, ye do it unto thy God."

Attunement could not be pursued solely by isolated moments of going apart. Only a mind and spirit which was fed on "His things" would know what to embrace in quiet. So attuning would blossom with study of history, biography, the scriptures, and the great teachings of the human spirit,[127] just as it required rites of symbolic renewal and affirmation. But above all it required a caring heart able to receive others and cherish them, despite their awkwardness and harshness, with the kind of listening which ever completes loving, because it provides the knowledge which turns goodwill into deep engagement. Here attunement stepped toward its twin, service.

For the readings the call to service, in life after life, was a call to love the world as God's creation, not to rise above it to ethereal heights, nor to stand across from it in lofty spirituality.[128] All things had their appointed destinies, and only one committed to the fulfillment of the very "blades of grass" (here the readings came close to Bodhisattva images from Buddhism) was hearing correctly the call to service. Likewise, the imperative was to honor not only individuals but their creations of institutions and culture, expressing impulses precious in the sight of God. No shallow do-goodism was enjoined, and the frailties of institutions were freely cited by the readings, but neither were individuals entitled to abstract themselves from their cultural skins. Rescue was one mode of service seen in Cayce's medical counsel, but so were reform and innovation which made rescue unnecessary, as seen in the productive careers enjoined on those who sought life readings. To lift up the broken and

---

[127]Note Bro, Harmon; "Can We Find the Lost Scriptures?" *Venture Inward*, May/June, 1985.

[128]Comparison is appropriate with Richard Niebuhr in *Christ and Culture*, 1951.

wounded was precious in God's sight. But just as dear was fashioning a world devoted less to crippling enemies or besting outsiders and more to freeing the potential of children and adults alike.[129]

In this view, one was to render service not only to the worthy or the respectable. Need was the criterion, as it had been for aiding the storied Samaritan. Indeed, committing oneself to the poor or the outcast in true solidarity of spirit might (in a biblical phrase) "cover a multitude of sins" for a life that had spent itself in orbits too small or protected. The command to do as one would be done to was near to the center of the spirit of service in the readings. Yet this was exceeded by the call to "self-bewilderment in Him," in which the criterion was not even fairness but radical and joyous response to the love already received from God. No long-faced or smug good works would do. Service needed the constant cleansing and renewal that only attunement could supply, until giving was as clean and fresh as Easter morning.

The Intent of Reincarnating, II: Covenanting

Supporting this co-creative lifestyle or spirituality, which the readings presented as the central purpose of reincarnation, were twin pillars which gave it a necessary foundation, to be built in life after life: covenanting and self-training.

Covenanting with God[130] was set forth as a process and a relationship which would continuously grow, much as love grows in a vital and purposeful family. Two patterns were at work here. One was just cherishing

---

[129]Although Cayce dealt with individuals, it is not inappropriate to compare aspects of his thought with Paul Tillich's concern for transforming the culture. See also, Bro, Harmon H., "Discovering a Lost World," *Venture Inward*, November/December, 1987, p. 51.

[130]See, as illustrative, the readings collected as reflections on themes in the Gospel of John, in *A Closer Walk*, 1974.

the divine as Friend and as Beloved, without Whose sharing no day's experience was complete. The invitation was "to glorify God and enjoy Him forever," as the old catechism put it. Only such an open delight would keep the relationship from being used for private ends. Yet in tension with this was a different process of entrusting God with keeping one's particular promises, needs, aspirations. Both the unfreighted joy of companionship and the deep relying on God's trustworthiness belonged together. "Know in Whom ye have believed," the readings counseled many, and that He is able to "keep unto the last day that which ye have entrusted to him."

Covenanting, as seen in the readings, was intensely personal, engaging the deepest desires and longing of the heart to be one "not conformed but transformed." Yet it was also social, and each had to find the reconciling of this tension. For as dreams showed, the human being was appointed not to solo life but to be part of a people, finding grace and transformation with others, though not without solitude. So covenants needed to be made and acknowledged before others, the "information" stipulated, just as in a marriage service, although the intent might be very different, as in a covenant to learn a skill for service, or to bear a burden of suffering until it yielded its secret blessing. And covenants needed the matrix of living tradition, as we could see enacted in daily references to the scriptures in the readings, not for decoration but for depth. Few passages were cited and paraphrased by the readings more often than Exodus 19:5, where the promise was "If you will be my people, I will be your God." Gifts such as Cayce's would be misunderstood if viewed outside his cherished tradition and covenants, both personal and corporate, because they would seem to be private attainments when in fact they were co-creations with a Creator God.

The practice of covenanting with God meant above all finding reconciliation between one's own daily will and the larger Will. "Not my will but Thine be done" was repeatedly offered by the readings as an essential theme of a life pledged to God. The intent was not to strip away individuality or earnest striving; God loved individuals by name and face, as he invited them to be His co-workers and co-lovers. Indeed, the readings frequently counseled vigorous self-assertion once the ideal for the life was firmly set in relationship to God and others. But since the will was presented by the readings as the one factor which more than any other made for soul growth or loss, its tempering and grounding in the will of God was crucial to the human journey, through the step which many feared most. Gently but firmly the readings insisted that yielding the will did not mean lessening of identity and potency, but enhancement of these, in a gamble which every soul must make, life by life. "Ye must believe He is, to find Him" was the command and invitation, recognizing that all real understanding is known by doing. Yet the belief should include the conception that God would not override the will, because the result would be an automaton, not a companion and co-creator with Him.

Since covenanting implied accountability, in which parties pledged to be faithful to what was entrusted to them, it required willingness to be weighed and challenged.[131] For the readings this meant heartfelt repentance and turning when needed in the assurance that God would keep His promises of utter forgiveness and no alienation. Such repentance was not reserved for public wrongdoers or criminals, for "all have sinned and fallen short." The sin in question was not naughtiness, but betrayal of the very Creative Force which gave humans life and offered each a unique potential. Playing God over others, or even over one's own destiny in contrived existence, or hiding from one's potential by living

---

[131]See Bro, Harmon H., "Finding the Way to Full Emptiness," *Venture Inward*, January/February, 1987, p. 34. Also, Bro, Harmon H., "What About Evil?" *Venture Inward*, September/October, 1984, p. 15. Compare Peck, M. Scott, *People of the Lie*, 1983, and Buber, Martin, *Good and Evil*, 1953.

through others and blaming others were examples of
sins of commission. By contrast, there were sins of omission just as serious, in one's toying with life, failing to
strike out in meaningful efforts, or ignoring the calls from
without and within to serve those in need. What made
the necessary repentance bearable and not a crushing
burden of guilt was the awareness, ever renewed in the
covenanting process, that God calls each by name, that
we are not solely our own and never were, and that the
Spirit "ever bears witness with us" to bring us before
God whole, productive, and lovingly connected to others.

Part of covenanting was trusting in guidance. If the
effort at attunement were regularly made, with a fitting
ideal, there would always be an answer, though not necessarily in the form sought. Whether through dreams,
prayer, impressions, or the prompting of opportunities
(or even readings), the response would be there from a
God faithful to keep His promises. Yet the aid would be
given to avoid loss of soul size, loss of depth and meaning and direction, not necessarily to avoid suffering. "Do
not attempt to go around the cross," the readings advised. One could put off some suffering and avoid much
else. But all that had been built as "carnal forces" in the
aggrandizement of self in many lifetimes (meaning not
so much passion as living to the flesh in shallow values)
would one day need changing. When it did, this would
come about not as punishment from an arbitrary God
but as the longing of the soul itself to be alive, awake,
and resurrected to larger life with and for others. In this
process suffering could ultimately be mercy and karma
be grace.

The Intent of Reincarnating, III: Self-Training

Implicit in the covenanting of a soul as a pilgrim down
the centuries was the other foundation which continuously supported a co-creating spirituality. It was training of selfhood as a kind of ongoing yoga or yoking to

the divine through life upon life.[132]

Growing as a person was not left by the readings to accident and impulsive self-improvement. "Study to show thyself approved, a workman not ashamed, rightly dividing the word of truth and keeping self unspotted from the world" was the closing passage, woven from scripture, in many a life reading. The task of self-training was presented not as collecting merit badges, but as a process of larger importance: "He that conquereth self is more than he that taketh a city."

Such training involved both balance and extremes, according to the need and capacity. On the one hand, the readings counseled moderation in all things, especially for building health and wholeness. Yet they also warned that one should not hold back from loss or even extravagance, when the purpose was sure and appropriate, and the need large. "Spend it all" was the counsel at times, whether the spending involved physical comfort and well-being or risking one's possessions and station in life. Each human asset, whether belongings, learning, fame, passion, or power, had its place in the development of the soul. But each had to be held lightly, and in covenants with God and one's fellows, lest the very blessing consume one.

A surprising motif in the readings' view of self-training as a continuous process was the affirmation that one's weaknesses could become one's greatest strengths if the energy were properly engaged. Anger and hostility could become boldness and courage. Stubbornness could become leadership, which endures where others quit. Deception could become true inventiveness. Sensuality could be turned to healing through rechanneling the life force itself. Pride of wisdom could become genu-

---

[132]See the selections of readings in Kidd, Worth, *A Way to Fulfillment*, 1973. A useful study of classic disciplines is Wells, Ronald V., *Spiritual Disciplines for Everyday Living*, 1982. See also, Bro, Harmon H., "To Be a Spiritual Leader," *Venture Inward*, September/October, 1986, p. 40.

242   Edgar Cayce: A Seer Out of Season

ine understanding used in sensitivity. The changes here
envisioned were not through amputation, but through
redirection of specific energies and urges, ultimately all
expressions of the one life force, using the centers or
chakras. To be sure, limits had to be set, for the needed
training was not magic. But the path to faithfulness in
the covenants of a co-creating lifestyle lay through
growth, in which impulses and habits were transmuted,
not simply overpowered, for the purpose of serving others and glorifying God. In the view of the readings, evil
was not poles apart from good, but "evil is just under
good, waiting to be lifted." It used the same energy as co-
creating but aborted it. Turning one's efforts to keep
promises well-made to God and others would redirect
and renew even violence, self-pity, willfulness, and crude
sensuality "in time and in patience."

The self-training, while essential, was not a burden to
be borne alone. Again and again the readings insisted
that the help of the Christ was available as coded energy
and Presence to any who sought it and kept promises
made in worthwhile covenants of love, work, politics,
and faith. "He did it all" was the assurance that no human predicament was too deadly for Him who had gone
through death itself. He would not force Himself on any,
but He was ever there as Elder Brother, offering both a
pattern and the vitality to keep it. What was required in
self-discipline, then, was hungering and thirsting for His
way, not simply learning skills and laws. "Love is Law, as
Law is Love," insisted the readings, pointing to a universe
run not by great mechanical forces, but by consciousness as tender and intimate as that of a friend.

Three blessings would be found accompanying the
Spirit of the Christ for those who would train across lifetimes for full stature.[135] One was "fruits of the Spirit,"
which the readings very often listed in Pauline fashion,

---

[135]On the Holy Spirit, Lindsay Dewar in *The Holy Spirit and Modern Thought,* 1959, has tried to connect ESP with its manifestations. See the Jungian treatment in Clift, Wallace B., *Jung and Christianity,* 1983.

with free paraphrases, to awaken in hearers a sense of the richness, and even glory, that could be theirs as co-creators with the Most High, starting right where they were "today, now." Another was "gifts of the Spirit," differently divided to each but appointed to every soul as birthright and promise, just as we were seeing in Cayce but could also find in ourselves, varying from prophecy to healing to administration, and much more. And a third was community of the Spirit, which would draw together those of like minds and purposes into friendships and families and groupings, some built centuries ago in prior lives and some quite new. Nobody was expected to make it alone in the view of this source, in which cooperation was the first spiritual discipline, and the backdrop was the people of God in the Exodus. There would be lonely times, as Jesus knew in the garden, but the passage was ultimately a lighted one, illuminated by the radiance of one's fellows and by helpers seen and unseen.

Finally, the large vista of training as an integral responsibility in a life pledged to God was neither an abandoning to the Spirit nor to the flesh. One could go too far either way. Humans in the earth plane were incarnations seeking to become expressions of the process in which the Word was made flesh, full of grace and truth as was their divine pattern. Earth was to be honored, with all its treasures and creatures given to be subdued and multiplied but not exploited. Souls would explore many other "mansions" in their long journey, but the goal of self-discipline and self-mastery was not simply to escape from the earth. Rather was the far vista one of greater and greater service, until one shared in the creation of worlds themselves, with the Source of all life. Since the journey was undertaken in great freedom, it might take many, many lifetimes for some souls, indeed, but none would be lost. Those who rebelled unceasingly would eventually be brought home to the Father but not "conscious of same" (and the Father would weep over what had been lost).

In these three processes of a co-creating spirituality, supported by convenanting with God and by training of selfhood, was the core of the serious business of reincarnation. But there was more to the rebirthing process exhibited in the readings. Three themes emerged as the essence of karma, or what was carried over dynamically from one lifetime to another as the soul undertook to grow in grace of co-creating with its Maker. They could be described as *talents, texture,* and *opportunity.*

Talents, of course, were all the abilities, interests, and understandings which had been developed sufficiently in past existences to surface in later lives. Texture (a term which I borrowed and modified from the psychology of William Sheldon, often discussed in our family circle) stood for the fabric of the personality—its richness, depth, and integration. Opportunities stood for those relationships, positions, assets, and projects which we often called chance but which might in fact reflect larger causation than we knew. All three offered features which might be overlooked in a view of the unconscious limited to one lifetime.[134]

The Heart of Karma, I: Talents

There was large drama in the notion of talents buried like pirate treasure just below the surface of conscious-

---

[134]A useful philosophic essay on reincarnation and karma is MacGregor, Geddes, *Reincarnation and Christianity,* 1978. Empirical data may be found in the studies of Ian Stevenson, such as *Twenty Cases of Reincarnation,* 1966, and Stanislav Grof, in *Realms of the Human Unconscious,* 1976. Morton Kelsey, in *Afterlife,* 1982, concludes against reincarnation. Victor White, Roman Catholic Jungian, offers an approach to reincarnation via the *Incarnation in God the Unknown,* 1956, Part II, ch. 1. An authoritative summary of reincarnation in the views of Clement and Origen appears in Drummond, Richard, *Toward a New Age in Christian Theology,* 1985. Cayce's views are presented in cases by Cerminara, Gina, in her *Many Mansions,* 1950, and *The World Within,* 1957.

ness. It was exciting to consider that anyone of us might be a poet, a political leader, a scientist, a merchant, a healer, or even a seer, and not know it until our once-learned skills were called back into life by insight or need, ready for training and use. In Cayce's trance view such talents, if well developed, would so often surface again that life readings frequently traced for individuals two or more incarnations (out of four to six given prominence) with the same or closely related vocations. Whatever the century or the culture of their origin, the same gifts might spring to life afresh in teaching, home building, government, astronomy, cloth trading, sports, music, or any of scores of other occupations.

Yet today's inner promptings to these same talents, long ago so valuable, might be missed or misinterpreted. The individual might be sidetracked by family circumstance, illness, war, personal weakness, or indecision. Working within a reincarnation perspective, then, required all of us to consider thoughtfully each other's depths, watching for the flash of true talent in vocation, hobbies, and interests which might signal special endowments and potentials. Education, child rearing, and administration or management—all the arts of fitting people to jobs and stretching them to new potentials—might be conducted better if each child or employee were viewed as a seasoned veteran of one or more callings, and perhaps an artist at some, or ready to combine several for new directions. One woman writer had been, her reading noted, an actress, barnstormer, missionary, and emissary in lives stretching across centuries, in which she had never been a writer. Yet the total combination fitted her well for the reporting she was about to undertake now.

A great prize in talents from past lives was unguessed vocations. Cayce's counsel scored here repeatedly with readings given for small children, as early as a few hours after their birth. Over and over the "information" correctly outlined for these infants what later proved to be pronounced endowments and skills, offering suggestions on how to develop them and at what age. Not realizing such potentials, parents might mistakenly push their family traditions or expectations on the new soul that had landed in their midst. Several dozen of these readings for children, I found, could already be compared with what was surfacing in the lives of those now in their teens and twenties, in which Cayce's trance ability was impressive, correctly foreseeing the gifts of a physician, a gymnast, a musician, a salesperson, or a spiritual leader, when all he had before him was a sprawling infant. If Cayce could do it, surely the laws could one day be learned for doing it through open vision without his aid, as he recommended.

Easier to verify as hidden talent were cases when Cayce's counsel led an adult to change vocations and achieve striking success because of a past-life capacity. Gladys Davis's brother, for example, had moved from an unrewarding occupation in the newspaper business to a new career in the manufacturing of uniforms, in which he rose to the top of his field and financial prominence, as the reading predicted. A telegraph operator became a successful commercial artist. An engineer developed his own enviable firm. A cripple became a concert harpist. Several dozen cases in the files showed people moving successfully to completely new lines of work in response to readings about past-life talents. Photos of some of these pilgrims through the centuries hung on Cayce's wall, and the appealing lore of their stories of fresh starts was part of the working tradition which helped him to keep going. Others had risen high in their callings, who felt they might not have done so had not Cayce and their inner confirmation of his guidance convinced them of exceptional talents from former lives. A number of these told me their stories: a psychologist, a financier, an author, a publisher, physicians, teachers, and salesmen.

The social implications were exciting. The natural hope for social change, as when reading Cayce's biography while guarding my part of the Manhattan Project, had been that the Cayces of the future might find new deposits of ores, new agricultural methods, new manufacturing designs to cure economic want. Talents such as his might design new political systems of justice, as well as undercut the machinery of war to bring a peaceful social order. But the life readings were suggesting an additional or even more central path toward the same end. Progress in social change did not have to be speeded by using seers of the future to solve economic and political problems. It could come by identifying the hidden talents of potential leaders in many walks of life who had brought with them unsuspected gifts from past incarnations.

Ultimately it was individuals who made social advances possible, in any case. Somebody always had to lead, to invent, to draw new pictures, to develop new worldviews, to pull others into new groupings. The key to a new social order might lie in specific individuals: the best miners and farmers, businessmen and inventors, politicians and artists, preachers and financiers of the future. If we could find them and draw forth their prized resources from past existences living on in the present, we could be headed into a heroic journey for our people and our times. Perhaps this was also why Cayce's readings insisted on taking one person at a time, in whatever mode each sought aid, rather than developing grand schemes and theories which nobody was on hand to turn into reality. If reincarnation were real, this was a way to harvest centuries of achievement right under our noses. No other national resource, no asset of nature or technology or culture, would be quite like this one: the unguessed talents of past ages walking around in our midst.

Consequently, reading after reading also pointed to drawing gifted souls into families through special preparations by parents-to-be. Just as Sarah had prepared the way for Isaac, Hannah for Samuel, David for Solomon, and Mary for Jesus, the universe was so designed that the life quality of parents would critically determine which souls would be born to them. A focus on great

music might draw a gifted musician, as a focus on engineering or politics or spirituality might draw a leader in
any of those respective fields. The key to this process
was not mechanical absorption in a given interest,
though Cayce encouraged parents to steep themselves
in the best they knew in a chosen field as they prepared
for childbirth. The actual texture of the parents' lives was
more decisive for recruiting a gifted soul, because it provided a promising climate for talent. Harmony, adventure, humor, faith, outgoing aid to others—all of these
and more made up the dynamics of a family which an
ample soul might want to enter. A number of the couples
around Cayce were taking him quite seriously on this
challenge. Parents and grandparents fished together in
the sea of souls for those who might bless others around
them.

The Heart of Karma, II: Texture

Besides talents, karma also engaged the texture of the
self: the character and temperedness, the complexity and
integration, the essential desire of the whole person. In
Cayce's view the universe was organized to help develop
the potential texture of souls fashioned by the divine at
the start of creation and destined to become conscious
co-creators with the Most High after eons of adventures.
Some of these souls—millions of them but by no means
all—had used their God-given powers to play in the garden of the earth, finally disturbing its creatures and cli-
mates for their own indulgence so that the earth-mired
souls lost their contact with their Source or found their
contact growing dim. A way was set up for souls to use
earthly experience better, gaining its lessons and incarnating its patterns by a series of anthropoid existences
in which they would have the imagination and intelligence to build whole cultures and civilizations yet have
free will which would bring them step by step to their
full stature and texture. Karma was the appointed pro-

cess to turn the whole vast venture into education, by ever stretching the quality of each soul through the challenges and predicaments, the rewards and trials, which came before the evolving person or entity. Talents and powers would be important, because they would express the God–given creative energy of each soul. But ultimately love—wise love—for the whole of creation would be the prize of texture that crowned the journey.

What was important to know about one's own past existences? Each of Cayce's life readings included a reminder that the "information" carefully selected incarnations and details of past biography to make the counsel "a helpful experience" for the seeker. Transcripts from the files suggested an outline of Cayce's typical portraits based on the unremembered past.

Often a half-voiced comment from the unconscious man opened these multi-life panoramas as he took his bearings on the person coming into view. He might describe a great hall of records, or the events of the individual's birth in this lifetime. One reading for a member of our staff, for example, reported that in Bokhoma, Oklahoma, one would never commit suicide after living with its earth underfoot: "something in the soil." More often he would leaf through the years of the person's present life, starting at the present and working backward to identify crises and inner hopes. He would murmur, "prolonged illness," "loss of parent," "business triumph," "hopes for a fresh start in college," "death of baby brother"—each item would be accompanied by the exact year, creating for the listener an uncanny sense of being known intimately not only by Cayce but by whatever transcendent source supplied the data he was inspecting.

The formal reading began in response to a suggestion which Mrs. Cayce regularly repeated to her husband:

> You will give the relations of this entity and the universe, and the universal forces; giving the conditions which are as personalities, latent and ex-

hibited in the present life; also the former appearances in the earth's plane, giving time, place, and
the name, and that in each life which built or retarded the development for the entity; giving the
abilities of the present entity, that to which it may
attain, and how. You will answer the questions, as
I ask them.

First the quiet voice from the couch assessed how well
the person was fulfilling his or her unique promise, the
relationship to the universe and the universal forces, or
what in other language might be the soul's response to
its original call from God. The summary comments varied widely, as my literal or paraphrased notes for a week
showed. "One who will ever be marked by the experience of having been healed by the Master." "This is a soul
who has drifted far from the purposes for which it entered, and must make amends soon if it would continue
in this sphere." "Nobody who comes close to this poetic
soul will soon forget it." "Busy, almost too busy—yet ever
longing to do the right thing in whatever it undertakes."
"The birth crippling here was an accident, not karma,
and somebody will pay for the carelessness." Just as diagnosis and prognosis opened the medical readings, so
this initial material sized up prominent features of the
person, tagging the most striking problems and conflicts
before moving on to more detailed analyses, for example, "This person is a blossom, and should in fact work
with flowers."

Next the typical reading described the unique texture
of the person. For the material on personality structure,
the trance counsel subordinated the influence of past
earth lives for a larger sketch, as skilled playwrights (such
as G.B. Shaw) introduced their key characters with suggestive notes, sometimes paragraphs long, meant only
for the actors and director to read before plunging into
the circumstances of the play. This opening overview in
the reading offered portrait highlights, noting (for example) how assertive and how guarded, how consistent

and how swerving, or how decisive and how reflective this individual was.

Then came the astrological patterns, set forth as influences from between-life existences, and after these the rich drama of earthly incarnations still being lived out in the texture of the person. Here the entranced Cayce spoke, as he did not in the opening material on disposition and interests, of the soul gaining or losing in its long journey Godward. Earth, he said, introduced new factors in personhood not present in between-life sojourns. These were emotions and will. He saw the passions great and small as motors and music of human life, making choices of earth life more difficult but more significant for soul stature. Incarnation in the flesh was a laboratory for taming and directing the emotions with the mind and will, harnessing them to high values. Because the vital drives and the great elemental feelings were linked directly to the endocrine glands, how they were used left their mark on the invisible fields of the soul, affecting for future lives the person's growth, illness, and central motivation, as well as transcendent states of consciousness.

Values from a given lifetime might turn into their necessary opposites, or go into eclipse for a time, for the intent of karma was full nurture of the texture of the soul. Both temperament and talents had to bow before the demands of values, the jewels of the soul. A one-time gifted mathematician from France now found himself mentally retarded, utterly dependent on the care of others and unable to use his talents, because he had scorned the work of others in a past life and needed to learn the mysteries of interdependency in the human pilgrimage. More than one person whom Cayce described had held power in ancient Rome but laughed at the torment of Christians sacrificed to gladiators or animals in the arena. Now they were back in crippled bodies, learning the hard lessons of powerless pain and restriction. But the central concern with values worked the other way, as well. Those who had wisely used beauty or power or wealth were often given it again to learn further lessons of responsibility and creativity. A woman who had used her hands generously to nurse others injured in battle, he reported, returned with hands so lovely that she could be paid to model with them. Always the thrust of karma was toward soul growth, not mere retribution or reward.

The poetic justice in the texture dimension, which Cayce described in some of these cases, was awesome to contemplate. Someone blind to the needs of others in a medieval town was now back blind. A man who had gossiped about homosexuals in the French court was now back as a homosexual. An entertainer who used her charms on the American frontier to manipulate others was here again with the desire to be an actress but chained to an office desk by financial need. A woman who misused her power in the turmoil after the French Revolution had returned as a widow with a child; she was now poor and anxious about her future. Another woman, who had committed suicide in Persia and thus deserted her child, now was a kindergarten teacher charged with caring for the children of others, but herself lonely and unmarried. A man who had fought with a woman in a Scottish feud of clans was back with her as his feuding sister in this life.

Was the universe shown in these accounts merciless? The readings insisted over and over that the cosmos was as loving as it was unshakably just. We must "pay every jot and tittle for that done which is destructive to others and to self," yet the operation of karma was not blind external punishment. Instead, souls surveyed their total journey between earth lives and chose the kind of incarnation which they most needed for their growth and the growth of those who might have to care for them or be cared for by them. Karma did not deal out punitive blows. It offered slow and effective education, awakening new dimensions of the soul for permanent gain. Often the readings repeated, "God hath not willed that any soul should perish."

Was there a means of escape from karma in the graphic journeys reported in these readings? The answer seemed to be that not all behavior consequences of chosen past deeds might be avoided. One who hurt others might need to experience the same kind of hurt, whether in body or in epithets or attitudes of others, to learn the laws of existence. But the escape always possible lay in the meaning of the experience that followed on past excesses. Every wound could be made to yield greater sensitivity to the needs and predicaments of others. And the alienation from the divine which so often accompanied wrongdoing (as did alienation from one's best self) could be utterly removed, even while tempering trial and hardship might remain. For this was the true grace of God. Asking for transcendent help and giving help to one's neighbor in affliction like one's own—these were the keys to grace which took precedence over karma, speeding up its slow learning until suffering either did not matter or dissolved.

Karma was not all hurts. It also created permanent gains. A lovely voice once used to inspire others in song and speech, a reading reported, appeared in the present as vocal talent that lifted others to memorable heights. A fiery gift of leadership for the oppressed of an earlier time was present as know-how in command which others recognized today. Any of the great human values won in the past might surge forth in the present existence: beauty and its cultivation in art, truth and its cultivation in learning, justice and its cultivation in the social order, love and its cultivation in family life or caring for the wounded, holiness and its cultivation in faith and intentional community. The real treasures of life, once they were earned, did not need to be won again, except by application.

Often karma derived from natural unfolding of a previously chosen treasure. Each great human quality required complementary values to give it richness and balance, as justice required mercy, love required wisdom, individualism required participation, freedom required responsibility. What one chose in ancient Rome, then, could find its complement and fulfillment in later Denmark, though the outward walks of life might be very different. In the long view of the Cayce counsel, all karma was good karma, meant to bring growth to the person and capable of yielding precious fruit. Even painful or restrictive karma, so–called bad karma (the readings did not use this term), was good in its intent. Physical crippling or mental illness or social hardship or loneliness could be seen (if one looked closely) as only a narrowing of the focus of one's life, so that a smaller range of reality would receive fuller attention than might otherwise be the case.

The Heart of Karma, III: Opportunities

In the universe of the readings, talent and textures were regularly met by appropriate opportunities to develop and use them, as though by laboratory and gymnasium. For me, trying to understand how this might work was not easy. To be sure, certain accidents to the body could be initiated by the psyche, as in the accident–prone person whom Freud and others had described, unconsciously seeking to punish or limit the self. And psychosomatic illness, or even a disposition to chronic or symbolic illness, could be created in the deeper recesses of the mind. One could imagine how certain relationships and interpersonal conflicts would flow from the dynamics of the unconscious. But Cayce in trance was describing an even larger and more complicated network of karmic causation. He was suggesting that events themselves came under law, through the general principle that like attracts like, or what in other language would be described as the all–encompassing providence of God.

Primal opportunities as karma were the other people in one's life, since they were not merely our own creations, as were imaginary playmates. They were gifts, fresh events, true opportunities for choice and growth and love. Parents, for example, were chosen by a soul for each particular lifetime, with some advance vision of what would flow from that choice. But most of the other charged relationships of a lifetime would also offer opportunities prepared by past lives, such as friends, lovers, siblings, children, and even enemies. In the view of the readings, no major relationship came by chance.

Souls, the unconscious Cayce reported, typically chose to incarnate together, taking on the various roles and bondings of the family molecule. In scores of readings Cayce traced the specific opportunities from being married to a former brother, or having a child who was previously one's parent, or caring for someone long ago ignored in the family circle. Further, he described souls as incarnating in groups or waves coming from the same culture into another period of history, which allowed them to work together on the same social problems. Those who had sought freedom in the American colonies had often been together taking away freedom in the name of spirituality during the Crusades. And souls often incarnated in groups to advance causes to which they were committed—medical care, education, opening new markets, or perhaps international peace. Even to begin to conceptualize such patterns in which the chance meeting of strangers might not be chance, it seemed necessary to postulate ESP fields within which signals flashed from person to person, and joint thought forms created to last even across lifetimes.

The opportunities of karma most vivid to contemplate in the reports of readings were often intimate relationships.[135] Men or women who had been unfaithful now found themselves incarnated with the partners they had once betrayed, sometimes unfaithful to them in turn. Cayce counseled the forgiving love which would be ap-

---

[135]McGarey, William A. and McGarey, Gladys, *There Will Your Heart Be Also*, 1975.

propriate in such tangled events. A woman forced to
wear a chastity belt in Europe in an earlier century by
her husband gone to the wars was now back with the
same man, but chronically angry with him and unable
to perform sexually; he now had to learn to deal with
the frustrations once visited on her. Parents in another
case who had once used a daughter as a seductive spy
now had her back as an epileptic, requiring the unstint-
ing care they had withheld before. Those who had hastily or recklessly taken celibate vows, or taken vows of
revenge on the other sex, found relationships with that
sex now disturbed, he explained, as they learned the
need for constructive vows, not just willful self–assertion. Those who had persecuted blacks as slaves often
returned as blacks in hardship. Those who ridiculed or
cartooned others were now systematically ridiculed. Yet
karma worked also to preserve and enhance opportunities by bringing back prized relationships, just as cherished friends often sought each other out in the course
of one lifetime. Those lovers who built good marriages
together, for example, had reason to think they might
find one another again in a different century.

As with opportunities in relationship, so with those of
station in life: souls who showed they could use prominence or wealth or power for the benefit of others were
given the chance again. In general, the picture in the
readings was that individuals in leadership or authority
were there because they had once proven their capacity
for serving well in such positions, even though they
might utterly misuse what came their way in the present
lifetime. It might be difficult to imagine how the robber
barons of nineteenth–century industry, or Franco or
Hitler, were souls who had once used their talents well
for others. But Cayce specifically affirmed that even Hitler
had begun with large potential for good (when asked
about it in a reading), shocking those around him who
were steeped in war psychology. Yet he condemned the
choices Hitler made once in power.

Situations of privilege or luxury, however, did not

necessarily represent rewards. Opportunities of wealth could provide subtle testing for the mettle of the soul. The same warning against oversimplification applied to those in poverty or suffering discrimination. Circumstance alone would not tell the state of the soul, which might have chosen hardship for service or a spiritual lesson. In general, unhappy circumstances in the view of the readings seemed less random and mindlessly cruel than most of us held them to be, although it was difficult to conceive how such widespread pain as the Depression or the present world war might be individually appropriate as karma, or even fitting for groups of souls who had chosen their destinies together. Clearly the readings did not use karma as an excuse for social neglect. Not to act on social injustice which came within one's reach, in the view of the counsel, was to fall into sins of omission, which created painful karma as truly as chosen cruelty.

Linked with opportunities of station were educational and vocational opportunity. Openings commensurate with talents would tend to surface, if consonant with the soul purpose for the lifetime. But such openings might not appear as the individual expected them. Cayce, for example, had a present opportunity to exercise gifts of healing and guidance which he had developed in earlier lives. But now he had to do it in the unwelcome mode of falling unconscious. The key to recognizing and claiming vocational opportunities, as many other kinds of karmic treasures, lay in the formula often cited in the readings: "Use what you have in hand, and the next will be given to you."

Health offered, in this view, yet another type of karmic opportunity. Those who used their bodies well, keeping them in balance and offering them in productive service of others, might come back with a body fitted for a model, a dancer, an athlete, one who could bear children well, or one who could endure much vocational stress. But the body might also reflect a very different opportunity when handicap or illness narrowed its capacities.

Because so many turned to Cayce for aid on intractable ailments, he often had occasion to note karmic roots behind chronic, life-distorting disabilities. By no means all hardships of the flesh were so tagged, but those which were long-standing, including birth defects and chronically disturbed functions, were often singled out as karmic. A man who had tortured and blinded others in Persia was blind now. A woman once an athlete ridiculing those overweight was now compulsively overweight, while one who had shed much blood as a ruler in Peru was now anemic.

It was not easy to imagine how souls would choose such hardships for themselves, even to the extent of being crippled or robbed of normal human experience. But the readings stressed the reality of such choices, urging many of the severe sufferers who came to Cayce not to blame fate or others, but to take responsibility for the quality of their present limited lives and start constructive action. Such dire circumstances should not be seen as punishment, though the readings noted in biblical quotes that "the law of the Lord is perfect, converting the soul," since "God is not mocked, and that which ye sow ye shall reap." Opportunity was the key, not blind reaction to pain from a wheel of rebirth.

By putting attention as far as possible on the welfare of others, one could make any stumbling block into a stepping-stone for soul growth. Indeed, the effort to give away to others whatever limited energy and love remained at one's disposal, even from a wheelchair or sickbed, would place the troubled individual under what the readings called the law of grace instead of the law of karma. Sins, which were usually at the base of restrictive karma as some form of selfishness or indulgence, could truly be forgiven when that forgiveness was sought in a penitent heart and enacted in a steady effort to reach out to others. The hardship might or might not be taken away, but the spirit of suffering self-pity, and the sense of distance from God and one's fellows, would be removed. In exceptional cases death itself could come as the mercy of God to a pain-wracked body or a mind trapped in darkness. A few readings described a death in just such terms, aided by concerted prayers of goodwill from others. This was hardly a conventional view of effective prayer. But then, not much about the Cayce view of the soul and its destiny could be called conventional.

Mental illness described in the readings could also express karma, carrying from one lifetime to another the opportunity to choose new values. A nun who had self-righteously condemned others was now back as an alcoholic. A woman who had been intolerant of the followers of Jesus long ago, and later of those suspected of witchery, was here again with a chronic depression for fourteen years. Hallucinations, phobias, psychoses, neurotic defensiveness, sexual dysfunction all at times were traced to karmic themes, though they also had physiological and psychological components from the present life.

Less threatening to contemplate were karmic opportunities from attraction to locales and special interests. Frequently someone's passion for the Southwest, for the ocean, or for farm country was traced to happy experiences there in past incarnations. And the weight which others felt about such institutions as the church or the hospital or the halls of government was also at times assigned to past experiences, with encouragement to build upon the best in that heritage. Hobbies and special interests, from pets to coins and even travel and hypnosis, came under scrutiny as past-life preoccupations, often with tips on how to develop them safely again, sometimes into vocations but just as often into refreshing side interests. In the light of such patterns of opportunities, the efforts of older people to gain further education, or to take up new interests in later years, might not be wasted as many thought. Ventures begun now with a stout purpose could be harvested in the next life.

Becoming the Law

What was the ultimate purpose of the whole, vast drama? An affirmation in the readings suggested the answer. The final goal of the soul, as seen in this counsel, was not simple obedience, the classic motif of so much Western faith, though obedience to the laws of existence was learned in life after life. In the language of Cayce's readings, the goal was not just "keeping the law" but "becoming the law." Each of us was beckoned to grow toward responding lovingly, wisely, justly to life's predicaments and challenges, becoming not simply well-behaved persons but persons of stature, on fire with such love as the Christ had known.[136]

Three dimensions of lasting soul gains had emerged in these readings: a co-creating lifestyle supported by covenants and self-training. Giving flesh to them were three kinds of karma: talents, texture, and opportunities. It was time now to explore how these strands were woven in one illuminating case: the past and present of Edgar Cayce.

---

[136]Cf. Augustine, whose Latin may be translated, "Love—and do as you like."

CHAPTER 10

High Priest and Scoundrel, Warrior and Shepherd of Souls

The Cayces and Gladys did not often speak of their past lives, even in the small talk of mailing, meals, or errands. They brought up the subject about as often as someone else might cite childhood memories or absent relatives. In the past they had studied with great care their profiles and interactions given in readings, but by now the novelty was replaced by the challenge of living out the directions suggested to them, elaborated by their dreams and hunches. Evidently reincarnation was not for them a cause, but just a valuable backdrop for each day's living, much as the physiology and anatomy of the medical counsel supplied a backdrop for their daily food and health choices.

There were light-hearted exchanges about living many lives. Gertrude would come rushing into the reading session directly from the post office and announce that she had just made for herself a pile of bad karma by getting angry at a clerk. Edgar commented that he was a "grandfather sandwich," because his small grandson had earlier been his Kentucky farmer-grandfather, in a reading's report. And there would be animated discussion when a reading suggested that someone had been centrally involved in their own far past existences. They had been collecting for years the names and identities of those who had been twelve advisers to someone called "the Young King" in ancient Egypt. Seven had turned up again in life readings so far. The Egyptian period in which the family felt they had played central roles was a kind of archaeological jigsaw puzzle for them, and they would listen wonderingly to new bits of artistic, religious, military, political, or scientific patterns from that time which might pop up each month.

I was grateful for a hardworking, expansive, and bright volunteer in the office, Mae Verhoeven, who took the time to brief me on the Cayces' past lives and conflicts, going over their life readings with me. Reincarnation was her specialty, since she felt it had helped her understand so much that was both difficult and exciting in her own life, as well as in her large Gimbert clan of Southern Baptists in nearby Oceana, where her father was a proficient carpenter. She was in her early thirties, childless, and recovering from a difficult prior marriage (to a demanding man whom the readings surprisingly described as having been Louis XIV of France, and she one of his unfortunate mistresses). Not particularly happy in her present marriage, she threw herself into working for Cayce with energy and flair. Possessed of a striking face and figure, as well as a throaty, blues-singing voice, she bicycled several miles to work with us each day, often in shorts and with a flower in her hair, catching smiles and whistles from servicemen, who never failed to notice her. Her vibrant presence seemed to give Cayce a lift, though she never presumed on the relationship, despite the indications in readings that she had been his companion in more than one lifetime. I turned to her often for details, since many of the crucial pieces about Cayce's prior lives were to be found in readings given for others, which interlocked with his own.

For her and for the Cayces the central fact of Cayce's present life, his trance counseling, was strongly derived from his past incarnations. This view did not diminish for them the sense of gift and privilege in what he did or the conviction that he exercised his talent in a living relationship with the divine or the Creative Forces. It was rather a way to think about his unusual activity as a lawful process instead of as an incomprehensible marvel. Others who visited or studied Cayce might associate his giving of readings primarily with hypnosis, as had his biographer. Or they might associate it with prayer, stressing his boyhood mystical experience, when his peculiar talents first showed. But while not denying these critical processes, their thoughts turned first to what he had done or failed to do in other centuries and places.[137]

Cayce's Egyptian Legacy

No lifetime had been more influential than the Egyptian, when he was reported to have been a high priest named Ra Ta or perhaps Ra–Ptah. The general date assigned by the readings for this incarnation was 10,500 B.C., a time hopelessly in conflict with the dating of archaeologists at the University of Chicago, who considered that period as nothing but the Stone Age, more than seven thousand years before the start of thirty dynasties of evolving Egyptian high culture. Part of the Cayce dating was his identifying the Great Pyramid of Giza, and the associated Sphinx, as having been built in the latter part of Ra Ta's service; Egyptologists saw the same construction as having taken place under Khufu, thousands of years afterward (c. 2634–2494 B.C.). In later years I would find the discrepancy even more glaring, when I spent time in Egypt with the world's outstanding authority on the Giza complex, Mark Lehner.[138] As someone deeply interested in the Cayce Egyptian reports, especially a repeated claim that a chamber of records of earlier civilizations such as Atlantis could be found bur-

[137]On all of Cayce's claimed or possible past lives, see Church, W. H., *Many Happy Returns*, 1984. Note that the author speculates freely.

[138]See Lehner, Mark, *The Egyptian Heritage*, 1984, and "A Unique Approach to Unraveling the Secrets of the Great Pyramids," *Smithsonian*, vol. 17, no. 1, April 1986; also the controversy reported in *Venture Inward*, "Ra Ta: Myth or Reality," vol. I, no. 4, March/April 1985, and "The Great Pyramid Reveals Her Age," vol. II, no. 3, May/June 1986.

ied not too far from the forepaw of the Sphinx, Lehner
mapped every foot of the Sphinx and studied the associated Great Pyramid complex, as well. To his dismay,
nearly a dozen years of work turned up nothing significant to support the Cayce dating. Instead he found many
kinds of evidence to support (or only slightly modify)
the standard historical view. The most telling of his evidence proved to be carbon dating of mortar fragments
containing organic material, which he dug out by hand
from far within crevices in the Great Pyramid and others. This work did not sustain the Cayce readings, leaving him wondering whether the very large body of Cayce
material on Egyptian events and personalities of the Ra
Ta period were only mythology, or perhaps took place
in some realm of thought forms, or were modeled on
Theosophical Society speculations about the Great Pyramid current in Cayce's time.

The story of Cayce's reported past in Egypt, whatever
its literal truth (I learned later to be careful in judgment,
after the Dead Sea Scrolls gave a different light to another apparent historical error), was at least a great adventure epic, comparable in sweep and moral lessons
with Arthurian legends. For their parts in this tale, Cayce
in trance had been picking players for twenty years with
no little skill. Whether in the present life those who got
life readings were artists or artisans, mothers or
monastics, tradepersons or bankers, Cayce's account of
many of them in Egypt often fitted well their present
talents and interests, as well as their conflicts and ambi-
guities. It was surprising to me how many of them reported dreams and reveries of Egyptian content, apart
from what readings offered.

As a young man in the Caucasus region (today in the
Soviet Union and Turkey), far north and east of the Nile
Valley, Ra Ta (so his readings reported) had shown prophetic leadership gifts which included instructing a portion of his people to emigrate to Egypt in preparation for
the coming breakup of Atlantis and the consequent need
for a new civilization. King Ararat in the Caucasus took

the counsel of the young priest and led his people to a mountain in today's Turkey, later named after him. There he prepared for some nine hundred of his subjects to go on to Egypt under his young son and friend of the priest, Arart, who had been a shepherd but proven himself in the arts of war and politics. Accompanying the procession were not only warriors but animals trained to attack: bulls, bears, leopards, and hawks. Even more strange were creations of the Atlanteans known as "things": animals modified into partly human form to serve humans (such figures as legend had long celebrated in mermaids and minotaurs, which I would find dramatically paralleled decades later in the Star Wars film epics).

When the fierce-looking invaders arrived in Egypt, the local King Raai wisely capitulated after receiving assurances that the invaders intended no widespread slaughter, but a fresh start in accordance with the precepts of the Law of One (one of two great teachings and groupings that had spread from Atlantis, the other being the Sons of Belial). Arart became the first of the Egyptian "shepherd kings" from the North, sharing his authority with the priest, now twenty-nine, and with a talented local scribe and philosopher, Aarat, popular with the local natives. Wanting to mollify the Egyptian population, the invading king surprisingly abdicated to his son named Araaraat, only sixteen, who as the Young King would share his power with the native scribe and with a council of twelve advisers or "judges." Putting together these pieces told to me and described in readings created a cast, for not only was Ra Ta reported as the modern Cayce, but the second shepherd king, or Young King, was his modern son, Hugh Lynn Cayce, and the local sage was Morton Blumenthal, chief philanthropist of the Cayce hospital but eventually Cayce's antagonist there.

Migrations were underway from Atlantis, with the emigrants carrying an advanced technology that neither the native Egyptians nor the northern invaders yet knew how to use. Others came to settle in the fertile Nile area (according to Cayce's counsel) from as far away as India, Mongolia, Persia, Arabia, Assyria, and Greece, providing a huge challenge to the leadership of the Young King and to Ra Ta, whom he employed not only for religious guidance but for many other kinds of inspired counsel (ranging over topics not unlike those covered in Cayce's present readings, though broader). It was a time not only of ethnic conflict among the incoming groups, but of racial arid caste discrimination, particularly against the humanoid "things" whose bodies showed animal appendages, fur, or scales.

In the dramatic account of the readings, Ra Ta provided guidance on mining, communal granaries and storehouses, domestication of wild animals (including some who had been used as attack beasts, whose likenesses could still be found on Egyptian artifacts today), architecture and engineering, transportation and electricity. He also helped to select, with his unusual capacity for ecstatic perception, those who had special talents needed to develop the emerging culture. And he specified the introduction of the monogamous family in place of dormitory–like dwellings of the separate sexes brought together under state auspices for mating. All of this he did in a developing lifetime which the readings reported was not uncommon for the times, running several hundred years. (This detail did not make it any easier to imagine the entire saga.) Ra Ta was notably responsible for developing two temples at Giza, near the present site of the Great Pyramid and the Sphinx, whose human-animal blend represented more than mythology, in the view of the readings. The Temple of Sacrifice was described as one of the first great hospitals and health centers of the world, where individuals not only recovered from illnesses, but underwent surgery to remove unwanted appendages, scales, or feathers from the ill–defined bodies created by Atlanteans. In this temple, psychological and spiritual cleansing was also part of the holistic healing, which even extended to curing racial prejudices, lust, and violence. The other temple was one which the readings likened to a modern university, the Temple Beautiful, where individuals who had been cleansed and purified underwent training in vocations and the art of living, under a strongly monotheistic tradition.

Ra Ta traveled, the readings continued, to the other developed cultures of the time, collecting ideas and spiritual lore for his people. But while he was gone, some of the temple and political leaders got caught up not only in avarice but in what the readings called "the fleshpots," so that when he returned and set about cleansing temple activities and personnel, he made enemies. The masses were devoted to him, and these leaders had to find a devious way of discrediting him. They chose a classic means of undoing Ra Ta's power: the charms of a woman. A beautiful dancer who was the favorite of the Young King (and now Gertrude Cayce, as she explained to me with an arch and teasing smile) was persuaded by the priests to present to Ra Ta a plan for speeding up the evolution of more perfect bodies, on which Ra Ta was embarked with some of the temple leadership. Perfecting bodies had been an interest of his since two prior incarnations in Atlantis in androgynous form, combining two genders in one body (another detail difficult to imagine) until the advantages of separation became clear. The dancer, named Isris, was to offer to create with him the perfect child. The result, the readings commented wryly, was that he "fell for the whole proposition."

Unfortunately for him, one of his great reforms had been instituting marriages and homes by choice and devotion rather than by state assignment for procreation. He had set a model by his own marriage. When he took the dancer as a concubine, he broke his own law. The action enraged the Young King, who let his jealousy over the lovely dancer influence his judgment, under pressure from some of his counselors including the native sage. He banished Ra Ta to what is now Libya with a retinue and associates numbering two hundred and thirty. The dancer went with Ra Ta and eventually replaced his former wife. But the king, in spite, kept their child, Iso (today Gladys Davis, as she explained), and she died in loneliness at the age of four. (Now, it appeared, the cast was complete.)

In his new country, Cayce's readings reported, Ra Ta encountered a peaceful matriarchal society much in need of his technical knowledge and prophetic guidance. He went into seclusion to attune himself, and from a state similar to that of Cayce's present consciousness for readings, he guided an extraordinary series of accomplishments: tapping volcanic energy and shaping new developments in geology, horticulture, agriculture, medicine, and astronomy.

Back in Egypt, leaders in various walks of life learned of his achievements and called for his return. Invading Atlanteans with superior technology were planning to take over the country, and there was widespread agreement that only Ra Ta could help the Young King stand up to them. In the meantime the king had been faced with rebellions, especially by a northern group that featured animal worship, which split off into a separate kingdom. Under pressure from his father, the older king who had originally brought the Caucasian throng into Egypt, the younger monarch persuaded Ra Ta to return. The procession was triumphal—an event which Cayce today felt he had vividly recalled in a dream.

But Ra Ta had aged greatly, and there was much concern that he might not provide the needed leadership for long. His response was to employ electrical and other resources from the two temples he had created in a novel effort to rejuvenate his whole body. He succeeded, and there followed a period of cultural flowering which the readings observed had influenced (partly through leaders in later centuries who would dimly recall their Egyptian experiences) all of Western history, as well as reaching out to other cultures as far away as Eurasia, the Orient, and what would become the Americas, including the Incas. Individual homes and family units were restored to their prominence before Ra Ta's shame, and women were given advanced position and privileges unknown in this region. (However, in his later years Ra Ta still took a series of female companions, creating a pattern that would haunt him in later lives.) Large–scale social insurance was developed, as well as vocational associations or unions. Technology harnessed the Nile, and there were new breakthroughs in metallurgy and electrical power, while the two temples produced un-heard–of developments in medicine, including diets, surgery, drugs, arts therapy, and athletics, alongside an elaborate system of education with special degrees.

According to the readings, spiritual principles were developed at such depth that they contributed foundations for the forming of Judaism, Christianity, and Islam, to come much later, while local centers of the Temple Beautiful were staffed throughout the kingdom to put the teachings into practice. A flow of emissaries began between Egypt and the other developed lands of the time, reaching all the way to the Orient for mutual sharing of advanced religious and technical ideas. A great library was begun at what later became Alexandria, and a huge pyramid constructed over a three–hundred year period at Giza, to be a repository for records of the civilization and a place of initiation for spiritual teachers. Its designer and architect was a highly evolved soul named Thoth, whom the Greeks would later call Hermes (and who would one day in the cycle of reincarnation become Jesus). Nearby, the Sphinx and its associated structures were erected to guard temple records and artifacts, at what the readings described as one of three such depositories around the world (and one which the readings insisted would be opened before too long in the modern era, creating a new view of ancient history that incorporated both Ra Ta's period and Atlantis). In time Ra Ta "ascended in the mount and was borne away," not as a divinity but as a highly developed soul. By now his name had been changed to Ra, which Egyptian mythology would long after associate with the sun god. And his consort, Isris, had become Isis, herself destined to appear in later Egyptian myths.

What was the effect on Cayce of the whole rich account, abounding in unverified details? He appeared to take the Egyptian epic seriously, though not obsessed by it, and it seemed to be a burden on him. The saga made him into a figure of world history, or of prehistory, and set before him a huge inheritance, while he held to the middle-class round of a family man in modern America. To be sure, the scope of this drama made his giving of readings more thinkable, as expressions of soul gains from service long ago. Such a view could help him come to terms with his lot as a seer in an age without seers. On the other hand, his limited present circumstances, in which he held no power, had no attendants or treasuries, celebrated no ceremonies and pronounced no edicts, would seem to warn him that he was a long way from his full stature and capacity for service, in a kind of exile more grievous than the one which had supposedly sent him long ago to Libya. His readings now told him that he "must enter again in 1998." One could not help wondering whether some of his fierce determination to keep the flow of his readings going at their maximum now might reflect a passion to start that lifetime without having to make up for failures in the present.

Might the entire Egyptian panorama unfolded by the readings be an ego trip for Cayce, devised by his unconscious as it played with archetypal motifs? The centrality to the story of sobering themes of unfaithfulness, betrayal of trust, and banishment might seem to work against that view, as did Cayce's desire to turn his Egyptian inheritance into today's daily medical service. The great Egyptian drama, which his readings described as a major foundation for all his work in the present lifetime, including his efforts at a hospital and university like the two temples of old, was not offered to him for self-congratulation. Rather it was presented and accepted by him as a reminder that he should once again seek that covenantal alignment with the divine which had been his as Ra Ta.

If there were ever proven substantial truth to this complex account, one could view Cayce's reaching for responsible authority in this life—whether in oil wells and a hospital, or just ordering us around in the office— as his reaching for the old force, the old bearing, the old stature which had once been his when he laid some foundations for Western monotheism. His restless impulse to take charge would not then be mere power drive, but the surging longing to stand once again as the full man, the centered leader, rather than as one whose stature was complete only when he was absent in trance. Edgar Cayce today would be first of all a soul in search of a lost inheritance. The ultimate issues here were texture, not talent, since by his attempting in Egypt to force the process of evolution toward more perfect bodies in the white version which he himself exemplified, he had violated his own covenant with the divine, and brought about what the readings described as the first great uprising between church and state, when he turned to "the fleshpots" with his concubine, and created "a mighty struggle" in the land, through his "aggrandizing of lusts of the body." Reading the yellow carbon copies on my stool in the cement vault, not unlike a burial chamber itself, I thought I had before me at least a myth of mankind's lost royalty or fall from grace, embodied in Cayce.

Dismissing the entire account would have been easier, but for Cayce's dreams recorded over two decades. There one could see mummies, pyramids, great processions, vast halls, creatures partly human, advanced technology, and creative social projects. Readings taken on these dreams confirmed that many elements were actual recall from Egypt. To an observer it seemed that if his unconscious were merely dramatizing in the night the epic which his readings offered, it was doing this with no small skill and detail. And the psyches of his wife and son and secretary and colleagues were dramatizing the same story under the same spell. In addition, their waking lives evinced some of the actual patterns suggested

by the readings as originally from Egypt, such as sometimes strident competition between father and son today, as priest and king in one family circle, and adoption
of the forlorn young child Iso, as secretary made part of
the family. But more familiar Freudian patterns might, of
course, account for much of the same dynamics.

Answering my questions with reserve and what
seemed to me palpable humility, Cayce made it clear that
he had accepted the Egyptian story from his readings as
probably accurate, though not without several years of
struggle against its inherent unlikeliness when it first
appeared. Yet right beside this towering structure of his
inheritance, he pointed out, like a ticking time bomb
within him was a legacy from Colonial America, much
closer to his present life, and as far from the Egyptian
leadership in moral and spiritual qualities as it was in
centuries.

Scoundrel in the New World

He was referring to John Bainbridge, who had already
been cited in a couple of recent life readings I heard,
where the dry comment was made, "Here we have another of the illegitimate offspring of John Bainbridge."
Knowing how unflattering were these items from Cayce's
reported past lives, we chuckled when we heard them
and did not hesitate to point them out teasingly as soon
as he wakened from his trance. Dates given for this
Bainbridge material were so conflicting that the only
possible explanations were inaccuracy, or two different
lives with the same name and general character (not
uncommon in the life readings). The time was 1625, assigned in a comment by the reading taken on a dream
that came to Cayce just after he debarked from a train
on arriving at Virginia Beach in 1925. In an astonishing
observation on karmic cycles, he was told, "Now, in this
first, we find there are just three hundred years to the
day, hour, in which time, space, as known in the earth's

plane, passed since the entity landed in this place, see?" Details given chiefly in readings for others made it clear that Bainbridge was an English adventurer or soldier who came to the area now Virginia Beach (adding "Hence the call always of the coast country") on his way to nearby Jamestown, where famed Captain John Smith had developed a settlement starting in 1607, making friends with the Algonquin chief Powhatan, whose lovely daughter Pocahontas would become legend, eventually going to England. In the trance account, Bainbridge later developed an irresponsible sexual liaison with an Indian woman named Rising Star, half sister of Pocahontas, about whom a reading observed that "only through the inactivities and the littleness in this Bainbridge did the entity then lose, in losing faith, hope, and confidence in the peoples of that color." Other readings linked Cayce-as–Bainbridge with the survivors of the earlier lost colony of Roanoke Island, where the first English girl was born in the new country, Virginia Dare. How Bainbridge died was not reported.

For whatever karmic reason, perhaps to try to undo doubtful patterns in early colonial America, Cayce emerged in another life time as John Bainbridge, where the decisive date of 1742, perhaps for his arrival in the colonies, was given in a reading for himself, not for others. He was told that he wandered through "many of the scenes that the entity experienced," presumably a century before. Apparently this Bainbridge was a charismatic person of considerable talents, born in Cornwall, England, and sent to Canadian military service in punishment of a crime. He escaped from Canada and landed in Virginia, again in the Virginia Beach area, where he began his travels as what his readings called a "wanderer" and "adventurer" and "wastrel," adding that he "considered only self," so that "many suffered in his wake," through "many escapades that have to do with those of the nature of the relations with the opposite sex." Among the women he reportedly seduced and used was his present wife, Gertrude, as an Indian woman of

some means whose wealth he plundered. Another was
our office volunteer, Mae, with whom (she explained to
me) he lived a rough-and-tumble three years as a gambler in the Lake Michigan location later, in 1803, to become Fort Dearborn, predecessor of Chicago. She, then
named Mae Umbor, served in a dance hall, or tavern.
Neither of them withheld their favors from others. The
reading spoke of "the activity in the inn that was known
as 'You Know—*you know!*' Somewhere in the mid-1750s,
when Bainbridge was presumably in his mid-thirties, the
French and Indians combined to destroy the settlement
in the French and Indian Wars that began in 1754, as the
Indians would again destroy the actual fort under British urging in 1812. Bainbridge and his lover and others
fled for their lives, hoping to get to Tidewater Virginia,
where Bainbridge felt safe. They made it as far as a raft
besieged by Indians with canoes and flying arrows on
the Ohio River, where Bainbridge lost his life by drowning, but not before helping Mae to save hers. The only
worthwhile talent which readings ascribed to this wasted
lifetime was an ability to deal with detail, especially in
following instructions supplied by others.

How could a soul who had been the visionary and
culture-transforming Ra Ta have come to this estate? The
readings' answer was supplied in part through reports
on Cayce's intervening lives. But one comment in a special reading was provocative: "As Bainbridge, the entity
in the material sojourn was a wastrel, one who considered only self; having to know the extremes in his own
experience as well as of others." The Cayce before us,
with his intense love of people, and his strong emotions
and tendencies to extremes, might indeed be seen as capable of trying almost anything to see where it would
lead him, testing the limits of his license and plumbing
the depths of the human condition. The photographer
who made such able portrait studies as to win regional
prizes with them might conceivably open the lens of his
soul to whatever caught his eye in the love of experiences for their own sake which Jung has described as

characteristic of intuitives preoccupied with the nonrational possibilities of human experience rather than with evaluation and system.

Whatever the truth in the hardly inspiring account of the two Bainbridges, Cayce had his own waking recollections which seemed to him to confirm it. He thought he could remember operating a shell game in a carnival and actually making the pea jump from shell to shell by intense concentration. He had gained money then but lost the ability to influence not just token objects but healing of the flesh itself, which had been his in other lives. All he could do now, he told an Army captain friend of mine, was rub warts and make them go away; he demonstrated it on a willing but surprised subject. In the same way, he thought he could recall being terribly hungry on the river raft where he met his death as the second Bainbridge, unable to land for food because of hostile Indians. He took me to a nearby barber shop, where the barber's small son when sleepy had one day offered him a bite of his sandwich, remarking that he and Cayce had been very hungry on that raft. The barber was amazed, but it seemed to Cayce a mutual recollection between himself and the boy. More vivid were some of Cayce's dreams of violence and seduction, in which the plot might fit anyone's dreams, but the trappings had colonial clothing, weapons, and settings such as frontier towns, gambling tents, and sideshows.

The disclosure of these lifetimes to Cayce, with his impressions that seemed to confirm them, had a chastening and even disheartening effect on him. If the account were accurate, he had betrayed his Egyptian inheritance. Now he had something to make good, well dramatized by versions of a repeating dream of his in which he tried to bring back to life an Egyptian mummy of a noble young woman, presumably an emblem of his own true creativity, as dreams of the opposite sex often represent. Further, the Bainbridge biographies put him on notice that in this life unwelcome drives and impulses could take charge of him. "To many peoples," one of his

earliest readings on himself observed, Cayce would today seem "very contradictory in thought, action, and
deed," "very eccentric in many ways" and showing "very
little of the moderate" while spending much energy in
whatever he undertook, at times bringing "destructive
elements and misunderstanding." If he proved unable to
control himself better than he had as Bainbridge, he
would find his temper (which I had already tasted) betraying him, as his "wrath brings misunderstanding." Yet
if he could hold to positive action in this lifetime, he
could become "the great dynamic force" in the present,
making a success of almost any line of endeavor, "especially the healing arts, or the higher spiritual arts." Readings on the Bainbridge karma pulled no punches,
rebuking him for his present outbursts and his constant
worrying, as well as for eating "so much like a pig," and
noting the burning of physical desires in his feelings toward a young woman office helper of the past. The
legacy of his life in colonial America could detonate
within him, damaging both him and others.

Illegitimate in France

As if to underscore for him how much misery irresponsible parenting might generate, a sad little lifetime
in France was reported in his own life reading, coming
right between the two Bainbridge dates. There he was
seen as an illegitimate child—though definitely a "love
child," his readings insisted—of the second daughter of
the last absolute monarch, Louis XIV (1638–1715) and
Queen Marie Therese of Spain (Maria Theresa of Aus-
tria), the queen in a marriage of political convenience
(since her father was the king of Spain) that included a
number of mistresses of the king. At seventeen the lovely
young daughter, named Gracia in her mother's tongue
(and the same soul who would be Gladys Davis later),
fell in love with the king's cousin, something of a liber-
tine, the Duke of York from England. Although married,

he was described as having really loved her, but only briefly, then deserting her with her boy child, a past incarnation of Cayce with the name of Dale or Dahl. Since the child, though illegitimate, was capable of being used by others as a pretender to either the French or British thrones, he and his mother were put out of the French court. His life was spared, but his mother was forced into a convent at age twenty, where her heart ached with longing for the child, and she developed a distrust of men which would continue into her modern American lifetime. Ten years later her lover returned to France, not now as a duke but as King James II of England, allowed to remain there until his death, not without efforts at regaining his throne. The readings do not report that the two ever met again but instead that Gracia died of a broken heart in the convent at age thirty.

In the report of the readings, the child suffered with great longing for its mother, a twist of karma that repeated the anguish of the young Egyptian daughter of his, Iso, left behind when he was banished to Libya; the same soul was now his lost French mother. From the viewpoint of the readings, the lifetime was one in which his soul was meant to grow in strength of character and texture of personhood by enduring suffering. Apparently his station in life could have given him significant leadership potential as an adult. Instead the child died at age five, in what the reading called "faltering" and seemed to suggest was a more or less deliberate withdrawal from the body (not unlike what had happened in a prior Trojan incarnation of Cayce's). However, the lad took with him a measure of commitment to principle and a compassion for children, which in Cayce would manifest as the cry of his heart to be helpful to children in his earliest mystical experience. But the youngster, Dale, did not learn enough in this brief life to keep the soul from the excesses of what the dating would suggest as the second English incarnation as Bainbridge, not long after, when angry self-pity could turn into self-indulgence.

Warrior-Ruler in Persia

Long-ago Ra Ta and the John Bainbridges of the colonies and the frontier represented (in the view of the readings) two poles of the modern Edgar Cayce, not simply as past portraits but as present trends very much alive in him, shaping not only his talents but his personhood, and marking the opportunities and relationships he would draw to himself. What provided the central integration between these poles now? Several intervening lifetimes, according to his readings, supplied the necessary dynamics. None was more decisive than that as a warrior-king or ruler of an ancient city located astride far-reaching trade routes in Persia near the modern Iranian city of Shustar (where his preserved bones, they added, could still be found today in a cave).

Coming after the long Ra Ta sojourn in Egypt, which had been given a roughly central date of 10,500 B.C., was a lifetime as Uhjltd (pronounced "yoolt") for which the dating in the readings was ambiguous but unlikely for a period as early as 8000 B.C., which Gladys estimated. The reading described him at the height of his leadership as tall and straight with a heavy brow, adding that all who met him felt they were being "heard by a master, a figure among men." When Cayce spoke of this Persian lifetime, I sometimes felt he smiled inwardly, as though this were his favorite personal chronicle and the least flawed. From this life, his trance counsel traced his "deep love to others in any or all positions or stages in life" (a quality I had already seen) and added that this incarnation brought him "the greatest force in present earth's plane" through the expression of psychic and occult skills in his medical aid, brought over from that life.

Cayce as Uhjltd started his life as a warrior, a vocation which would be no help to him as Bainbridge the English soldier gone to the New World. His largely nomadic people engaged in raids or wars on surrounding peoples, tribes, nations, though it was the fabled wealth of the ruler, as well as his cruelty, that lured warriors such as

his brother, Oujida. Oujida captured the adopted daughter of the king in the dynasty that would one day yield
Croesus (d. 546 B.C.) and eventually made her his wife,
only to have her kill herself after bearing a daughter,
Inxa. This daughter was the same Egyptian concubine
that had been Ra Ta's downfall in Egypt (destined one
day to be Gertrude Cayce); now abandoned, she was tast-
ing the pain of desertion which she had brought to the
young Egyptian Iso. Inxa grew up beautiful and able to
command others with the spell of her eye, not always
wisely (the same eye she would long after lose as
Gertrude Cayce, if the report in the readings were not
sheer fantasy).

At thirty-three, after a period of studying healing in
Egypt, the land of his mother, Uhjltd made a bold move
toward peace and commerce by riding alone to the
stronghold of the king. At the gates he met and was offered aid by a lovely young woman, Ilya, destined to be
his lover and queen. (The story identified her as the soul
who had been his twin in Atlantis and would one day be
Gladys Davis; it read dramatically enough to become a
movie script—as a reading later obligingly developed it
on request.) Treachery led to his being made a prisoner
rather than treated as an emissary of peace, but Ilya
eventually befriended him and engineered his release
down a tower wall. For this act she and a companion
were pushed over the same wall. Uhjltd rescued them
and took them to a desert oasis, where they recovered
by practicing the healing he had learned. Meeting a
younger brother, he learned that his tribesmen had
turned against him but had a vision that he would build
there what would be called "the City in the Hills and the
Plains," or Is-Shlan-doen, as a great center of healing and
commerce. That night took place the consummation of
his love, described with unusual tenderness in a reading
among those Gladys gave me to study:

> With bodies oiled and dressed from the cave
> spring, they repair to their couch of skins, and

there watch the sun's slow sinking over the desert
sands. And in this fading hour they first find the
answer of body to body in the soul's awakening,
as they melt into one; giving then an offering to
the world, who, in the form and in the stature of
the great leader, gave the first philosophy of life
and love to the world, coming from this union.

The leader described here was their child Zend, an
early incarnation of the Christ soul, whose offspring in
turn would be called Zoroaster, followed generations
later by one of the same name (flourishing in the sixth
century B.C.), who would bring the monotheistic Persian
faith of Zoroastrianism, or Parsi religion, in his life and
in the teachings of the sacred book compiled from very
ancient traditions, the Zend Avesta.

Uhjltd recruited helpers from Egypt, where he traveled in a kind of exile, often meditating upon the sands
and skies. As a result of the spiritual attunement which
came naturally to him, he developed into a teacher, a
healer, and in time a ruler. He used methods of irrigation
brought from Egypt, located precious stones and miner-
als, and the city prospered. Emissaries came from many
lands to study methods used here, as they had those of
Ra Ta in Egypt. In the words of the readings, Uhjltd was
"an excellent teacher" whose teachings were later preserved in the famed library at Alexandria before its burning. Through his desert attunement, not unlike that of
the Hebrew prophets who would come centuries later,
he developed the ability to get guidance from beyond
himself, carried into his present life as Cayce in the ability "to aid, counsel, advise," even to "speak as oracles to
that Throne" of the Most High.

The Persian king, of course, was not happy with these
developments, and undertook several raids against the
city, but found his own stronghold conquered by Uhjltd
and himself forced to abdicate to his young son, who
negotiated a more prosperous though temporary peace.
It was Greek traders who next coveted the city, and de-

vised a plan to infiltrate it with the aid of the Persian court. Greek maidens came first and were well accepted. Young men followed, and the setting for assassination and conquest was prepared. When Uhjltd and Ilya paid an official visit to the distant Persian court, they were mortally wounded. She was beheaded and he was left to die in the desert.

A reading noted that the woman would ever after fear knives (true of Gladys Davis) and that the man would distrust friendships (true of Edgar Cayce, in that he kept a certain reserve even with his closest associates). However, it took him three days to die, and Uhjltd by intense concentration succeeded in raising himself above the pain of his body, laying the foundation for the trance state which Cayce would enter for his healing service many centuries later. He did not succeed in rising above his hatred for the betraying Greeks, however, and in his next major incarnation showed up in Troy as an enemy of the Greeks, a warrior "with a vengeance, attempting to wreck." The working of karma to allow the soul the lesson it chose even at the very end of life seemed here dramatized, in what was otherwise an exemplary life in ancient Persia.

An unusual reading in the files encouraged Cayce to fast at a time of difficult decisions in this life by addressing him in exceptional fashion as "O Priest, O King," which called forth both Ra Ta and Uhjltd as present realities in him. From the Persian experience he felt he could locate the true authority, the royal bearing, which those of us around him saw when he was at his best, and for which his dreams showed he inwardly longed. If as Ra Ta he had been a channel, a vessel for awesome knowledge and guidance (but not fully in charge of himself and others, leaning to the unconscious at the expense of individuated personhood and ego strength), he found in Uhjltd the necessary complement, a man of action able to call on the inner world but not be possessed by it. While in texture Ra Ta had been at the mercy of his own nature as son–lover–reformer, drawn to the

feminine as conquest and vehicle, Uhjltd was also father–provider, finding in the feminine a fitting companion and peer.

For Cayce's close associates in the present, who knew
of his past lives, the Persian incarnation seemed an inheritance to rally around, a wire frame on which to
sculpt his present service in the medical readings; he had
done it all before and done it even better. To help him
build a hospital and an entire university seemed reasonable. His leadership so long ago, when not a few (including my wife and myself) were told they had been with
him, had been whole and balanced, as truly political as
intellectual, with his best energies focused on helping
others in pain. Yet for Cayce it seemed that the drama
from that life added to his feeling exiled in the present.
He took it seriously, but the price had to be not only a
kind of nostalgia but even outrage that he had gotten so
far from it, and had now to continue its work in the
nearly ridiculous state of being unconscious twice daily.
At times when he paced the floor, smoking a cigarette in
irritable puffs, it seemed believable that we had on our
hands royalty without power, remembering a lost estate.
I thought of King Lear on the moor and wondered what
Cayce would give to undo what he saw as his Bainbridge
excesses.

Chemist and Warrior in Troy

When Edgar's readings set forth his next life in Troy,
they brought him onto the lighted stage of history, although it was, to be sure, Homeric history of the twelfth
and thirteenth centuries B.C., which might have remained legend and mythology but for the modern archeological vision and labors of Schliemann, showing
how much of Homer demanded to be taken seriously.
Cayce's trance counsel placed him in the city under siege
by the Greeks for nine years, seeking to retake the beautiful Helen from Paris who had lured her from her hus-

band, King Menelaus of Sparta. The dates given were 1158 to 1112 B.C. (following the correction of Church, the imaginative chronicler of Cayce's past lives),[139] with death occurring at age forty-six for Xenon, the reincarnation of Ra Ta and Uhjltd. The lifetime was intended to teach him "strength, the power of resistance in the face of adversity," precisely that full selfhood and healthy ego development which seemed overwhelmed by trans-personal forces in Egypt, but had been built in Persia. Yet this was not to be the outcome; quite its opposite followed.

Hector of Troy was pictured less favorably in the read-ings, and Achilles the Greek attacker better, than per-haps Homer rendered the two. Studying the accounts of these men, better known in poetry than established his-tory, led to the shock of finding the readings assigning to Achilles a follow-up lifetime of the antagonist of Ra Ta in Egypt, as the local sage who had been raised to share power with the Young King and had worked for the high priest's banishment. This meant we were seeing as Achil-les (the Cayces explained) an incarnation of Morton Blumenthal, the modern stockbroker who had first been Cayce's benefactor and then his relentless enemy in evis-cerating the Cayce Hospital. One might expect that life readings might have Morton turn up at decisive points in the Cayce past-life saga, for he was evidently a bright and deep man, impassioned in his convictions (as I would find when I later interviewed him). But giving him a legendary role in Western history strained credu-lity, even for events on the grand scale which the Ra Ta epic unscrolled. Hector, too, appeared in the account of the readings, as the widely read philosopher-printer who brought Cayce to Dayton, Ohio, and drew out of him the first life readings and the entire reincarnation perspec-tive. Whether or not Cayce in Troy had really known these two classic warriors of ancient times was a ques-

---

[139]Church, *op. cit.*, for these and other datings of Cayce's lives.

tion made sharper for him by a dream in which he saw with a photographer's vivid and gory detail, as though he were there, the destruction of Hector as he was dragged around an arena behind the chariot of Achilles, with his brains smashed out against a stone.

The story of Uhjltd reborn as a person was easier to imagine than was the epic Trojan account. The young man Xenon was "first the student; the student of chemistry, the student of mechanics, the student of those things in the arts" yet later "forced, against its [the soul's] *own* will, into active participation in an open conflict." Whereas memories from Egypt and Persia initially suggested an aptitude for chemistry and sculpture, the calling of warrior appeared to catch up the note on which the Uhjltd incarnation had ended, a mood of violence and revenge. Xenon was placed in charge of the gate to Troy and showed repeatedly his skill at repulsing the invaders. Then the wily Greeks left their great wooden horse at the gate and withdrew in their ships. This was "subtlety which had not been the experience of the entity" Xenon, and trusting too much in his own prowess rather than in spiritual guidance through "the abilities of self to maintain that at-oneness" with the divine, he let the horse be brought in, whereupon invaders leaped out and brought down the city. Xenon became "an outcast, as one dishonored, as one thought little of: at last losing self through self-destruction." Suicide was his way out, a sullen act in which the warrior overpowered the potential leader who also lived in him. The consequences for the soul who would later become Cayce were crucial, according to the readings. After prophesying that some from the Troy period would be met again (as indeed Blumenthal as Achilles was), the early life reading for Cayce continued, "And this is the *great* barrier, the great experience which the entity must meet in the present," seeking "a regeneration from that." The manner, under comparable trials of shame and regret, would be the same as for every soul: "In Him put thy trust."

Evidently real damage to the soul's growth had been

done by the suicide, in the readings' view, leaving a wound of self-doubt which could correspond to what we encountered at times as Cayce's hunger for attention and confirmation just below the surface of his personality. And the self-violence of suicide had magnified, the readings indicated, a tendency to a "quick temper," with its "unexpected" flashing out at even those closest to him. A series of readings given on him in Dayton, when he first encountered the concept of reincarnation, had noted "the ultra forces, Uranus and Neptune, given strength in Jupiter and Mercury." What had enabled him to push so far in service in Egypt and Persia could push just as forcefully in other directions not so promising. Mentioning his predilection to secret romantic affairs, the reading summed up that without reference to the activity of his will (which in this viewpoint was always decisive), Cayce would in the present tend to be "always very good or very bad, very wicked or very much given to good works." He would be "ultra in all forces," becoming "very poor or very rich" and "scaling to heights in intellectual ability and capacity, or groveling in dregs of self-condemnation" with the latter seen in Troy and not absent from Bainbridge. The same reading, however, assured him that he would find the "greater strength in spiritual forces and developing," and that it was possible for him "to make manifest much of psychic and occult forces" in order to "bring joy, peace, and quiet to masses and multitudes through individual efforts." The warning in this self-portrait of a seer serving individuals was stern. But the promise was ringing.

Cayce rarely referred to the Troy lifetime, yet his few comments on it suggested that he felt the central public struggles of his life, in the building and loss of the hospital named after him, came partly from failing in his leadership there long ago. By contrast, little that was prominent in Cayce seemed connected to what was described as a brief Grecian incarnation as Armitidides the chemist, under Aristotle. There the soul that would be Cayce met Alexander the Great, for whom Aristotle was tutor, and about whom the readings said that he had the capacity to make the world one nation but instead "ran wild" in using his power for self-exaltation. This was the soul drawn in again as Thomas Jefferson. In the same Aristotle incarnation he met the governess of Alexander, daughter of Socrates, now his wife Gertrude. There she had developed the power of reasoning (something which all of us around Gertrude knew well) but found it warring at times with her better spiritual impulses, needing reconciling by more attention to "quieting within" so that the "greater powers" could arise.

Shepherd of Souls in Asia Minor

The next lifetime described for Cayce evinced strong continuing Greek elements but had its start in North Africa, as though the soul were touching back to its Egyptian roots.[140] Lucius was born in Cyrene, now Libya, to which the long-ago Ra Ta was exiled. He moved when young with his well-to-do Greek and Roman father and Jewish mother to Asia Minor, in the city of Laodicea, famed for its black goats and trade, and not far from Ephesus and Antioch. The period was contemporaneous with the life of Jesus and the period of the early Church, and found Lucius witnessing before he died the Roman destruction of Jerusalem in A.D. 70, as well as the widespread martyrdom of Christians.

If the Ra Ta life dramatized for Cayce the origins of his unusual counseling talent, enriched by further use in Persia, and the life as the ruler Uhjltd dramatized for him the best texture of his personhood and manhood, then it was the Lucius life which emblematized the spiritual center for his soul journey. When Cayce spoke of

---

[140]For a novelized treatment of the Cayce readings on the time of Jesus, see La Croix, Mary, *The Remnant*, 1981. For the Lucius incarnation novelized, see her *Sons of Darkness, Sons of Light*, 1987.

this lifetime, it was with awe and joy, not so much for his personal attainments then as for the fact that he had been with Jesus through much of "the Master's" ministry, even sent out by him as one of the seventy commissioned to heal and teach in his name.

Knowing Cayce's devotional life and deep personal faith, grounded in the Bible he loved and taught, helped me understand why the Lucius lifetime meant so much to him. Part of his wonder and gratitude over this sojourn lay in the assurance from the readings that Lucius had taken materials gathered by his mother's brother, Luke the physician, and actually written the gospel credited to Luke by the similarity of their names, together with the Book of Acts. But Cayce made no special fuss or claims today over this supposed contribution. What mattered much more was the strengthening of his sense of companionship with the living Jesus. Not infrequently his dreams had cast him in adventures with Jesus which touched him deeply. But his prayer times had also brought him what he felt were genuine encounters with the living Christ, typically assuring him, "Be not afraid; it is I," when Cayce was overwhelmed by the privilege of the meeting. There were other times when the man in trance suddenly lowered his voice and in a tone of deep respect advised the others in the room that "the Master is here" or "the Master passes by." Nobody close to Cayce could doubt that the person of Jesus was central to his most precious values and relationships, nor that Cayce felt his work was entirely subsumed under the broader process, also engaging others in their own special rounds, of "preparing the way" for Jesus' return to earth in modern times in his risen body.

In taking up that relationship, the Lucius lifetime appeared to be focusing on the deepest spiritual currents of Cayce's soul, according to his readings. These currents reportedly went all the way back to his first appearance on the earth millennia ago, when "the morning stars sang together" as "man became a living soul." And they picked up the one fragment of Hebraic experience cited by the readings for Cayce (though there may well have been others, since the readings selected only those they found most helpful for his present life). When he was about to undergo the equivalent of trial by fire in the loss of his hospital and the alienation of some of its backers, Cayce had dreamt of being with "Mr. and Mrs. Lot" at Sodom, accompanying them as they fled and watching in horror as the wife was stricken by heat, as "came from the fire from heaven" which all of them encountered. A reading taken on this vivid little dream affirmed that he had in fact been there as a messenger sent to warn Lot, and had survived the tragedy. The dream memory had come, he was told, to prepare him for his own personal suffering, coming in relation to his hospital.

Given Cayce's deep connection with biblical faith, the circumstances of his receiving the Lucius incarnation were strange. All the other major lifetimes were specified in 1923, shortly after he came across the concept of reincarnation in his own counsel, while living in Dayton, Ohio. But it was not until 1938, fifteen years later when he was sixty years old and living at Virginia Beach, that the Lucius experience emerged, first cited incidentally in a life reading for someone else. When asked for an explanation of the delay, Cayce's trance source commented unflatteringly that he "would have been puffed up" if the New Testament lifetime had been given earlier. However, by the time I came to know Cayce, five years after the disclosure, he gave no signs of arrogance based on the Lucius report, seeing the lifetime instead as a challenge to further growth and service, since it had been a journey not without character flaws and problems.

Lucius began his life inauspiciously as a soldier of fortune and a "ne'er–do–well," presumably picking up on the military adventures of Persia and Troy. But in his travels in the Holy Land, Lucius heard Jesus preach and became a "hanger–on," initially with the intent of participating in what he saw as a coming rebellion against Rome and its legions. Perhaps because of this doubtful motivation, as well as his essentially Greek background, he was disregarded by the devout Jews close to Jesus, though selected by the Galilean himself to go out with several dozen others as teachers and healers. He was close only to Thomas among the disciples. After the crucifixion and resurrection, he was apparently present at Pentecost in Jerusalem, and there underwent an experience of genuine transformation, after which he sought in earnest to help the new movement of the Way. But when the deacons were chosen and Stephen was martyred, he was rejected for a post because of his close previous association with the persecutor Saul from Tarsus near his own home in Laodicea—the Saul who later became Paul.

In the report of the readings, Lucius was often welcomed at the Bethany home of Mary, Martha, and Lazarus, all of them close to Jesus. His helpfulness there served him well when he returned to Laodicea, after Paul began establishing his churches in Asia Minor, for he was accepted by Paul and given authority in such centers of the new Christian sect as Antioch. On his return to his home in Laodicea to build a church there, Lucius brought with him a young Jewish woman named Maiererh, whom he had married in Jerusalem. Her presence brought divisions and bitterness back in Laodicea, for Lucius had already formed there in earlier years a liaison or marriage of sorts with a lovely and much desired woman of Greek and Roman descent connected directly to the royal house in Rome, who had borne him two sons. He wavered in his loyalties, even having a daughter by the patrician Vesta, cousin to the Caesars. Paul, ever preferring unmarried church leaders, challenged Lucius's authority in church circles, given his entanglements with women, while Lucius affirmed of Paul that "many of the things propounded by him were unstable."

Nevertheless, in due time Lucius became bishop, presbyter or "shepherd of souls" of the Laodicean church, as one to whom all questions were taken in matters of theology and religious laws, serving as the last word unless appeals were made to the apostles or to the church in Jerusalem. What might be considered the old authority from Egypt and Persia came back to him, and he guided the church well, in addition to serving as collaborator with his uncle, Luke, on a record of the life of Jesus and the early people of the Way. His Palestinian Jewish companion rejoined him after a despairing period away, and gave him a child, so that before his death he experienced periods of mellowness and great content, until persecutions from Rome cost the lives of his two sons by Vesta, now preachers in the new faith, as they did the lives of the leaders in the Jerusalem church, while Paul and Peter were martyred in Rome.

The consequences of such a life for the man Edgar Cayce would seem considerable. Here he might find the roots of his long determination to serve in churches, if indeed he could see himself as present at the birthday of the church at Pentecost, and guided then into new life by the fiery Holy Spirit. And here he might locate his deepest authorization for giving readings, in which he would continue to advise, teach, and awaken people to their full potential in a resurrection process, even though public religious office and the leadership of worship were not available to him. Was he in fact tempted to be puffed up by the knowledge of this supposed incarnation? It did not appear so, for he made no special claims on the basis of it in the earnest exchanges of his teaching. There were brief times when he could be haughty, imperious, or thoughtless. But these seemed derived from a larger struggle for identity and centering, in which the voice of an early shepherd of souls within him would be only one voice, not derived from spiritual pretensions as such. That larger struggle was the drama of the present Edgar Cayce, still learning the price of sustained open vision.

Part III

The Life:
Wrestling through the Dawn

CHAPTER 11

Rely on the Promise

Edgar Cayce was born in a farmhouse on March 18, 1877, near Hopkinsville, Kentucky. His father, Leslie (then twenty-three), and his mother, Carrie (then twenty-one), both shared in the duties of the family farm owned by Leslie's parents and dominated by the ancestral house. For the next eighteen years young Edgar would be a farm boy, as he often pointed out when asked to describe himself in later life. He not only shared in planting, harvesting, and curing the dark tobacco for which the region was famous, but took his turn at caring for farm animals, gardening, carpentry, repairing farm implements, and canning fruits and vegetables. He also rode horseback well and hunted quail, as well as fished in the stream that ran by the farm.

His deep engagement of the earth and its creatures, with the flow of the seasons, gave him several lasting gifts. He learned how to create jointly with natural energies as the foundation for the co-creating style which was at the heart of his lifelong spirituality. He learned something of timing and patience, which would never be easy for him. And he learned how to find joy in solitude, often by using his hands while his thoughts ran free. Nobody who knew him well in his later life could doubt the depth of his ties to the earth, which led him to plant a rich variety of flowers wherever he lived, as well as to cultivate vegetables for the family table and basement reserves. From his farm days, too, came his ease with pets. He would always have a dog and often own cats, pet birds, goldfish, ducks, or rabbits. Not entirely joking, he told friends in later years that he could instruct one of his pet chickens to lay an egg—and it would.

Alongside his gifts from nature came security and a sense of identity from a large clan of Cayces (the name derived from the Norman French *Cuaci*) that spread over several counties and was represented by towns with the family name in both North Carolina and Kentucky. He was named after an uncle, and farmed for two others as he grew up. Everybody around him in childhood recognized the family name and its reputation of hard-working, churchgoing people. In the South, not much more than a decade since the end of the Civil War, traditions of courtliness and social graces were still strong, and each person also knew where he or she fitted in the order of things. His father was elected justice of the peace during Edgar's boyhood, becoming Squire Cayce for the rest of his life and finding the title congenial to his expressing opinions on politics and many other matters at his brother's country store, which he soon took over. Young Edgar found that neighbors placed him easily and that his family's lack of means was no great social barrier.

What he drew in position from his father was not equaled by intimacy and affection, for the Squire, though a well-meaning parent, was frequently stern and aloof, as well as disapproving of his son's early fantasy life. He had no use for the unseen playmates which the boy reported, and objected vigorously to Edgar's relatively unimpressive record in school, derived in part from the lad's daydreaming. While the father was no intellectual, he was sensitive about the family image. It seems likely that the nickname of "Old Man" which others bestowed on the growing boy came from his having to discover and exercise his manhood for himself, appearing prematurely older.

Edgar's mother, on the other hand, was someone he described as having been his best friend, sweet and gentle, yet ultimately a stronger person than her husband, with considerable natural wisdom and spiritual insight. She was a homebody with a sense of humor, who did not disguise her affection for her son, called "Brother" by the family in the style of the times. Whatever may have been young Edgar's karma with the feminine, he was early surrounded by it, for he also had four devoted sisters, starting with Annie, eighteen months younger, Mary, Ola, and finally Sarah—twelve years his junior. Annie in particular adored him and would fight his battles in school spelling competitions, while he offered in turn to take the blame in incidents that led to spankings from their demanding father.

As so often for a sensitive, imaginative child, the grandparents were young Edgar's special sponsors. His grandfather took him fishing and told him stories he usually kept to himself, including accounts of seeing and talking with the recently dead. He showed the boy how anything green would grow for him and how (as the recognized dowser of the county) he had found well sites for many farms. Less known was his ability to make brooms dance and tables rise by concentrating on them, a use of unseen energy that he warned the lad about: "I don't know what the power is, but don't fool with it!" The loss to young Edgar was cruel when he watched his grandfather accidentally trampled to death by an upset horse. Only having the old man seem to return a number of times after death to talk with the boy softened the blow. His grandmother took these visitations as real, just as she did Edgar's imaginary playmates, and couched her encouraging comments in images of faith.

Always a Book in His Pocket

Young Edgar started school late, at age seven, and walked each day two and a half miles with his eldest sister to the little red schoolhouse where he would in time complete eight grades, and only eight, because no further education was available in their rural area. He did not do well in his studies because he was often not interested, though he was obviously bright and loved to read. As his sister later told me, "He always had a book sticking out of his pocket." Fiction was his favorite, and he kept two Dickens books (one was *Oliver Twist*) in the little lean-to he built for himself (partly to get away from his sisters) around a willow tree near a rivulet in the meadow. Most of his reading was not as literary. He delighted in every issue of *Youth's Companion* and liked American history, but his preferences were entertainment and diversion, poems, and stories. He made his sister read poetry to him and then showed her how to be more expressive. In later years he would buy his wife a complete set of the romantic novels of E.P. Roe. At the end of his life, a small bookcase in his front hall held the full collection, while the shelves in his office library were largely bare. Blood-and-thunder adventure stories held less appeal for the boy, and scientific inquiry did not draw him, but he wore out two big red books of illustrated Bible stories. In his teens he took to reading the *Louisville Courier Journal* daily, keeping up with current events. International affairs interested him more than local politics, and he got to know the editor personally when he wrote intelligent responses to editorials. Following the articles on issues of his times, he was drawn to the underprivileged and tried to treat the Negroes on the farm strictly as individuals with principled goodwill and fairness. But his passion was foreign missions, which he read about in church papers common to the day. He would mention specific foreign places when asked to give the mealtime blessing.

Young Edgar was not outstanding at ball games, spinning tops, or marbles, and he would simply withdraw from squabbles among playmates, partly because when pushed he was capable of his father's explosive temper. Often he preferred to be with older people, but not always, since he enjoyed games with both boys and girls. In his early years he was, as his sister put it, "right sweet on a lot of little girls." When it came time for parties, he was timid and disliked dancing. He did not take up smoking or drinking early.

Where the Bible Speaks

Where he shone was in church life. His earliest memory, according to his journal, was going to church services with his mother at about age four. (Significantly, his father was not in this bit of charged recall.) Southern church activity in his youth was actually a second track of education and community, as potent or more so than schooling. Each Sunday brought sermons on wide-ranging topics at Old Liberty Church in South Christian, about eight miles from Hopkinsville, while Bible classes and revival meetings carried the discourse even further. The church was his source of history, philosophy, geography, ethics, social criticism, biography, and poetry, as well as homespun sayings mixed with literary allusions. Often a guest preacher was invited home for Sunday chicken dinner, and some stayed for brief periods with the family, where they would be vigorously engaged by young Edgar and his mother. Discussing sermons was an art form of the time, both recreational and serious. Here Edgar was not shy at all, and stood up to imposing figures, to his sisters' awe. Not infrequently the exchanges mirrored his reading both in the Bible and in the tracts and magazines which were common in the Christian Church.

Years later I found he could discuss animatedly the issues that grasped church leaders of the period: biblical authority, the status of ex-slaves, excesses of the Industrial Revolution, musical instruments in worship (when a boy, his church voted against an organ as not scriptural), the validity of missionary societies, the five-fingered "plan of salvation," immersion baptism, communion open to all believers, alcoholism, personal idealism, service to the poor, and more. His religious tradition, the Christian Church, had been founded out of two native American movements that were offshoots of Presbyterian life only decades before. Its two principal leaders, Alexander Campbell and Walter Scott, had actually met for the first time at the Old Liberty Church, which carried the memory with pride. Determined not to be a denomination, the Christian Church eschewed creeds and sought to restore Christian unity among all sects on the basis of New Testament faith, especially devotion to Jesus Christ as Lord and Savior.[141] The reform program was bold and exciting, still young, and caught the imagination of Edgar.

If farm life gave him a feel for primal creative energies, and his clan and family gave him identity, it was faith that caught his imagination. Whether he was drawing on ancient patterns of teaching by Ra Ta and Uhjltd and Lucius, or just finding the first real challenge to his young mind and adventurous spirit, he found in the religious world horizons of excitement and awe. In his church tradition clergy were treated with respect but not deference, since they were simply named elders like any other, but given special assignments of leadership. Among the adults in his church the views of an informed and earnest lad could readily be heard, though not without the bemusement that older members adopt when the young catch their attention and respect.

He learned that the church needed a sexton and volunteered for the job while yet so young that he had to climb on a chair to reach the bell rope summoning neighbors to services. As he later remarked, he came to work in the church when he could only reach up to its front door latch, and stayed until he could reach the top of the door. In the meantime he made himself a genuine if youthful authority on the content of the Bible, crucial to his tradition, in which one central affirmation was "Where the Bible speaks, we speak; where the Bible is silent, we are silent." Evidence of the centrality of that earnest biblical thrust could be found in the hymns he sang, in which reference to the Trinity was at times omitted as not in the scriptures.

---

[141]De Groot, A.T., *The Restoration Principle*, 1960. See also Garrison, W.E., *Alexander Campbell's Theology*, 1900.

It was an old black woodchopper on their farm who first ignited Cayce's interest in the Bible, before he could even read, by telling him fascinating stories which led him to beg his mother to read more to him. At ten, while only in the third grade, he asked for his own Bible, and his father brought him one from town, donated by the bookstore owner, Mr. Hopper, who felt that a lad with these interests should be encouraged. Before long he had his mother sew a little "hind pocket" (as he called it) on his overalls, where he kept a small New Testament. When he was twelve, he drew from a visiting preacher the idea of reading the entire Bible once for every year of his life, and for months seized every hour he could from chores and schoolwork to go through the entire Bible, Genesis to Revelation, over and over again. By the time he was thirteen he had finished his twelfth round and was starting afresh. So deeply did he enter into the world of the patriarchs, judges, prophets, kings, psalmists, and wisdom teachers, as well as the disciples and apostles, that he formed a view of biblical faith that would stay with him all his life.

It was not the conventional Bible perspective of his times, in which good but often ignorant men and women served a Jehovah of law and wrath, in a pilgrimage that led up to the Gospel of love. Instead the entire account was for young Cayce a kind of two-tiered drama, divided not horizontally by time, but vertically by aspiration. What mattered in any period of biblical history was those who reached up to put their trust wholly in God, even though they sinned much and repented much. These persons walked by the light of trust and faith into exciting deeds of collaboration with God, to be celebrated as the author of Hebrews had done. Aspiring to their level but often falling back were the others who put their own interests and notions first. Decades later, when I often heard Cayce teach the Bible, he was still working from this framework, which carried the electrifying sense that anyone, anywhere, anytime, could step into intimate converse and co-creating with God. Moses was not less privileged than Paul, and Paul not more privileged than any of the rest of us. Cayce's own astonishing abilities by then made the picture believable to his listeners.

Even as a youth, Cayce had his own compelling intuitions about the reality and availability of the ultimate Companionship, whether these surmises were grounded in past lives or in his daily rounds with the farm creatures and with family members who loved him—or all of these. Later biographers and commentators would misunderstand his deep cherishing of the Bible as conventional piety and as "fundamentalism"—a reactionary movement which had not yet appeared on the American scene. He was not in fact absorbed in defending Bible inerrancy as a boy or later. How many days or eons creation required did not weigh heavily on him, or details of the plagues of Moses or how Joshua stopped the sun. Nor did he struggle over the Virgin Birth or the Resurrection, which seemed to him quite possible for a God whose ultimate nature was love. He was so caught up in the drama of real closeness to a living God that mechanics were not the issue. For him the prophets and the disciples of Jesus were so near he could almost hear them breathing, and he felt he might with daring guess the spirit of their visions, healings, trust, and prayers. Many who later read of his life would assume that as a suggestible youth he was entranced by stories of miracles, which led him to aspire to his own feats that might glorify God. His youth, on the edge of puberty when he first waded into the rich streams of the Bible, surely was important, yielding for him the intense idealism so often celebrated in teenagers. But his aspiration was relationship, not powers. He wanted to serve God and to love Him, to delight in His Presence and share His abounding goodness, not show off for Him.

The generation which would follow Cayce's life and thought with interest after his death put its attention on states and powers of the mind found in dreams, meditation, ESP, and past-life recall, as well as in hypnosis and

mystical consciousness. The focus was natural in a psychological century that first blossomed with discovery of
the unconscious, and developed into an era of drug–in-
duced states, as well as giving attention to right– and
left-brain hemispheres, and to near–death experiences.
But at a deeper level the focus embodied the modern
Western preoccupation with mastering and using whatever came to hand, in the assurance that greater technology would conquer both outer space and inner space.
Cayce's absorption in the Biblical saga was typically seen
by thousands later drawn to his story and concepts as
his provincial quaintness, replaceable by formulating
universal laws that could be accompanied when needed
with a few Bible quotes. The passion which was Cayce's,
even as a youth, to be utterly present to God in the most
ordinary pursuits of farming, play, and family life, tutored
by the biblical treasure of biographies, sacrifices, teachings,
and thanksgivings, has often eluded his later admirers.

For Cayce as a youth the Bible was not a spiritual
handbook that stood by itself. It was the record, charter,
and the promise of people and community—the living
church. When he was still very small, red-cheeked and
round-capped, his sister told me, he would go early to
the church building with his mother, who baked the
communion bread, and climb up into the "Amen corner"
of the balcony, where he played Uncle George Cayce, the
oldest member of the congregation, or mimicked some
other Cayce relative. Later he rode several miles to Sunday school and church with his sister in a cart drawn by
a horse named Tig, for Tiger. If they got there early, he
climbed up behind the pulpit to be the minister, his
dearest aspiration. His first sermon, he told her, would
be on "God so loved the world," though sometimes he
thought it should be from the Sermon on the Mount,
which he loved most of all. Whatever the text, the theme
was immediacy of relationship with God, not miracles.
Indeed, the concept of miracle was hardly real to him
because it implied natural law overridden by God, and
natural law was an abstraction foreign to him.

In his world, crammed full of biblical events and
phrases by his ardent reading, there was only one law,
and that was God's. The church was the household of
faith which trusted and loved that law, reaching far
beyond the Old Liberty congregation. Just over the
shoulders of the choir, or of the elders presiding at communion, were the rest of the larger church, in skins of
many colors at mission stations, and as doctors and
nurses at hospitals, or pioneers fighting for child-labor
laws. Other denominations were also there, of course,
since the Christian Church had been born to unite them
all in simplicity of New Testament faith. His memoirs
told of his friendships with many pastors during his farm
boy school years: Methodist, Baptist, Presbyterian, Christian, Unitarian, Congregational, Mormon, and for some
time a Catholic priest.

Worship for the teenage Cayce was not a duty but a
delight. He sang—as he told me—of walking with Jesus
"In the Garden" and bringing his burdens to "The Old
Rugged Cross." He joined in "Nearer My God to Thee" at
funerals, and bounced along in happier tunes of "Show-
ers of Blessings" or "Shall We Gather at the River" in Sunday school. Decades later, when I stood beside him in
worship, sharing in the responsive readings and the
loved hymns of faith, I found it easy to grasp why his
dreams often showed him in church services, and why
he reported some of his most precious mystical experiences had come in the pews. His faith was not a private
attainment, but a corporate gift renewed with others in
both attunement and service.

The family was another locus of spiritual community.
There were always table blessings, which not only the
parents but the children were expected to lead. Family
prayers in the evenings were customary all through
Edgar's school years, although the practice later tapered
off. The father was a good Bible student and would often
retire to the back sitting room with a Bible after supper.
The mother encouraged the children, while still very
young, to start each day by thanking God for caring for

them through the night, so they made it a habit to offer
thanksgiving on their knees before leaving their rooms
to hurry through breakfast and off to school. Edgar also
had his own special prayer life, as his sister recalled for
me. When faced with a problem, he would go off by
himself and then return to say, "I talked with God, and I
know where I'm going."

In his elder sister's view, this intimacy of communing
in prayer was partly responsible for her brother's independence of thought: "He was not a leaner." Yet he did
not force his ideas on others, though he had "definite
opinions," and when he was convinced of the rightness
of a course of action, "he usually went through with it."
In groups at school and play he was not a leader, but his
direction was felt as what she called "an undercurrent,"
though she remembered well an incident in the school
when he stood up to his mocking fellow students, warning them to be understanding of an alcoholic teacher
and reminding them of Noah's drinking.

Whether because of his ardent prayer life in which
God was more companion than judge, or because of his
sense of unfolding creative energies in all that grew
around him on the farm, the young Edgar was not
caught in the preoccupation of being saved from hopeless sin, which so profoundly marked segments of small-
town church life in his times, as it had frontier churches
earlier, when conversion was the dramatic thrust of camp
meetings and revivals. He was well aware of sin, the subject of heartfelt pastoral prayers and sermons alike, just
as it was of family table discussions. And he searched his
own soul as he read the Bible, finding there many like
himself who stumbled often or acted rebelliously or self-
ishly. Yet he did not undergo the typical teenage crisis of
fearing for his soul, and no reference to a born again
experience appeared in his later memoirs. The pattern of
spirituality which made sense to him was one of slow
growth more than sudden transformation, though he
relished the dramatic tales related by evangelists. His
spirituality, in the language of a much later age, was first

creation centered in order to be redemptive.[142] It would stay that way throughout his life, as well as be reflected in his readings, which expressed little of the Calvinist conviction of human depravity, although often affirming "All have sinned and fallen short" in one lifetime and in many.

I Had a Religious Experience, a Vision and a Promise

Coming home from church one Sunday afternoon, not long after completing his marathon reading of the Bible twelve times, he was keyed up by the preaching and the simple but pregnant Lord's Supper that crowned each service. He had been baptized by solemn immersion not too many months before, in 1889, going under the waters, as he was told, into the death of his old self, and rising with Christ into a new life. The promise of simple but genuine resurrection of his best nature was still very real to him. That afternoon he went off for a time to his hideaway in the meadows and prayed, as he had often done recently, to be used by God in service. The willow tree and its creatures seemed very close to him, he later told me, in that communing with the Creator out-of-doors which so often centered him later in life. Back at the house for supper, he was tutored in his lessons by his father, who had until recently done some of the teaching in the little schoolhouse. When he prepared for sleep, he knelt by the bed to pray. Before he fell asleep, he saw a vision, a figure of radiant light (having no special gender, he explained to me). Thinking it might somehow be his mother, he went to her room, then returned; and the being of light was there again. He was asked

---

[142]See Fox, Matthew, *Original Blessing*, 1983, and *Whee, We, Wee, All The Way Home*, 1981. A different approach to similar themes is in Pannenberg, Wolfhart, *Christian Spirituality*, 1983.

what he sought, and stammered out that he wanted to
help others, as he had seen in the Bible could be done
with God's grace—especially to help children. The response given him, as nearly as he could recall, was "Thy
prayers are heard. You will have your wish. Remain faithful. Be true to yourself. Help the sick, the afflicted." He
rushed out into the moonlight to give thanks at his favorite retreat spot, where two squirrels, he remembered,
came down the tree at dawn and hunted in his pockets
for nuts.

Awake through the night, he was in a daze at school
the next day, still amazed at what had transpired. When
his Uncle Lucian, the current teacher, called on him to
spell the simple word "cabin," he gave it two *b*'s and outraged his uncle, who required him to stay after school
and write it correctly five hundred times on the black-
board. Worse, his uncle notified his father, who was waiting for him when he got home, determined to teach the
boy spelling by whatever means was necessary. After
supper the squire set about quizzing the lad on word
after word, methodically and angrily knocking him out
of his chair at each miss. For an exhausted lad trying to
cope with the ecstasy of the night before, the jars to his
nervous system were considerable. Later researchers
would comment on the likelihood that delicate *chakras*
were jolted into life the way accidents or blows had affected other gifted subjects. Cayce later told me of the
incident as he also wrote about it in his memoir.[143]

As the evening dragged on toward eleven o'clock, he

---

[143]For verbatim excerpts from his unpublished memoirs, used by
permission of Cayce and his son, Hugh Lynn, see the unpublished
1955 doctoral dissertation by Harmon H. Bro, *The Charisma of the Seer:
A Study in the Phenomenology of Religious Leadership*, University of Chicago: By University policy, this dissertation has been available for
decades to any who would pay the cost of duplicating a copy. For
extensive treatment of the memoirs in narrative and paraphrase,
see Millard, Joseph, *Edgar Cayce: Man of Miracles*, London: Neville
Spearman, 1961. This book is built almost exclusively on personal
writings of Cayce and his father, but is popular, not scholarly.

began to doze while trying to recall words, winning more cuffs from his father. Then something seemed to speak to him from within, saying "Rely on the promise." He asked to sleep for just a few minutes, and his father let him. First he prayed, remembering his experience of the night before, and then put his head down on his book and briefly slept, while his father went to the kitchen for a drink of water. Awakening, he triumphantly handed his father the book and began to spell not only the words in the assigned lesson, but any word asked him from anywhere in the book—adding where it was located on the page. Not surprisingly, the father rewarded him with another blow, thinking the boy had been holding out on him. But young Edgar was delighted, not only with his performance there but in school the next day, and with all his studies. For he quickly learned that he could memorize passages from any of his books the same way. None of his classmates could keep up with him, his elder sister told me years later, because when it was time to recite, he could see the pages as though they were before his eyes.

The boy's new ability remained with him during the two last years of his country schooling, as it did throughout his life. When I asked two of his sisters how his classmates felt about his astonishing ability, I got a charming reply, reflecting the pragmatism of children. They all got used to it soon, and rather than dwell on the marvel, they grumbled at his lucky advantage, then gave it no further thought. The squire, however, was elated. At last he had found something to be proud of in his son, whose temperament was so different from his own. To show the boy off, he had him memorize, while sleeping, a speech by a local politician that ran an hour and a half, then give it at school exercises. Everyone was bored except the political figure, who was delighted.

What is striking in the story of learning by sleeping is, of course, young Edgar's bewildering ability. But it is too easy to overlook the deeper setting of the covenant in which it appeared, the first of several in Cayce's life. He felt he had made promises and that promises had been made to him in return, as well as demands—not the least of them his having almost at once to appear partly a freak to relatives and teachers. Looking back much later on the covenant dimension, he typically led into the events by recalling how intensely he had studied the Bible that year, and how close God had become, until "I had a religious experience, a vision and a promise."

Although friends thought he simply fell asleep on his schoolbooks or whatever else he needed to memorize, he actually needed to turn each time to that promise and the sense of Presence and loving care it brought. He prayed in the spirit of that relationship, and then he could fall asleep and awaken with the text. Years later, when he prayed before giving readings, he still touched back to rely on the same companionship promised him as a boy for service of those in need.

The "First" Reading

Two years afterward came an incident which presaged his ability to give readings, well described by his biographer Sugrue. He was playing a ballgame common at the time, called Old Sower, in which he had to stand with his back to the pitcher when he struck out and have the ball thrown at him. He remembered nothing of what followed, but the blow on his head or spine must have jarred the nervous system considerably, because after school that day he was so disoriented that his sister had to lead him home.

On the way, she told me, he was noisy and shouting, climbing in trees, rolling in mud, and stopping passing teams of horses. At home he took a pan of roasted coffee beans and sowed them in the yard, frightening his mother. The squire came home and they put him to bed, where he fell into a coma. After a while he spoke clearly and authoritatively, although unconscious, telling his parents that he needed a certain kind of poultice to be

put at the base of the brain. He prescribed the ingredi-
ents and urged them to hurry so that no damage would
occur to his brain. Looking back, his father remembered
more, as did other members of the family. Lying in bed
and seemingly in some kind of a trance state, the lad
spoke of a number of matters he thought would be helpful to his parents: how the school board appreciated the
principal and the assistant, the man's sister, and what
their past and future held. His father thought the boy
was out of his senses, yet could not help listening when
he went on to describe some trends in the national financial and political scene—ever a preoccupation with
the squire. Ruefully, the father noted later that he might
have made money in the markets, had he taken seriously the strange information pouring out of young
Edgar. Cayce told me that he thought this might have
been his first reading.

For the boy of fifteen, the strange incident meant only
that friends and neighbors had another excuse for thinking him queer. A special blow came when the girl on
whom he had a crush taunted him: "Dad says you are not
right in the head." Her father was the local country doctor, who told Edgar kindly and firmly that he would never
be normal, since injuries of one sort or another were
doubtless behind his strange experiences; he should leave
girls alone and not think of marriage, because he would
probably be unable to have children and die insane. The
prediction worried young Cayce for years despite his
mother's assurances that his spiritual experiences meant
instead that he would be able to help people.

In his most subjective memoirs he later told of taking
a fling at going to carnivals and dances with a rough
crowd of farm boys older than he in the effort to prove
that he was normal and a he-man. Whether this was the
first emergence of a Bainbridge-like pattern that would
recur in his life is questionable, but he lived dangerously enough to be accidentally shot one night while
watching black men play craps on his way home from a
dance. The bullet lodged near the collarbone and was

safely removed by a doctor in a not-too-near town where his friends took him. The degree of his rebellion was evident in his not telling his parents why his shoulder was so sore for weeks, but the incident ended his brief rowdy days in the farm setting as suddenly as they had begun.

I Must See Something of the World

His parents decided to move to Hopkinsville in order to get further schooling for the girls. The squire took up selling insurance. Young Cayce stayed behind to work on his uncle's farm, supporting himself and sending money to help the family, as well as saving a bit toward his goal of education for the ministry. Then came a second powerful spiritual experience, when the same presence he had seen as a figure of light now approached him and told him to leave the farm and go to town, since his mother needed him. He left at once and began the difficult adjustment of changing from a thoroughly rural life to town life, in a community dominated in his age bracket by students at local academies and a college.

With typical originality he got a job in Hopper's bookstore by offering to work for nothing until he showed his value. The scheme worked, and became the prototype for many an imaginative and creative business step in the years ahead, as part of his emergent lifestyle of co-creating in whatever he touched. But the shift was not easy, as he later recalled; constantly meeting people and handling books, stationery, pictures, picture frames, wallpaper, window shades, vases, and statuary was far from what he had known all his life as a "clodhopper," "tending flocks as well as work mules and horses, spreading of manure, and seeding, reaping, and harvesting of crops." Under the pressures of trying to find himself, he had another run at Bainbridge-like sporting life, keeping up with a fast college crowd until the fling ended embarrassingly when a bartender who knew of his Sunday school work and liked him refused to serve him a drink, though his companions got all they wanted.

His interest in church work continued, with unexpected encouragement from the famed evangelist Dwight L. Moody, who came to town to preach in the capacious Sam Jones Tabernacle. How much the encounter meant to the young Cayce may be seen in Moody's appearance in his dreams throughout his life. Going out one morning to fetch his cow, given the lad by his aunt when he moved to town, he found Moody sitting by the side of a stream reading his Bible. They talked of the Bible and of Cayce's religious experiences and sense of promise. Moody did not make fun of him but instead related similar experiences of his own, becoming the first person apart from Cayce's mother to urge him to view his visionary times as a serious call from God. The respected evangelist suggested that whether or not the young Cayce could achieve his goal of becoming a minister with his painfully limited finances, he could become a genuine authority on the Bible. So Edgar put the advice into action, volunteering as a Sunday school teacher in the Ninth Street Christian Church and sometimes supplying the pulpit for circuit-riding Methodist preachers of the area. Members of the class came from other churches of the town, as well as his own. His teaching, though he was still in his teens, so affected his listeners that *over half* of his early class of thirty-eight eventually entered foreign-mission service—a remarkable record. They went out to China, India, Mexico, Africa, and Tibet.

As he began to develop a measure of social graces, he fell deeply in love with a sparkling black-haired socialite named Gertrude Evans. She was a member of a distinguished architect's family who lived in a spacious Southern mansion, surrounded by relatives who gave Cayce his first access to the professional world of the arts, medicine, and literature. From the viewpoint of his past lives, he found with her opportunities completely different from his farm upbringing, completing but not replacing it. In this perspective he began to move into his own inner world of Ra Ta, Uhjltd, and the offspring of French royalty. Whether he could have kept his head in this climate without his early grounding in nature and farm community life might reasonably be doubted.

In Gertrude he discovered his complement in a sharp and orderly mind (according to later readings, the daughter of Socrates!) as committed in spirit to idealistic service as his was, yet contrasting with his intuitive leaps and surmises. He also found a young woman of great strength of will and personal discipline, an articulate introvert who would in time become his business associate in photography and even more his colleague in the giving of his strange readings. Her nature allowed her to step easily into the world of masculine activities and decision-making in an age when gender roles were usually stereotyped. But alongside her obvious talents she also represented to him a potential of smoldering sexual feelings (she would one day be reported as the dancing Isis who was his companion in Egypt) which he found in her fluid walk and gestures, as well as in the tossing of her long hair. Her very glance could melt him, as his sister Annie later told me, remembering how keenly she had felt displaced by her brother's new focus. Edgar was to find in Gertrude a spirited and passionate lover, but one whose deepest purpose was to nurture and take care of those in pain, even in her slim patrician body. Not for nothing would she one day be called Muddie by her family. Impressed by Edgar's spiritual depth, she was never awed by him and in later years became the only person other than their elder son able to take him on when he needed rebuking.

Cayce was twenty when he proposed, but so poor that he could not see his way to marriage any time soon. This did not stop him from buying her an expensive diamond that required months to pay off. Nor did it keep him from a gesture that revealed his own inner sense of stature, already emerging, when he sent it all the way to Rumania to be cut. Reluctantly he began to give up his plan of education for the ministry. Marriage to the right girl seemed more important—although his mother was dismayed at the choice. His life now revolved around Gertrude, so much that his sister recalled that he was suddenly useless around the house, except when he bargained for his sisters' aid in arranging his dates. He rode a bicycle to the Salter mansion, where Gertrude lived, and kept each date even in pouring rain, often bringing her books from the store where he worked, since she was a more systematic reader than he. Suddenly losing his job at Hopper's through a change in ownership, he worked for a time in the shoe department of Richards Dry Goods Store but felt he was getting nowhere. So he took a bold step into a large city.

His oldest sister, as she told me later, had finished high school and gotten her first full-time job as a bookkeeper; she could now help to support the family, so that Edgar's income was not needed as it had been while he worked at his uncle's farm and in the two stores. So he decided he must "see something of the world," as he later recounted it. Louisville, Kentucky, was the place he picked out, and the story of how he got a job at a book and stationery company made me chuckle when I heard him tell it several times. He sent for their catalog and began memorizing it, by sleeping on it, a few pages at a time. Forty-five years later he could still recall its entries for me. Meanwhile, he went to all the professional people he knew in the town—judges, physicians, ministers, teachers—and had them systematically send telegrams of recommendation to the Louisville firm every few days. The surprised company, which had first turned him down, wired him to stop sending messages and report for work, then found him a great asset because of his uncanny knowledge of the firm's extensive catalog. It might not be too far-fetched to see in this delightful story a bit of Ra Ta creativity in action, or at least his lifelong sense of faith that something could always be done, starting with what one had in hand.

Moving to Louisville took him on his first train ride, and the streaming city streetcars, buses, and throngs of people at first bewildered him. But the two years of active urban life which followed were to give him a confidence and sophistication in dealing with larger institutions which he would never lose. The farm boy was not replaced, but rather joined by an inner self who would have been at home in a Persian city, in Troy, or in affluent Laodicea. He advanced in his firm, worked in a prestigious Christian Church, and began with his minister what became a lifelong practice of visiting those in jails and hospitals. But with his typical (and also lifelong) style of spending whatever he earned, he did not succeed in saving enough for marriage. His salary did go up some when he landed the account of one of the wealthiest families in the city—as well as landed the attractive daughter of that family, who shared in his Christian Endeavor work at his church and was a member there with him of the Glad Helpers Society. The conflict of affections for two women at once mirrored what his life readings would later describe as a soul riddle for him, and gave him distress when he let himself think about it. Finally, during a Christmas visit to Hopkinsville, he decided on his hometown fiancée. He was glad to accept from his father an offer of a job as an insurance salesman, which would base him in Hopkinsville near her but take him on short trips. The Louisville wholesale bookstore convinced him to take along a line of their products to sell.

Speechless in the Studio

Then, while he was on a business trip to nearby Elkton, the whole fabric of his vocational and marital plans was torn apart when he stumbled into a calamitous illness that began with violent headaches and briefly being out of his head. He lost his voice for a period that stretched on endlessly, month after month. His sister and wife later told me that this illness was the greatest trial in his entire life, prompting him to spend

much time by himself in Bible reading, prayer, and questioning whether he had been using his "promise" correctly. It was a classic initiatory illness, when seen in the
perspective of religious biographies and even shamanis-
tic gifts,[144] as he worked silently each day at the only job
he could get, making frames and then taking and developing pictures in a local photographic studio. Whatever
he might have known as a chemist in Troy and Greece
(where his readings would later report that he had been
close to the woman now Gertrude) might be seen as
making it natural for him to mix the darkroom brews
and nurse the prints to life. Since he could only speak in
a hoarse whisper, his church school teaching was gone,
and his marriage plans seemed to him hopelessly threatened by his inability to give Gertrude a normal live. Although she stood by him and his family was solicitous,
his only real recourse was his personal faith and sense
of God's closeness, as tormenting in its uncertain outcome as it was still real in His silence. Edgar was twenty-
three, the same age I was when I met him long afterward,
and I shuddered as he retold the story.

The loss of his voice became a recurrent illness in his
life, as I saw only months before his death. What kind of
karma might lie in this seemingly arbitrary disability was
of course the subject of family discussion when reincarnation came into their worldview. His elder son associated it with the Ra Ta period, when the high priest had
used his will—associated with the throat center—to force
the course of evolution of human bodies toward his own
idea of perfection rather than listening to inner guidance. Cayce himself was not averse to linking it to his
Bainbridge experience as a sideshow barker, misusing
his voice to fleece people out of their money. Whatever
the origin, the result for the young Cayce was an opportunity to hold fast in the face of adversity—just as his
readings would later claim he had been destined to do

---

[144]See Eliade, Mircea, *Shamanism*, 1964.

instead of taking his life in Troy, or withdrawing in dismay as a French child. The kind of healthy and tempered ego strength which was not automatic for a privileged high priest was now demanded of him. Perhaps partly because of the character of Lucius, the New Testament bishop whose times had become so real with young Cayce's intense Bible study, he held his ground inwardly, also drawing on the perspectives of his farm solitude. The consequences proved to be wildly different from anyone's expectation.

Specialists examined him and tried to treat him, not only in Hopkinsville but in Nashville, Louisville, and Cincinnati. Wealthy church friends in Louisville even arranged for a noted physician from abroad to come and care for him. Nothing worked, and months dragged past in a procession that seemed surely destined to leave him speechless for life. One of those who learned of his disability was the so-called Professor Hart, a showman whose public demonstrations in the new and exciting field of hypnosis captivated the town. He offered to restore Cayce's voice for two hundred dollars or accept nothing if he failed. Friends of the young man put up the money, and a local physician agreed to supervise. Hart succeeded in getting Cayce to speak clearly under hypnosis, but he could not get him far enough into trance to accept post-hypnotic suggestion to speak normally afterward. The hypnotist tried a variety of approaches on the young man, even succeeding in one astonishing episode with getting Cayce to play the piano effortlessly (a skill he knew nothing about and never evinced again), but he could not restore the voice. A local psychology professor brought the case to the attention of a New York specialist in hypnosis, and the physician came to Hopkinsville to work on Edgar, also without success. But among those drawn to the case was a Hopkinsville hypnosis enthusiast who was taking correspondence courses in osteopathy, a frail man who kept the books for his wife's millinery firm where Annie Cayce worked.

Al C. Layne took the young man under his wing and

got him to explain how he felt when he was being hypnotized. The state, Edgar reported in his hoarse whisper,
reminded him of how he felt when he put himself to
sleep to memorize books; he wondered whether he
could just hypnotize himself. Layne encouraged him to
try and offered to give him post–hypnotic suggestion to
recover his voice. But Cayce's parents were firmly against
any such experimentation, and the young man soon was
unable even to whisper, while a physician referred to his
illness as "galloping consumption." Finally, on a Sunday
afternoon in March, 1901, Edgar and Layne went to the
latter's store and Edgar made himself unconscious; the
older man asked Cayce to see himself and explain the
problem. The answer came in a full, even voice, explaining that there was a partial paralysis of the muscles of
the vocal cords, coming from nerve strain.

The quiet, firm voice of the sleeping Cayce then directed a procedure of hypnotic suggestion to increase
circulation to the affected area, which promptly turned
bright red, and waited for nearly twenty minutes before
informing the amazed Layne that the cure was completed—as indeed it proved to be. Wanting to be sure
that his voice stayed, Cayce did not tell his parents until
the next day, when he walked into his mother's room (as
his sister recalled it) and said firmly, "Good morning,
Mother!" The local paper ran a head line story:

Voice Restored

Edgar Cayce Suddenly Relieved of a Terrible Affliction.
Vocal organs paralyzed a year ago made well as ever.

The news column continued, making no mention of
Layne or hypnosis, as Cayce himself undoubtedly did
not either, referring to him as "son of Mr. L.B. Cayce" and
"a very worthy and deserving young man." It told of how
on Monday morning:

*Overjoyed, he rushed into his mother's room to break
the good news. All day yesterday he was on the streets*

*talking to his friends and receiving congratulations . . .
It had been a month since he took any sort of medicine
and his power of speech was restored as suddenly and
unexpectedly as it was lost.*[145]

Talk, Talk, Talk

Layne was delighted, suspecting that he had found in
Cayce an example of the medical somnambulism or traveling somnambulism described in the largely European
literature of early work in hypnosis. These accounts told
of subjects, often uneducated, who could diagnose illness and prescribe treatments for others while in trance.
Newspaper features and magazine articles of the day
carried reports of cases going back to 1794, when Western attention was first drawn to the strange sleep like
phenomena made famous by Franz Mesmer. Victor, an
uneducated French peasant boy, when "magnetized" by
one of Mesmer's pupils, the Marquis de Puysegur,[146] was
reported to have correctly described the physical ailment
of someone sitting next to him, and a fad of diagnosis by
somnambulists stirred Europe for a time, although it was
ridiculed by physicians of standing.

In America there was the well-reported case of Andrew Jackson Davis, the Poughkeepsie Seer, who made
many hypnotic diagnoses for over a decade and achieved
national fame until the 1850s, when the beginnings of
American Spiritualism, with the Fox Sisters levitating
tables and producing "rappings," drew attention to something more bizarre. In Massachusetts there was Lucius
Burkmar,[147] uneducated hypnotic subject, who per-

---

[145]*Hopkinsville Gazette*, April 2, 1901. (This publication has been discontinued and copyrights elapsed.)

[146]See Sugrue, Thomas, *There Is a River*, 1942, p. 5.

[147]Kemp, C.F., *Physicians of the Soul, A History of Pastoral Counseling,* 1947,
p. 161.

formed the same kinds of services in the 1860s at the hands of Phineas Quimby—the same Quimby who was stirred by his Burkmar experiences to ideas and practices that started the widespread New Thought movement in America, and under whose tutelage it was reported that Mary Baker Eddy, the founder of Christian Science, had first developed her ideas.

Given this background, it was not surprising that Layne should want to experiment further with Cayce. He decided that the best method was to offer himself as the next subject for inspection and treatment, since he had a chronic gastritis problem. But Cayce, who had been poked at and experimented on for nearly a year, wanted no part of the effort, apparently fearful lest he lose his newfound voice. Still he felt indebted to Layne.

Under hypnosis (again self-induced in prayer that relied on his first promise and covenant) he produced a full medical diagnosis, together with prescriptions of certain drugs, diet, and exercise. The results dumbfounded young Cayce, who had never studied physiology or anatomy or chemical compounds. He feared he might make Layne worse or even kill him. But when Layne followed the instructions, his condition improved so dramatically that in a few months he was a well man. Cayce was frightened and disturbed, questioning what it all meant and wondering whether it was connected to his childhood experience of a promise from God. Mostly, he told me emphatically, he was ashamed of the whole queer business.

He refused to go any further, but after a few months his voice began to fail again, and so he needed Layne's help to restore proper circulation to his throat while he was in trance. This put him in the hypnotist's debt, and he hesitantly agreed to try to help some sick persons as Layne asked. The results were extraordinary, for he gave instructions about others as readily as about himself and Layne. One instance which his sister later recalled as removing the opposition of her parents was having her brother locate a celluloid collar button in a baby's throat, on which it was choking to death. The doctors had understandably missed it with X-rays, and young Edgar saved the child's life. Layne promptly opened an office without waiting to complete his correspondence-school training, and began administering the varied treatments which the young photographer described. Townspeople were critical of Layne's presumption, and those who recalled young Edgar's sleeping on books in childhood suggested that he was queer, despite his personable ways in the Bowles Studio.

"Talk, talk, talk" was how he later recalled the time. Layne kept pulling him into his office on behalf of sick people as often as five or six times a week, and word spread all over town. Young Cayce did not even know the people whose lives fell into his care, and he wondered if it was all a fantastic trick of some sort. He refused to talk about it further with his family, as his sister recalled, for he had decided that whatever the process was, he didn't believe in it.

Because Edgar had to return to Layne for periodic aid to keep his voice going, friends added a new fear, that Layne had him in his power and wouldn't release him. He was tormented by the question of the real spiritual significance of his ability. Despite her doubts about Layne's competence, Cayce's mother continued to insist that her son had some sort of gift from God which he must use to help others, similar to gifts he had read about in his beloved Bible. Gertrude's aunt, the outspoken Carrie Salter, joined her in affirming to the troubled young man that he had a gift which God would see was not misused. But to most of his associates it seemed preposterous that a local boy, just one of the large Cayce clan, should have anything at all in common with gifts of the awesome figures of biblical times. When even people in nearby towns began making what he called "smart cracks" to Cayce about his irregular ways of "sleeping," he was angered and noted later, "It didn't set very well with me." A friend located a job opportunity for him in an idyllic college town of some ten thousand residents, Bowling Green, Kentucky, and Edgar jumped at it, partly because it took him back to the familiar setting of a bookstore, where he would be working with pictures and frames, notebooks, and the volumes he knew so well back at his first job in Hopkinsville and then later at the wholesale firm in Louisville.

Before he left, Layne persuaded him to undertake an experiment to explore his clairvoyance at a distance. He had Edgar follow a group of Hopkinsville businessmen and their wives who were just then on a trip to Paris. Cayce described with precision the shops and streets, using French names, and went on to recount their visits to can-can shows that embarrassed the residents on their return (as Gertrude later told me with mischievous delight). There was no instruction book that came with his peculiar ability. He also discovered, when Layne found him hunting in the woods and begged for emergency aid in response to a wire from a Chicago man, that he could give his peculiar counsel simply lying there on the frosty ground. The subject died of internal bleeding, however, as the reading warned, and the young man encountered a new problem: his aid might instruct how to save lives, but the counsel would be useless unless people were able to get exactly the treatments he prescribed.

He took the train to Bowling Green with the intention of an entirely fresh start in his life, free of all the hypnotic weirdness that had given him so much trouble. He would be normal. He would send for Gertrude and be happily married. He was twenty-five years old and ready. But a little girl would change his mind and require that he undertake a new covenant with his Lord.

CHAPTER 12

It Should Be
Thoroughly Tested

In Bowling Green, Cayce stepped into the world of professional people, businessmen, and community leaders which he would not leave for the rest of his life. The farm boy was pushed further into the background, though he would have to touch back to it often when he needed to find renewal. But his fellow roomers at Mrs. Hollins's boardinghouse framed his life in new dimensions. His roommate was a young medical doctor who specialized in eye, ear, nose, and throat ailments. There was also a dentist, the executive of the local YMCA, and another M.D., John Blackburn, who became a special friend for many years. He joined the Christian Church and its interdenominational Christian Endeavor group for young adults. And he began associations with academic people, those in legal professions, and a widening ring of doctors who had formed what they called the E.Q.B. Literary Club—the kind of society common among physicians that reads and discusses current books. It would not be difficult to argue, from the perspective of Cayce's yet unknown past lives, that he was starting to claim and use the heritage of Uhjltd, the gifted healer and city builder of ancient Persia, who was a strong and balanced person, adding this subsystem to the core of the Lucius incarnation from New Testament times which had infused Cayce's Bible-fired youth.

At the same time, Cayce's focus for the next eighteen years was to be the familiar tasks of young manhood: getting married, turning a house into a home, providing for his wife and children, establishing himself in voca-

tion and reputation, engaging peers, and joining groups.
The call of nature for perpetuation of the species, and
the first deep cries of the adult heart to give and receive
love, supported by security and public identity, would
engross him—though not without pain. Whatever his
karma, it would be woven on a loom of desire and passion appropriate for his age and station in life. His ambitions were personal, not institutional, and certainly not
for seership in an age without seers.

Help the Sick, the Afflicted

He expected to leave Layne and the queer readings
far behind him, and he did—for two weeks. Then his
voice began to fail again, and he had to take the train
back to Hopkinsville for the weekend, filled with doubt
and fear. Layne suggested that he would come up to
Bowling Green on Sundays, exchanging his aid and train
fare for Edgar's counsel on patients, and the reluctant
young man agreed, taking his guest to his room each
week and hiding what went on there. His understanding
of the promises in his childhood mystical experiences
did not include continuing as a freak in this fashion. He
had asked to serve those in need, especially children,
and he expected to become a minister or evangelist, not
a somnambulist. Nothing in his deepening prayer life
during the dark days of working alone and voiceless in
the photography darkroom had quite convinced him
that God would not sooner or later rescue him and give
him a happy, respectable life of love, work, and church.
He had kept his part of the covenant which asked him to
"remain faithful" and "be true to yourself," and he had
thought that "help the sick, the afflicted" meant precisely
the visiting of hospitals and jails which he had begun
regularly in Louisville. Now he seemed trapped in an
embarrassing kind of service to the ill, not at all as so-
cially acceptable as the ministry or being a respected
Bible teacher. What did God really want of him? Had he

broken the covenant that had so centrally marked his life for a dozen years? Why did God not rescue him from periodic voice loss and from unwanted collusion with Layne in procedures frowned on by public leaders in Hopkinsville, which his new Bowling Green friends would doubtless despise?

The beginnings of a deeper covenant developed, as he might have expected, in response to the needs of a child—one of those he had originally prayed to help. Several months after a fresh start in his new location, a phone call came from one of the most respected and loved public figures back home in Hopkinsville. It was from the former superintendent of schools, C.H. Dietrich, pleading for aid for his six–year–old daughter, a hopeless case for the past four years. Edgar took the train to Hopkinsville and went to the Dietrich home. He did not know whether he would disgrace himself in front of the town's leading citizens or regain some of the self-respect that had been his as a Bible teacher. The results affected him so profoundly that in later years when he prepared a booklet about his work, he included a deposition by Dietrich in every copy given to inquirers for over twenty years. It was still in the text sent to the thousands whose letters were stacked high when I arrived. In medical terms the case was not any stranger than many hundreds of others who would come to him. What mattered was that in this instance his own faith took a decisive step forward. Here is what the girl's father later volunteered in the kind of formal statement that others also spontaneously supplied to the young Cayce, and later filed with the American Society for Psychical Research, in New York:

State of Ohio
Hamilton County

as:
Personally appeared before Garrit J. Raidt, a notary public in and for said county, C. H. Dietrich,

and after being duly sworn, deposes and says
that:

Aime L. Dietrich, born January 7, 1897, at
Hopkinsville, Ky., was perfectly strong and healthy
until February, 1899, when she had an attack of La
Grippe, followed by two violent convulsions, each
of twenty minutes duration. Dr. T.G. Yales, now of
Pensacola, Florida, was the attending physician.
Convulsions returned at irregular intervals with
increasing severity. She would fall just like she
was shot, her body would become perfectly rigid,
the spells lasting from one to two minutes.

This went on for two years, or until she was four
years old. At this time she was taken to Dr.
Linthicum in Evansville, Indiana, and Dr. Walker,
also of Evansville, was consultant physician. They
said a very peculiar type of nervousness was all
that ailed her and proceeded to treat her accordingly, but after several months treatment, with no
results, the treatment was stopped.

In a few months, Dr. Oldham of Hopkinsville,
Ky., was consulted and he treated her three
months, without results. Later he took her for four
months more treatments, making seven months
in all, but without results. She was now six years
old but getting worse, had as many as twenty convulsions in one day, her mind was a blank, all reasoning power was entirely gone.

March 1, 1902, she was taken to Dr. Hope of Cincinnati, O., who made a most thorough examination. He pronounced her a perfect specimen
physically, except for the brain affection, concerning which he stated that only nine cases of this
particular type were reported in Medical Records,
and everyone of these had proved fatal. He told
us that nothing could be done, except to give her
good care, as the case was hopeless and she

would die soon in one of these attacks.

At this point our attention was called to Mr. Edgar Cayce, who was asked to diagnose the case. By auto-suggestion he went into a sleep or trance and diagnosed her case as one of congestion at base of the brain, stating also minor details. He outlined to Dr. A. C. Layne, now of Griffin, Ga., how to proceed to cure her. Dr. Layne treated her accordingly, every day for three weeks, using Mr. Cayce occasionally to follow up the treatment, as results developed. Her mind began to clear up about the eighth day and within three months she was in perfect health, and is so to this day. This case can be verified by many of the best citizens of Hopkinsville, Kentucky, and further deponent saith not.

[signed] C.H. Dietrich
Garrit J. Raidt, Notary Public
Hamilton Co., O.[148]

Here were all the elements Cayce would so often see in sufferers during the years that followed: tragic symptoms, frantic parents or relatives, a procession of physicians in various cities, no hope, and then precise diagnosis and instructions for care or treatment in a reading, followed by unbelievable recovery. The pattern was still there in the cases I worked with daily, so many decades later. In this instance the drama hit the young Cayce with decisive force, because he knew the listless child (as did people all over his hometown) and could see her fully cured, playing with her dolls, in a matter of weeks. The reading had reminded the parents of a forgotten injury to the child's spine in a fall from a carriage at the time of the "grippe" that allowed infection to set in. Follow-up readings for a few days kept after Layne to

---

[148]Cayce, Edgar, *Edgar Cayce, His Life and Work,* 1943, pp. 4–5.

make the correct osteopathic adjustments until the trance counsel approved them. Edgar's sister, Annie, later reported to me that she was so uneasy about what her brother was trying to do in this public case that she couldn't even go to church that weekend.

Although the case was well publicized in Hopkinsville, it somehow did not get back to Bowling Green, where Edgar was allowed a normal existence as a popular bookstore clerk for nearly a year. Nobody at all knew of his Sunday afternoon readings for Layne, and he felt secure in getting married and moving on with his life despite his still meager bank account. The wedding was held in Hopkinsville at Gertrude's home, the Salter mansion, and performed by the minister from the Christian Church. One of his doctor friends and another roomer from his Bowling Green boardinghouse went along to support him in the ceremony. When the four returned by train that night, they were met at the station by more than a hundred cheering, rice-throwing friends from Christian Endeavor. The local paper wrote up the wedding in the society columns under the heading "PRETTY WEDDING AT HOPKINSVILLE" and described the groom as "Mr. Edgar Cayce, the popular salesman at L.D. Potter's bookstore, this city."[149] It had been six long years since the diamond sent to Rumania had started their engagement, but their respectable future in a new city seemed assured. Their newlywed home was in another boardinghouse across from the first.

Our Physicians Are Deeply Puzzled

But in a few days their situation would change suddenly. Never again would they be entirely free of public attention. Events moved so swiftly that one might sus-

---

[149]*Bowling Green Times Journal,* June 18, 1903. (This publication has been discontinued and copyrights elapsed.)

pect a kind of destiny or karma had only been waiting for Gertrude's strength to be added to his before shoving him into a new round of life. On the next Sunday they ate with Edgar's old friends at Mrs. Hollins's place, and Layne was there. So was Judge Roup, who rode a circuit as a magistrate and also served as a newspaper reporter, occasionally boarding at the house. He pressed Layne as to his meetings with Edgar, remembering a news account of the Dietrich case. The truth about the readings came tumbling out, to Gertrude's horror and the utter astonishment and skepticism of Cayce's medical friends sitting around the table. They adjourned for a reading at once, and the results appeared in the Bowling Green *Times Journal* for June 22, 1903. Less than a week after his happy and hopeful marriage, he was an unwanted celebrity and once more an oddity, a doubtfully marked man:

Dr. A.C. Layne, osteopath and magnetic healer, was in the city Sunday from Hopkinsville to have Edgar Cayce, the well-known salesman at L.D. Potter and Company, diagnose a case for him.

This sounds peculiar in view of the fact that Mr. Cayce is not a physician and knows nothing in the world about medicine or surgery . . . it was done in the presence of several people at Mr. Cayce's home on State Street.

The patient is not here, but is ill in his home in Hopkinsville. Cayce went into his trance and then the doctor told him that the patient's body would appear before him, and he wanted him to thoroughly examine it from head to foot and tell him where the diseased parts were located.

In a moment more the doctor commenced at the head and asked Cayce minutely about every part of the body. He answered, telling of the location of blood clots that one lung was sloughing off and detailed other evidences of disease. It was as if the body was immediately before him, and he could see through it and discern plainly every ligament, bone and nerve in it.

Dr. Layne was thoroughly satisfied with the diagnosis, and when it was completed had Mr. Cayce diagnose several other cases of less importance, and then left for home and will base the treatment of each case on the diagnosis as given by Cayce.

Mr. Cayce does not know what he is saying while in the trance, nor when it is over has he any recollection of what he said. He does not pretend to understand it and is not a spiritualist in any sense of the word, but an active member of the Christian church.[150]

Blackburn and the other doctors were genuinely impressed and excited with what they had seen, but they warned Cayce that he and Layne had been fortunate not to hurt anyone so far. Because of Layne's inadequate training they turned in Layne to the state medical association, which promptly closed his office in Hopkinsville. However, Blackburn persuaded them not to press any charges, and the Association actually helped Layne get set up in the Southern School of Osteopathy at Franklin, Kentucky, where he could properly complete his education. He left for the school at once. Edgar rejoiced to be free at last of the whole strange business, since nobody but Layne had ever guided him in trance. He prepared to put it all behind him as just a peculiar development in his life, not unlike his sleeping on books, and picked up with relief his church work as his proper public identity, along with his place in the bookstore.

Again his voice suddenly failed him—and he was desperate. He turned to Blackburn to guide him through a trance experience of renewing the deep circulation to his throat. The obliging physician promptly enlisted the aid of his colleagues in the E.Q.B. Literary Club, and de-

---

[150]*Bowling Green Times Journal*, June 22, 1903.

veloped a plan for methodically studying Cayce's abilities and recording the results. Over the next six years Cayce was taken through more tests and experiments by competent professionals than at any subsequent period in his life. The results were consistently positive. Nearly a year later the local paper again reported on him:

Strange
Power of Mr. Cayce Again Tested by Local Physician

Some time ago we published an article regarding the peculiar power Mr. Edgar Cayce, of this city, has of going into a trance and describing the physical condition of people miles away and whom he has never seen . . .

[A] few days since a local physician tested Mr. Cayce's powers. He says that Mr. Cayce simply lay down on his operating table and relaxed himself thoroughly, and in a few minutes appeared to be in a deep sleep.

The physician then told him that he wanted him to describe a certain little boy, a patient of his, who had pneumonia, calling him by name. Mr. Cayce had never seen the boy and did not know him, and the little fellow was then on a sick bed in another part of the city.

Notwithstanding he went right on and described the boy's condition . . . The statements, the physician says, were absolutely true. He also described the condition of several other patients and went on to tell of the circulation and talked about the spleen and accurately described its functions, and during his talk showed a wonderful familiarity with physiology and anatomy, of which he knows nothing when not in trance.

The physician is at a loss to explain the matter. It is not hypnotism, for Mr. Cayce does all the work himself without suggestion from the physician, but what it is he does not know.

There seems to be no doubt whatever, that when in these trances, Mr. Cayce in some way can look through and through the human anatomy and tell what he sees as accurately as if it were all on the outside. He also suggested a remedy for some conditions he saw, told what kind of medicine to use, and when asked what should be done to remedy other conditions he would say that he "could see no label."

There is something extraordinary in Mr. Cayce's power in this respect and it should be thoroughly tested and developed by our medical and scientific people.[151]

A Nashville, Tennessee, paper sent a corresponding reporter to investigate, who filed this story:

X-Ray Not In It With This Bowling Green Man
Edgar Cayce Startles Medical Men
with His Trances

Edgar Cayce, salesman in a bookstore here, has developed a wonderful power that is greatly puzzling physicians and scientific men. He is a quiet young man of the strictest integrity of character and thoroughly reliable in every way, and would not knowingly be a part to a deception. He some time ago discovered that he could relax himself and go into a trance and while in this condition could tell what people whom he did not know were doing miles away. . . . The physicians have been using his power to help them diagnose their cases. Several evenings ago, one of the most prominent physicians here, in company with the college professors of the city, tested Cayce's powers and are surprised and mystified by the result . . .

[151]*Bowling Green Times Journal,* March 25, 1904.

Cayce remembers nothing he has said when he comes out of the trance, and it is all a perfect blank to him. He does not pretend to account for his extraordinary power, does not understand it in the least, and is not using it to make money. Further tests will be made by our physicians, who are deeply puzzled over Cayce's strange powers. Mr. Cayce formerly lived at Hopkinsville, but has been here for several years.[152]

Tests are what Edgar got. According to his memoirs, nearly every one he met while with these doctors sooner or later wanted a reading from him, whether for entertainment, scientific experiment, or real medical need. A priest wanted to know what he had in his sealed package (it was altar candles). Somebody had him predict the sex of unborn babies (correctly), and a doctor wanted a minute description of the hospital room, as well as the interior of the patient (he got it). The Psychology Club at Potter College, with Dr. Blackburn, sent the sleeping Cayce's mind to Louisiana to solve a crime committed in the home of one of the members—and gave Cayce a gold watch for his successful effort.

Somebody sought help in locating buried treasure and actually succeeded in digging up some under Cayce's trance guidance, but another inquirer was told (as the elder Cayce reported it), "This land does not belong to you and it would not be right to give you the information. This land belongs to another (here he called the name of the rightful owner), and it would be right to give him alone the location of the treasure." Edgar's later memoirs named more than a dozen Bowling Green medical doctors who used him to diagnose a variety of difficult diseases (including appendicitis, typhoid fever, and poliomyelitis) so effectively that many turned to him

---

[152]*Nashville Times*, March 29, 1904. (This publication has been discontinued and copyrights elapsed.)

repeatedly. Often he prescribed complex medications, including one that pharmacists present insisted could not be compounded—until one tried it and found not only that Cayce was correct, but that the unusual prescription had been used elsewhere for precisely the condition at hand. The absent patient in Nashville recovered and was overjoyed.

Famous visitors such as Nikola Tesla and Elbert Hubbard investigated the young man when they lectured at the local college. So did Thomas Edison (whose experiments with him Cayce later described to me). He tried to record readings on his talking machine but was blocked each time he put his speaking tube over Cayce's face, which would suddenly terminate the trance, as though an important unseen connection had been severed.

Alarmed at Cayce's growing notoriety, the official board of his church called him up for questioning about possible fraud. This action hurt him deeply, given his long church background and his active teaching of the Bible in the church school. He was grilled for hours, and told his story forthrightly, drawing on his impressive biblical knowledge to make the point that "God moves in mysterious ways, His wonders to perform." Happily, he also had a prominent defender. "A professor in the Bowling Green business university, Mr. Dickey (who was later president of the school), came to my defense—as he had obtained readings for his wife, daughter and himself, through Dr. Blackburn's experiments, and I was exonerated." Indeed, Cayce went on to become in time an officer of the church. But the event shook him in a different way than all the medical tests, because it again raised the question of his own covenant with God, based on the promises given him as a child. What did God want of him?

To Live a Normal, Useful Life

He and Gertrude prayed earnestly for guidance, and reached what seemed to them a sense of peace with God about how to handle his readings. Evidently they were not to be just an episode in his life, but part of his service of his Lord, as they had both begun to suspect many months before in the touching case of little Aime Dietrich. He would continue to give them only in his spare time and charge nothing, since the ability was a gift to him and not something he had earned. He would seek no publicity or promotion, since God's work was His, not theirs. He would refuse no reasonable request under proper medical auspices, and he and Gertrude would put up with the notoriety and embarrassment as best they could. But they would expect God to protect the recipients from harm through the readings, as well as to bring them aid as He saw best. The young couple also felt they could count on God to protect him while in his vulnerable state. Above all, it was their understanding that they were to be allowed to live a normal, useful life, rear a family, earn a living in other ways, and participate in church and community events exactly as their friends did.

A burst of creative energy seemed to come with this new covenant of promises. For a YMCA occasion, in which Cayce was a member of the entertainment committee, he invented a game called "Pit," or "Board of Trade," based on his friends' noisy boardinghouse exchanges about grain investments, which had often delighted him. The Bowling Green paper noted the results with interest:

The Pit

Copies of Game Invented by Bowling Green Man Received Here.

Copies of "The Pit" or Board of Trade, the parlor game invented by Edgar Cayce of this city have been received by the Bookstores of Bowling Green and are in big demand. The game is played with a deck of sixty-four cards and its object is to corner the market.

The people of Bowling Green have begun to play the game and it has already proven quite popular. The game is having a big run all over the United States.[153]

Other newspapers carried items about his card game, noting that it should "net him considerable money and bring him much fame," as "soon as a copyright can be secured." But as Cayce later related to me, he had sent the invention to a game company and received back as payment only complimentary copies. The loss of potential income apparently did not bother him. He had devised something in an evening which would be played by nearly every educated child or youth in the country for decades to come, and exhibited once again that rich vein of co–creating originality which was central to his faith.

In the same spirit he jumped into a new business, one which he already knew well from Hopkinsville. It became his vocation for many years to follow. A relative of Potter, the bookstore owner, joined him in buying a photographic studio. There a side room was fitted with a couch and chairs, where he could meet with his physician friends in the evenings and give needed readings. But his heart was in making the studio successful. Calling on the patterns of hard work which he had learned as a farm lad and relying on the extremism natural to him, he put in tremendous effort. Gertrude helped as a receptionist and began the painstaking tinting of prints— the only way to get color into his portraits, which soon drew praise and customers. Money came pouring into their lives for the first time, and they hired two assistants. They found a cottage for a home, and their prospects looked bright.

One New Year's Eve, while Gertrude was visiting relatives in Hopkinsville, the necessity for rest and balance

---

[153]*Bowling Green Times Journal,* date uncertain; clipping in file of the Association for Research and Enlightenment.

(which was still a central problem when I knew Cayce so many years later, and clearly was an issue in his death) tripped him up. His inner controls, whatever they were, knocked him unconscious and brought him to the edge of dying. All the doctors who tried to help him that night gave up—except Blackburn, who pulled him through. The next day a floral wreath of sympathy was actually sent to Gertrude. Their covenant had not included an understanding of proportion in their efforts, and he had now to try to add it, though he would only periodically achieve it. The self-training which his readings would later spell out as part of any deep relationship with God was beginning to be demanded of him, a tougher challenge than simply bearing stares and jibes for his ill-defined gift.

Their efforts prospered, and Gertrude told him he would soon be a father. A few months later he opened a second studio near the college and Potter went to run it. Then disaster tested their faith outrageously. Edgar had never believed in extensive insurance, although his father sold it and he had briefly done so himself. His sister later told me that he believed God was his best insurance. So he took no special precautions when he sent for a $40,000 consignment from New York of paintings, prints, and watercolors which he exhibited in his second studio. On Christmas Eve in 1906, after three and a half years of growing success in Bowling Green, "the new studio burned down, leaving him buried in debt. Later he would see this, like other fires that hit his studios, as connected with the Bainbridge lifetimes, when he felt he had despoiled others in con games. But for the present he had no choice but to work harder than ever and to wonder, when he let himself, whether his covenant with God were still intact. However, he had not asked for any special favors, only for the opportunity to live a normal life. He felt what had happened to him was not unlike the sufferings of others, and could make him more understanding of those who sought his aid, if he survived the strain.

He almost did not, for after one reading when he was exhausted, Blackburn could not bring him back to consciousness, and both he and Gertrude thought Cayce was surely dying. For a time, just before his thirtieth birthday, he slowed down (though money fears drove him, as they would all his life) enough to enjoy the birth of their new son on March 16, 1907. They named him Hugh Lynn, after two of Gertrude's relatives. It would never have occurred to them to see in him the soul described much later in life readings as the Young King who exiled Ra Ta for taking his cherished dancing girl in long ago Egypt, or as an intimate follower of Jesus in Galilee and a sponsor of Lucius in the latter's final years. But the closeness to the lad, which Gertrude felt at once, would be recalled when a life reading eventually indicated that she and Hugh Lynn had been twin souls together in Atlantis.

Potter sold his interest in the studios to Edgar and a partner, with Gertrude's Aunt Carrie (who had always believed in him) lending the young couple money. Trying to increase their earnings, Edgar took a summer course in modern photography and darkroom methods at a photographic school in McMinnville, Tennessee. The move was typical of his readiness, so often seen in his life, to take a risk, try something creative and promising—part of his faith lifestyle in which the readings themselves seemed deeply embedded. While in Tennessee he lost his voice again, and this time the president of the school helped him out with the trance. Understandably, the man wanted to secure some full-fledged readings, but they could not find a physician to be present as Edgar regularly required. No doctor in the city wanted anything to do with these irregular proceedings.

Back home, Edgar found that his other studio promptly burned. This time he was better insured, and soon back in business, but still in debt. His partner decided to get out, which threw the firm into bankruptcy—one of the darkest times in the lives of the young Cayce couple. They resolved to pay off every cent. Meantime, unpaid experiments and tests for the community's physicians continued, trying to determine the nature and limits of his abilities. The president of the McMinnville school wrote for Cayce's aid for his brother, vice-president of a railroad, who was concerned about accidents on his rail line. Cayce's readings described precisely the person responsible and then predicted ominously that if the individual were not discharged, he would be responsible for another accident "before the first of December" in which the vice-president would be killed, and it would happen "in Virginia and West Virginia." The executive decided to ignore the strange prophecy, but the fatal accident occurred through negligence of the guilty employee right on schedule and just as the train was crossing the line between the states named. Cayce and Blackburn were shaken up. Equally startling to them was a totally inexplicable development in which Blackburn fell behind in making notes during a reading for a polio patient, requested by the founder of the Osteopathic College which Layne was attending. The noted osteopath was present, as well as a dentist. When Blackburn wanted the entranced man to speak up, and not so rapidly, the dentist put his hand over the center of Cayce's body and said, "Up, up—not so fast." The body reportedly floated up to his hand, completely unsupported, staying there until the astonished man pulled back. Telling of the incident in his memoirs, Cayce reported that for several days he was almost in a state of nervous collapse, not knowing what damage might have been done to him by the thoroughly unbelievable levitation.

The damage that finally did occur from the wide-ranging medical experiments was much more obvious. A committee of experts was formed to conduct a demonstration reading before a large meeting being held in Bowling Green for local and out-of-town physicians.

The entranced Cayce presented the symptoms, the diagnosis, the causes, and the treatment for the chosen patient, even giving the temperature and pulse rate. He then waited while the committee went and checked the absent patient, returning to pronounce his findings all correct. Stunned and outraged physicians jumped up onto the stage, pushed Blackburn aside, and began to test Cayce's hypnotic state, presumably to prove fraud. One shoved a long hatpin clear through Cayce's cheeks, while another peeled back the nail of his little finger. The man in trance neither bled nor showed any pain. However, when Blackburn finally regained control and brought him back to consciousness, Cayce lost much blood and his finger hurt violently. In great anger he told the whole company off and stormed out. To add to his dismay, the finger became infected and bothered him all through the next year. When I knew him, the nail was still slightly deformed.

From Poison for a Baby to Horseraces

Why had he not been protected, as he thought he would be while giving readings? He and Gertrude finally concluded that he was authorized to help the sick and afflicted but not to try to persuade skeptics. Jesus in Galilee had refused to prove himself with signs, and Cayce would refuse too. From now on he would give readings only to those who requested it with a clear need.

But determining what was a clear need was not always simple. He had no trouble deciding to go to Hopkinsville for Gertrude's Aunt Carrie, who had been so helpful with his studio. Married to Thomas House, who was both a medical doctor and an osteopath, she was frighteningly ill and diagnosed as having a tumor. This was Edgar's first attempt to help a seriously ill relative, and he felt mouth-drying fear at the prospect. The reading insisted she had a locked bowel, not a tumor, and prescribed a fitting treatment. It also observed that she was pregnant—though Dr. House assured him that was impossible, since specialists had repeatedly established that she could not bear children. The treatment for the bowel quickly restored her health, while the delivery took place some months later, producing a baby boy, to the delight of all the relatives and most of all Carrie. When the child fell ill with convulsions some months after the birth, Edgar returned to give a reading which to his shock and that of Dr. House prescribed a lethal overdose of belladonna, followed at once by an antidote. No physician would administer it, so Carrie did it herself, secure in her confidence in Edgar's gift. The child recovered nicely, but Cayce would always remember watching this very special woman giving fatal poison to her own baby, trusting absolutely in a process he himself often still questioned.

Then there were other requests for aid more difficult to decide on. His father came to see him, pleading that the family and his younger sisters needed money, and asking for readings on the wheat market. A syndicate of investors had formed in Hopkinsville and agreed to include the squire in exchange for Edgar's trance aid. The son felt such assistance was out of keeping with his understanding of his gift and his promises to God. With great reluctance he finally agreed, insisting that he was not personally to profit. The subsequent readings gave him a headache, as so often when something went on in trance of which he did not really approve, headaches served him as an instant warning device. The wheat investors piled up profits at once, but when Edgar eventually told them a man he named would corner the market and cause a complete crash, they ignored him—and got wiped out. The incident created some lasting bitterness against the squire, whom they felt had overly promoted his son.

The elder Cayce would not be stopped, however, and began pushing his son to solve crimes, especially those with rewards. Edgar wanted no part of the money but found he could be tempted to use his readings to break cases whose solution eluded everyone else. A Canadian slaying involved two elderly sisters, one of whom was shot by a prowler whom the other one described minutely. No sign of the man could be found. The reading

shocked the authorities by claiming that in fact the surviving sister had murdered the other one in jealousy
over a suitor and had thrown the gun through the window, where it landed in a rain spout and had been carried into the mud beside the house. Police found the
gun exactly where the reading specified, but instead of
arresting the sister they wired Kentucky authorities to
hold Edgar as the murderer, convinced that only the
criminal could be so specific. Eventually, when confronted with Cayce's virtually eyewitness account of the
crime plus the motive and the gun, the sister confessed.

The elder Cayce's memoirs reported another case from
the same period, when a reading tracked down a black
man who had shot and killed the town marshal of a
small railroad town a short distance from Hopkinsville.
The reading located him working in a coal mine, but (as
so often seemed to happen in such cases) the man moved
on that very day. Further readings trailed him until he
was successfully arrested. A different, more colorful case
involved a missing female employee, suspected of having taken several thousand dollars in bonds. Her boss
filed a wanted-person report with the police, and a de-
tective pressed Cayce—who disliked getting into the matter—to locate the woman. Finally Cayce agreed on
condition of his anonymity and promptly found the
reading describing not the employee but the boss's wife,
who had run off with a lover and the money. The detail
in the reading which clinched the description (and made
me shake my head when I heard of it) was so unique
that it startled Cayce and his father: two of the woman's
toes had grown together, after a burn on her left foot.
The embarrassed husband filed a new complaint, and a
series of readings followed the runaways until they were
located in Columbus, Ohio.

Readings of this type upset Edgar, because they
seemed to leave in him a residue of violence. But once
he had begun using his ability for nonmedical purposes
that would profit someone else, as did rewards for the
criminals, it was difficult to know when to stop. His sis-

ter later told me that when she stayed with her brother
and his family in Bowling Green for a couple of weeks,
everyone seemed to want to use him for something to
their own advantage. But Edgar was still struggling to
pay off the bankruptcy debts. She urged him to look out
for himself by making his fortune with his readings in
New York, as she had long felt he should. If her sense of
his connection with New York was intuitive, it would
prove sound, because twenty years later extensive funds
would come for his work from there. Meantime he was
approached by a young friend named Joe, who also felt
he should interest New York investors in his gift. The
details that followed fascinated me with their precision,
when I heard Cayce tell the story more than once. The
young man located a Manhattan speculator, and Dr.
House conducted the reading on him. It began by describing the house and the time of day in New York (observing daylight time as Bowling Green did not), then
followed the subject step by step as he went to his office.
At 9:30 in the morning he bought a cigar that was unusual for him, and when he got to his office building
and its elevator, the reading observed, "We will have him
walk up so he will remember it." Walk up he did, whis-
tling "Annie Laurie" (I liked this touch) and finding a man
waiting for him to discuss a real estate parcel that the
reading described and stipulated would be called in sur-
rogate court that afternoon at three. The man found on
his desk three specific letters detailed in the reading: a
bill, a business letter, and a letter from his sweetheart
whose beginning the reading quoted. The telephone
rang and the reading promptly identified the caller.
When all of this was sent to New York by wire, the astonished recipient wired back that it was absolutely correct and that he was leaving for Bowling Green at once.

Experiments in Kentucky followed, with participation
by officers of the local bank, and money was put up to
send Cayce to New York, where he could give his remarkable readings and all would make a killing. But
Gertrude objected vigorously, citing their conviction of

promises made with God. How could he be sure he
would not lose his gift if he used it to make money for
himself, when he had been so strongly convinced that
he should not? So he decided against the venture.

Yet the lure remained. While he was suffering so much
with financial distress, it was impressive to see that his
gift could attract others who had money. From the perspective of the later life readings, the Bainbridge incarnations seemed to be surfacing with remarkable force
and suddenness, once he got back into the aura of gambling and speculating. Then Joe returned, offering to pay
off Cayce's last remaining bank note from the disastrous
fire if he would give him three readings on wheat. Cayce
finally consented, stipulating that Dr. Blackburn must
conduct the reading and be paid for his time. The young
man made twenty thousand dollars on wheat in three
days—more than three times what Cayce would ever
make in a year for the rest of his life. The sum would
have bought Edgar and Gertrude both a comfortable
home and a studio, at the time. Not surprisingly, Cayce
listened when Joe showed up once more, this time to
suggest readings on horse races. They went to the track
at Latonia and secured readings for three days. Most of
the outcomes predicted were exactly correct—although
results were refused them on races that the readings said
were fixed. Joe made hundreds of thousands of dollars
and lost his mental balance, having to be put into a state
mental institution for the rest of his life. Cayce was a
wreck, and found to his horror that he could no longer
give readings at all. His health failed, and he coughed
constantly with what seemed to be tuberculosis. In despair he closed his studio—out of bankruptcy but penni-
less—sent Gertrude and his son to stay with relatives at
the family home at Hopkinsville, and soon followed her.
He decided he would quit all his experimenting with his
unusual ability and try to take stock of his life.

Once Again a Sick Child

Besides, he truly thought at the time (as he later told both me and Sherwood Eddy, who wrote about it) that his unusual ability would never return. Month after month went by, in which he could not secure readings even for the most critically ill. To him it seemed gone forever, forfeited by his impatience and lack of trust in God, and mocked by what proved to be the enduring insanity of the young man who so suddenly had made so much money. He had not only failed to keep rescuing the ill, he had used his gift to create a terrible illness. Through seven long years he had lived in the college town, ending up with just as little as when he started. Now even his special means of serving God had been taken from him.

Back at his old home he rested several months, earnestly studying the Bible and praying. He realized that when he had taken up speculative readings, he had undergone a precipitous change in his whole being, developing new tastes and values, as well as taking on new associations. In later years he would see all this as expression of his Bainbridge karma, but at the time he could only wonder at what had happened to him, finding his heart crying out for a new beginning. Finally he went alone to Gadsden, Alabama, taking a job with a young photographer and staying with the man's devoutly Christian parents, who affected him deeply. In the spring he took a post with a small firm in Anniston, because he knew it would keep him out of doors much of the time. He wanted to be alone and in nature as much as he could. His duties were to take pictures of school classes, as well as other conventions and meetings in small towns.

He was thirty-three, a father, and torn open by pain. Trudging down the roads and through the woods, carrying his camera, tripod, and flash powder, as well as his suitcase and Bible, he sought his way back to his real relationship with God. What had he learned in Bowling

Green? He had made scores of friends but none who shared his spiritual perspective. Blackburn was someone he would cherish as a friend, but where were those who would work with him in the light of biblical faith? No minister or church group had taken his gift seriously. Faculty people and scientists had been fascinated with his now lost ability, but they had offered him no fellowship, no community. Bankers and business leaders thought they might use him—that was all. He needed to have people close to him and Gertrude who, like those idealists in his early Hopkinsville Bible class, were ready to set out across the world in principled service. A covenant with God meant a covenant with God's people—but which people had a place for him?

Although he was tired and despondent, he was stronger than when he had started in Bowling Green. Running his own business, the studio fires, the overwhelming debts, the public testing by doctors and experts, and even the mistakes made in toying with murders and markets had tempered him. He had learned detachment when he walked away from it all. Somewhere inside him was a quiet force that could stand off his own extremism and worry when he chose it. He might have lost his gift, but he was beginning to gain himself.

In the solitude of nature his prayer life had returned, and God felt as close again as He had long ago during the hours of quiet at his tree house in the meadow and during the year without speech in the photographic darkroom. He was ready to start again. Once again it was a sick child that finally brought forth a reading, on a Sunday afternoon in a small Alabama town, over eleven months after the capacity had completely deserted him. It was helping children, as with Aime Dietrich, which could always guide him back to his own primal covenant with what he felt was the God of Abraham, Isaac, and Jacob, made on that May night when he was a boy.

CHAPTER 13

Why Shouldn't I Dread Publicity?

Almost at once his life turned around. He was catapulted into national fame. In Hopkinsville he had met a doctor, an M.D. named Wesley Ketchum,[154] and had done some readings for him while in Bowling Green. Ketchum's initial response had not been promising, since he thought the medical counsel was preposterous, but pointed out that he and Cayce could make a lot of money offering it. He changed his mind, however, when the evidence compelled him—beginning with a reading on himself. After Edgar's gift returned, Ketchum began using him on difficult cases. Whenever Cayce came home on the weekends from the countryside to see his wife and child, he squeezed in readings for Ketchum. Then, quite unknown to Cayce, Ketchum (without naming him) delivered a report on him at a medical convention of some seven hundred doctors in the National Society of Homeopathic Physicians, meeting in Pasadena, California. Significantly, Ketchum challenged his colleagues to test his account:

> I would appreciate the advice and suggestions of my co-workers in this broad field as to the best method of putting my man in the way of helping humanity. I would be glad to have you send me the name and address of your most complex case and I will try to prove what I have endeavored to describe.[155]

---

[154]Ketchum, Wesley H., *The Discovery of Edgar Cayce*, 1964.
[155]*New York Times*, October 9, 1910. Reprinted by permission of the publisher.

A specialist in the audience invited him to deliver a paper before the upcoming meeting in Boston of the American Association of Clinical Research—a solid and respected professional association. Ketchum wrote his report with care but felt he was too busy to attend and had it read by a widely admired medical colleague, a contributor to the *Journal of the American Medical Association*. The response was immediate, beginning with this notice in the *Boston Herald*:

Strange Hypnotic Case

A remarkable case of hypnotic endeavor was described before the American Association of Clinical Research at its meeting in the rooms of the Society of Natural History. A report from Dr. W.H. Ketchum of Hopkinsville, Kentucky, stated that he is employing an illiterate young man who can go to sleep at will, and in that condition accurately diagnose a disease and prescribe the correct course of treatment, whether it be a medical or surgical case. He then uses technical language without any hesitation, but when he awakes he knows nothing about the patient and nothing about medical phraseology.[156]

Reporters quickly discovered Cayce's identity, and in a few days the staid *New York Times* ran a long article on him, with photographs, that occupied nearly a full page:

Illiterate Man Becomes a Doctor When Hypnotized
Strange Power Shown By Edgar Cayce Puzzles Physicians

The medical fraternity of the country is taking a lively interest in the strange power said to be possessed

---

[156]*Boston Herald*, September 30, 1910. Reprinted by permission of the publisher.

by Edgar Cayce of Hopkinsville, Kentucky, to diagnose difficult diseases while in a semi-conscious state, though he has not the slightest knowledge of medicine when not in this condition.

After describing the circumstances leading to Ketchum's report, the article continued:

Its presentation created a sensation, and almost before Dr. Ketchum knew that the paper had been given to the press he was deluged with letters and telegrams inquiring about the strange case.

It is well enough to add that Dr. Wesley H. Ketchum is a reputable physician of high standing and successful practice in the homeopathic school of medicine. He possesses a classical education and is by nature of a scientific turn, and is a graduate of one of the leading medical institutions of the country. He is vouched for by orthodox physicians in both Kentucky and Ohio, in both of which states he is well known. In Hopkinsville, where his home is, no physician of any school stands higher, though he is still a young man on the shady side of Dr. Osler's deadline of 40.

Dr. Ketchum wishes it understood that his presentation of the subject is purely ethical, and that he attempts no explanation of what must be classed as mysterious mental phenomena.

Dr. Ketchum is not the only physician who has had opportunity to observe the workings of Mr. Cayce's subconscious mind. For nearly ten years his strange power has been known to local physicians of all the recognized schools.

Excerpts from Ketchum's extended paper followed, with this summary of his experience so far:

After going into detail with a diagnosis and giving name, address, etiology, symptoms, diagnosis,

and treatment of a case, he is awakened ... Upon
questioning him, he knows absolutely nothing
that he said, or whose case he was talking about. I
have used him in about 100 cases, and to date
have never known any errors in diagnosis, except
in two cases where he described a child in each
case by the same name and who resided in the
same house as the one wanted. He simply described the wrong person.

The article next turned to Cayce's own account of how
his skill worked, as reported by Ketchum:

When asked to give the source of his knowledge, he
being at this time in the subconscious state, he stated:
"Edgar Cayce's mind is amenable to suggestion, the
same as all other subconscious minds, but in addition
thereto it has the power to interpret to the objective mind
of others what it acquires from the subconscious minds
of other individuals of the same kind. The subconscious
mind forgets nothing. The conscious mind receives the
impression from without and transfers all thoughts to
the subconscious, where it remains even though the conscious be destroyed." He described himself as a third
person, saying further that his subconscious mind is in
direct communication with all other subconscious
minds, and is capable of interpreting through his objective mind and imparting impressions received to other
objective minds, gathering in this way all knowledge
possessed by millions of other subconscious minds.
    In all, young Cayce has given more than 1,000 read-
ings, but has never turned his wonderful powers to his
pecuniary advantage although many people have been
restored to health by following out the course of treatment prescribed in his readings while in a state of
hypnosis.
    President James Hyslop of the American Psychic

Society has made suggestions in regard to the development of the subject's powers. Other psychologists in Europe and America are seeking information, and Dr. Ketchum's plan is to have a committee of scientists of the highest standing come to Hopkinsville and investigate in a most rigid manner and make a report as to the truth of what is claimed but not understood. That this will be done in the near future is certain. Several men in this city have attended Mr. Cayce's readings and are ready to testify to the truth of the representations made.

After recounting verbatim the text of an entire reading observed by a reporter, the article closed:

His experience does not fatigue or exhaust him. On the contrary it seems to refresh him. Sometimes he would be feeling tired and will take up a case to read, dropping off to sleep for the purpose, and when aroused will feel greatly refreshed.

The question of distance is not important, as he has given successful readings with his subject a thousand miles away.

Mr. Cayce will not disclose the names of his patients, if they may be called patients, but he says he is ready to submit any necessary facts in aiding the fullest investigation.[157]

More than Twenty Thousand Letters

Purged by the suffering during his Bowling Green stay and the subsequent lonely year of soul-searching, Edgar was ready for the sort of careful and thorough inquiry described in the article. With over a thousand readings

---

[157]*The New York Times,* October 9, 1910. Copyright 1910 by *The New York Times Company.* Reprinted by permission of the publisher.

behind him, he needed to know how his ability worked
and should best be used. But he found Ketchum an ambitious man, eager to show up his colleagues and the
whole medical profession, while still hoping to make
considerable sums of money. The doctor also felt the
sting of being a Northerner from Ohio in the conservative and sometimes parochial world of small-town Kentucky. Instead of the research effort so timely and
appropriate, Ketchum proposed a profit-making firm
made up of himself, a local hotel owner named Noe who
would put up cash, and Edgar's father, who would serve
as conductor for the readings. The project reflected not
only Ketchum's understandable desire to make a name
for himself, but the ethos of the country in 1910, when
legends of railroad barons and banking tycoons were
part of the American dream. Cayce's open vision had no
real place in such a time, and no community of inquiry
or service wanted to take him on: no hospital or clinic,
no university, no church. His own missionary spirit
found no mission field and no farsighted sponsors.

Edgar was stuck with a huge flood of mail and telegrams from incurables and curables all over the country.
Over two thousand dollars in money, checks, and money
orders had arrived at his home, and more than twenty
thousand letters. The scene, when he returned from an
Alabama trip photographing schoolchildren for the
Tressler Studios, was the same as the one near the end of
his life—signs of unending pain. With his own emotional
suffering from failures still very near, he was stirred by
compassion for the sufferers turning to him from all over
the country. His solution reflected his own growing sense
of stature, for he took his situation to prominent public
citizens across the state. He was no longer the uncertain
farm boy or the groping studio owner. Instead he was
beginning to search for patterns to put his life together
in a responsible design worthy of the calling which had
been renewed in him.

His greatest desire was for a research organization,
which would help him sort out what was valid in his gift

from what might be, as he said, "bunk." But no hospital or university showed interest. Trying to be responsible, he went to judges of Kentucky courts—state, circuit, county, and city—and asked them to be present at readings, then give him a written opinion (to be filed with a society for psychical research in New York) as to whether his readings should be considered valuable before public opinion and the law, or discarded as the work of a charlatan. Their response was strongly positive. Reluctantly, he accepted the only offer made to him, which was a business partnership his father arranged that proposed to handle data generated by his readings yet earn income for the three backers: Dr. Ketchum, Noe, and his father. Stenographers were hired as Cayce insisted, and every bit of money in the thousands of mail inquiries sent back with a careful explanation of what was offered and what was not. Transcripts were made of readings and submitted to him for study, but he simply did not know what to do with them. There were no protocols or specialists for research on seers in Hopkinsville.

The new firm was to provide him with a studio for his photographic work, and spend five hundred dollars on his equipment. That was all. He still saw himself primarily as a photographer wanting to support his family and live a normal life in the community. In exchange for the rent and equipment, he would give daily readings in a room just across the hall from where he took portraits. What was absolutely new for him was this financial dimension. Ketchum would bill patients for his own medical services that included readings (part of the reason for getting legal opinions in advance) and split the net proceeds in agreed proportions with his partners—though not with Edgar. Persons without means would receive readings free by the terms of the contract. Deciding to receive any benefits at all was a giant step for Cayce, especially after the disastrous horse race attempts. But he was determined to serve the sick who turned to him, to do it under proper medical care, and to make it a regular part of his life as a way of quietly glorifying God where he could. The side-by-side design of the second-floor walk-up studio and consulting office mirrored the split in his vocation.

Young Man with Good, Honest Eyes

His partners were not as inclined to modesty as he, and his father—ever the promoter—was delighted to have an impressive and expensively furnished office in which he would conduct the readings, even if this meant standing to conduct them beside a high table where Edgar lay. The table, suggesting a vaguely surgical setting, was raised for deliberate dramatic effect despite Edgar's objections. In a reading taken on how to proceed, they were all told that Edgar should be located at Virginia Beach, Virginia, to do his best work, but of course the partners ignored it, and Edgar had never heard of the place.

Case after case across a remarkably wide spectrum of illnesses, injuries, birth defects, and mental disabilities got presented to the entranced man on the high table. His photographic studio proved successful, as well, for he had talent that was quickly recognized, as it had been in Bowling Green, where he had won prizes for portraits submitted in competitions as far away as St. Louis, and had one award-winning work reproduced in *Ladies' Home Journal*. His later life readings traced the artist in him to a lifetime in Troy, where he had been first a sculptor. Further, he was dealing with bodies, his old preoccupation for healing and genetically perfecting as Ra Ta, in two constructive ways at once—medical care and camera studies. And significantly for his future, he was striking out in new directions with his photographic creations, fashioning portraits that revealed what he saw as the essence of each person or family grouping brought before him. That he was already moving toward the life portraits in readings to come could be argued with some reasonableness. If the return to Hopkinsville meant the return of that part of him which was Lucius from the early Church, as the renewal of his Bible teaching in the Ninth Street Christian Church might suggest, it was now accompanied by some of the battle-tested strength which could be drawn from Uhjltd the warrior king.

His partners wanted all the publicity for him they could get and welcomed a series of articles in 1911 for the *Chicago Examiner* by the respected and articulate reporter Roswell Field, who came to Hopkinsville to study him. The first piece, as so many before and after, played up the ignorant and country-bumpkin angle, despite Cayce's established brain power in his weekly church school teaching:

Psychist Diagnoses and Cures Patients Ignorant of Medicine, Turns Healer in Trance Kentuckian New Puzzle for Physicians

Admits He Can Remember Nothing That Occurs in Hypnotic Sleep Remarkable and Successful Treatments Are Sworn to in Affidavits

After explaining what Cayce did and how, Field turned to the location:

> Near the end of Main Street in Hopkinsville, at the side of a narrow flight of stairs, is the sign "Cayce Studio." At the head of the stairs are two doors, one of them leading directly into a photographic establishment, the other indicating a suite of rooms on the glass entrance of which is painted "Edgar Cayce, Jr., Psychic Diagnostician."

The partners, without consulting him, had decided on a name for his talent and had added a gratuitous Junior to distinguish him from a local uncle by the same name. Field continued with some history that began:

It was rumored that although a simple, easy-going modest young man, with very little education, he possessed marvelous psychic powers.

Like many others, he saw Cayce's simplicity and modesty as coming from lacks in his makeup, not from the disciplined commitment where they actually originated. Field went on:

His appearance was neither conspicuously encouraging nor disappointing. His photograph, which is an admirable one, bears out the impression of a tall, slender young man with good, honest eyes, sufficiently wide apart, a high forehead and just the ordinary features.

The article continued in a long dialogue with Cayce, and concluded with Cayce speaking, in a vein less pretentious than his partners':

"I don't account for it. I don't know anything about it. I simply know that they show me the copy when I get up, and it's all Greek to me."
"Have you attempted any other kind of psychic work?" "Yes, but I don't like it. I really think that if I were to trifle with this gift God would take it away from me." (They say that Cayce is extremely religious.)[158]

The series developed into several long and fair articles, concluding the last in an upbeat note:

The laymen of Hopkinsville, the old acquaintances, friends and school mates of Cayce, have only the kindest words for him. He grew up there, has been personally known to them for years and they speak

---

[158]*The Chicago Examiner*, February 18, 1911. (This publication has been discontinued and copyrights elapsed.)

enthusiastically of his nature, his character, and his
spirit. They tell the same old story—"We don't know
what to think," but they believe in the man's personal
integrity.

Meanwhile, Cayce is going along looking after his
wife and boy . . . and incidentally photographing the
beauty and chivalry of Hopkinsville.[159]

Buoyed by the favorable accounts, Edgar and his father accepted an invitation from a Chicago newspaper
to spend two weeks in that city giving readings. They
were ensconced in the bridal suite of the La Salle Hotel.
Cayce was at first asked to locate a missing girl whose
disappearance had been widely publicized, to do magic,
to bring back the spirits of the dead, and to levitate an
elephant. When he finally arranged for an appropriate
medical reading on a patient, the stenographer stormed
out, refusing to take down the preposterous material,
and the attending doctor who conceded the diagnosis
was correct refused to agree to apply any recommended
treatment or even to allow his name to be mentioned.
Father and son left the city, with Edgar bitter and disillu-
sioned, negative about publicity for most of the rest of
his days; as he wrote in his published life story: "Then
why shouldn't I dread publicity?"[160] Once more, his New
Testament perspective told him that producing signs to
impress people was not the way of Jesus, and it should
not be his. Genuine research he could handle; fanfare,
parades, and promotion he could not. God's way was a
strength found in weakness.

When a fully qualified expert came to expose him in
Hopkinsville, Cayce stood his ground. He opened up
everything he had done to inspection and answered all
questions, as well as sent the man to interview knowl-

---

[159]*Ibid.*, February 20, 1911.
[160]Cayce, Edgar, *Edgar Cayce, His Life and Work*, 1943, p. 10.

edgeable people throughout the city. The visitor, gruff
and hostile, was Dr. Hugo Münsterberg of Harvard, one
of the most respected psychologists of his time and always ready to expose mediums as charlatans. Annie
Cayce later told me that she was so frightened of this
man that she stayed home from work. He was an intimi-
dating figure to the whole family. After hearing readings
for himself, Münsterberg encouraged Cayce not to be
afraid to continue his readings, but added (wisely, as it
turned out) that he was mixed up with the wrong crowd,
since his efforts should not be oriented to making
money. Decades later Cayce's son would point out to me
that this able man had been the first of a number of
academic psychologists to investigate his father firsthand
with objective scientific care. In Cayce's subsequent long
years of service, none ever did so with the outcome of
charging fraud or triviality.

Will Anyone Ever Understand?

The judge of his readings that Edgar had to face next
was much more severe: himself. His wife presented him
with a new baby son, Milton Porter Cayce, and they were
both delighted, feeling at first no great concern that the
infant was constantly sick and crying, expecting him to
get over it. But the attending physician stunned them
with the information that the baby had developed colitis and was dying. When Edgar frantically sought a reading, he was told it was too late, and informed of the hour
when the baby would die, as it did. The young father
was overcome. Why had he not sought a reading earlier? He had served hundreds on hundreds of others in
medical need but ignored his own son.

Once more he took to long hikes out-of-doors, trying
to make peace with himself and his God. He expected to
be taken care of when he was doing what he felt God
wanted. But that arrangement did not mean he could
neglect to use his own best resources. How deeply his

failure to use his readings for this second child wounded him could be seen in dream material that would haunt him years later. Yet it also opened him afresh to the sufferings of others who lost battles with death.

Gertrude had her own struggles of guilt and dismay over the baby's dying. She could not seem to get her strength back after the birth and grew pale and listless. A cold turned into pleurisy, and then into tuberculosis. Both Cayce and she told me long afterward of the shock he experienced when Dr. Jackson, her family physician since girlhood, had called him aside and said, "If there's anything in this monkey business you've been doing with these fellows around here, you'd better try it on your wife." Gertrude was now not only ill but expected to die within the week. He wrote about his panic in his autobiographical booklet.

> Will anyone ever understand what it meant to me to know that I was taking the life of one near and dear to me in my own hands, and that the very forces and power that I had been wishy-washy in using for years must now be put to the crucial test?[161]

Still shaken over not even trying to help his infant son, he was unsure what he really thought would happen when he went into his unconscious state for this purpose. Would he be judged for all his floundering and found wanting? The reading diagnosed her carefully and accurately but prescribed drugs which the attending physicians said could not be compounded. However, when the problematic compound was given to her as directed, his wife's hemorrhages stopped, and she began a steady recovery, with the aid of an unusual remedy that would later prove helpful for other sufferers of simi-

---

[161]*Ibid.*, p. 6.

lar respiratory infections: the fumes of apple brandy in a
charred oak keg.

I Told Them I Was Through

For both of them this reading was one of the few most
significant turning points in their lives, leading directly
toward a much more serious covenant than they had yet
contemplated. Edgar's readings would one day be not
simply his part-time outreach as a serious Christian, but
his sole vocation. Gertrude's illness drew them closer to
each other, and they found shortly that they needed one
another's strength to face an unwelcome change. Edgar
began to have headaches again, always his warning that
something was going wrong in the reading process. He
could not figure out the cause, since he insisted on reviewing the transcripts of daily readings, and they
seemed in order. But his intuition told him something
was wrong, and he began to write and telephone recent
recipients of readings typed out for him. To his horror,
he learned that some had not received any such aid. He
confronted his father and the other two partners, with
consequences that gave him one of the greatest blows of
his life.

What he discovered was that they had faked some of
the transcripts in order to secure readings instead on
how to invest money, which they felt was coming in far
too slowly with the number of free readings and the
process of securing only two a day. Edgar felt betrayed
and used, especially by his own father, and promptly
ended the partnership, telling them he was through. The
others were not willing to let him go, and he had to sue
them to get released in a series of court actions that left
bitterness all around. He got no money or equipment at
all from his studio.

It was not only Münsterberg who had warned him.
As he told me later, a tall figure of darker complexion
dressed in white and wearing a white turban walked up

the stairs to his studio one day, looked him earnestly in the face, and said, "You are with the wrong people." The man then turned and went down the stairs. Cayce was certain he heard his footsteps, but when he recovered his composure enough to run down after him, the townspeople standing on the sidewalk nearby assured him flatly that nobody—absolutely nobody—had come by and entered or left the studio stairs. He thought the figure was Hindu, but a reading taken much later would explain that it was Persian. The startling visit from the stranger was not to be his last; in the decades ahead it was to recur at crucial times.

The Happiest Period of My Life

Calling on the capacity for detachment and swift turning which had been aroused in him when he departed from Bowling Green, he simply walked away from the whole debacle in June 1911, bitter but determined on a completely new life. He took a job in Montgomery, Alabama, working for the Tressler Studios, his employer when Ketchum had made him famous. Without money, he had to leave Gertrude and Hugh Lynn behind with relatives. Two years had gone by with the partners in his hometown, during which he had been both financially secure and nationally famous, though he had been sharply tried by the needs of his dying baby and his gravely ill wife. Once more he was right back where he started. This time the gift had not been taken from him. But now he himself wanted to give it up.

He was sick at heart over his inability to find trustworthy associates who shared his faith perspective. Indeed, he prayed to be released not only from whatever he had done wrong in his covenant with God, but even from the covenant itself if God saw fit. He had been through enough, and he wanted only to be a good photographer, husband, father, and church member in a place where nobody knew of his peculiar past endowment.

Tressler soon sent him to Selma, Alabama, where they wanted to open a studio and have him manage it, on shares of the profits. In addition, he was offered a part-time job at the local hospital, reading and interpreting X-rays, at which he had always been excellent (physicians were still bringing them to him when I knew him). As a photographer he also was to take the X-rays. He soon discovered that his uncanny abilities had not left him, for he could not secure a proper plate. Double femurs appeared, multiple hearts and spines, twisted organs. Some kind of energy seemed to go from him directly onto the plates, producing the strange results. He never figured out what it was, for he promptly lost the job and had to rely on the studio for income.

Customers were few at first, and he turned to the kind of quiet attunement which seemed essential to his peace of mind throughout his life, taking up his Bible reading, prayer periods, and church work. As he reported of the time, there was little business, and he knew few local people, so he could review his whole life in a prayerful, meditative spirit. For the next eight years his gift went relatively unexploited though not totally ignored, and there were almost no newspaper stories, local or national. It seemed to him that his prayers to live a normal existence were at last being answered. Indeed the time in Selma was to prove (as he later told me) "the happiest sustained period of my life." He functioned as a constructive leader, organizer, and teacher in the city's activities in a fashion which might be expected from Uhjltd, which might be seen as the central karmic inheritance of this period in his lifespan.

Edgar made out well as a photographer, and he was soon able to send for Gertrude and Hugh Lynn. He then bought out the studio where he had begun work and set up business for himself in a roomy three-story building under the name *Cayce Art Company*. By now he knew a great deal more about running a business than he had when he had started in photography back when his voice first disappeared. His wife did the delicate retouching of negatives and the laborious tinting of prints, always a natural talent for her. They made money, and he devised amusing and highly creative promotional schemes such as installing a large clock in front of the studio with the names of local citizens posted where numerals should be. Interest was often keen when the clock began to slow, because citizens at whose name the clock stopped when it ran down would receive free portraits. Technical processes of photography interested him, and he put his ever inventive mind to work on new types of lenses, new developing solutions, and even a process which once successfully produced colored photographs—unique for his time. Turning again to art concepts in his photography, he designed costumes and sets for his biblical subjects and undertook nude studies, as well—a bold step for a Selma churchman. Both kinds of creations won him prizes at exhibitions throughout the South.[162]

His work in the Christian Church was a constant joy and, except for the office he held in a fraternal organization (as treasurer for Woodmen of the World), occupied much of his spare time. He regularly taught Sunday school. His class, the Sevens, produced a church newspaper, the *Sevenette*, full of personal items and timely reports that were eagerly read by hundreds from many churches of the town whenever it came out. It proclaimed (as local citizens told me years later), "Our greatest aim is to show man his true relationship to God. In so doing, we claim that character will be builded, morality improved, and vice subdued." To facilitate discussion he invented a horseshoe-shaped table for church school classes, which was widely copied. In March 1912 he became a deacon. The Junior Christian Endeavor (young experts on the Bible) from his church, whom he taught, became state champions.

---

[162]See the portraits in Leary, David M., *Edgar Cayce's Photographic Legacy*, 1978.

His enthusiasm, organizing skill, and ability at impromptu speeches soon won him a prominent state office in Christian Endeavor work. He felt much at home in it because of the emphasis upon unity among denominations, long a concern of the Christian Church "Brotherhood." According to his church associates of that period, he was much in demand as a speaker at dinners and conventions—someone earnest and likable who had a knack for making the personalities and teachings of the Bible seem as real as his photographs. Recruiting medical missionaries for foreign service again became his passion, and during the time he led Christian Endeavor work in the state, more such missionaries went out than ever before or since for that region. He told me later that he could count eighty such recruits from his lifetime of church work. Many of them wrote to him for years and in time turned to him for medical counsel on difficult cases of obscure diseases in Africa, China, India, Tibet, or Latin America.

His religious thought matured, as seen in the reports of associates from that period whom I interviewed. Original sin was real for him but not as a result of ultimate dualism, for the Oneness of God was a central conviction. He spoke of God as Father and did not dwell much on the divine within, yet always thought gifts and wonders were real and natural—because he knew he could do them. Jesus was to be personally known, not just talked about. His resurrection and crucifixion were never in question. Adult baptism by immersion was for him the biblical mode of signifying one's full trust in the risen Lord. Partaking of the Lord's Table each Sunday was deeply meaningful, nurturing him for the week to come. For him survival of death was completely real, but he did not emphasize it in his teaching nor lean at all toward fostering Spiritualist contacts with the dead. His concern for missions was commitment to service, not saving others from damnation. In his view, other religions probably held real merit, although he saw them all as subject to guidance and transformation by the Christ.

He did not press for special healing prayers or services in church, yet he taught his classes and associates
to always pray heartily for those in distress. He himself
found it natural to pray for those recently dead because
he felt he could see their need. Despite his remarkable
history, he did not promote psychic awareness or talent
in the church setting or anywhere else. Instead he preferred to speak of guidance and the Spirit. His approach
to faith was mystical in the sense of embodying the intimate closeness of the divine, yet both he and Gertrude
called upon the rational mode of doctrinal analysis
which his Campbellite tradition accepted from Locke.
Although his thought usually ran down traditional road-
ways, friends drew him (for the first time) to an interest
in astrology late in his Selma years.

Busy as he was, he found time to play with his son,
Hugh Lynn, who recalled for me that he loved the romp-
ing but disliked the way his father could read his mind
whenever he got into trouble, as he did in later years
when Hugh Lynn first smoked, drank, played hooky, and
skipped his chores. Edgar was delighted with the birth of
another son, named Edgar Evans, partly after him. This
was a soul, according to the family's account to me from
later life readings, who had been involved in advanced
Atlantean technology. As he grew up, his careful and
sharp engineering mind would prove to be a needed
balance in the family circle. In Selma the new youngster
joined a crowd of children who seemed always underfoot at the studio. On Sundays Edgar took the family for
long walks, and as the boys grew older he often took
them to cliffhanger serial movies on Saturday mornings.
In later years he arranged hay rides, box socials, parties,
and auctions for them. Gertrude and he enjoyed entertaining friends and offered the spacious studio rooms
for church parties. He played croquet well and bowled
often.

Members of the family later told me that he once tried
a Ouija board before a roomful of people and got a
variety of messages, including one striking tip which

located the body of a drowned girl for her bereaved parents. By the time I knew him, Edgar would have nothing to do with such a device or any other dissociative method, nor would he discuss stories told me by his family about mysterious rappings at the studio in Selma. He considered his ability in self-induced trance to be sufficient mystery for one lifetime.

Readings without Promotion or Pay

On some Sundays he began quietly to give readings for friends and relatives from Hopkinsville who pleaded with him for aid. Gertrude's brother, who worked in nearby Anniston, came over to conduct them. His first reading for a Selma native was for a crippled girl. As always, it was the young he could not resist. A friend (who was a freight agent for the Southern Railway and much interested in hypnotism) conducted the reading, while a physician, Dr. Gay, took notes and agreed to treat the girl as prescribed. Within a year she had fully recovered. The doctor was cautious but in time sought a reading for his own father. He received a prescription which alleviated the elderly man's cancer of the head. Many years later Cayce would report Dr. Gay as one of those who came to see him in a nighttime visit, after discovering he had just died. The good doctor also seemingly broke into a reading with friendly counsel from the next plane.

The freight agent conducted a number of readings and decided on his own to help Cayce with publicity by taking a reading that Edgar thought was for someone else. He used it to prepare a movie scenario entitled "Through the Subliminal" for a production to star a fetching young actress named Violet Mersereau and promoted by Carl Laemmle in New York. The producer called a press conference to announce the psychic script, and the Manhattan papers gave it appropriate publicity. Cayce was outraged, feeling once again he had been betrayed while unconscious, as he had been by Ketchum and his father. He feared there would be publicity of the sort that had burned him in Chicago. Fortunately, no public word of the movie plan got to Selma, but he never let the man conduct another session.

Inevitably more readings followed, but Cayce would not allow any public report. He still did them only irregularly in his photographic studio at night or on weekends, seeing the process as part of his Christian service, like his visits to the local jail. They were in his covenant with God, but only as a resource for emergencies, not as a vocation. He took no pay. Readings led Dr. Gay to admit that he was twice wrong about appendicitis in the Cayce family. Once he stipulated that Gertrude should have surgery, but the reading said not, and again, when he concluded that Cayce's own cramps and nausea were not serious, a reading insisted—quite correctly—upon an immediate appendectomy. The young couple were learning to rely on "the information" for themselves as readily as for others, mindful of the episode of their lost child.

Their commitment was given a painful test when young Hugh Lynn heaped up some of his father's flash powder and ignited it. The explosion badly burned his eyes, and he lost his sight. Shortly, consulting physicians insisted that they must remove one infected eye if there were to be any hope for the other. The boy himself asked for a reading, at which thirty people from the Christian Church were present, joining in the Lord's Prayer. The amazed physicians reluctantly agreed to the treatment of applying tannic acid dressings for fifteen days, insisting that the acid itself would ruin his eyes. It was a long and frightening fifteen days for the parents, but when the dressings came off, the lad was completely healed and without scars. The reading was one of a handful of the most significant in their lives, as Edgar and Gertrude both told me later, not only because of the incredible help it yielded but because it enabled them to see the peculiar readings exactly as other pleading parents saw them. From the time of this deeply personal assurance of

God's loving care present in their lives, the elements of a
new covenant began to form in their hearts and prayers,
finding expression only when Edgar left Selma on a different sort of pilgrimage than they yet guessed.

In the meantime, readings continued. A Sunday
school teacher got a series of readings that led to the
recovery of his mentally ill sister. In a pneumonia case
the sleeping Cayce horrified his listeners by stating in
passing that the attending physician would be dead in
six months and six days—which proved exactly correct.
Less threatening but just as puzzling was the reading
given in response to a letter from a member of the Italian nobility. Since the letter was written in Italian, a local
fruit vendor was called in to translate it. The counsel was
given entirely in Italian, which the frantic stenographer
did her best to set down phonetically. The next day they
asked for and got the same reading in English, which the
fruit vendor indicated was a very good translation of the
first material. The family was astounded at the entire incident, because Cayce neither knew the language nor
had ever heard it continuously spoken. They were somewhat less surprised when a reading for a Cuban began
in excellent Spanish, and soon stopped the sleeping man
to redirect him to English.

Edgar gave his first astrological reading in 1919, not
too many months after the war ended. A newspaper editor in Cleburne, Texas, had corresponded with him and
asked for his birth date and time. He followed up by
getting twenty-one different astrologers to cast Cayce's
horoscope. They did their work from points as distant as
India, Europe, South Africa, and Singapore. Cayce was
impressed by their character analysis of him. When he
found they agreed on a date in 1919 as a remarkably
auspicious time for him to secure a reading that could
have far-reaching consequences, he decided to try it and
prepared a list of questions about himself and his trance
counsel. Among them was a question about the general
validity of astrological influences. He was shocked to find
the "information" asserting their reality—never greater

than the free will—and their value in charting vocational directions and character analysis. What was then offered about himself from just such an astrological perspective seemed all too fitting and not wholly flattering. He laid aside the possibility of such readings for others, however. Four years later, when the subject of such influences would come up in readings at Dayton, Ohio, he found it a useful bridge into the concept of other hidden influences from past lives—not too outrageous in the light of his first Selma experiment in vocational counselor "life reading."

Called to Washington

Cayce's memoirs of the time spoke cryptically of a highly unusual development as World War I drew to an end, and I puzzled over the entry as I read it. He reported that he was called to Washington not once but twice, to give readings for "one high in authority." The family, sworn to secrecy, refused to discuss these incidents with me, but Cayce's lifelong friend, David Kahn, insisted that the requests came from President and Mrs. Wilson, the place was the White House, and the subject was the peace program which became the Fourteen Points. The contact was someone Kahn knew well, a cousin of Wilson's whom Cayce had met in Atlanta. Cayce was not the only psychic whom Edith Wilson brought to the White House (as presidential historians have noted). Noteworthy was the deep respect for Wilson in readings given later. There the trance counsel insisted that in essence the Christ had sat at the peace table in Versailles through the spirit shown by Wilson. It also admonished that the United States should have joined the League of Nations—and made it work.

A Whole World at War

The way had been prepared for such unusual read-

ings by a new development in Cayce's counsel. A reading had mentioned that war would be declared, and
when it was, the boys in Edgar's Sunday school class
asked him to try to get information on the conflict. He
was hesitant but finally agreed to try, on a Sunday afternoon in his studio, with the boys there and the reading
recorded on a revolving cylinder Dictaphone, modeled
on the instrument Edison had tried to use on him years
before. A whole series of what were filed later as "world-
affairs readings" followed, detailing the breaking up of
the Western Front, how the war would end, the fall of
the Russian government, and the rejection of religion in
Russia with the Revolution, adding that out of Russia
would come a religious development to have worldwide
influence for the good of mankind. Shocked listeners
asked in a later reading if this meant Communism and
were told crisply that Communism was not a religion.
On the nearer targets the new type of readings proved
consistently correct, but there was no way to test such
long-range prediction. Besides, the "information" insisted
that free will could always shape the future in fresh directions.

Selma boys grew up and went to war like others their
age. These lads took with them stories of Cayce, and soon
he was receiving requests for medical aid from all over
the country and across the world—India, Turkey, England, and places he couldn't even pronounce. In one
day's mail (he noted in his later memoirs) he found these
letters: five from Texas, one from Arkansas, two from
Oklahoma, two from Missouri, one from Chicago, three
from Ohio, one from Kentucky, three from New York,
one apiece from New Jersey, Maryland, Virginia, and
North Carolina, and six from Georgia. Among those who
often turned to him for readings were a top steel executive, a U.S. senator, a leading automobile manufacturer,
and the heads of a dozen other industries. None of these
requests came from newspaper or magazine publicity,
but only from word of mouth, a pattern he trusted because it was the way of the Gospels and Acts.

Hundreds of letters poured in to get his help on locating soldiers and sailors missing in action, just as I saw in a later war. Readings advised against it, describing such counsel as "like sharpening a pencil with a razor," damaging the razor. Further, Cayce was told that there were "many things which might be done that would be better left undone"; he should concentrate on the living and not be vulnerable in trance to someone's longing for connections with the dead. Shell-shocked veterans were something else, and readings indicated that much could be done for them if the right kind of facility were available for the complex treatments needed. Gertrude and Edgar began to wonder what their responsibility might be for securing such a medical facility, and again the elements of a new covenant stirred within them.

The terrible suffering of the war affected them greatly, just as I saw in the midst of a later worldwide conflict. Instead of shielding them from their times in a cocoon of wonders, the readings drew them closer to their fellows, prodded their prayers, and called on them for bolder action, just as their biblical faith did, in which prophets cried out against unholy alliances and the suffering of the downtrodden. In the psychological age that would follow long after Cayce's death, his efforts would often be misread as guides to private spirituality and soul development, far from the pain for a war-shattered world which he knew in Selma and again in Virginia Beach.

He reflected later on his questioning on what he should do in a period of widespread tragedy: "I had not yet claimed anything for myself (and still don't)." Readings advised him cryptically, he reported to me, "Use that in hand. Start where you are. You will go the rounds again." They added that a medical institution should be built on his work.

How deeply he felt about those killed in battle was evident in a dream that came when he lost his voice again. He had been overtired, and while in trance a local hypnotist had tried to make the old instructions work—

and failed. Gertrude tried guiding him herself, at first without success. But then he awoke and told a dream in a clear voice. He had seen all the graveyards of the world in one staggering but beautiful vision. First he had been drawn to India, where a voice said, "Here you will know a man's religion by the manner in which his body has been disposed of." Coming to the graves in Flanders fields of Europe, where the war dead had been buried, he saw three boys from his Sunday school class who told him how they had been killed, showed him their graves, and sent messages to friends and relatives in Selma. When he asked whether he might see his dead son, Milton, his vision showed him tiers of babies, and in the third tier from the top was Milton, who recognized him and smiled. Back at the graveyards of home, an old flower lady gave him a message of encouragement and asked him to do a favor for her surviving daughter. Then he talked of church life with a friend who before his death had been an official in the local Christian Church. He wakened with a strange aftereffect that was still with him when I knew him. Whenever he came to a cemetery on his travels around the country, he could name and often describe those buried there, once given some inscriptions from tombstones anywhere in the cemetery to start him. He had no idea why it worked and why no reading was required, but he took the experience as a strengthening of solidarity with those who suffered and died needlessly, in what his faith called "the communion of saints."

What New Covenant?

Then it was 1920. The war period was behind him, and he felt himself ready for a fresh challenge of service. The fact that something important was beginning was signaled when he gave eight extra readings at one session which had not yet been requested but whose pleas turned out to be in the mail. He was forty-three years old, and currents deep within were stirring. For eight long years Selma had been good to him. His family had been profoundly nurtured. His trance abilities had improved. His sense of inner authority had taken him to the nation's high places without his yielding to a longing for public attention. Best of all, for the first time in his life he had an authorizing community of people of faith like his own. Though his local Christian Church took no official role in his readings, he found himself loved, trusted, and encouraged by one after another of its leaders. Respected graduates of his classes were all throughout the congregation. He had been repeatedly asked by people from this church not only for his medical counsel but for his larger counsel on public life. Now he was ready to risk for his Lord in new directions. But what directions? Would photography still be his livelihood? And who would help them? He and Gertrude still had nobody close to work with them, and memories of his Hopkinsville partners still echoed somberly in their minds.

As so often when they were ready, and as his readings had suggested in the recent counsel, they found the answer already being prepared: "Use that in hand."

CHAPTER 14

Untouched Oil Pools in Texas

Five years earlier Cayce had gone to the university city of Lexington, Kentucky, to give a reading for a wheelchair cripple, a woman named Mrs. DeLaney, who suffered from severe arthritis. The conductor, reading instructions to the entranced Cayce from a little black notebook, was the teenage son of Mrs. DeLaney's neighbors—the Solomon Kahns. Afterward Edgar stayed on to give readings for the Kahn family and found himself especially drawn to the son, David, as well as to the mother, Fannie. He answered their many questions as best he could and found that as Reform Jews they at once saw his ability as a gift from God. David was in the process of deciding on his future and saw no reason why Cayce should not give him vocational counsel. If the readings could deal with sick bodies and troubled nations, they could surely deal with the son of a Kentucky grocer.

Cayce was uncertain at first but remembered the astrological reading he had taken on himself. So together they made up a suggestion for what they called a "vocational, mental, and spiritual reading," with a list of questions, and attempted the reading. It was a dramatic success. After describing the young man's character and talents, as well as principles for his conduct, it turned to his future and indicated he would leave his family and go into uniform, eventually taking up a line of work that none of them expected. Since this was before the war, David thought the reference was to police or firemen's uniforms and most unlikely, but the rest of the reading was convincing. It also informed him that he would have much to do with Cayce's work. Edgar remembered that he had been told in Hopkinsville, when struggling with Ketchum and Noe, that his efforts would find their greatest success when he worked with a Jew. Years later the explanation would be given that God still kept His covenants with the Jews and offered each new spiritual work or promise first to them.

Back in Hopkinsville, he kept in touch with David, who went to the University of Kentucky and planned on a law career but was interrupted by the predicted military service. Again and again Edgar secured vocational and decisonal readings for David, often wiring or telephoning the findings, and following him through a successful military career that made him an officer. Some of the counsel gave him information about troop movements and command decisions which David used well but could not explain to his superiors. When he was discharged from the Army, he came to Selma, smartly dressed in his captain's uniform. His brother Leon had just died because no physician could be found to administer the treatments Cayce described. David was determined to help Edgar establish a hospital, a subject which had already come up often in their talks together. And he had the plan to do it. They would go to Texas and make money by locating oil.

Cayce was hesitant, remembering his unpleasant experience with his father's syndicate on wheat markets. But Kahn contrasted securing oil from new, untouched pools with simply gambling in speculative futures. A reading confirmed that money could be secured for a hospital in this fashion but warned that all involved must be in accord as to that purpose. Edgar was elated, remembering that Layne had once located a successful coal mine at Nortonville, Kentucky, by using a reading taken without his permission. He had only learned of it from the new owner, Frank Mohr, who came to Hopkinsville to get readings for his niece and then proposed buying out Ketchum and Noe to move Cayce to Nortonville and build a hospital there. Mohr was so sure he could finance the project that he had the basement for the hospital dug and half the foundation laid, although the partners who held the contract for Cayce still resisted the sale. Then Mohr was severely injured in a mine accident, and when he could find nobody in Nortonville to treat him as the readings advised, he went to his earlier home in Ohio, and his fortune eroded. For a short time Cayce had been ecstatic with hope.

Great Million-Dollar Institution

The first attempt at oil, done by telegram for a Texas friend of Kahn's, located through the Cleburne editor who had secured Cayce's horoscopes, was incredibly successful. It described exactly what the drill would encounter at successive levels, when to use liquid nitro, and resulted in six hundred barrels a day for the owner, though no income for Cayce or Kahn. Sure that they now had a plan that could not fail, they lined up potential investors among Cayce's relatives and Kahn's friends, and organized the Cayce Petroleum Company.

Cayce had for years felt a growing desire, which he often discussed with interested friends such as Mohr, to be associated with a hospital where all the treatments described in his readings could be conducted in one place—surgery, osteopathy, medication, rubs, baths, exercises, packs, irrigations, diets, massages, and more, including intercessory prayer. Too many people like young Leon Kahn had died since his first reading for Layne nearly twenty years ago, because they could not find a cooperative physician. Others had suffered needlessly, in the report of his readings, because of the lack of precise care that was stipulated. He knew how desperate he would have been had they not found physicians willing to use the counsel from his readings for Gertrude's tuberculosis and his son's eyes. Building a hospital was something active he could do for his Lord, beyond just lying down and becoming unconscious. Here at last was a way to turn his strange avocation into a vocation.

Seen from the perspective of his past lives, still unknown to him, he could be described as claiming the full promise of Uhjltd, the healer and teacher who built an entire city of healing in the Persian hills and plains. But he could also be seen as entering for the first time into the larger inheritance of Ra Ta, one of whose reported gifts had been locating ores for mines, and one of whose major achievements had been reported as creating the hospital-like Temple of Sacrifice, as well as the university-like Temple Beautiful. If these were his emerging patterns, it would remain to be seen whether the stable and royal Uhjltd would anchor the inspired but impulsive and sensual high priest within him. And since he was leaving home for an unknown daring adventure, he could well stumble over the Bainbridge karma that had flared in the rowdy episodes of his youth and returned in Bowling Green when he was drawn to the New York speculator and the horse race gambler. Crucial for the outcome might be his ability to continue tapping, without Gertrude beside him each day, the deep spiritual springs of the Lucius incarnation, which had flowed so freely in his church life, his teaching, and his generous readings at Selma, as they had long before in his farm boyhood.

Whatever the karma, the motivation upon which it would now be spread was like that of the medical missionaries he had so long recruited: seeking to build resources where they were sorely needed. His hospital would be modeled on the hospitals, orphanages, and schools they founded overseas. If the years since he started at Bowling Green had been built upon the desires of his heart, focused on the nurture of his family within its supportive community and church life, then what was at hand now was noble ambition, a worthy cause. All that had long ago stirred him to be a minister or a missionary came back now, not as a boyish dream but as an adult challenge, in which he could engage his full strength and experience, toughened by many fail-

ures and disappointments. He could even grin about the
loss of his voice, his studio fires, the yearlong disappearance of his gift, the bitter newspaper exploitation in Chicago, and the quarrels with his father and Ketchum, if
they had prepared him at last for his new and difficult
task. He would not be split between a photography business and the business of his readings. He would be one
man.

His covenant with God up to this point had been to
serve with his gift and bear its embarrassment and awkwardness, but only part-time. Now he felt God would
enable him to serve full-time, drawing his support from
efforts based on his readings. More important, he would
provide leadership. He would ask God to protect him
and those who got readings, as always, and to care for
his family. But now he would ask for helpers worthy of
the effort in front of him, starting with the ever optimistic yet canny Dave Kahn, who seemed effortlessly to
make friends in high places of finance and government.
Cayce, the willing servant, always stepping into the background to allow something unseen and unknown to be
done through him, was gone. Cayce, the leader of men
had arrived—he hoped ready to be guided wherever God
wanted him sent, even to the hard fields of Texas that
covered black gold, and on to a place of clean white uniforms and compassionate care of the "afflicted"—as they
had been described in his childhood promise.

His new boldness, as well as the ebullience of Kahn,
was reflected in a news item in the Selma paper for September 14, 1920, eight years after he had arrived in the
city. He no longer resisted the publicity which Kahn felt
was essential to secure investors, even though it exaggerated the interests of friends into actual offers of hospital sites. For the first time in public, he also spoke of
training others to serve as he did, though he did not
mention a project the size of a university.

Cayce Leaves to Promote Hospital
Great Million-Dollar Institution to
Be Built by Selmian And His Partner—
Will Develop Psychic Diagnosis
of Baffling Cases

Edgar Cayce on the eve of his departure for Nashville and New York this afternoon, spoke with confidence of the work which lies before him, in raising large funds with which he and his associate, David E. Kahn of Cleburne, Texas, and Lexington, Ky., propose to build a great hospital or sanitarium where the invalids of the nation, rich or poor, whose cases have baffled science, may receive treatment.

In this humanitarian work Mr. Cayce will associate himself with a corps of able surgeons and physicians, who have complete charge of administering the hospital; his work is to consist exclusively of diagnosing the troubles of those who have sought long and hopelessly for relief.

Record of Cases

Substantiating the claims of Mr. Cayce, as a discoverer of elusive and undreamed of ailments, whose treatment alone is necessary to cure seemingly hopeless cases, are records and affidavits from many reputable men and women, who testify to the benefits received, when physicians followed Mr. Cayce's diagnosis.

Many cities have already offered hospital sites, among them Tulsa, Jefferson City, Shelby Springs, Pensacola, Nashville and Memphis, besides several small towns in Alabama.

Selma is not offering for the hospital, and if such offers were made there would be no chance of securing it, stated Mr. Cayce, as Memphis and other cities have made such flattering offers that it is probable a much larger city will be selected.

Float Cayce Oil Co.

As means to financing the hospital project Mr. Cayce and Mr. Kahn intend to exploit large and untouched oil pools in Texas, through the Cayce Petroleum Company, organized in August under the laws of Texas with a $2,000,000 capital. Mr. Cayce is president and Mr. Kahn secretary and among the Board of Directors are three bankers and a leading physician of the southwest.

The development of psychical diagnosis which is considered a unique gift of Mr. Cayce's but which he declares is a power within the reach of many others who follow certain training, is a dream of Mr. Cayce in connection with the organization of the great hospital. Another phase of Mr. Cayce's work, which he intends to stress, is the treatment of shell-shocked and maimed soldiers, in which he has been highly successful recently.[163]

Edgar clearly had in mind at this point an institution like that which was actually developing on the Minnesota plains as the Mayo Clinic—to which he would be referring patients when I knew him much later. However worthy the ideal, some of his native extremism was showing in his Selma departure, to a degree that might appear hubris in any but a high priest. Significantly, this was his first major move that was not born in part from his own suffering, hours of penitent prayer, and earnest Bible study. Ever affected by his times because of both his intuitive nature and his outgoing biblical faith grounded in the prophets of Israel, he was expressing the expansive spirit that would later develop into the

---

[163]*Selma Star,* September 14, 1920. (This publication has been discontinued and copyrights elapsed.)

Roaring Twenties, infecting all who would associate with him in his exciting new enterprise.

Leases, Boots, and Guns

He recruited his father to come to Selma and run his business; Leslie was having trouble with alcohol and came without his wife. Edgar also hired a photographer to take the portraits. Then he and Kahn took off. Their new base was in Comyn, Texas, where readings indicated an underground oil deposit that would be the largest in North America. Oil men and investors flocked to them from Dallas, Fort Worth, and other Texas areas, hearing of Cayce's amazing readings and sure that he could not fail. He and Kahn bought up all the leases they could afford in the area and began the expensive drilling. Others competed for the promising leases and drove the prices up. Edgar wore boots laced knee-high and a big Texas cowboy hat, drove an open touring car, and lived the tough life of the oil fields right beside the operators and riggers—ate their food, matched their stories, laughed with their bawdy humor, and gave readings even lying on the bare ground where oil was suspected below him. The life he and Kahn shared was often necessarily coarse, dirty, and dubious. It had none of the Sunday school serenity and family rounds of the peaceful days in Selma. Whatever could be described as John Bainbridge in him had arrived to stay.

There were interminable, expensive delays in the drilling. Three initial wells brought only partial success, and others produced water, which happened to be sorely needed for the current drought. On their major well the readings kept describing what they would find at each stage, and the results were sufficiently accurate to keep them going, yet seemed to shade off into vagueness at crucial points. Local backers proved to be far less interested in a hospital than Cayce hoped and far more caught up in the financial prospects. They promised to buy him whatever he wanted, but first they had to hit the big oil strike.

As months dragged by, quarrels and suspicions developed. Cayce and Kahn lived in metal-roofed sheds on the property of two brothers, rough men who worked at the well and had an interest in the enterprise. The brothers began to suspect Kahn of delaying the well until the leases ran out, when he could then buy them all for himself. In addition, Kahn had proven a dashing figure who constantly drew feminine admirers, and one of the brothers suspected his wife of responding to him. A showdown came which Cayce managed to convince them to arbitrate by a reading. In a dramatic scene in a shack one night, the principals laid their guns on the table, determined to shoot Kahn if he proved guilty. Both Cayce and Kahn were so nervous that they could not get Edgar to the requisite depth for a reading, and postponed the event to the following night, when tempers had built up even higher. Murder was in the air. The reading exonerated Kahn and pointed to sabotage by unnamed others but warned that the project would not succeed in any case unless all were of one mind and one ideal, consistent with the purpose which had brought Cayce to the site.

Bits of tombstone, string, and tools were found in the well when the drill repeatedly broke up; the driller turned out to be in the pay of a large oil company, though Cayce's company had him on what was then a huge salary at one thousand dollars per month. Many wanted the leases to run out so they could buy them for themselves. Cayce held onto his hope. He was offered, he told me later (perhaps with a touch of extravagance), a check for a million dollars to buy out the Cayce Petroleum Company and give readings for nobody else. But he turned down the offer quickly, sure that his readings would not fail him and that he would make a great deal more.

The First Apparent Failure of His Readings

He still had not grasped the essentially collaborative nature of his counsel, in which everyone involved had a part in the delicate attunement process. The readings seemed outwardly to be his private gift, for which the right conductor was important, as well as a worthy purpose, yet with him in sole charge. But this perception proved a costly error. He did not have Gertrude to help him in his attunement for counsel, or even his loyal if promotion-oriented father, and certainly not his mother or Gertrude's Aunt Carrie, who had backed him and focused his covenant in spiritual terms. He did make a few devoted friends, later reporting that these relationships were "as beautiful as any that have ever existed." Among them was a handsome woman of considerable bearing, one of Kahn's recruits, who was described a number of times to June and me in later years by Cayce's elder son, who knew her well. She presented him with difficult choices at a time when he was vulnerable because of the mounting defeats in oil drilling, and low in spirits. Very different from Gertrude, tipped more to the lover side of the feminine than the maternal, and more of an action person than an intellect, she fell deeply in love with him. She was willing to risk with him to steal light from the gods for mortals. Cayce was drawn to her, with feelings that he would later credit to his karma from Egypt, Laodicea, and the Bainbridge legacy so prominent in the entire oilfield venture. But he felt he had to turn away and disappoint her, even though his withdrawal helped create what he later described as "crosses" and "resentments" among his Texas companions.

Seeking investors, he traveled widely. His letters home grew fewer and fewer, and he sent no money—indeed, he often had none. Because of the huge expenses of the company, he was never paid a salary as its president, relying instead on gifts for sporadic medical readings. Gertrude and the boys moved back to Hopkinsville to live with her relatives, the only course they could afford.

It was painful to leave Selma and all their friends, and even more painful to face the questions of relatives in Gertrude's hometown. It was a time of heartbreak and confusion for the small family.

As the second year of the fruitless odyssey passed, Kahn arranged for Hugh Lynn to come visit during the summer. The boy of sixteen was charged with bringing his father home and did not succeed. But he evidently touched something deep within Edgar, who began to question the choices he was making and to confront his situation. Oil was never found, although the readings kept insisting it was there. For the first time he had to consider the frightening possibility that his readings had become flawed. Some of the geologists told him that the trance descriptions of underground formations and deposits were excellent—for a period of perhaps three hundred thousand years ago. Others such as Dr. House, who visited under Gertrude's pleading, suggested that the dubious intentions of so many drawn into the project, combined with Cayce's shifted values, might have drawn into the reading process the thoughts and energies of dead prospectors who wanted the oil to remain hidden, which they had so long sought in life. Whatever the reasons, his trance counsel had finally gone wrong, or become so unclear as to be useless. It was a tremendous shock. After more than twenty years of its unfailing reliability and clarity, since Layne had first used him as a traveling somnambulist, he had ended up not simply losing his ability this time, but having it fail him. How could he ever be sure again that it might not distort on medical counsel and cost the life of someone ill, perhaps a suffering child? The possibility tormented him, and when he let himself think about it, he suffered keenly.

Leases expired, creditors pressed, one of his companions proved to be a criminal and was apprehended, and eventually Cayce gave up, bitterly disappointed, as well as humiliated to face his investors—some of them relatives and others people who had trusted his readings for years. It did not ease his pain when he later learned that a competing company found oil in a few of the places his readings had originally described, though never the great oil pool. But he was comforted in later years when a number of the men who lost heavily in his oil company continued to turn to him for medical and business guidance for themselves and their families.

Six Months Alone in a Birmingham Hotel

Defeated in the oil enterprise, he was not ready to give up on the hospital dream. Mohr wired him from Columbus, Ohio, that he was now able to finance the hospital, and sent Cayce the money to come there. However, the reading taken in Columbus firmly stipulated that the location should be Virginia Beach, and Cayce was inclined at the time to honor his trance source on the conditions for his success. Having taken too lightly the insistence that all must be of one mind and high purpose, he was now ready to look more carefully at the requirements. But when the publisher of a Denver newspaper offered to bring him and Kahn to that city, he jumped at it. After hearing readings, the influential and wealthy man offered Cayce a thousand dollars a day—an impressive sum for the times—to give readings solely at the publisher's direction in a robe and turban, supported by such amenities as a Cadillac and chauffeur. Wherever else Cayce had proven he could be tempted, he had never wavered in keeping sole control of granting his readings, and he turned down the offer promptly. (I would hear him do it again when a cereal company proposed putting him on the air daily for readings they would direct and pay for generously.)

Word caught up with him that a women's club wanted him to lecture in Birmingham, Alabama, and he agreed to do it in exchange for telegraphed railroad tickets. Then he stayed on alone in a hotel for six long months to give readings, lecture, and consult with community leaders about his hospital plan. For the first time (and the only

time of which I could learn) he ran a newspaper advertisement about his work. The item included his picture,
his Birmingham hotel address, and the caption "PSYCHIC
AND MYSTIC," followed by "AIDS THE SICK" and a letter
from someone he had once helped with a reading.[164] He
was growing desperate to capture his hospital dream.

An item in the Birmingham paper, however, suggested
that he was turning away at last from the commercial
spirit of the past two years and more, toward the spiritual footing where he had put his trust in the past:

A Hospital of Last Resort Proposed
By Invalids Served by Edgar Cayce

For thirty [sic] years or more Edgar Cayce, healer
and mystic, has been besieged by invalids seeking a cure
for diseases that have been given up by physicians . . .
Patiently, but assiduously, this gentle, kindhearted man
is doing all he can to relieve distress locally. Constantly,
throughout the day at his headquarters at the Tutwiler
Hotel, he is being appealed to for aid. Three times daily
for a month he has appealed to that hidden sanctuary for
diagnosis and for treatment of the diseases that come
before him, and there is no record of failure. Whatever
may be the spiritual nature of the sources on which he
draws, Mr. Cayce is convinced through thousands of
cases of cures obtained through his "readings" that he is
but a humble instrument of God.

The spirit was considerably different from the trum-
peting that had accompanied his hope-filled departure
from Selma with the expansive David Kahn.

---

[164]*Birmingham News*, date uncertain; clipping in file of the Association for Research and Enlightenment. This publication discontinued and copyright elapsed. Material from *Birmingham Age Herald*
used by permission of publisher.

Through his success with local invalids, friends of Mr. Cayce have convinced him that Birmingham is the logical site for the establishment of that hospital and sanitorium for which he has planned and dreamed for more than twenty years. Citizens of Denver, Colo., of Columbus, Ohio, and other cities that have entertained the healer and have been benefited by his service have besought him to locate elsewhere. But being Southern-born and loving the South, he has decided that if Birmingham wants the hospital he will stay here. And, in explanation of that statement, it should be said here that Mr. Cayce has nothing to sell; that he has never commercialized his remarkable powers, and never proposes to do so. Himself a man of simple life, "contented with small means, seeking refinement rather than fashion," seeking above all to serve the wretched ones of earth, and desiring above all else to have a hospital where all who need his services may come, certainly there should be a sufficient number of persons here to back him financially in this beautiful venture he proposes. One thing is definitely sure: that unless his clients who have been comforted and healed and unless the public at large give that support in this emergency, some other hospital somewhere will be occupied by him.[165]

The financing looked hopeful at first, with sixty thousand dollars raised in a few days. But the rest of the needed money did not develop, and Cayce (often with his father) went to city after city, wherever anyone would pay his way to give medical readings, with any interest at all in helping him build his hospital—New York, Pittsburgh, Chicago, Kansas City, New Orleans, Memphis, St. Louis, Indianapolis, Cincinnati, Philadelphia, Florida, and elsewhere. Still separated from his family, he went back to Birmingham, not Selma, and gave readings again in a

---

[165]*Ibid.* See above.

hotel room, for which the recipients were asked to make
freewill offerings in the tradition of his church life. Now
that he was forced by circumstance to spend more time
alone, the old Lucius character and conviction appeared
to reassert itself. Another Birmingham news item reflected the perspective that had governed most of his
earlier life:

Power Credited to God
"Healer" Says His Work
Is Done Through Divine Gift

"Whatever powers in healing I may possess I at-
tribute to God working through me for the welfare of
the afflicted" declared Edgar Cayce in an informal address to the Psychology Club Tuesday night at the courthouse. "I regard the religious phase, and not the psychic,
the most important part of the work. To me the challenge continues that I must practice discrimination in
the cases I treat, and that whatever is done must be done
for His sake: that whatever feeble powers I possess must
be dedicated to him."

A substantial audience greeted the Selma mystic in
Judge Smith's courtroom at 8 o'clock and many questions were asked the speaker concerning his healing
work. Since his return to Birmingham after almost a
year's absence, Mr. Cayce has been in constant demand
for his, "readings," which are declared to be remarkable
by his friends and those who claim to have been cured
by his diagnosis and advice.[166]

He lectured extensively for the first time outside of
church circles, speaking not only to the Women's Club,
but to the Writer's Club, the Theosophical Society, Unity

---

[166]*Ibid.* See above.

Church, the Applied Psychology Society, the College Club, Businessmen's Club, and others.

Burned Clean in Personal Fires

Finally Cayce looked at his life in weary repugnance and turned home to Hopkinsville to seek his wife's forgiveness—and to forgive himself—as well as to gather together his family. They returned to Selma, after he had been away three years, to see what could be salvaged of the photographic business. He later reported of his return that it had taken great effort to bring him to it, as an expression of "normalcy" in his life. The events and relationships of the Texas venture had made him doubt his fundamental ideals and even his covenant with God. He questioned whether he was ever meant to have a hospital, or whether he had just missed the boat by not selling his company when large sums were offered. He agonized over how best to serve others with his "phenomenon" that was both his blessing and his torment. What came clear was that his life had to change totally.

Alone in his hotel room for many hours, he had taken up his Bible again and renewed his prayer times. God had been faithful in sending him helpers but had required of him much more leadership and strength than he had expected. Building a hospital had proven infinitely more difficult than putting on a series of Christian Endeavor rallies or even developing his studios. He had expected (as the newspaper articles showed) to be a spokesman for a worthy cause, to which supporters would stream. Instead he had found himself having to take on each person drawn close to him for the enterprise, and required to define and shape the nature of each day's association and labors. He had been unable to serve merely as an adviser or consultant on a beautiful dream, but forced instead to be captain of an expedition he had not thought out. Further, his readings had proven not to be a private arrangement between him and God, but surprisingly dependent on the motives of those who joined him. Whatever he tried in the future would require a solid core group united in faith and ideals, just as the missionaries he had recruited had gone to shared mission stations, not to personal adventures of evangelism.

He did not think in terms of karma at the time, but later would look back to discern how he had managed by what he saw as God's grace, despite the shame of failure, not to fall into the self-destructive patterns of Troy. His personal and public life had come apart with the collapse of the oil project, but he had not withdrawn into suicide, however tempted, or into the longing for revenge that long ago troubled the dying Uhjltd. He had not turned to the gambling, alcoholism, or cynical exploitation of others that Bainbridge knew so well. And he had discovered much about the patient love of God, including the great freedom given him to make choices on his own, though not without consequences, and the compassion that assured him of utter forgiveness of his excesses once he had halted them. He had been burned clean in personal fires he had helped to ignite, but his medical counsel proved as reliable as ever.

Gertrude and Edgar's relatives were more than half ready for him to give up his hospital dream and settle down in Selma, which had proven more their home than anywhere else they had lived. He was prepared to charge ten dollars a reading for the first time in his life, and a reading approved the decision he made. An item in the Selma paper suggested that he might consider an outcome of settling down, though he still felt that God had promised him a hospital for the best use of his readings:

Edgar Cayce, Psychic Wonder,
To Spend Summer in Selma
Patients Here Awaiting Diagnosis[167]

The story noted that he would be "spending his time between making pictures . . . and making a few of his world-famous diagnoses."

But as so often at turning points in his life, he had failed into success. Once he had gained control of himself and renewed the inner spirit of his covenant, help appeared.

---

[167]*Selma Star,* June 15, 1923.

CHAPTER 15

The Great Influential Institution

First came Gladys Davis, eighteen years old and the sister of a former member of his Seven class in the church. The spiritual community he had lacked in his travels, but now regained, served him well by providing him with a member of the nuclear core upon which he would build for the rest of his life. What he saw was a bright, attractive, and capable blonde stenographer who could take down his readings where others failed because they were rushed, confused, or frightened by the strange trance process. What he did not see (until his readings pointed out the patterns not many months later) was the soul who had been his twin in Atlantis, the neglected child of his union with Isis in Egypt, then his beloved wife in Persia, and finally his convent-driven mother in France. Miss Gladys, as the entire family addressed her in the Southern custom of the time, soon became a part of the family circle and stayed in it until his death, though not without challenges that none of them foresaw. Her faith was strong, her loyalty deep, and her capacity for details was incredible. Her companionship brought to the family not only good judgment in daily decisions but hard work. Although her usually good spirits were occasionally marred by times of depression over the woes of her family, struggling for income, and coming from the wrong side of the tracks, she had a happy capacity to laugh at herself. An introvert like Gertrude, she carried for Edgar the action-oriented, daughter-lover female pole that completed Cayce's sense of the potent feminine anima.

Kahn stayed available. He moved rapidly upward in

his career as a New York manufacturer, which would lead him to combine "wood and metal products" as readings precisely suggested, becoming the largest maker of radio cabinets in the country at a time when every living room had to feature a set on its own table or a waist-high console. He remained intensely loyal to Cayce, whom he called *Judge* because the name signified the respect he felt. Over the years he sent scores of his business colleagues to Cayce for various types of readings, just as he presented the Cayce story to major political and military figures. His conviction of the goodness in the readings never faltered, nor did his personal devotion to Cayce. A core group of those with similar purposes and values was building.

Then Arthur Lammers, a wealthy middle-aged printer from Dayton, came to Selma for trance counsel. He started with a horoscope reading not unlike the one Cayce had already secured on himself four years ago. Lammers had read widely in such arcane subjects as astrology, the kabbalah, the mystery religions, and versions of Hinduism, as well as Theosophy. Convinced that Cayce's ability was genuine and far-reaching in its potential, he sought readings on the nature of human existence rather than on medical problems or personal needs. It did not surprise him that he got full answers, but the new dimensions of his gift thoroughly shook up Cayce, though they also interested him. When Lammers offered to pay all his family's expenses and secure numerous readings if Cayce would come to Dayton, Edgar was ready almost at once, despite the fresh beginnings they were making in Selma. Within a few months he sent from Dayton for his family, leaving Hugh Lynn to finish out his school year. He saw in Lammers only an affluent businessman with a highly speculative nature and an impressive presence, not his old warrior associate of the Trojan wars, Hector, as the readings would soon indicate.

Cayce insisted that Gertrude sell his photography business at once, although the sale gained them very

little and disheartened Gertrude, who had labored with
him to buy each piece of equipment. But he was impa-
tient to move on, and the sense of his renewed covenant
with God to provide leadership and to build a hospital
was strong in him. Now he would promise God to implement that covenant in a new way, by trusting the direct
income from readings to provide the sole support for his
family. No big company with heavy investors was required. He would simply put down his cameras and developing trays, and place his whole trust in going
unconscious each day. Those who sought readings still
mostly gave him only the offerings they chose, from next
to nothing all the way to twenty-five dollars—which he
finally settled on in Dayton as the recommended gift.
But the freewill offering kind of income had been sufficient for the ministers of his youth and often for missionaries in far lands. He was ready to trust it when
seekers could not afford the full fee. So the family took
Gladys and moved to the North. Their future seemed
secure under Lammers' care, as they got an apartment
and rented a hotel office in which to give readings.

Utterly New Ideas

Almost at once, as if in response to their earnest
gamble, a new type of reading emerged—the "life reading." Their first hint was a remark in an astrological reading for Lammers that he "was once a monk." Follow-up
readings spelled out a coherent view of reincarnation in
repeated human—not animal—form that was supplemented by between-life existences in specialized spheres
of consciousness. Edgar was staggered at the departure
from familiar biblical concepts and the Christian Church
teaching of the plan of salvation, although he was also
intrigued. Either his readings were again failing him, as
they had seemed to do in the oil fields, or he was entering an entire new continent of human meaning and adventure. He had to convince himself that he was not

collaborating in deception or helping to propound a view that would harm others. The answers offered in the new vein of readings, he was told, came promptly in the same clear, natural, and firm voice that usually described someone's arthritic limb or ruptured spleen. There was no marked shift in language, except for new terms, and the syntax was as unruly and the sentences as complex as ever. There was no pause for answers, no fumbling. Replies came as crisply as ever—only on new subject matter. But here he was discoursing on moral law, history, the soul, and God.

As Hugh Lynn later told me, Cayce's greatest question was whether the new views pouring from him in trance could be congruent with biblical faith, not whether empirical evidence could be found in psychology or daily experience. All of that could come later. The first question was whether the teachings distorted the deep relationships with God that were at the heart of the biblical saga, or might turn people aside from the great commandments to love God and their neighbors with their whole selves. Did the new concepts deal squarely with sin and grace? Did they temper justice with mercy? Did they place too much emphasis on righteousness of works? Did they offer a way of salvation so mechanical that it excluded the saving role of the Christ? Did they affirm the value of the church and its ordinances as the household of faith? Did they glorify God with the psalmists, preach Christ crucified with Paul, fulfill and yet transcend the Law in love?

Day after day, evening after evening, the little band of Edgar, Gertrude, and Gladys wrestled with these questions, feeling that the integrity of their souls and their devotion to God was at stake. Sometimes they were joined by Lammers and his male secretary, Linden Shroyer, who served as conductor of the trances. They sought further readings, which unfolded sweeping vistas of their own soul journeys, not without embarrassment as they recognized the stuff of their intimate passions, unvoiced hopes, and painful excesses laid out before them in this new mode. Gradually Cayce's anxiety lessened as he discovered that the One God of the patriarchs and prophets was still central to the picture given, and that the pattern of Jesus' self-giving service was described as the destiny of all. The crucified Christ was the risen Lord for one life or for many, for earth or for experiences in dimensions of Jupiter or Mars. Other religious traditions were treated with respect not common in the church circles in which he had so long moved. But illustrations of principles in these readings were drawn directly from the Bible again and again, and his counselees who requested the new kind of guidance were urged to study that Book. Just as important, the spirit of prayer, meditation, and devout worship which had always brought him to his best self ran through this new material, keeping it from being a mere speculative system. And the ethical content was uniformly high, focused on outgoing, generous service of one's fellows as children of God.

This time he did not have to make the ultimate decisions alone, as had been the case in the recent past. Gertrude and Gladys made a primary team with him, soon joined by Hugh Lynn, whose good mind was showing even at the age of seventeen. Edgar Evans was only five, but Hugh Lynn gave his parents enough trouble for two when confronted by the new concepts. He was outraged that they had sought a reading on him without his consent, and not at all consoled to learn that he had been an Egyptian pharaoh as the Young King of Ra Ta's times, nor uplifted by the affirmation in the readings that he had been Andrew, the disciple of Jesus, after first following John the Baptist. Hearing that most of his subsequent lifetimes (except one as a monk) had been marred by violence, including the persecuting ventures of the Crusades, did not help to soften his attitude either, for the reports came too close to fitting the explosive temper which was already his—like his father's.

Suddenly Lammers was out of their lives, landing in a series of lawsuits which ended his support and left them

stranded when he moved away. He had successfully arranged for the boys to go to the best private school along
with the scions of Dayton's rubber and auto families, but
he had not arranged for clothing or allowances appropriate for those circles. The boys suffered doubly, both
from being outsiders from Alabama and from the lack of
suitable suits and graces. Gladys was down to one brown
dress, which she wore day after day. The family was often rescued from a supper which looked dismal only by
an unexpected request for a reading. They shivered in
the cold climate where none of them had ever lived and
began wearing newspapers under their clothes to keep
warm. On weekends they undertook outings that gave
them brief if hilarious release, and eventually the
weather got warm enough for picnics and rambunctious
croquet.

Dream Doorways to the Past

Although Cayce had been through misfortune before,
and no stranger to hard times in Texas, he found that
watching his family struggle without adequate food and
clothing wrenched him hard. They fell far behind on
rents. The requests for readings which he expected would
follow him to Ohio did not appear, because the hundreds of families which had so often relied on his medical aid in the past simply could not locate him. He had
no reputation at all in Dayton, and the Christian Church
which they attended proved cordial but totally
uninterested in his peculiar work. There were no doctors
familiar with his cases, and nothing even remotely approaching the hospital he wanted. He could not help
questioning the promises given and received with his
Lord, in which protecting and caring for his family had
always been a part. The situation seemed unfair. He had
turned his back on photography in order to put his
whole vocation into his readings. But the risk was turning into a disaster. Their distress was heightened when,

on a trip back to Hopkinsville, he was stuck between
trains in Cincinnati and ran so hard to catch one pulling
out of the station that he contracted a lung infection
which left a permanent weakness, ultimately contributing to his death.

His readings consistently told him and the others to
be faithful, since God had not forgotten them. But their
suffering and humiliation were not lessened by the additional information that he was back in the Ohio area
where as John Bainbridge he had exploited so many,
defrauding them of their means as he was now bereft of
means. Once again, however, the lack of business served
him well, for he had time to pray, go for walks (when not
frozen), and read his Bible. Once again he was not bitter
(most of the time) or self-destructive. With the Texas venture still fresh in his thoughts, he did not turn to new
commercializing of his gift. He just held on, and his
household with him.

They kept careful records of all his trance sessions,
and filed them away neatly for the first time. Often the
readings had been transcribed in the past, but usually
for the convenience of recipients, without copies for his
own edification. Typically he had not wanted to know
what had come out of him, feeling that the added knowledge was only a burden. Now, with Gladys's help, he was
more careful. Only about five hundred transcripts were
in the cartons where they were unceremoniously kept
from the thousands upon thousands of readings he had
given all over the country. He had created afresh each
time, like a photographer fashioning portraits that belonged to those who posed for them. But now he had to
study a large system of laws that he now saw in his Bible
in sayings such as "God is not mocked; whatsoever a
man sows, that shall he also reap," or "He that lives by
the sword shall die by the sword," or teaching's that Elijah
had come again as the Baptizer, or questions put to Jesus
as to why a man had been born blind. So for the first
time he took care to keep copies of all the readings.

As though answering his need for understanding, another kind of reading promptly appeared, offering ways of reaching directly to memories of past lives and for depicting time–transcending karma.

These were readings that interpreted dreams, following one which urged him to keep track of his own and study them as a means to greater understanding of human nature and destiny with the divine. In a time when dreams were largely ignored by thoughtful people as mere secondary phenomena of the mind and emotions, with no more value than any other omens or superstitions, his readings developed a full theory of their function in the psyche and helped him understand not only relationships to past lives within himself and others, but psychic experience, health concerns, business judgment, cultural change, and spiritual growth. None of them was familiar with the work of Freud, whose epochal *Interpretation of Dreams*[168] had been published the same year as he gave his first readings. Only later would they find Freudian dynamics and processes abundantly evident in the dream interpretations, though subordinated to an approach which magnified spiritual growth and often gave dreams external reference. If reincarnation within Christian faith were their required study course, then dreams were the accompanying laboratory that saved them from feeling victims of strange, seemingly occult concepts beyond their reach to verify except in large speculations. They concluded that his trance counsel might be failing him in some way they did not understand, but if that were the case, it was doing so richly and methodically, not sputtering into vague references such as those in the later oil well guidance.

A Seer in Search of a Destiny

Although it would be some time before they under-

---

[168]Freud, Sigmund, 1901.

stood the full implications, Cayce could now be seen as reaching the full stature of his Ra Ta incarnation, when he had been a spiritual teacher. He would continue giving medical counsel in Ohio and Virginia right up to the last months of his life, and always view it as central to his calling. But from now on many would view him in a new light. He was for them not simply a psychic, just a good man whose gifts helped those in pain—not alone a specialist in facts of the distant or buried, past or future. As a psychic diagnostician of health problems, he might be paid for his services and forgotten as one does with other medical specialists. Even if his aid rescued someone from an incurable disease or condition, only a certain surprised respect was called for.

But as a character analyst and moral teacher, he was someone to be reckoned with, especially because his readings saw no incurable psychological or spiritual problems. Selfishness, impatience, frustration, indulgence, or loneliness could all be reknit into larger, clearer life patterns, according to the "information." He was inevitably seen by some as a revealer and a teacher of spiritual realities. The change would strain his beloved church ties and leave him once more vulnerable to the need for an authorizing community. There would also be those like his own mother (who never sought a life reading, convinced that it was unimportant or irrelevant), who looked away from the strangeness of the new concepts in the ability they had cherished. Medical people, so often his friends and sponsors, would relate to him more guardedly, feeling that his irregular diagnostic and treatment methods gave them enough to handle without getting into his odd worldview. Businessmen, never quite sure they might not become butts of taunts because they sought his advice, would now often pull back, as would most political figures. He had asked God for a hospital where truth could be sought in disciplined research. The response given him was a life-shaking challenge as to whether he even wanted truth at all when it might lead him in such drastic new directions.

Groaning, he decided to take up the burden of the new teaching and insight in his life readings and related material. Though he would have considered the term strained at the time, he had become a full-scale seer—but a seer out of season in the bustling, expansive postwar Twenties. He was a seer still without a home base or nurturing community anywhere in his own land, after having traveled it widely for four years in search of his destiny and capable companions.

To Virginia Beach at Last

But then, in August 1924, Morton Blumenthal appeared with his younger brother Edwin, encouraged by the ever promoting Kahn to get readings for Morton's ear trouble. Morton was young, only twenty-nine, slightly built and short of stature, with an earnest face that dominated his slim body. He was the keen-minded introvert, and Edwin was the busy, outgoing extrovert. The two had grown up in a conventional but genuinely religious Jewish family in Altoona, Pennsylvania, where their father ran a store and their mother gave the family its essential strength. Morton had gone for a time to the University of Pennsylvania. Now the young brothers were successful stockbrokers in Manhattan, making money steadily in the rising markets of the mid-1920s. For Morton the life readings were heady material, awakening the interest in philosophy which had compelled him in college, while for Edwin the prospects of learning how to be psychic in the stock market offered the most immediate challenge.

Life readings told Morton that he had been the native sage in ancient Egypt of Ra Ta's time, sharing power with the young king and pushing for the exile of the high priest. Later he was the opponent of the Trojans, as Achilles, who shamed Xenon (now Cayce) into suicide by the device of the famous horse. He had also been among the rebuilders of Jerusalem after the Exile, where he had been an assistant to Ezekiel. By contrast, Edwin was told he had been a merchant who could rise to prominence in the world's financial circles, and that he was once Jude, the younger brother of Jesus, who doubted him until after the resurrection. All of this made adventurous treasure maps for the two young men. Both were natural idealists capable of generosity and sacrifice for principle, as I would learn for myself when I interviewed them in depth later in Virginia Beach. They responded quickly to Cayce's idea of a hospital and the insistence of the readings that it be located in Virginia Beach.

What they honored in Cayce was his longing for larger service purged of personal ambition by the Texas failures. Their instinctive trust of him was strengthened by what they felt were latent memories of his towering stature as a gifted high priest, quite capable of building both a great hospital and a place of training. Morton especially liked the idea of an institute, which would do research, hold classes on the great ideas of the human family, and sponsor the hospital. He saw, as Edgar did, that the gifts of the man from Selma required duplication in others to reach their full effects. And he was committed, as Edgar always had been, to serious encounter with professionals in the worlds of medicine, education, religion, and business. Further, his interests reached to the welfare of distant peoples, as his dreaming of China showed, and to the aiding of underdogs—despite his Wall Street profession which kept him among the affluent. The spirit of Jewish prophetic traditions was easily aroused in him, both as a means to understanding Edgar's calling and as an imperative to build a more just world. Yet this spirit was often overshadowed by the more speculative philosopher in him, eager to solve riddles that had troubled the minds of the great thinkers for centuries.

Morton found the centrality of the figure of the Christ in the readings a major stumbling block. Yet his unconscious seemed to take up the task of unfolding the mystery of the Incarnation without losing his essential Jewish

monotheism when it gave him dreams of God with human compassion like that of his father, or of God as a
middle-aged businessman of keen vision and great presence coming to visit him in his New York apartment. Or
they led him into dreams of vivid and touching encounter with Jesus as Elder Brother, modeled on his personal
love for Edwin.

Within just a few years he would be married, having
his courtship and even his honeymoon monitored by
readings given on his dreams. He was told by Cayce's
counsel that he would have a son who could bring back
prophecy to Judaism—if he could hold his family and
faith intact. His deep love of God, combined with the
adventurous spirit of his years (not yet thirty) and the
expansiveness of the postwar country around him, made
all of this somehow believable—however strange the
trance source.

The two brothers sought successful medical readings
for members of their family, got the blessings of their
mother, listened to the stories of years of fascinating
readings told by young Kahn, and brought Cayce to New
York to meet with them and their friends. Shortly afterward Morton came to Dayton with the keys to a house
he had bought at Virginia Beach for the Cayces. He arranged to pay their expenses to move to the edge of the
ocean, where the trance counsel insisted that Cayce
would do best. Gertrude would also, they were told, find
the sea helpful to her spirits.

The move came none too soon. It was not their finances which now troubled the Cayce household, for
readings had caught the interest of business executives
and industrialists in Ohio who would in turn become
lifelong friends. Edgar had even developed an arrangement to give readings for banks that went on for a year
after he left Dayton. He was now giving his counsel in
his home, and those who had so often sought his medical aid in the past were catching up with him. Some of
these (but by no means all) were genuinely interested in
the life readings. Having once dealt with the utter

strangeness of Cayce's aid, they were prepared to follow it wherever it took them, provided that the new concepts were as ethical and spiritual as they had found the readings in the past.

What strained the Cayce household, now back in the Ohio River territory where Bainbridge had wandered (never marrying but making many alliances with women), was the mutual attraction between Edgar and Gladys, now reaching her full womanhood. It was enhanced by the Southern patterns of romantic idealism which they both knew well, and not made easier by Edgar's periodic despondency over the financial hardship they had all experienced in Dayton. The "information" sought to help them by showing how their feelings were based on their long journey together as twin souls in other lives, especially the passionate lifetimes as husband and wife in Persia, where both had been killed by treachery and deprived not only of the joy of bringing up their gifted son, Zend, but of their own deep mutual love. Yet the readings advised great caution, strong willpower, and much prayer. As always in such matters, the perspective of the readings was that "All love is lawful, but not all is expedient unto good works," reminding them that excesses could dishonor their labors but that the choices must be theirs.

Gertrude kept her bearings while all of them grew in understanding the complexity and force of karma. Her role was not made easier when she fell down a flight of stairs in their Dayton home and injured her eye, eventually losing her sight and somewhat marring the beauty of face that had always compelled the attention of those who met her. Nor did it make her path much easier to be told that this was the eye she had used to command men in Ancient Persia and that she had known her own excesses as the Egyptian dancer who captured Ra Ta or as a charmer in France at the time of Louis XIV. By the time I knew her, Gladys had become for her just a loved daughter—as Edgar also clearly saw her. In the account of her elder son, as in observations of others who knew the family well, Gertrude grew the most of any of them in these post–Selma years. She learned to love with great patience and insight, and developed such strength of character and faith of God that the lives of all of them were increasingly centered by hers. When Edgar had a dream of their move to Virginia Beach that showed Gertrude as the engineer driving the train, a reading told him to let her plan and execute the logistics of the move, since she was more competent than he realized. Much later, when he first wrote Hugh Lynn overseas in the Army, it was about appreciation for his wife: "She's made out of steel wire—pulled, twisted, drawn, purified."

For his own part, Cayce learned how deep–seated was his pattern of finding his soul projected on a compelling and compassionate woman, and set out on a journey of inner transformation that would result in his lasting free-dom from the inclination, freedom to love without be-guiling projection—as I saw when I was with him. That the journey was not always easy he pointed out with some humor in telling me of a time, not long after Day-ton, when he was staying at an estate of wealthy friends in a New York suburb. One of the house guests was a beautiful young Hollywood actress who was fascinated with the story of his life. She invited him to come to her room and tell her more. He went. Just as he turned to-ward her, in the privacy of her room, the figure dressed all in white, wearing a white turban, suddenly appeared. It was the same imposing presence that had warned him of his partners in Hopkinsville. No word was spoken, but Cayce left at once. Nobody else saw the man, but the memory of him and the warning stayed vividly in Cayce's mind.

By Vast Atlantic Waters

Edgar's dreams, and the readings taken to interpret them, held out great promise for the move to Virginia Beach. One, for example, showed him and his backers

and physicians fishing off the coast with much merri-
ment. The trance interpretation was that he and others
could indeed draw much spiritual nourishment from the
waters of the Spirit and build together "the great influential institution." The wanderings since Selma were
coming to an end, and he found himself able to imagine
his hospital actually being built at last. His enthusiasm
spilled over into his dreams again, when he saw himself
lecturing to women's clubs around the country about
the new institution, as he had in Birmingham when it
was only an idea. However, the reading taken on the
dream warned him that this approach was too laden
with ego. What was required was quiet labor for principle, not fanfare.

What they found at Virginia Beach, when they moved
in mid-September 1925, was a desolate winter. Their
modest house was on 35th Street, not far from the ocean
but a couple of miles from the only shopping area at
17th Street. There was no housing or resort activity near
them, although before long the large and expensive
Cavalier Hotel would be built nearby. Groceries had to
be ordered, in the practice of the time, by telephone,
which were then delivered (if the vehicle were coming
their way) that day. They had no car. The house was essentially a summer dwelling, not insulated and without
a furnace. Sometimes they patrolled the long beach for
wood scraps or collected discards at construction sites.
Gertrude found a pile of used bricks which they trundled
home and used to construct a walk in place of the muddy
entrance path. It rained constantly, and they were often
cold. Gladys had to scribble down questions for Morton's
frequent readings while in the chilly hallway, and her
fingers were so numb that she could barely do it.

In the town were mostly boarded-up wooden hotels
and Victorian buildings. There was no recreation except
an occasional silent movie. So they took to organizing
their own. In the evenings they played Rook and
Parcheesi, or card games in which they didn't have to
concentrate so hard that Edgar could read their minds.

They staged debates (usually with Gladys and Edgar against Hugh Lynn and Gertrude) on all sorts of topics, especially the issues raised by the life readings. Most difficult for Edgar was the question of possible past lives for Jesus. They listened to a table radio, and Edgar found the one person he ever described himself as wanting to meet—Bing Crosby. And they had family prayers every evening after supper.

When the weather finally grew warmer, Edgar worked outside with his hands, making repairs on windows and steps, putting in a garden of both flowers and vegetables, and raising chickens. Inside he repaired chairs and dressers, as well as framed pictures. He installed a doorbell. His emotions and his worries were best controlled when he could keep his hands busy. The world of physical sensations and activities was often the doorway to the deeper levels of his unconscious because it was an inferior or less developed side of his nature, compared to his intuitive gifts.

He still found himself subject to bursts of temper and harsh criticism, as he had been all his life. Gladys would later report in her memoirs[169] how capable he was even now of abruptly ordering her to leave permanently, and how difficult he found it to ask forgiveness. He disliked receiving criticism but had trouble translating this into steady restraint of his remarks to others. The boys, however, found him as always a companionable father, usually just and tender, as well as playful and inventive.

Once again the people who had sought readings from him for their own or relatives' medical needs found him difficult to locate. On principle, he did not advertise or send out mailings, and the word of his location had to pass from individual to individual. Morton used him regularly and Edwin occasionally. Though the two frequently sent him fresh contacts among business

---

[169]Davis, Gladys, with Mary Ellen Carter, *My Years with Edgar Cayce*, 1972.

acquaintances, the income was barely enough for survival. They were back at the Virginia scene of the irresponsible adventures of the first Bainbridge, and the price again seemed to be the lessons of financial hardship.

Lacking visitors, friends, and daily need of readings, Edgar had time to think and to pray, as well as to read and ponder his Bible. The vast ocean, only a few blocks from their home, lifted his spirits with its ever-changing hues and constant motion, where ships from the ends of the world appeared first as specks on the horizon before passing majestically into the entrance of Chesapeake Bay. He had before him in these ancient and endless waters a living emblem of the Eternal, different from humans yet close and vital. He dreamt at night of its majesty and power. Slowly he found himself able to present his failings of recent years before God, seeking forgiveness. He found it, and his table discussions of the Bible reflected it, as they still did when I knew him. Bible character after character had proven sinful and arrogant, even King David himself. Yet when truly repentant they had found Jehovah full of mercy and ready to help make their paths straight. He laid before God his seeking of power and attention in the Texas fiasco, as well as the impulses of his heart for ardent companionship. He grew stronger and more confident. God did not ask of him perfection all at once, he felt, but only that he sincerely keep trying. And God sought from him not just decorum but wholeness and full manhood, which entailed risks and frequent failures. He could keep going and could understand, more fully than ever before, the weaknesses of others which so often lay behind the ills of the flesh that brought them to readings. He noted that his counsel was clearer and deeper than before, partly because Gertrude was now serving as conductor (which she had begun in Dayton) and also because he was regaining his composure—ever mirrored in the quality of the readings.

The family sought a church home, first traveling to Norfolk to reach a Christian Church but finding prohibitive the regular cost of train fares for all of them.

They next turned to the local Baptist Church—not too different from their own—but found that the church leaders had heard of his readings and were doubtful about granting them memberships; Edgar never returned. The local Methodist minister of the time seemed stuffy. They ended up at the Presbyterian Church, where Edgar was soon teaching an adult Bible class on Sunday mornings that would continue until just before his death. Worship fed them all, as did the familiar rounds of church suppers, socials, and programs by missionaries and evangelists. Edgar joined the men's club and Gladys joined the choir. Gertrude took an active role but kept her membership in the Hopkinsville Christian Church. Having reasoned out the principles of Christian faith, she was not about to change them without better persuasion than she found. Edgar began visiting the jails again, as he had not done since Selma, and Hugh Lynn found occasion to join him.

Readings on Death, Stocks, and Philosophy

Readings took interesting new directions. Some of them described with great precision exactly how real estate would develop in the next decades at Virginia Beach, naming streets and sequences and recommending purchases. Edgar had no money to invest, or he would have been able to leave his family assets that yielded great wealth. Morton was busy with the stock market. Besides, the predictions that this nice little resort town would become a great resort city (adjoining what would reportedly become the world's largest port) seemed farfetched. Readings set forth the course of coming weather changes in large patterns, and opened up the subject of future earth changes that would later preoccupy a number of persons who sought his aid.

Money began to come in at last, so that they could buy a car and Hugh Lynn could go to business school in Norfolk. Young Edgar Evans, nicknamed Ecken, now had more decent clothes. The Blumenthals often came to stay at the expensive Cavalier Hotel, seeking two kinds of readings: those on business prospects and those (which Morton loved) on survival after death, which was then the primary question of psychical research in England and the United States. Dave Kahn came when he could, requesting business counsel and bringing his intelligent and well-read wife. Formerly an actress who had striking beauty and poise, she took her Judaism seriously but also found herself at home in the teachings of Hinduism. She also entered easily into the world of psychical research. All of these visitors found that the trip to Virginia Beach was a mini-pilgrimage that quieted and refreshed them (just as readings had said it would), combining an overnight train ride with a final ferry journey across the water and ending at the magnificent ocean whose clean expanse of beach was unsurpassed on the East Coast.

In October 1926, Edgar's mother became gravely ill. The reading taken on her condition described how and when she would expire. He sent a rather unusual wire to his sisters, telling them she was about to die and asking them to hold her for his arrival. Then he hurried home to say good-bye to her. Although he was forty-nine and had not always kept close to her in recent years, she still was dear to his heart; she had first and always believed that his readings were not just psychological oddities but gifts from a loving God. Within a year Leslie, the squire, came to live with the family, staying there until his death and attending all the reading sessions. He often told visitors his many stories of his son's achievements with expansive flourishes. Hugh Lynn went off to college at a school with impressive Southern traditions, Washington and Lee. There, his readings told him, he would meet individuals important to him from past lives. At his fraternity initiation he suddenly saw his roommate, Thomas Sugrue of Connecticut, as a cowled monk he had known long before. It was the first of many episodes of what seemed wide-awake past-life recall which would occur to him all his life.

The Blumenthal brothers swiftly made money, with Morton using his dreams for leads on particular stocks, and Edwin using his intuition on the trading floor. They bought a seat on the stock exchange and, while still in their early thirties, became millionaires. Morton studied William James on religious experience,[170] as well as Hudson on the laws of the mind,[171] Ouspensky on the reincarnation philosophy,[172] and training exercises of Gurdjieff. He asked so many questions about these works that Cayce's entranced unconscious reacted as though it knew them and recommended the books for others to read. The "information" enabled Morton to keep in loving touch (through his dreams) with his grandmother who had died, with his wife's mother at her death, and with his father after his death. With the latter he formed a highly unusual partnership of joint effort to build the Cayce Hospital; one of them was dead and the other alive, but both committed to service of the needy.

Slowly, Morton made progress with his attitude to women, who were so often just sex objects to males of his times and social circles. A delightful dream showed him chorus girls kicking and coming forward in turn to do their individual numbers in a creative attitude that the readings identified as "service, service, service"—the ultimate cure for his too-narrow fascination with the feminine. As he grew in texture of personhood, so did his dream guidance for his work. One dream placed him under a lamppost at night, and the light turned into incredible illumination as a gift from God. He saw in one brilliant vision all the stocks of the Stock Exchange with their individual quotes and their tendencies to advance or decline correctly.

---

[170]James, William, *Varieties of Religious Experience*, 1902.

[171]Hudson, Thomas J., *The Law of Psychic Phenomena*, 1896.

[172]Ouspensky, P.D., *Tertium Organum*, 1944.

As Morton made money, he gave more to Edgar, manifesting a generosity which the entire Cayce family later confirmed to me and which I found believable when I interviewed him at length. He also struggled (as had nobody before him) to understand both the philosophy and the operation of the readings. His winsome young wife learned through her dreams to slip at times into a state where she could talk helpfully in her sleep—even briefly matching that of Edgar's trance (as his reading confirmed). Morton's earnest efforts laid the groundwork for much research that would follow Cayce's death (which years later led me to dedicate to him a book I wrote on dreams).[173]

The World Seemed Fair

The brothers pushed ahead on the hospital project, enlisting the help of Kahn and some of Edgar's able business friends from Ohio and Chicago. Morton found himself led by his psychic dreams right to the doors of New York contributors willing to help. The first step was the incorporation of the Association of National Investigators in May 1927, with a sweeping motto which reflected the scale on which all of them were thinking: "That We May Make Manifest Our Love for God and Man." The direct focus of the new organization was to be psychic research, but the larger aim was to use well whatever could be learned though responsible psychic sources in every walk of life. Money was flowing in, and the world seemed fair to those in business circles. They joined in an ambitious effort to conquer the psychic arena reflecting the spirit of the times, when Henry Ford was showing the world what mass production and American know-how could do. In their minds they would be the ones to apply this know-how to the little-known area

---

[173]Bro, Harmon H., *Dreams in the Life of Prayer,* 1970.

of psychic phenomena, starting with Cayce's readings. Plans for the institute called not only for a hospital but a lecture hall, a large library of the world's religions and occult systems, and a staff of librarians and researchers to correlate the readings with other systems of thought and with current research. A magazine, called *The New Tomorrow*, was planned and soon became a reality. Morton put together his thinking in a densely written little book which he then published, entitled *Heaven on Earth*.

The Association purchased land for the hospital on a knoll two blocks from the ocean that was stipulated by readings. It was the highest point in Virginia Beach, well removed from developed areas, with a sweeping view and the potential for a beautiful multilevel terrace and added buildings. A skilled architect designed the building, which was surprisingly large and imposing for its times. Four stories held not only many beds but complete offices and laboratory facilities, as well as a vault for readings and room for research. Its cost then was the equivalent of millions today. Cayce was thrilled and enjoyed helping with the carpentry, as well as supervising each stage of the development. A feature picture of the nearly completed building appeared in the Norfolk paper toward the end of October with the caption "CAYCE HOSPITAL TO BE DEDICATED" and an accompanying report:

> Rapidly nearing completion at 105th Street on Atlantic Boulevard [now 67th Street and Atlantic Avenue]. The building is of stucco and shingle exterior, containing 30 bedrooms, library and lecture hall, doctors' offices and living rooms. It is built by the United Construction Company of Norfolk for the National Association of Investigators [sic], Inc., at a cost of approximately $150,000.[174]

---

[174]*Norfolk Ledger Dispatch*, October 30, 1928. Reprinted by permission of the publisher.

A longer article in the same issue described the psychic aspects of the hospital, while New York papers carried full reports, such as this one in the *New York American:*

New Psychic Hospital
To Find Ailments
Offers Diagnosis of Physical Troubles
by Mental Method, Even to Absentee Patients

A group of American men and women, including three New Yorkers, have made an endowment of over $100,000 for a "psychic" hospital, the first of its kind to be built in America. Ailments of the body will be diagnosed at the hospital by means of psychic concentration. It will not be necessary to be at the hospital for "readings." They may be thousands of miles away and still be diagnosed.

The hospital, to be known as the Cayce Hospital for Research and Enlightenment, will be formally opened November 11 at Virginia Beach, Va. Two of the three New York sponsors are Morton H. Blumenthal, a broker of No. 50 Broadway and David E. Kahn of the furniture industry.

Named for Investigator

At his office last night Mr. Blumenthal explained that the hospital was named after Edgar Cayce, known by many for his probings into the subconscious.

The method that will be employed was discussed by Mr. Blumenthal, who is president of the organization, known as the Association of National Investigators . . . "A competent staff of physicians will be associated with the hospital to provide treatments; if the individual prefers his own doctor he is at liberty to go to him for treatment . . . "

"It is our intention to demonstrate to the individual

the relationship existing between his own indwelling spiritual being and his physical being and thus bring to intellectual man an awakening of the internal cosmic character. Through our demonstration the individual may gain the realization of that internal part of himself called soul."[175]

In Morton's mind the urge to enlighten easily outran the urge to research, despite vigorous warnings from readings, which insisted that "knowledge not lived is sin."

Just as the hospital was being finished, Edgar had one of those rare experiences in which someone from beyond the grave spoke through him before he was awakened from trance. He had been planning to install a fountain as a memorial to his mother but had not invited the aid of Annie, called Sister by the family, or his other sisters. The poignant transcript he handed me and I copied was like a brief scene from the end of the play *Our Town* by Thornton Wilder:

> Mother! Mother is here—and you haven't written Sister yet, and told her—Sister wouldn't like it, Brother—and she'll feel hurt! Write to Sister, tell her, and Sarah and Ola and Mary—they will all want to have a part, and they'll feel just as you do—and after a while when everything is straightened out it will be so nice for you all, to know that Mother will be right with you! Be a good boy. Write, Brother! Talk to Mother. Be good to Papa. He will be home before long. But write to Sister—and tell the children Mother loves them all.

All of the sisters contributed to the memorial. And just as indicated, the squire died not too long afterward.

---

[175]*New York American*, October 22, 1928. Reprinted by permission of the publisher.

Though a small event in a lifetime, the little episode of loving greetings from beyond the grave represented the kind of unusual happening which made Edgar's world different from that of others, and contributed to his constant need to keep himself in balance.

The shiny new hospital was dedicated on Armistice Day 1928 with a stirring address by Hugh Lynn's psychology professor from Washington and Lee, Dr. William Mosely Brown, who had heard sufficient readings to be greatly impressed. The first physician was Dr. House, whose experience with the readings dated back to Bowling Green, and whose wife and child had both been plucked from threatening illnesses by them. His wife, Carrie, was the dietitian. Finding a doctor with both a medical and an osteopathic background had not been easy, and Edgar had been spurred on by a vivid dream showing himself, Gertrude, and Gladys swimming in a very large tub of hot water—hardly a difficult warning to interpret. Dr. House held both degrees, and Edgar trusted him not to misuse the readings as he felt Ketchum and other physicians had. Nurses and other staff were hired, and patients admitted from a waiting list of desperate people (who had already applied from all over the country) with a variety of serious ailments that defied diagnosis. Cayce could see for himself that finally all the types of treatments recommended in his readings were promptly available in one place. His joy was beyond words. This joy was still in his voice when he later told me of the first crippled woman who came in on crutches and walked out unaided.

A University to Study the Whole Person

Treatments were not the only activities. Blumenthal, though only thirty-three, had big ideas and the money to act on them. He wanted to move to Virginia Beach and start work for the Association full-time, but a reading dissuaded him, arguing that he could do more good by staying right where he was, continuing to be both a successful businessman and a responsible spiritual person on Wall Street. This would say something important to those who asked, "What good can come from the Street?" A reading pointed out Jesus as a model because he had immersed himself in the common life of his times and not stayed aloof with the Essenes. So Morton continued his studies in the readings by mail, getting almost daily counsel. He came down to lecture in involved prose at the hospital on alternate Sunday afternoons. On the intervening Sundays Cayce, in homey but articulate style, lectured on topics he felt he knew something about from experience: telepathy, life after death, healing, soul growth, the subconscious, and co-creating with the Holy Spirit. The local paper carried the full text of his addresses. He was happier than his sister Annie had ever seen him, she later told me, because he had fully joined his personal vocation to his readings, and because his readings were doing more good than ever before. Besides, he saw for the first time a setting where others might eventually be trained to do his kind of work.

Training was on Morton's mind too, and he recruited psychologist Dr. Brown to serve as the first president of a new campus, Atlantic University. Brown recently had been an unsuccessful Republican candidate for governor in the overwhelmingly Democratic Southern state. He was widely known and respected in Virginia. They secured a charter, and Blumenthal put up the necessary money to hire a genuinely impressive faculty at high salaries, recruited from all over the country. Doctorates were the rule among them, and degrees from such institutions as Harvard and Yale were common. A full liberal arts program was designed and an attractive catalog issued. Over two hundred students enrolled when the new university opened in September 1930, two years after the hospital started up. Classes met in hotels, where students were also housed, while foundations were poured for a full complement of academic buildings across the boulevard from the hospital. The new school had all the

features for a promising future, with its own expensive
football team and dramatic productions, as well as a literary magazine, research laboratories, and yearbook.
Cayce was on the board of trustees, his work was discussed in classes, and the faculty were committed to psychical research, as part—and only part—of a plan to study
the whole person, which was not only fresh for its times
but anticipated much to come in American higher education. This effort, however, seemed brash to some, such
as the *Baltimore Sun*, which (in the first of several articles
written from its New York bureau even before the school
opened) equated *psychic* with *spiritualism*.

Spiritualistic Research Aim
Of Atlantic University

Proposed Virginia Beach Institution Inspired by
Work of Psychic Healer,
Morton H. Blumenthal, Chairman, Reveals

The proposed Atlantic University at Virginia Beach,
Va., is being backed by a group who are deeply interested in psychic research and spiritualism and it will be
the only university in this or any other country to undertake psychic work, it was revealed today.

The University will be headed by Dr. William Mosely
Brown . . . Dr. Brown in his announcement of the aims
and ideals of the university a day or so ago listed a full
course of the liberal arts and sciences and relegated psychic research to a footnote. However, Morton H.
Blumenthal, whose brokerage offices are at 71 Broadway, New York City, and who is chairman of the board
of trustees, said today the idea for the inception of Atlantic University really had sprung out of the work of
Edgar Cayce, a psychic healer.

Mr. Cayce runs the Cayce Hospital for Research and
Enlightenment at Virginia Beach and diagnoses patients

who may be hundreds of miles away and whom he has never seen. According to Mr. Blumenthal Mr. Cayce does this through his "subjective mind."

Boards Almost Identical

Back of the Cayce Hospital for Research and Enlightenment is a board which almost exactly duplicates the board that will run the new Atlantic University.

Thus Mr. Blumenthal, his brother, Edwin D. Blumenthal, also of 71 Broadway, and a member of the Stock Exchange; David E. Kahn of this city, a furniture manufacturer; Thomas E. Brown, of Dayton, Ohio, an engineer, and Franklin P. Bradley, of Chicago, a paint and varnish manufacturer, will finance and control Atlantic University as they now do the Association of National Investigators—the name of the organization behind the hospital.

To Study Mediumistic Work

Morton H. Blumenthal occupies the key position, however, inasmuch as he is chairman of the board of the university and president of the investigators' group. There also is another of the family connected with the investigators—Adeline Levy Blumenthal.

Furthermore, it is planned to make the hospital where Mr. Cayce's patients are treated an integral part of the university. That is, the students will be given an opportunity to study his mediumistic work.

Spiritualist Is Considered

From other sources it was learned that an Englishman—William G. Hibbins, B.S.A., a spiritualist, is being considered for the post of psychic research professor. Mr. Hibbins tried unsuccessfully to have the University of Sheffield, to which he is attached, install a similar professorship. He has written a preface to Mr.

Blumenthal's book entitled "Heaven on Earth" and published by the Association of National Investigators. The book has a brilliant purple cover.[176]

Cayce's cup was full, and while some might object to the nature of Blumenthal's philosophic ambitions, he had the hospital for which he had prayed and worked so long. As a bonus he had before him a serious new university. His lifelong passion to relate his ability to competent professionals, starting with his friend Dr. Blackburn in Bowling Green nearly thirty years ago, had found fulfillment. Then his cup began to tip. And finally it spilled.

Falling Out

Morton was paying all the bills. The Great Depression had hit in late 1929, and the two brothers had not heeded the seemingly farfetched warning in a reading taken shortly before October's Black Friday to get out of all their holdings. They still had investments in real estate, however, and money in the bank. Morton even traveled to Europe at the height of the panic, boasting that he had a million dollars in bank accounts. But the Crash and its aftermath hit others hard, so that Brown could not raise the money he expected to secure for the university, and the hospital board faced the same problem.

In addition, Morton had been finding it difficult to secure readings as often as he wished, since Cayce put the daily hospital counsel first. The practical trance guidance and even more the instruction on far reaches of the soul's journey meant everything to him, and he complained. He got more readings but far less than the preferential treatment he genuinely thought he deserved.

---

[176]*Baltimore Sun*, April 16, 1930. Reprinted by permission of the publisher.

Kahn seemed to get readings promptly, as Cayce's long-time closest friend, and this irritated him. Finally he turned to the apparently mediumistic talents of his red-haired secretary in New York, Patricia Devlin, and began getting regular counsel from her. He brought her to demonstrate her skills to classes of the university. Almost at once he was warned by her source away from Cayce, and began to see flaws in Edgar's efforts, whether real, imagined, or both. At one point he presented Cayce with an ultimatum "from Jesus" that Kahn should receive no more readings. The selection of who would get readings was one point on which Cayce would not budge and never had. He responded that the day Kahn could not get readings would be the day "Eddie will be six feet underground."

Over a decade later, I interviewed the Blumenthals in depth and found fault enough to go around for everyone. Kahn contributed only furniture to the hospital, yet to the Blumenthals his sweeping style made it seem that he claimed to be a crucial benefactor. Try as he might, Brown never developed an adequate financing plan for the university. Cayce had hired relatives to fill posts all through the hospital, including not only Dr. House and his wife but the husband of his youngest sister, Sarah (as the bookkeeper), and later his sister Annie as dietitian. In his mind, after a lifetime of being disappointed in his associates and needing a harmonious climate for his readings, this was sensible. To others it was indefensible nepotism.

He had been extravagant, with the disregard for money that might be expected of a high priest given national treasuries at last. He was expansive, he was generous, he was an extremist. A huge bill had been run up at the florists, food accounts appeared to have been padded by someone, and a friend had tapped into the hospital's water system for free service—discovered by Blumenthal only when a visitor stumbled over a partially hidden pipe in the ground.

To be sure, Morton had been caught up in the same

spirit for a time. He and Cayce had only looked at the sandy expanse in front of the hospital from its spacious porches one day and remarked that the area would look lovely as a lawn. The next day Cayce had ten thousand dollars worth of sod delivered and installed, to Morton's pleasure. Cayce kept no special sums for himself, although his elder son worked briefly in the library during a summer vacation, and his wife and secretary were each paid small salaries for helping him with the readings, while a second cousin worked in the hospital as a technician. Cayce was paid only $3,400 a year at the height of running the operation.

Edgar was not a manager. He was a leader, a visionary, the basis for the entire enterprise. But he could not delegate and got into every area of the hospital's operation—yet without a mind for details. He did not know how to set policies, conduct orderly hiring and supervision, keep records, or evaluate service delivery. Worst of all, he did not know how to pull others to work together. Whatever he may have known as Uhjltd, when he had reportedly forged a people out of Bedouin nomads that threatened the empire of the line of Croesus, he could not find it in the present—perhaps because it had been a talent squandered in Troy, as well as in colonial America—right where he lived now.

The board took little responsibility, dazzled by the plans they all had. An effort was made to find a competent manager, but none appeared at hand, and Cayce all too willingly continued running the full operation while giving the heaviest schedule of readings in his life. He was so busy that his daily devotional times suffered, compounding the problem. As a result of all the stress, the day arrived when he gave a reading for Blumenthal's aunt, accurate in all but the crucial detail that she had already died. As with the oil wells, his precious trance resource was again slipping in time—so often a trap for psychics. Morton was incensed, as he told me, and his fears were made worse by the counsel of the new osteopathic physician hired to replace Dr. House after the latter unexpectedly died. Dr. Lyman Lydic had little experience of the readings and told Morton not to trust Cayce very far.

In essence, the members of the group fell out with one another. Financial problems were severe but not hopeless. What undid the enterprise was suspicion, competition, and pride. One doctor also reportedly got involved in affairs with nurses. No one person and no spiritual community or tradition was strong enough to hold it all together. The brothers supported the university for one semester, then stopped their payments and the school dragged on for another year. Then the Blumenthals asked that the hospital be put in their names so that they might deploy it as an asset in the difficult financial markets that threatened to drain all their resources. At a crucial September board meeting in New York, Cayce urged that it be given to them, and walked away, never looking back on the decision. In the quarrels that followed, Blumenthal and Cayce were both deeply hurt. Morton sued Edgar for a door and some windows. Suits and countersuits were instigated in New York, where Morton had Kahn briefly jailed. In the same week Morton and Edgar were both reported as wanting to die. When one suit was tried at the Princess Anne Courthouse outside Virginia Beach, Cayce might have won the hospital back because local people were in sympathy with him, including the jury. But he felt the Blumenthals were entitled to it and again fully released it. The last patients were sent away, and the hospital closed on February 28, 1931, shortly before Cayce's fifty-fourth birthday.

Edgar was so low that nothing could hold his interest. A reading taken on his serious gall bladder infection warned that he was very near death, and one was interrupted by voices from "the other side" asking him to come over there, where he would be welcome. Morton and Edwin watched their fortunes slip away, and both found themselves sued for divorce by their wives, with the same mediumistic secretary named as co-respondent. Divorces followed, and the two brothers took up the faith of the woman and her husband, Roman Catholicism. The son who was supposed to bring prophecy back to Israel was placed in the custody of Morton's wife and grew up to mental illness, spending years in an institution while lacking the stable home base which readings had stipulated was essential for him. The brothers moved to Virginia Beach, where for a time they sold sandwiches on the boardwalk to survive, far from their Stock Exchange wealth and prestige. Later they entered into a printing firm with the former secretary and her husband, where they were working when I interviewed them. Although Cayce sent with me a message indicating he would welcome reconciliation, they wanted nothing to do with him.

The ending of the hospital and university was the darkest time in Cayce's life since the first and seemingly hopeless loss of his voice long ago. It had been seven dramatic and exhausting years since he had left Selma, determined to provide leadership to the work done through him and around him. He had seen his hopes fully realized and then completely destroyed. A reading indicated that his own mismanagement was partly responsible for the outcome, and he carried the pain of that awareness until he died. He later wrote of the time in a publication on his life which he sent to all who inquired about his services:

> I am only human. Humanity is doomed to failure when it trusts its own weak self, and most of us have that failing. Besides giving two "readings" each day and talking with hundreds of people who came asking for "readings" and enquiring about the hospital, I attempted to handle for a time much of the business details of the institution . . . I look back over the turmoils and tribulations, the disappointments and periods of despair . . . In February, 1931, the Association of National

Investigators, Incorporated, through some of its directors, felt it necessary to close the hospital and discontinue the entire program of the organization. I tried to take stock of myself and the work. Even then I wondered, "Am I all wrong?"[177]

But once again he failed into success.

---

[177]Cayce, Edgar, *Edgar Cayce, His Life and Work*, 1943, p. 10.

CHAPTER 16

There Is Nothing New Here

What developed in a few months was a new type of reading, just as the life readings had suddenly emerged in Dayton after Cayce released the oil well effort. This time the trance counsel focused on the formation and nurture of small, self-led study groups or training groups. These were to use daily disciplines chosen by the groups, together with regular prayer and meditation, to engage a succession of biblically based themes in spiritual growth, such as serious mystics had long developed in devotional manuals. Starting in September 1931, special readings continued for thirteen years and expressed the heart of Cayce's fresh covenant with his Lord.

The new counsel emerged quite unexpectedly when Mrs. Barrett, a Norfolk housewife, brought together a group of friends in her home to secure readings from Cayce on how to develop psychically. What they got was a training regimen that taxed them severely and paid far less attention than they expected to psychic talents as such, except as guidance and healing which the information described as normal for deep and regular prayer. They were assigned the task of writing a modest two-volume book together, which would (in the humility associated with spiritual movements of the past) be published anonymously. They were not to claim any special authority from Cayce's unusual process, but to affirm in the book's simple introduction, "There is nothing new here. The search for God is as old as humankind." Though they could quote brief passages of readings now and then, and build the book on themes that actually came from readings, they were to appeal only to a pragmatic criterion which headed the introduction: "Try living the precepts of this book." Readers in other study groups that would follow were to explore for themselves such quiet processes of spiritual growth as those in the book, sharing their findings at weekly meetings not unlike those of Wesley's prayer bands, and similar to the small gatherings in homes that marked the fourteenth-century Friends of God in the Rhine Valley, or the best of the German Pietists in the seventeenth century.[178]

Nothing in the books was to be presented as self-authenticating, whether from the Bible or the readings, although a general Christian perspective was used. To make that point about the sources of truth very clear, both explanations and illustrations were to be written up from the actual experience of group members, not simply quoted from Cayce's readings, and the text was to be their own, however pedestrian or plain. Twelve chapters, or lessons, were to make up each volume. Each was prefaced by an affirmation suggested in the readings for regular use in meditation and in studying the chapter's theme. There was no indication that the two volumes were the only such devotional study books or manuals which might be developed from themes in the readings.

The process which the readings initiated for the manual was striking. After each new theme was introduced, the group was brought together monthly for a reading which examined their lives one by one to discern and report how authentically they were living the substance of the chapter. No new material would be given them until they passed this inspection. As a result, eleven years were required to complete the small

---

[178]See Underhill, Evelyn, *Mysticism*, 1911, and lnge, W.R., *Christian Mysticism*, 1956. On the Friends of God, see Jones, Rufus, *The Flowering of Mysticism*, 1939, and comparisons with Cayce groups in Bro, *Begin A New Life*, 1971. For an influential viewpoint on group life, see Bonhoefer, D., *Life Together*, 1954.

maroon–colored and neatly bound books; one theme
occupied an entire year before a reading would give
them further material. Slowly members grew in capacity
to evaluate themselves, using prayer, journals, dreams,
visions, and earnest responses to one another, shaped
by biblical motifs. Such means were enjoined as part of
the entire spiritual growth process, capable of replacing
evaluations from readings. Cayce's years of teaching the
Bible, in which he struggled to make its use empirical
and relevant, were mirrored in the training themes suggested by his readings for whatever serious lovers and
servants of God might choose to work with the little
volumes, entitled *A Search for God*, Books I and II.[179] The
plan from the beginning was that no charge would be
required for membership in groups which might use this
material. Since the inspiration required to complete it
had been a gift to all of them, no fee was appropriate,
other than the cost of the book.

Service toward others ran as a bright thread through
the new training readings, setting the resultant volumes
apart from many comparable manuals that have emphasized self–development and perfection of soul as the
major goals of spiritual growth. But service here was not
undirected busyness. To stress the necessary attunement,
each volume opened with an illuminating but undogmatic chapter on the ancient art of meditation as a
complement to prayer and corporate worship. The original small group, in which Edgar, Gertrude, Gladys, and
Hugh Lynn were members, was composed of persons
thoroughly immersed in church life, who would have
been surprised (as my notes on interviews with them
indicated)[180] to consider that anyone would use their
little books without fully engaging in such community,

[179]Published by A.R.E. Press.

[180]See Bro, Harmon H., "The Saving Secret," *Venture Inward*, January/
February 1988, p. 49.

where discerning preaching, sacraments, and outreach to the needy or threatened embedded their search for depth in faith. The effort directly paralleled the rise of tens of thousands of lay-led study groups in Latin America, fifty years later, as Christian Base Communities, constituting one of the most important religious and reforming movements of modern times.

Why was Cayce's new group-centered type of reading important? Seen in context, the focus on small search-and-share spiritual training groups came directly after the failure of the hospital and university. It addressed the heartbreaking dynamics of such failure, showing an initiative uncommon to seers. All of the principal figures in the hospital-university venture had received life readings, frequently with further detailed accounts of individual lifetimes. Yet knowledge of karmic themes and tangles had not prevented them from falling out. All of them had been continuously coached by readings to strengthen family ties, by depending on the love and judgment of those close to them. Yet the Blumenthal families had broken up, at terrible cost to the brothers and their spouses and children, while affairs had distracted some of the medical staff.

All of them had been prodded continuously by readings to claim the full measure of their religious heritages: Judaism for the Jews and Christianity for the Christians. The readings were not oblivious to conflicts in the two traditions, which they addressed with care, but neither were they bent on evangelism or the kind of conversions which for centuries had been forced on Jews. In the perspective of the trance counsel, there was so much in the common heritage of prophetic faith to build upon that if each participant took this challenge seriously in synagogue or church, they would have their hands full and grow in stature before God. Yet participation in spiritual communities had failed to command the humility of the participants in the debacle.

All of them had also been members and leaders of the nonprofit and idealistic Association of National Investi-

gators, bent upon service of mankind for medical and
psychological purposes, as well as for philosophical and
theological truth. Yet this fellowship had not proven
strong enough to deflect quarrels and evoke cooperation born of love when differences of opinion and status
developed. Obviously a much deeper and more effective
method of life transformation was required for any who
might seek to build together in the future, and these
readings took up exactly that need. They were the
equivalent, though with a markedly different sort of assumptions, of the disciplined efforts emerging in America
at the same time as psychoanalysis, which would generate in time its own legacy of small group processes.[181]

With these readings, known as the "262 series," supplemented by an entire series on healing with prayer and
meditation (the "281 series") that generated the Glad
Helpers group (named after a church group in Cayce's
past), Cayce's work entered the mainstream of serious
mysticism. It joined the efforts of devout men and
women across centuries of Western faith that had gathered in small groups and prepared manuals for growth
as they steeped themselves in prayer, study, and helpful
service.[182] Cayce's new counsel developed a systematic
sequence of archetypal motifs[183] grounded in daily activity. Though he would remain essentially a seer in his

[181]For a survey of psychoanalytic and other schools of group efforts, see Shaffer, J.B. and Galinsky, *Methods of Group Therapy and Sensitivity Training*, 1974.

[182]See Bro, Harmon H., *Begin a New Life*, 1971, for comparisons. An
important book on group training at the time was Heard, Gerald,
Pain, Sex and Time, 1939. See Clinebell, Howard, *Growth Groups*, 1972.

[183]On the sequence, see Bro, Harmon H., *Begin a New Life*, 1971, and
Edgar Cayce on Religion and Psychic Experience, 1970, both of which are
built on it, as is Mark Thurston's *How to Interpret your Dreams*, 1978,
with his two manuals, *Experiments in A Search for God*, 1976, and *Experiments in Practical Spirituality*, 1980. For verbatim Cayce excerpts,
see *Library Series*, vol. 7, *The Study Group Readings*, 1977, and vols. 17
and 18, *Expanded Search for God*, Parts 1 and II, 1983.

method of individual counseling all the rest of his life, his trance aid now reached beyond alleviating personal suffering or crises of vocation and business to shaping a path of growth Godward. Upon his death a New York paper would headline his obituary not as a psychic, but as a mystic.[184] The distinction was accurate and important.

Yet the change did not give him, as an untimely seer, a firm place in American society. Protestant church life of the time was taken up with the antimystical though deeply felt Neo-Orthodoxy of Barth[185] and others, while Jewish religious thought was a bit more responsive to mystical currents in the thought of Heschel and Buber, yet in American synagogue life the Hassidic heritage[186] was more often seen as a form of ardent Orthodoxy than as a viable perspective on faith for most urban Jews. Russian and other forms of Eastern Orthodox traditions with strong mystical currents were still so strongly ethnic as to not often engage in dialogue across communions, while Roman Catholic life had its own heritage of mysticism, but not in forms that could take on Cayce's deviant reincarnation approach. As a consequence, he remained a seer out of season, more often known and sought for his skill with practical unknowns than for his new group-based teaching and coaching, however sophisticated and rich these efforts were. Yet a reading told him that he was now doing more good in several directions than he had as Ra Ta or Uhjltd.

---

[184]*New York Herald Tribune*, January 4, 1945. Reprinted by permission.

[185]Barth's major work is his *Epistle to the Romans*, 1950. A representative anti-mystical viewpoint of the time is Aulen, Gustaf, *The Faith of the Christian Church*, 1948. Tillich's work, which combined what he saw as mystical and prophetic strains in Christian faith (as in his *The Courage to Be*, 1957), was not yet widely studied.

[186]For example, Buber, Martin, *The Legend of the Baal Shem*, 1955, and *Hasidism and Modern Man*, 1958.

An Association of Plain People

The corporate vehicle for Cayce's new readings emerged several months after the closing of the hospital when some sixty friends gathered in his home on 35th Street; the date was June 6, 1931. As before at turning points in his life, he had wrestled with himself and God for weeks after the hospital was shut down and the last patients were sent home. He prayed, took long walks, read his Bible, dug in his garden, and slowly regained a will to live. Then he took a step similar to that in long ago Hopkinsville when he had sought written opinions from judges and other public figures on the validity of his work. But at that time the need was to handle the flood of pleading letters that had followed the first widespread newspaper publicity on his work. Now the need was to decide whether to continue with his readings at all. He did not this time turn to public figures but to his own constituency, those he had served for so many years. Gladys pulled out names from the files, and he sent a letter to scores of friends, asking whether they thought he should continue with his readings after the dispiriting collapse of the hospital. Uniformly they responded with encouragement, often with touching details of how readings had transformed or even saved their lives.

Those who lived in the Virginia Beach and Norfolk area, called Tidewater Virginia by local residents, gathered with him on the June afternoon. Except for Dave Kahn, the New York men and women of means on whom Cayce had depended so heavily were largely absent. Dr. Brown was there with his dean and some of his faculty, still trying to keep the university going, and ready to start a promising summer term in a location at nearby Oceana. So were a few solid Norfolk businessmen. But the rest were mostly plain, ordinary people: teachers, nurses, real estate agents, housewives, business persons, a Naval officer, and more. No physician was present, and only one minister from out of town, Dr. Scattergood. Cayce had not yet developed in Virginia Beach the kinds of professional ties once his in Selma.

Edgar spoke first, looking back over his life and sharing responses to his readings which had meant much to him. Then Dave got up, and in his enthusiastic way shared his perspective from sixteen years of intimate work with Cayce. He was only thirty-one but tested by military service and impressive business experience. One after another, people spoke their pieces in a spontaneous outpouring of appreciation and affection for Cayce that stirred him to the soul. Soon a consensus developed that a new organization should be formed to receive members and help him carry on his work. Edgar saw, seated on the stair landing, the tall figure in white clothing and turban who had appeared to warn him of his associates in Hopkinsville years ago. This time the figure nodded in encouragement, and Cayce drew strength from his presence, though nobody else saw him. Dr. Brown suggested a name, drawn from the former hospital, and in a few days the Association for Research and Enlightenment was incorporated with a board made up largely of local people who had little experience with boards but strong conviction that they should help Cayce.

In the months that followed, various men were considered as possible managers, and one served a term in this post, but little significant organization and planning were accomplished until Hugh Lynn volunteered for the assignment, having completed his college studies and a major in psychology the year before. He turned out to be just right for the job, with a natural flair for recruiting helpers that the few who knew of his life reading (he kept it from public knowledge all his life)[187] traced to the disciple Andrew, and with a take-charge competence that led some to see the Young King from far-off Egypt.

---

[187]The A.R.E. first appeared to suggest it after Hugh Lynn Cayce's death in a 1984 collection of his lectures entitled *The Jesus I Knew*, but the detailed identification was made by Church, W.H., in his survey of Edgar's past lives, *Many Happy Returns*, 1984.

He spoke in public with easy grace and well–thought-out ideas, and he wrote clear and compelling prose,[188] as his life reading had indicated he would when given to him as a teenager. He had a remarkable skill at leading small groups, which soon made him valuable not only to the Association but also to the Boy Scouts, whom he served for years as an innovative and much loved local Scoutmaster. Prosaic as Scouting might seem as a laboratory for learning how to lead others in work built on Cayce's unusual gift, it turned out to be helpful for focus on principles, growth through disciplined achievement, fellowship, and religious ethos.

He plunged in with vigor and kept the post until he left for military service twelve years later. Money was never available to him beyond his immediate needs, because the little Association barely scraped by. Times were often hard for the entire Cayce family in the Depression period; they lost weight, lived frugally, and ran up a grocery bill of three hundred dollars which hung over them for years. They moved to rental houses twice before they finally managed to buy a home with practically nothing down, and in 1940 added office space, with Edgar doing much of the carpentry. The father kept the funds, in a pattern of a family firm, giving Hugh Lynn cash when he asked for it but never a salary. Edgar loved to give people money, whether family or strangers, but because he worried so much about having enough, he was slow to arrive at the practice of regular wages for them. However, by the time I joined him, that had changed.

Anonymity

In the covenant that had shaped itself around the events of leaving Selma to finance and build a hospital,

---

[188]Best seen in his *Venture Inward*, 1964, and his *Faces of Fear*, 1980.

Edgar had asked God for helpers so that he could provide fitting leadership. They had been given, some as blessings and some as trials. First came Dave, then the oilfield friends and his father. Next came Gladys, followed by the Blumenthals, and in the hospital Dr. House and Carrie, as well as his sisters Annie and Sarah, with Dr. Brown and the talented faculty of the university, such as Dr. Job Taylor, skilled in classical languages. Now there was his elder son, the most promising of them all for the aid he needed. It might be expected that with such assistance he would push on to reclaim the hospital or build another. But his best inner guidance looked another direction. It was time for a new covenant.

He would not ask for an institution or for public position; that pattern was over. Now he would lay down striving to build something notable and concentrate on another goal: training and equipping others to work with the ideas and the life-transforming processes in his readings, especially in the small groups suggested by his new form of counsel. He would take on his own son to share with him all he could, although they often clashed, since both were strong-minded and hot-tempered. He would build up the plain people of Tidewater who responded to his efforts. And he would ask God to send him others, not now for a cause, however worthy the hospital project had been. He wanted those who would make a difference in their own walks of life, most of all those ready to work with one another in their growth and training. This much he could already see from the mistakes with the Blumenthals; he had been quick to draw on their generous and idealistic aid, but not quick enough in personally training them, other than through readings, or quick enough to fashion full spiritual community with and for them. He took full responsibility for his mistakes in letters to friends and promised himself he would not make the same errors again.

In his new covenant he would lay aside his old hungers to do something important to validate himself and his peculiar gift, now accepting anonymity. There would be no hospital or foundation named after him. The change to this new focus took time, but once in place it never really wavered. And he discovered as he made it that he could ask as never before to be cleansed and made whole himself. In the past he had prayed for God to protect him and his family, as well as to protect those who received the readings he could neither hear nor control. Now he was ready to ask for more than sheltering love. He wanted deep and lasting growth in his own mind and will and heart so that he could be the person he asked others to be. His earliest spiritual experience as a lad had brought him a promise which included the instruction: "Be true to yourself." More than ever before he was ready to reach for his best self. This part of his new and final covenant would, it turned out, be honored as fully as the other dimensions of it, though not without his suffering.

From the viewpoint of his karma, he could be seen as returning to the source where he began, as Lucius the Greco–Roman follower of Jesus down the roads of Palestine. This incarnation had first seemed evident in his compelling Bible teaching as a young man on the farm and in Hopkinsville, where so many had chosen service in mission fields. He was claiming afresh what he came to see as the stature of the seasoned bishop or presbyter of the church at Laodicea, where he had been a peer in his own way to Paul and Peter, and a laborer on the Gospel of Luke with Acts, addressed to Theophilus so long ago. It was a lifetime still unknown to him but soon to be disclosed in a reading because he was living it. He had retrieved the leadership potential of Uhjltd in Persia as best he could with the damage done to it by self-destruction in Troy and by the exploitation of Bainbridge among the colonies; his recent public failure at Virginia Beach (worse than unsuccessful oil wells) had pruned his ambition and humbled him for everyone to see. He had called on the heritage of Ra Ta both to locate oil and to unfold life readings, as well as to build two institutions that mirrored the two Egyptian temples. Now he was coming home to his central self and vocation from the adventurous and Spirit-filled times of the New Testament, with his son a long ago companion of Jesus to help him be his best self.

The impulse for unfolding his karma would be different from what had challenged him before. As a young man he had sought to nurture intimate love for his family, together with the earnings and position that would support them. Then as a man of early mid-life at forty-three, he had set out to fulfill a worthwhile public ambition by building his hospital. Now, as a mature man of fifty-four, he would choose a different framework, in which the key word would be service. There had always been a service motivation in his giving of readings, of course, just as there was in the creation of the hospital and university. But at this point he would seek a richer kind of service: selfless service without public recognition. Instead of helpers boosting him, he would try to boost others.

The task seemed more possible because the companionship of Jesus as a living Friend and not merely a past leader was becoming more and more real to him. He met the one he called the Master in dreams, in visions while giving readings, in prayer times, in church worship, in the act of talking with somebody troubled. His readings assured him these were real contacts, not just lovely symbols, but the sort open to every soul who would prepare for them. With Jesus at the core of his devotion, he sought to walk in his footsteps and partake of his loving creativity and willingness to sacrifice for others. The success he wanted in his new covenant was relationship to this Christ, more than he had longed even for his cherished hospital of last resort for the wounded and broken. From such a companionship many outcomes could flow, wherever they seemed best to his Lord.

As a step toward that precious relationship, he told me (as he also wrote to friends in letters), he had completely forgiven the Blumenthals and hoped someday to

be forgiven by them in turn. How could he expect to
grow in grace if he held grudges? The riddle of what had
happened to his soaring hopes with young Morton
haunted him, however, right up to the last few days before his death. He knew that his life readings had depicted him and Morton as antagonists in Egypt, when Ra
Ta had brought on scorn by his indulgences, and again
as antagonists in Troy, when the imposing figure of
Achilles had shared in the defeat and shame of Xenon,
the guardian of the gates. But there was a piece missing,
which came to him only on his deathbed. There he
roused himself to tell Mae Verhoeven, panting with the
effort and his voice weak, that he had seen in a vision
how he had mistreated the soul now Morton when he
was unfair to him in another task of building long ago. It
was the rebuilding of Jerusalem after the Exile, in a lifetime not given him by his readings, but indicated for
Morton. Then his own arbitrariness and unkindness, he
felt, had laid the groundwork for suspicion to develop
suddenly between them centuries later in Virginia
Beach—or so it seemed to him as suffering altered his
consciousness and appeared to lift the veil of past-life
memory.

Ousted and Jailed

Readings had commented that those who would grow
the most often suffered the most at first. He quickly
found such suffering, not as masochism but as agony of
confronting his own limitations. Morton instructed him
to move out of the house which he thought was his as a
gift. Since Morton had never bothered to transfer the
deed, Edgar and his family had to move on short notice.
The only house they could find was just down the street
toward the ocean from the hospital building, where they
watched in horror as it was turned into the Princess Pat
Hotel and eventually made a nightclub. The nurses'
quarters, a spacious three-story residence, became a

rooming house. Meantime the university dragged to a close, leaving faculty stranded at Virginia Beach in the midst of national hard times that held no jobs for most of them. They piled up bills at the grocery, then ran out of food, and friends who were townspeople had to take up collections to keep their families from starving. The memory of their pain and shame stayed with Edgar the rest of his life, since they had joined him to build a new world in which gifts such as his would be understood and more widely developed, but left him when they were hurt, bewildered, and sometimes bitter. Often he asked himself why he had not fully grasped the debacle coming or been able to prevent it with inspired leadership of his contending backers.

Pain in a different way was his humiliation in New York when he went there on a final fruitless mission to secure money for the university. A policewoman in disguise pressed hard for a reading and signed an application, then arrested him for fortune-telling when the trance was over, also arresting Gertrude as conductor and Gladys as secretary. A reading later taken on the incident indicated that it had been set up by his former New York associates but did not specify names. The three were bitterly embarrassed not only by being unceremoniously jailed until Kahn got them out on bond, but by tabloid newspaper features that cut Gertrude out of photos taken at the jail entrance to suggest that Cayce and his blonde secretary of twenty-six were lovers. When the case came to trial, it was dismissed on the grounds that they were conducting psychic research for the new association each time they gave a reading with a signed consent. The *New York Herald Tribune* story ran this lead to a full and sympathetic article on Cayce's life and ability:

Research Plea Voids Charge of Fortune Telling
Edgar Cayce, Wife and Typist, Freed in Court as Members of Association Leader's Power Released
Said to Learn Contents of Books While Unconscious[189]

Cayce was in shock over the event, wondering whether his understanding or covenant with God, which had always included protecting him when he gave readings, had somehow been broken. As he walked down a New York street alone trying to calm himself, he told me later, he came to a construction excavation, where he stared at the large machinery and the workers for a time, then started to go on. Coming toward him on the sidewalk was the figure in white clothing and turban. This time passersby saw the striking sight, and a crowd began to gather. The dark–complexioned man in white came up to him and then knelt before him, saying nothing. In a few moments scores of people pressed in so tightly to see the strange sight that Cayce had to be rescued from the crush by a nearby policeman. When he looked back, the white–clad figure was gone, and he never saw him again.

One Honored by Jesus

Edgar took comfort from the apparent blessing after his jail ordeal. But the total impact of the current blows shook him. As before in his times of hardship, the consequence was a measure of vulnerability to the femi-

---

[189]*New York Herald Tribune*, November 17, 1931. Reprinted by permission.

nine, in which he might find renewed the pulse of man-hood so threatened by his public failures. Gladys had encouraged a young woman close to her family and two years her senior to move to Virginia Beach during the operation of the hospital. She got a job as a secretary and stayed on, eventually joining Cayce's Bible classes and the *Search for God* group, as well as carrying responsi-bilities for the Association that entailed her hearing many readings. Bright and winsome, with a lovely sing-ing voice and what seemed at times buried sensuality, as well as strong spiritual intuitions, she was frustrated in her hopes for marriage and inclined to be hard on her-self. Her first life reading in 1929 left them all incredu-lous by reporting that she had been Mary, the sister of Martha and Lazarus in Bethany, where she had "chosen the better part" by listening to Jesus not once but many times. This reading and subsequent ones insisted that the Mary of Bethany had earlier been known as Mary Magdalene, operating a house of ill repute for Roman trade and arrested for adultery by Jewish elders who planned to stone her, then released by Jesus. She had developed a deep mistrust of men which would haunt her in later lives, including one in the French court. But in the Holy Land she had eventually served among the early followers of Jesus with such faithfulness that Jesus appeared first to her after his resurrection. Her ties to Cayce's incarnations, Gladys told me, appeared not only among early Christians but in Egypt, where she helped to arrange the return of the high priest, and in Uhjltd's Persia.

Slowly Cayce, starting over in his post-hospital cov-enant, found himself drawn to her, first as one he could train. Had not this soul been honored by Jesus? She in turn fell deeply in love with him, and her touching de-votion was evident to all those around him. Of his own feelings, Cayce dreamt as early as 1932, a few months after the jail episode that he fell into water over his head and could not climb out, so shouted for aid. When they could not rescue him, Gladys ran for help while he tugged at the feet of the other woman. She asked, "Can't you climb up?" And when he answered "No!", she replied, "Well, pull me down." A reading called the dream a warning and counseled caution, as well as mutual prayer and meditation. The attraction deepened, and readings warned Cayce of that which was "uncomely" as they pointed out what he must still meet from his Bainbridge incarnations. For months during this strain Cayce's body moved jerkily in readings, as though mirroring the pressures within him.

In 1935 the gifted woman left to develop what became a productive married life of her own, while the Cayces were on a trip to Washington, D.C. Edgar shut off his feelings for her with the capacity for utter detachment which he had learned he could call up. She had been a presence before him for five years, as though in response to the cry in his covenant to be cleansed and made whole. By 1941 he had so firmly established his true feelings for Gertrude that he dreamt appreciatively of their relationship in an episode which he felt told the truth of their lives: "Dreamed I was looking over a lot of records, and I saw what would have happened if Gertrude and I hadn't gotten married. She would have died in 1906 of T.B., and I would have died in 1914 of stomach trouble." The night before he actually died a few years later, he roused himself from the coma where he drifted in and out, and asked Gertrude tenderly, "What have I ever sacrificed because I love you?" In the report of those present, she touched his head gently and reassured him that his love had meant everything to her. Nobody who knew them well and understood the profound love that had grown between them for so many years, not without pain, was surprised that she followed him in death only three months after his life ended.

Edgar was never driven again by the old karmic longing to find his soul mirrored in a woman. As if to bless his strenuous efforts to change, he found himself joined in 1938 by Mae Verhoeven, who came as a volunteer in the office to help pay for her medical reading, and stayed on working there until his death and after. She was immensely attractive and full of vital spirits, and knew it, but neither she nor Cayce distorted the relationship beyond affectionate teasing, even when they heard from life readings that she had been his patrician Roman wife or companion as Vesta, bearing him two sons and a daughter, and his companion again in the rowdy tavern incarnation at Fort Dearborn, where he had saved her life on the Ohio River as he lost his own. (Since readings indicated that I had been her son when Lucius was my father, we shared much all around joshing about her past lives and Cayce's, as well as many serious hours of reflection. Later, June and I named our first child after her.) Her reading noted her capacity to affect men, observing that she could make them fight each other for a smile and affection, and found it easy to wind men around her finger. In Atlantis she had been a high priestess. Her association in Virginia Beach with Cayce appeared to be a renewing of her ties with him in the early Church, when she had lived to a ripe old age and taught the young, becoming a deaconess at the direction of John the Beloved. Their companionship rewarded both in this life, and she helped Gertrude and others to care for Cayce in his final illness, including being present at his bedside when he died.

The Real Miracle

One more jolt which seemed to the Cayces to derive from the Bainbridge karma awaited them in Detroit, part of the area where the second Bainbridge had wandered. In November 1935, Edgar went there with Gertrude, Gladys, and Hugh Lynn to be guests of a family that had often been helped by readings. When their hosts asked for a medical reading for a sick neighbor girl, Edgar responded quickly, as he always did to the needs of children, but failed to get the permission of the father, who was not there. The angry parent went to the police and had them arrested for practicing medicine without a license—a charge to which they were clearly liable. Again they were jailed, a humiliating outcome from his desire to serve. The Detroit paper carried this notice:

Police Arrest Four on a Quack Charge

Four persons were arrested Saturday on a charge of practicing medicine without a license . . . They were taken into custody at 3046 Webb Avenue, where they have been staying for ten days following their arrival here from Virginia. Police said Edgar Cayce is president of the Association for Research and Enlightenment. Members can obtain an alleged diagnosis of illness by paying Cayce $20, police said. The diagnosis is furnished by mail after Cayce goes into a "trance" and thinks over the symptoms reported, according to the police.[190]

Released on bail after a night of incarceration, they sought a reading which advised delaying the trial for several months while they sought all the legal help they could get. When the case came to court, the others were cleared of all charges, but Edgar was found guilty and paroled in his own custody.

Hugh Lynn Cayce later described to me a remarkable scene in the barren and cold county jail, where they were locked up with drunks, thieves, and pickpockets, as well as a few strikers, and left to sleep on hard metal benches until arraignment the next morning. As the evening dragged on, Edgar began talking thoughtfully with those around him, where he stood in a corner. He spoke with quiet eloquence about the love of Jesus for the poor and the outcast, and how he had often found those of little

[190]Detroit, November 30, 1935; name of paper unknown (clipping in archival files of A.R.E.).

reputation were most ready to learn spiritual truths and to help others in times of need. Given the circumstances, he might have been angry and bitter, but he was not. Instead, his situation seemed to put him in touch with the very spirit of the Christ. The cell grew quiet, and soon the neighboring cells did also, as Cayce spoke with compelling but restrained fire to his fellow prisoners, telling some of his own hardships and failures. He spoke for thirty minutes or so, and when he concluded with a simple but heartfelt prayer, the hush hung in the air and some were in tears. He was learning what his readings insisted: God asked of each person, including himself, not so much perfection as willingness to try, getting up again after each fall, whether personal or public, to pursue a worthy ideal. The spirit of this assurance quickly reached people who got to know him well, all the rest of his life.

On the long train trip home he had a dramatic dream, which showed him reborn a century later, in a coastal city in Nebraska! [A later reading would suggest that the imagery was to indicate that regardless of what transpired in the outer world (e.g., being arrested for practicing medicine without a license), his work would survive.] In the dream, he assured scientists that he had been Edgar Cayce and that they could find evidence of his life and work, which they eventually did, taking him to far locations in a cigar-shaped spacecraft. The dream gave him the assurance that his life would not be completely lost from record, despite the distress of jail and other calamities.

Other dreams of the times put his work in larger perspective than public fame. In a delightful parable he dreamed that he and Gertrude and Gladys died and went to the next plane, where he found that people all around him knew little of their own identity, bearing only the name of Jesus on their foreheads (an image drawn from the biblical Book of the Revelation). He met Mae's father, Mr. Gimbert the carpenter, and had him build a dwelling where he set about giving readings. One by one he took people, some strangers and some he had known, and recalled for them their earthly identities and labors and loves, not to replace the name of Jesus but to enrich it with the unique individuality of each. Awakening, he saw the dream as a parable of the real purpose in all he did with life readings and in his Bible teaching. He was to remind people of their full accomplishments, nature, and destiny as individual friends of God, in one lifetime or many, called to grow into His presence.

A very different dream, even more visionary, had come during the period before the Detroit arrest when he was still struggling with his own emotional tugs. He described the scene and events with the eyes of a skilled photographer, but the climax was a note of faith which became the hallmark of his covenant through the rest of his days. The dream, which touched me deeply when I heard it, was modeled on the biblical story of Jacob wrestling with the angel, but also reflected the "Message to Garcia" story of delivering a message through painful trials, which he had heard in sermons and used in his teaching.

He saw himself on the way to an unknown military camp, carrying a message to the commander in a little leather case like those for spy glasses, slung over his shoulder. The taxing route led over a mountain, so that he did not reach his destination until just before dawn. Before him was a host of men clad all in white uniforms, making their breakfasts in groups of four. He asked the way to the man in charge and set out for a great white tent in the distance. Along the way he passed a dark ravine to the side, where the sound of someone stepping on sticks made him stop. Suddenly there appeared a second host, all dressed in dark garments, with an angel of light between him and them. They were joined by an angel of darkness, who insisted on a fight between representatives selected by the angels. Cayce was chosen to fight with the leader of the hosts of darkness, and they began to wrestle.

As they struggled, Cayce was haunted by the sense

that he had not delivered the message in his leather pouch. Had he waited too long? It seemed that the imp or leader of darkness would put him down in the dirt, and the prospect was unbearable. If he could only re-member it, he would be safe, but what was it? They wrestled on through the dawn. Then from the very cen-ter of him came the words of Jesus' promise that he had been charged to carry: "And Lo, I am with you always, even unto the end of the world." The soldiers of darkness fell back, and a great shout went up from the people in white. But as the angel of darkness fell back, he struck Cayce on the hip, so that he awakened with a great pain there.

Edgar did not see the dream action depicting him as a redeemer. Quite the contrary, the message of Jesus en-trusted to him made clear who the real savior was. What he saw was the struggle in his own soul, to choose the way of the Creative Forces, and to put his trust entirely in the Master. That his choices would affect not only him, leaving crippling pain from the struggle as seen in the dream, but affect others as well, he had no doubt, since in his worldview the choices of each person made a real difference in the larger outcomes of events. His own personhood was a battleground, but so were the personhoods of others all around him in daily life.

I found the dream poignant when I heard it near the end of his life, because so many signs indicated that he was not quite sure, all the way to his death, that he had fulfilled the trust placed in him. He wondered, inevita-bly, whether his own stumbling had obscured the help-ful, hopeful message that he wanted to share through his gift. He could see the good that had been done through him, and because of him, in the lives of thou-sands who had received readings. But was this enough? Was he supposed to have done more? Was a hospital appointed for him to build, but lost by his own limita-tions? Had he made clear that the aid which poured through him for so many years was not his own, but from the One who promised to be with His fellows always?

He knew well that he was no saint. He could not serve as a model of an ideal spiritual life. At best he could be seen as a warrior who kept fighting the darkness in himself as long as he could. For many who looked carefully at the story of his life, he knew that would not be enough. He knew he smoked too much, ate too much, lost his temper, criticized others arbitrarily, worried, rode his passions, forgot to put first things first, trusted too much in his own plans, failed to build community as he went. But in the dawn hours, when he so often read his Bible and prayed with his whole heart, wrestling, he remembered to try again to point beyond himself, trusting that his painful shortcomings would be obliterated by the radiance of a loving God.

The dream, and its promise that he could faithfully deliver what had been entrusted to him, came back to me many years later in San Diego when Hugh Lynn and I were lecturing together and he spoke to the audience about his father's personal struggles. "The real miracle," he said, "is not that Edgar Cayce gave *readings*. The miracle is that *Edgar Cayce*, with all the problems and tensions inside him, gave readings and kept on giving them."

His Visionary Abilities Grew

As the manager of the small Association, Hugh Lynn found that he had some three hundred people around the country who wanted more than just the privilege of securing readings. He began sending them a mimeographed monthly *Bulletin* that featured articles on subjects related to the content or operation of his father's counsel, plus book reviews and reports on the modest research projects which he developed, surveying not only treatment patterns in the readings for various diseases, but *A Study of Clairvoyance*,[191] as one mimeo booklet

---

[191]Cayce, Hugh Lynn, *A Study of Clairvoyance*, 1940.

was titled. His own passion was psychical research.[192] He saw it as a doorway to fresh understanding of spiritual realities in modern times, especially if psychic phenomena were presented as expressions of the soul and not as mere mental attainments. He got his father to visit Rhine at Duke, followed by the stay of the psychologist Lucien Warner at Virginia Beach, sent by Rhine. Warner arranged for a study of life readings by the other leading figure in psychical research of the 1930s, the respected psychologist at Columbia, Gardner Murphy. However, Murphy got sidetracked from the project, and they never received the full results of the study.

Determined to move into larger professional circles, Hugh Lynn arranged readings by his father for interested leaders in New York and Philadelphia. At one of these in the home of a professor at the University of Pennsylvania, he became so distracted that he failed to give his father the proper suggestion in time, and Edgar fell into a deep sleep for four hours, ending the demonstration in embarrassment. Later Hugh Lynn moved to New York for a period, falling in love and conducting a weekly radio show about psychic experiences that drew thousands of letters. Edgar backed him but with the reserve that came from his years of trying to find a balance between responsible presentations and fruitless publicity.

More to his liking were the annual Congresses of members of the Association, which Hugh Lynn began within a year after its inception. His son invited a wide variety of speakers to the June events, representing the medical field, psychical research, religion, and philosophy, with literary figures occasionally added in. Members from around the country, especially the East Coast and the Midwest, joined Cayce's longtime friends from Kentucky, Alabama, and Ohio for these conferences which lasted several days or a week, and Edgar drew

---

[192]Best exhibited in his *Venture Inward,* 1964.

much encouragement from their presence and responsiveness. He always gave at least one talk himself, less scholarly than those of the invited specialists, but animated and thoughtful, built on biblical themes. Many looked forward to these talks as the highlights of the Congresses. A pattern developed of securing two public readings for these annual conferences: one on some issue of public interest, and one on the nature and prospects of Cayce's work.

When I came in wartime to take Hugh Lynn's place for a while, the task of preparing for and conducting the Congress was one of my duties. At this particular event I arranged for Cayce to demonstrate something unusual. He agreed to use a morning period by going around the room, describing and interpreting auras of those sitting there. The results engrossed us all. Apparently the aura he saw for each person stretched around the entire body, enabling him to discuss injuries and medical problems, as well as to give health warnings.[193] But as he spoke of various patterns and bands of color, with subtle hues and infusions of troublesome gray, as well as shafts and swirls of light, he went far beyond the body, turning to vocation for many, and to issues of marriage and family relationships, as well as character development and faith themes. I interviewed those present afterward and found him stunningly accurate on details that could be confirmed. Other matters had to wait for years for their outcome, such as telling an able osteopath not to run for public office or he would be soundly defeated (he was), and assuring a musician that her talents would flower only much later in life (they did).

Those close to Cayce felt that his visionary abilities, both awake and in trance, grew in the dozen years that followed the loss of the hospital. He often reported

[193]A booklet ascribed to Edgar Cayce, *Auras*, 1945, was largely written by Sugrue, incorporating Sugrue's ideas, although Cayce contributed.

dreams and visions that came to him while he was unconscious during readings. Simpler in speech, even col-
loquial, was the dream during a session, which I heard
him report when it happened. It reflected his sense that
Peter would be incarnating to help out with the spiritual
renewal needed for present times:

> Went fishing with John, James, Andrew and the
> Master. I asked where Peter was. "Oh you know
> Peter ain't here!" said James. Thomas said, "Oh
> yes, I was a fisherman; don't let them fool you,
> telling you to quit fishing. We are all eating fish."
> All of us were in the nicest little boat on a lake.

The vivid little experience lifted his spirits for days,
and he took to eating more fish. He remembered that his
life reading had indicated Thomas had taken his part,
when as young Lucius he found the other disciples pulling away from him, put off by his Greco-Roman ancestry. However, he did not fish more, and the rest of us
were not wise enough to encourage him to take the
needed breaks, using the impressive collection of tackle
which friends had given him over the years.

A beautiful visionary account of the Last Supper
poured through him in 1932 when he was still suffering
from the hospital loss. He failed to awaken after one
reading, despite three repetitions of the suggestion. Then,
as though standing at the scene, he described what each
person there wore and how each appeared, as well as
what they ate and drank from what sort of vessels,
with the foot washing of Peter and the others, and the
challenge to Judas. His verbal portrait of the Master,
down to his fingernails and the sewing of his robe,
was memorable. He described the events and the impression created when Jesus broke the bread and poured
the wine in his covenant with them, and how they sang
a hymn—Psalm 91—before leaving for the fateful developments in the garden. In the years that followed, many
treasured this little account, shared as though his gift

had suddenly made him an eyewitness. [194]

Other experiences were sobering. He roused himself in horror after one reading during wartime and reported that he had just seen an entire company of American soldiers wiped out in North Africa. He had already seen terrible suffering in Manchuria the same way, and predicted a revolution in China.[195] The awful violence of the war troubled him and found its way regularly into the prayers he offered at afternoon staff devotional meetings. Hugh Lynn later told me how his father called him into his study one day after the start of the global war, and told him which of the lads about to travel across the country with him on a Scouting trip should get his special attention. They were the ones who would be killed later in battle—as indeed they were.

When asked by those of serious intent rather than curiosity, Edgar's readings took up the theme of possible coming earth changes.[196] Parts of Southern California would slide into the sea within three months after eruptions at Mount Etna followed by comparable activity at Pelee in the Western Hemisphere. Land would come up from the ocean off the eastern coast of the U.S. with artifacts from lost Atlantis. Much later Manhattan would suffer devastating earthquakes, and the Japanese islands would be largely wiped out by earthquakes. Through comparable activity in the Midwest, the Great Lakes would empty into the Mississippi. But with these predictions the readings constantly offered the assurance that human righteousness and prayer could affect even the course of geology.

Social changes to come also drew descriptions from readings, not fatalistic but with similar provisos of human freedom. They warned of the death of two

[194]Presented in Cayce, H.L., *Venture Inward*, pp. 105–106. Alternatively, the account is on file at the A.R.E., Reading 5749-1.

[195]Cayce, H.L., *Venture Inward*, p. 105.

[196]See Thurston, Mark, *Visions and Prophecies for a New Age*, 1981.

American presidents in office (seemingly Roosevelt and Kennedy) and widespread rioting in the streets (perhaps the sequel to Martin Luther King's death), insisting that a devastating depression was yet to come in the U.S., when the social machinery would collapse so completely that those without access to plots for growing foods would suffer and many would starve. Everyone, the readings repeated, should have a goal of a home with direct relationship to the land, even if this meant restructuring the shape of contemporary society. Social justice for minorities and full accounting for the rights of labor must become serious business for Americans, or there would come "that leveling" which could only mean revolution.[197]

The cause of peace received attention in readings, with Americans warned that unless they took the leadership in ending armaments and warfare, the course of civilization would again pass westward, as at American beginnings, but this time to the Orient. At a Congress reading on world affairs after World War II had begun in Europe, the sixty-seven people in the room were told that God was no respecter of size but of the heart. If they alone, few as they were, prayed constantly for peace and lived as they prayed, no invasion would come to American soil. The concept seemed appealing but unlikely to those present, as they never followed up on the recommendations; in any case, Pearl Harbor followed.

Seeing human affairs on an even more cosmic scale, a reading which I heard quietly affirmed that after the early 1940s no souls would be incarnated in the earth who had not encountered the reality and spirit of the Christ somewhere in their long journey. Humans were given a long tether, but God also provided them with aid. Social change would be accelerated and polarized by the reappearance of many, many souls, not a few in leadership roles, who had taken part in the advanced engineering and technology of Atlantis, misusing the

[197]*Ibid.*

energies they commanded in such a way as to cause the breakup of the continent.[198] Modern life would again see electronic and nuclear genius, as well as new sources of energy, with the transmission of electrical power across long distances without wires, and the widespread use of crystals for coherent energy modes. However, the same souls who brought these gifts would present today's civilization with critical value choices: to move away from mindless technological mastery of whatever portion of the earth they chose to plunder.

Challenges to Cayce's reading process appeared. After breaking into readings with messages several times, a source which called itself Hallaliel, who proclaimed that it had never been incarnated but could bring Cayce much needed wisdom, asked them to place the reading process under his guidance.[199] The event occurred during study group readings, and the group went through much soul-searching and division before the majority won out, who felt that the only attunement Cayce should ever directly seek was to the Christ. A reading quietly confirmed the wisdom of their decision, which had been left up to them. The group also experienced a ringing voice which called itself Michael, Lord of the Way,[200] identified in a biblical reference as the same angelic force as that which had contended for the body of Moses, and one who stood ever ready to guard the approach to the Lord from those with impure intent. This being, whatever it finally was, made no effort to take over Cayce's work, only demanding that they all be more serious in their efforts.

Cayce agreed again to seek buried treasure but found his own dreams warning him against it. The readings taken gave enough factual items to tantalize the seekers

---

[198]See Cayce, Edgar Evans, *Edgar Cayce on Atlantis*, 1968.

[199]See Cayce, Charles Thomas, "Evaluating Channeled Information Carefully" in *Venture Inward*, July/August 1987.

[200]See also the Michael message in Reading 3976-7.

at Kelly's Ford and elsewhere[201] but again grew vague at crucial points, as in oil well days. By the time I knew him, he could not be tempted, although an agreeable man arrived one day with a full-blown plan to finance all of the Association's research efforts through the recovery of a lost silver mine, which he was sure he had documented. Cayce was much more interested in mining the man than the ore.

Once more, Edgar was sought for political guidance, first by a representative of the State Department going to war-divided China, who received valuable counsel. Not many months afterward, I answered the phone to hear that the office of the Vice President of the United States was calling. The man who requested the trance counsel was Henry Wallace, Vice President under Roosevelt, soon to go to China, who wanted a whole series of similar readings. Cayce gave him appointments some months ahead, unable to fit him in sooner. Then Cayce's own illness and death prevented him from revisiting the circles of national leadership he had reportedly known twice with Wilson.

He never turned again to Wall Street, although he gave business readings to Kahn and a few of his associates. Edgar had his own leftover business riddles from the Blumenthal days, in readings of subsequent years which insisted that someone from England would take a deep interest in his work, and that in time he and Gertrude would benefit substantially from stock investments on their behalf. Neither ever occurred, and they never knew why.

Research efforts interested them all, and Gladys kept track of the daily temperatures for an entire year to watch for correlations with the quality of the daily readings. None appeared, but the spirit of inquiry set a pattern that after Cayce's death would often be buried under

---

[201]See the accounts in Cayce, Edgar Evans and Hugh Lynn, *The Outer Limits of Edgar Cayce's Power*, 1971.

the typical American imperative to "get out the word,"
even when it was not always clear what word was to be
gotten out, in response to the Cayce legacy.[202] Various
responsible people pressed Hugh Lynn to discover the
reaches of Cayce's gifts, and readings located the sunken
Lusitania for divers (precisely describing what they would
encounter when they entered its rooms), as well as
tracked the kidnappers of the Lindbergh baby and located the downed aviatrix Amelia Earhart (but not in
time to save her from death that followed shortly, according to the readings). Huge puzzles popped up at
times, as in the life reading I heard given for a man with
homosexual tendencies, which indicated that astrological patterns were relevant, and added that on the particular day of his birth, only twenty-three of the babies
born in the entire U.S. were males. The size of the research to confirm with hospitals the sweeping trance vision put it beyond my reach, and the issue of how all
this might be reflected in charts of the stars and planets
was even more forbidding to tackle.

Once in a while a life reading caught Hugh Lynn's attention with the stature of the soul described there, especially when the recipients were children whose
subsequent development might be tracked and correlated with the features described in the reading. Parents
of one lad were told he had been Franz Liszt and had
present musical abilities to cultivate with care. Another
couple was told that their child could provide spiritual
leadership to many, if kept in a completely normal round
of life and always in the church, as he grew up. He had
been, the reading indicated, Thomas Campbell, whose
biography Cayce knew well as the Scotch Presbyterian
clergyman who came to Pennsylvania with his son,
Alexander, also a minister. There, in a town not far from
Pittsburgh, they and others had issued in 1820 the Wash-

---

[202]Readings of the time counseled that "enlightenment" was getting
too far ahead of "research."

ington Declaration, which resulted in the religious grouping that had engaged Cayce most of his life: the Christian
Church, or Disciples of Christ. The earlier lives ascribed
to Thomas did not surprise Cayce, who knew that the
elder Campbell's mystical tendencies had been stronger
than those of his son. He had been, the reading indicated, the biblical Elisha, successor to Elijah and the author of more remarkable happenings than any other
biblical figure except Jesus. Before that, he had been Noah.
Not surprisingly, given Noah's record, the trance counsel
warned of the tendency to alcoholism which would
trouble the boy as he grew up. Cayce was interested but
not fascinated by such cases, and they were never published or given special attention. The choices to be made
by each soul were its own, not to be distorted by publicity. The same attitude prevailed with the case which Hugh
Lynn later called the Little Prophetess, because her life
reading indicated that if she chose, and if she received a
disciplined and devout upbringing, she could manifest
abilities which would considerably exceed Edgar's own.

People for the Covenant of Training

Cayce's covenant with God in the post–hospital period, which proved to last fourteen years, was built
around the sense that he should focus on training and
equipping others who sought such aid. They came. Some
were in the group that developed the small books entitled *A Search for God*. Esther Wynne, a schoolteacher, became skilled at teaching others how to work in small
groups. Florence Edmonds, a nurse, grew in the practice
of healing by laying on of hands, especially in groups,
and taught others how to do it. From the Tuesday night
Bible class which Cayce taught in his home came Eula
Allen, wife of a Navy officer; she took a deep interest in
the readings' accounts of creation at the beginnings of
time in the earth, and later published her version of these
processes, but her special gift proved to be working with

teenagers learning how to meditate and grow spiritually.

Hugh Lynn developed sufficient extrasensory ability, backed by systematic study, to become a guide to the safe unfolding of psychic talents by many, as well as learning the dangers in pursuing undisciplined psychic phenomena, which he later described with care in his widely read book, *Venture Inward.* The family told me with mischievous delight of Hugh Lynn's early experience of stepping into the shade of his departed grandfather, the squire, on the stairs of the Virginia Beach house. Although not many knew about it, Hugh Lynn also was surprisingly effective at removing unwanted influences from haunted houses, which he was called upon to do a number of times. However, his major focus was on guiding people through lasting spiritual growth, which he did with special sensitivity to meditation that seemed natural to him, and with great skill in group dynamics, in which inventiveness and a grasp of processes and barriers came easily.[203]

His managerial abilities for leading and building the Association grew as years passed, so that in the decades after his father's death he developed it to a membership of thousands and bought back the former hospital building to use as a headquarters. In time the organization under his leadership would sponsor lectures and conferences annually in over seventy-five American cities and many abroad, plus four months of week-long conferences each summer at Virginia Beach, using a part-time faculty of over eighty professional and lay speakers and authors. It would have its own press, physiotherapy department, overseas tour programs, summer camp, archaeological digs abroad, and periodical. It would even begin classes again in Atlantic University, whose charter he had kept.[204]

---

[203]See his *Venture Inward,* "The Place of the Small Group in the Spiritual Search," pp. 212–217.

[204]See www.AtlanticUniv.edu for additional information.

Others besides Hugh Lynn appeared in Edgar's life for coaching. Readings began referring sufferers for certain kinds of medical care in the New York area to Dr. Harold J. Reilly, a physiotherapist with impressive offices, staff, and equipment in the posh Radio City complex at Rockefeller Center in Manhattan. A hearty man with much wisdom about the body, which included nutrition and exercise, as well as treatment procedures with baths, sweats, and massages, he had drawn a clientele that by the 1940s included major figures in the entertainment and business worlds, as well as artists and scientists. He was startled to have clients come in with typed instructions for their care which made sense to him after he examined them but whose origins made no sense: an unconscious and uneducated man in Virginia. He sought Cayce out and they became good friends and colleagues; he treated scores of the ill whom readings sent him, and worked out for himself an understanding of the Cayce health patterns which he published after Cayce's death, receiving a wide readership.[205] In his later years he also undertook the training of many young massage therapists, which eventually led to the Cayce/Reilly School of Massotherapy at Virginia Beach.[206]

In New York also were several physicians whom the readings picked as expert osteopaths, while another, Dr. Henry George III, volunteered his aid from Delaware, and a gifted woman osteopath who later taught in the Philadelphia school of osteopathy joined the growing list of scores of cooperating physicians, most of them interested in the entire outlook of the Cayce materials, along with the Cayce medical counsel. Dr. Frank Dobbins of Virginia Beach, a highly competent osteopath (as I learned for myself), was often suggested in readings, and delighted the Cayces with what he called the Dobbins method for using

---

[205]Reilly, Harold J., *The Edgar Cayce Handbook for Health Through Drugless Therapy*, 1985.

[206]See www.EdgarCayce.org for additional information.

the readings: doing exactly what they stipulated.

Edgar finally found at Virginia Beach a minister appreciative of his work and his personal struggles for growth in faith and grace. The man was Joseph Clower, the theologically sophisticated pastor (later to become a religion professor) at the Presbyterian Church where Cayce taught the Sunday morning adult class. Never committing himself to the concept of reincarnation, yet always interested in the accounts which Hugh Lynn and others brought him, Clower gave the Cayces and Gladys welcome pastoral care and support. He enjoyed coming out to the house for long theological discussions, he told me, even though he failed to convince Gertrude that she could safely abandon her Christian Church convictions for Presbyterian doctrine and practice; they both enjoyed the tussle over beliefs. In Edgar he found a Bible resource whose command of scriptural themes, not just scriptural passages, never failed to stir him. Not surprisingly, it was Clower whom the family chose to conduct the memorial services at the deaths of both Edgar and Gertrude.

The person with whom they shared the most on religious perspectives and reports in the readings, however, was Hugh Lynn's college roommate, Thomas Sugrue, who first came to hear readings, highly skeptical, in 1927. He was Roman Catholic, a Connecticut native, and possessed of both an exceptionally keen mind and lyrical writing skills. As the editor of *The New Tomorrow* magazine, published by the first Association during the height of hospital activities, he was already showing the writing and editing skills which would take him to the top of his literary and critical profession in New York, where he wrote first for the *Herald Tribune* and then for the *Saturday Review of Literature*. His essays, and eventually his books, starting with *Stranger in the Earth*,[207] would draw wide attention, among them *Watch for the Morning*, which he

---

[207]Sugrue, Thomas, *Stranger in the Earth*, 1948. See also *A Catholic Speaks His Mind*, 1951.

wrote as an account of the new state of Israel, traveling there in a wheelchair to which he was confined in later years by arthritis.

Sugrue was centrally interested in the religious concepts in the readings, which he found refreshing after his Catholic upbringing, but also confirmative of aspects of his faith, such as the Virgin Birth and the Resurrection, as well as precepts that marriage vows should be observed with great seriousness and divorce undertaken only rarely. His avowed intention, as he later told me, was to secure Cayce's work and thought sufficient hearing to bring about reform and spiritual renewal for the larger church, not simply for Catholicism. He found the concept of reincarnation believable and useful, supported by his own dream and mystical experiences. As a lay person, he sought some way to set the Cayce concepts before thoughtful Christians, and settled on the device of ascribing to the readings the view (not exactly accurate) that Christianity could be understood as merely one of the mystery religions common to the Hellenistic period.[208] His intent was to loosen the dogmatic grip of the church he had grown up in, the hope he made clear in his earnest book *A Catholic Speaks His Mind,* in which Cayce's thought was not an important issue. His articulate questioning drew to him like-minded Catholics who shared his challenge to what they felt was rigid authority but also shared his deep love of Christ and the church. They became some of the American pioneers in the larger movement that found its fruition in the epochal reforming council of Vatican II years later.

By 1939, when he was in his early thirties, Sugrue was the victim of arthritis that left him bedridden. Living in Florida, he was married and out of money. Readings traced the causes to karma from Egypt and elsewhere

---

[208]Sugrue, Thomas, *There Is a River: The Story of Edgar Cayce,* 1942. "Philosophy," A.R.E. Press edition, p. 305.

but also spelled out treatment procedures which they indicated would markedly alleviate or remove the condition. The treatments were complex and demanding, requiring daily care that included lengthy massages. With the largeness of spirit that many (including myself) came to honor in Hugh Lynn, he insisted on bringing Sugrue to his home with his parents and undertaking that exhaustive care himself for two long years. The presence of Sugrue's discerning mind and aspiring spirit gave much to the entire family circle, even when it spilled over into his rage at his helpless condition. Cayce found in him the kind of leader he had prayed would be sent in the covenant he entered after the hospital disaster. And Sugrue undertook with immense commitment, given the physical limitations which required him to write in longhand while lying on his back, the task of a biography of Cayce, not as a promotional piece for Cayce's work (which Cayce did not want), but as a means for setting forth ideas and practices that seemed to Sugrue important for modern psychology, philosophy, and spirituality. He completed the book in two years, with Hugh Lynn often his collaborator, and found for it (not without the help of readings) a respected publisher, Henry Holt, which released the work in 1942. By then Sugrue had set out on a renewed New York career, walking and buoyant. His affliction would return in later years after Cayce's death, but his spirit and his graceful, penetrating prose did not flag.

His work on Cayce, written with high hope for a larger intellectual dialogue, received practically no public attention from theologians and scientists. However, it brought Cayce larger response in requests for readings than he had expected, and presented Edgar with the last great challenges of his life, completed by his exhaustion and death in less than three years from the book's publication. They were years of great joy for Edgar, as well as heroic activity and final engagement of what he saw as his complex karma. They were also years of deepened companionship with the one he called the Master, even in his own physical suffering where he found he could not do for himself what he had so often done for others since Layne had launched him into the unknown waters of somnambulism in Hopkinsville: defy death itself.

CHAPTER 17

Ask That the Life
of Cayce Be Spared

In the rush of publicity and the unending demands for help which flowed from publication of his biography, Cayce had to make decisions about the work of the little Association without the aid of his two sons. Hugh Lynn, recently married and delighted with his toddler son, Charles Thomas Taylor Cayce, had first been given deferment from military service as director of recreation for Virginia Beach, where he organized basketball teams of war-pressured workers and supervised the lifeguards. Then he was deferred to work with the U.S.O., which served the recreational needs of servicemen crowding the Virginia Beach area. Kahn, with his connections that reached to Eleanor Roosevelt, offered to try to secure him further postponement of military service. But a reading advised Hugh Lynn to go, as he felt he should, and he found himself before long in England, in charge of military recreation in his unit, then following General Patton across Europe. There he saw himself in a vision one day, in the midst of long-ago columns of the Crusades—the essential karma he felt he must meet in his wartime service.[209] Edgar Evans also was sent to military assignments, and Cayce turned to me to help him deal with the press of his work.

The war effort pushed us all.[210] Women did back-straining welding and construction in the Norfolk ship-

---

[209]Cayce, Hugh Lynn, *Venture Inward*, pp. 66–68.

[210]For a vivid account of daily life pressures in the period, see Terkel, Studs, *The Good War*, 1984.

yards, and industry everywhere worked on a schedule of a forty-eight-hour week or longer. Sixteen million new workers were recruited from the unemployed, youth, women, and the elderly. America's production of military hardware and supplies was widely seen as capable of tipping the balance to Allied victory. Gold stars for the dead appeared in more and more Virginia Beach windows; June and I knew well the Methodist households hit by the dread losses. Overseas, Mussolini had fallen from power, then been arrested, while half a million British and American troops had landed in Sicily and become stuck there. It was clear that sooner or later Il Duce's strident Fascism would end. Churchill, Roosevelt, and Chiang Kai Chek met at Cairo on their war aims, and there was hope in the air. One could see it in the way people walked, in the lowered crime rates, in the heightened drinking, in the love songs and marching songs, while all of us willingly cut back on rationed sugar, gasoline, and shoes, and rode in prewar autos or walked. Heroism in daily life was required of us all.

What Kind of Association?

Cayce felt the urgency, giving more readings per session than any of us had thought possible, and writing letters with two fingers on his portable until bedtime every night after a full day of dictation. He also took firm charge of the small but growing Association, shaping its programs and policies and refusing to commercialize any aspect of his work. I found out how serious his principles were when I did a cost study of the mimeographed booklets on various topics from the readings which we were selling at ten and twenty-five cents apiece. I took the figures into his study and showed him that the Association was losing about a quarter on each booklet. His response was to sell them at the low price anyway. We would get the money back in gifts or some other fashion, not from sufferers whose wartime budgets were al-

ready stretched. In keeping with his long church experience, he genuinely believed that God would provide as
long as we offered the best service we knew how. Eventually I went to Gertrude, and she finally persuaded him
to up the price a bit on a few, and only a few, of the
publications. When I developed a weekly newsletter of
interesting items from each week's readings,[211] sending it
to several hundred subscribers, he insisted that it cost
members only five dollars per year, including postage.

He would not allow me to undertake advertising or
mail solicitation to the many new inquirers. They got
the booklet about his life and work,[212] with its low-key
invitation to examine the Association's ideals and join if
they wished—nothing else. I kept pushing for research
funding, so I could engage cooperating physicians who
were not in the military, and get on with the indexing of
readings which our nurse volunteer had started for us.
Finally, when my mother and others joined in the
project, he agreed to let me write to a few longtime
friends, indicating that contributions would be welcome
to a Living Sponsorship for a research program. Several
thousand dollars came in, but he was unwilling to extend the effort.

Somewhere deep inside, he seemed convinced that
his ability was a gift of grace to him and others, not to be
marketed in typical American fashion. We could and
should prepare files of readings and selections on various topics for use by researchers who might inquire, but
not push these materials when they were not sought. I
kept probing the issue, wanting the means for recruiting
researchers to join me in sorting through the huge body
of unindexed transcripts in his files. But I listened with
great soberness when a reading taken on his work at the

---

[211]*This Week's Readings*, starting in January 1944, and later made
Weekly Reading Extracts, continuing through November 1947.

[212]Cayce, Edgar, *Edgar Cayce, His Life and Work*, 1943, partially reprinted
in *What I Believe*, 1946.

1944 Congress affirmed in strong language that we should not even "expose" his work of giving readings to those who did not of their own accord seek it out. Such a spirit of modesty and reticence was new to me as a social reformer who had always engaged in mailings, fund-raisers, picket lines, and news releases for good causes. But I took the warning seriously and tried to work with it in my own life during the years that followed.

He was not in the least concerned about the size of the Association, agreeing with the readings that numbers were not God's way. If we did our parts conscientiously and creatively, those persons would be drawn who could use it. I could glimpse some of what he meant by "drawn" when I studied the patterns in requests for readings. Not infrequently he would give a reading on a given day for a rare ailment, and we would discover that on precisely the same day one or more additional sufferers from the same obscure ailment also got their readings, as though scheduled by an unseen central bureau, even though the requests had come weeks apart from different points in the country, while Cayce was often unaware of their particular illnesses. What sort of far-ranging ESP or Providence might be involved in such grouping was difficult to imagine, but the process made it easier to understand his deep confidence that pushing to recruit numbers as such was not the nature of his work. Little incidents in the requests showed us an unseen network of good will supporting our efforts. A soldier stationed overseas wrote for a reading but could not remember where he had read about Cayce in a magazine article. The military censor passed his letter and then sent back to the soldier a copy of the article in question, my mother's piece in *Coronet:* the magazine published an account of the happy incident.

As he had throughout his life, except for the one advertisement in Birmingham, Cayce was content to let his efforts be reported among friends and relatives by word of mouth, even if it meant hardship for his family. That choice was not easy for someone who worried so much about having enough money. To be sure, he cooperated in Sugrue's biography, but as an effort to share what he felt was the love of God shown to him and to others, not as marketing strategy for his readings or to promote journalistic publications on them. I had only to witness a few occasions when he gave spontaneous readings in his trance (after completing those scheduled) for individuals whose emergency requests were not yet received, but came in a later mail, to understand his profound conviction that "our times are in God's hands." Whatever force for good jumped across time and space to save lives with his unconscious counsel could be expected to supply our needs without our forcing the flow.

To me it was tremendously heartening to see his determination not to let himself become the subject of a cult, so often the fate of a pioneering figure in religious circles. Familiar to all of us were the flamboyance of Aimee Semple McPherson, the West Coast evangelist, as well as the almost fanatical following of right–wing anti–Semites who held radio pulpits. Evidently there was something in the human heart which craved shortcuts, finding a way to God by attachment to a spiritual leader with prompt answers.[213] Cayce took up the question of cult one Saturday when he unrolled for me the plats of lots next door, which he had bought some time back. He would like, he told me, to gather friends to build a Christian Church there and have me as its minister. But he groaned and put the drawings away. People would misunderstand him as trying to foster a denomination, a sect, or even a Cayce cult. They should take on their own churches and synagogues, not a new religious grouping, and he should set the example. Others pressed him to build a modest lecture hall for conferences, in the same

---

[213]See the helpful and undogmatic analysis by Melton, J. Gordon and Moore, Robert L. in *The Cult Experience*, 1982. See also Woods, Richard, *The Occult Revolution*, 1971.

lots, and even started a building fund, but he did not
push it, determined not to provide any aid to cult dynamics.

It was not difficult to see the possibility of Cayce-ites
in the admiring attention of those who visited, wrote,
and came to the Congresses, as well as attended his lectures in other cities. Steinway Hall in New York was
jammed when he spoke in Manhattan in late 1943, repeating his lecture for an overflow crowd. His readings
combined high ethical and spiritual standards with just
enough novelty and drama to make his efforts a rallying
point for many, often those wounded by life and feeling
outsiders or anomic, as sociologists describe those invisibly alienated in modern times.[214] But readings were
sternly and repeatedly insistent that his work was not to
become a "sect, schism, or ism," allowing no appeal to
the strange nature of his counsel to validate it apart from
"application," the quiet testing by experience which each
interested person must undertake.

However, a few of those who came to his Bible classes
saw his readings as pronouncements from a modern
oracle rather than as the intimately dialogical acts of love
which in fact they were, and modeled their exchanges in
group settings on this base, making statements of solemn truths their expression of spirituality. It was natural
for them to aspire to the style of the awesome discourses
of a seer in their midst. Besides, centuries of pulpiteering
on the Bible had preceded them, and it was not surprising that they should simply lift from their churchly surroundings a pattern of quoting texts which they could
transfer directly to quoting readings. Cayce fought this
tendency, not only by refusing to cite readings as settling all controversies, but by the way he treated the
Bible, which was not for him a collection of pious self-
validated truths, but the record of real human beings

---

[214]Building on Durkheim's study of anomie in suicide. See
Riesman's effective use of the category in *The Lonely Crowd*, 1950.

trying to deepen their relationship with God in all the walks of life. Gertrude struggled against the cult tendency by incisive questions which blew away pretentious statements based loosely on readings in both class settings and in conversations. They both seemed to understand clearly that the hallmark of a cult or ism which they wanted to avoid was always private truth, and to take seriously the warning of the "information" that concepts from the readings should be presented "never on authority" of a special trance state.[215]

A Mountain About to Fall on Us

In the midst of global violence in 1944, we all struggled in our crowded little offices at the end of Cayce's home to be worthy of what was entrusted to us. People worked in every corner of the library, and two to a room around it, even in the storage room where the busy mimeograph was. We got on each other's nerves, and we barked at one another, though the two o'clock devotional time centered and united us for a while.

Those who got readings wrote back to us with endless questions on how to understand and use them. Others, waiting as long as two years for their appointments to come, pleaded for help in coping during the interval: what could we suggest for their pain, or where might we refer them? Visitors came to the door with great sores on their bodies, or the uncertain stares that followed brain

---

[215]See the important distinction between teachings presented in "communitas" and in "structure" by the anthropologist Victor Turner, who follows Buber in his analysis of "liminality," in *The Ritual Process*, 1969; there he presents cases studies of religious movements. See also, on authority claimed by religious groups, cults, and movements, Troeltsch, Ernst, *The Social Teachings of the Christian Churches*, 1981 ed., and Wach, Joachim, on sects in *Types of Religious Experience*, 1951. Note Maslow, Abraham, on the value of peak–experience knowledge, in *Religion, Values, and Peak Experiences*, 1964.

damage in combat, or shy confession that they had just been released from a mental hospital and wanted not to return. The combination of obvious need with the war-time drumbeat behind all our lives put each of us under pressure. Cayce was tired and sometimes short with those who sought to help him, including the Navy wives who could hardly grasp what he was doing. His critical comments and impulsive behavior were hardly consistent with what he taught in his Bible classes, and we dismissed his dark remarks as exhaustion or as the extravagance of expression which made him such a good storyteller.

All of us were trying hard to provide support, but in the backs of our minds was anxiety. These impossible readings, however laden with blessings, often seemed far beyond our comprehension. Each day brought some daunting challenge of swift outreach or strange concepts. And we seemed right on the edge of the overwhelming busyness which had led the trance gift to falter before. Would we precipitate such a crisis again? Cayce wrote to a friend his fear that we might be "smearing over" the essentials in readings, some now down to as little as five minutes from their usual forty-five. He felt my concerns, not made easier when the young woman married to a Navy flyer who shared a duplex with June and me came to us sobbing that her husband had just been killed overseas. Public and private pressures seemed to fuse for all of us. The day came when my needs and Cayce's to be in control of our respective efforts collided, and I learned something of how the collapse of the hospital had occurred, when idealistic coworkers fell apart.

In the monthly routine, I submitted my material for the *Bulletin* to him, since he monitored this closely, as he did so much else in the office, and asked that he give it to my secretary for stenciling, as usual. For some reason that I never fully grasped, perhaps just fatigue and oncoming illness, or perhaps what he might see as residues from Laodicea (where readings said I had been his son), he dropped it on my desk and ordered me to handle it:

"You type it! You wrote it!" I stared at him in outrage at what seemed to me hopeless arbitrariness, and then I flew at him to knock him down, shoving him fiercely and demanding with the poor sense that usually accompanies hot arguments, "Whom do you think you hired here?" He caught himself before he fell to the floor, and at once the heat between us was gone, though not the hurt. He went back to his office and called Mae in, asking, "Why did the boy do that?" I went on with my labors, tight-lipped, pounding out the stencil as required.

The next few days we were all stiff. It took me awhile to grasp how much his associates, including me, were inclined to expect of him. We always saw him with his voice and presence in readings just over his shoulder: infinitely fair, patient, helpful, yet able to be severe if needed. When he spoke harshly, it was like judgment from the gods. Who could be sure that he was not seeing some devastating flaw, some weakness of soul, from perspectives similar to those of his readings? But he had never heard himself speak in trance; he got the nobility and force only in dry transcripts. So when he felt like complaining or being bossy—and who does not?—he ran into what must have seemed incomprehensible touchiness in those around him. We saw a mountain about to fall on us. He merely felt a bit cantankerous, trying to get hold of the swirl of events. For the first time I thought I could recognize how Ketchum had ended up in lawsuits with him, and the Blumenthals had backed away so suddenly. The nature of a seer's calling threatened the very ties it brought into being.

Edgar fell ill almost at once with a virus or flu which ran a fever and left him coughing, robbed of his voice. All readings stopped. I felt hopelessly guilty but too unsure of myself to know what to say. After these many months of strenuous effort, was I to be the one whose excesses interrupted the whole process? Days went by, and a friend of ours from the Methodist Church, where June and I sang in the choir, heard of Cayce's illness and stopped at the back door with a pie. It was a simple neighborly gesture, and I was dumbfounded, sitting in the kitchen, to see Gertrude weeping after she thanked the woman for the gift and shut the door. Why? She told me that in all their years at Virginia Beach, no neighbor had ever brought them food as a gift of concern in the round of life's troubles. People did not feed a seer. They respected him; some even loved him. But pies and cakes were for ordinary folks, not for someone townspeople addressed as Dr. Cayce, uncertain what else to call him. Seeing the price of isolation she and Edgar had paid for their strange service, my heart melted, and I resolved to beg Cayce's forgiveness. But as though he read my mind, he appeared from upstairs in his bathrobe, still coughing and barely able to speak, to announce that he was going to New York for care by Dr. Reilly, and would be taking June and me with him. This proud man was bending very low to reach out to me, and I was grateful indeed.

The Time Must Be Used

Almost as soon as we got on the train, found our berths, and went to the dining car, he began to talk with us from his heart. His voice was scratchy and hoarse, but he was determined to communicate, as though the time must be used to the limit. For the next two weeks, throughout our entire trip and a series of visits to his friends in Manhattan, he kept up the generous flow, never pulling back into that absent space which so often bewildered those around him. I had my little notebook and drew him out at mealtimes, in elevators, in the hotel lobby, in taxis, during late-night snacks. But he needed little prompting. He seemed to want to share the shape of his entire life with us, going clear back to his childhood and his deep appreciation for his mother, through his mystical experiences, and on through each stage of his often uncertain journey. He enjoyed it—his voice grew a little stronger—and so did we. This time he was not entertaining us or holding us at arm's length, but unreservedly disclosing himself.

He told us tales that were outrageous and barely believable, then others that were simple and touching. He spoke of addressing a stranger on a Western street one day, calling him by name as a lark, just as the name occurred to him. The man nodded and went by, then came back puzzled and asked who Cayce was. They struck up an acquaintance and went to lunch in a fashionable restaurant. The man turned out to be a banker, and after hearing from Cayce something about his abilities, he dared him to write on a napkin the combination to the bank safe. Cayce promptly did, and they became friends for life. (I had seen the correspondence.)

He told of how he had drowned and been pronounced dead in his youth, and how the invisible playmates of his childhood had returned to him once as an adult. And he spoke with evident deep feeling about the day he sat alone in his office, wondering how he could ever finance the building of a vault in which to keep his filing cabinets of readings, when Jesus appeared, assuring him not to be afraid and telling him simply to write to those he had helped, stating his need. They would take care of it, he said, and of course they did but without knowing who had prompted the letter to them.

He told us about dogs he had loved, and his parrot and canaries, and the huge fish he had caught on ocean forays. He chuckled over the way he loved to read catalogs and to order from them trees for his garden, shirts, ties, tools, fishing lures; catalogs had been his delight since boyhood. He spoke of seeing the dead, seeing people in the garb of past lives, seeing the aura of a woman who would die that day in an auto accident if he didn't warn her (which he did, though she was a stranger, and found her life dramatically saved from the crash that followed). When I asked him about why he seemed never to read much except the Uniform Lesson material for each Sunday's church school class, he explained that it annoyed him to read a book in his later years, because he had only to start it and he knew the entire text, so that the fun went out of the reading.

He warned us that devoted women would come to the hotel, pressing to see him, and asked us to help protect him, as it turned out we needed to do. Yet one of these so touched him, with her gifts of flowers and cards and a book by Elbert Hubbard out of his earlier years, that he forced himself to go to the theater with her, despite his bodily weakness that made him perspire.

With obvious pleasure he took us to visit Reilly's impressive health facility in Manhattan offices, and left us there to interview him about cases while he got his treatments. He drew us into long conversations with Dave Kahn, to which I listened with fascination because Kahn had been in exactly my place when as a young man just my age he sought to help Cayce in another war. It was fun to watch them top each other with stories of current events in their lives. Cayce had learned that his biography was being considered for translation into Russian by a brother of Marshall Timoshenko, the general fighting with such bravery to drive back the Germans from Russian soil; everyone knew the general's name at the time. He told Kahn of the proposed Russian edition, and when asked who would do the translating, replied "Timoshenko," neglecting to specify which one. Kahn was briefly speechless for the first time in days, as he tried to picture the embattled Russian general finding time to work on the book at the Eastern front. Cayce kept a poker face but glanced at us. He loved dramatic effects, when they were called for.

My little notebook filled with items as the days went by. The stories yielded to thoughtful essays. With great patience he opened up his life and his convictions and guesses, addressing our questions about how he felt his past lives might have influenced the present one, and about the promises he felt he had made to God at different periods in his life. He shared his pain, as well, when a phone call home brought the totally unexpected news that his Presbyterian church had pushed him out of his

Sunday morning class after all his years of service. The
congregation was between pastors, and lay leaders, embarrassed at the publicity he had received since publication of his biography, voted him out, substituting an
attorney with the familiar oratory of such adult classes.
He told us he had taught Sunday school almost continuously for nearly sixty years and could not imagine his
life without the anchor of this activity. We could see his
grief, and it stabbed at us. Once more it was clear that
there was no sure place for this untimely seer in modern
America.

Yet he was not ignored, either. The New York trip
showed him welcomed by people of no small competence and station in life, as we met friends of the Kahns,
of Sugrue, and of the physicians who sent him their
cases. I was relieved. There were business executives,
editors, artists, and psychologists well informed on his
capacities and respectful of his spiritual stature. Most of
them saw Cayce's reincarnation material much as I did:
a surprising hypothesis worth investigating further. The
gap from my University of Chicago classrooms and his
sunny study in Virginia Beach was not the chasm I sometimes feared. Perhaps these friends in the mainstream of
intellectual and literary life would, when the war was
over, bring about the research which it was so frustrating to initiate and finance during wartime.

We knew well the Cayce of simple tastes, who could
be happy pounding nails in a railing to basement stairs,
wearing overalls. Yet here was the same Cayce as a man
of easy sophistication, an urbanite who gave orders to
waiters as though they had been born for just this opportunity, and beckoned cabs with crisp dispatch. He
seemed to require only a few moments to size up anyone he met. I could understand better why such a man
might want his little office staff to run exactly as he said,
whenever he said it. Had I not been told there was something like a Ra Ta in him, I might have had to make up
some such dynamic to get him into perspective.

Bow Thine Heads

Back home, he undertook his first reading in weeks, sought of course on his own health, because without that he could serve nobody. Work was stacked high. To catch up with the readings he had missed, he would have to undertake extra sessions on Saturdays and even Sundays. Perhaps he sensed that something serious might be coming, since he asked a number of us to join him for the trance counsel, and we squeezed into his sunny little study. His voice, ever vulnerable for forty years, was little more than a hoarse rasp. The reading began simply enough. Originally, he was told, he had developed an acid–alkaline imbalance, as poisons had been thrown into the lymph system "from anger produced by activities of environs about the body." I winced, remembering our fight.

There was now congestion in the soft tissue of the head, face, throat, bronchi, and even the lymph activity of the alimentary canal. Treatments were specified to rejuvenate and revivify the respiratory system, including regular walks in the open air, requiring breaks from work which I knew Cayce would find difficult to take. Consistency in his behavior was emphasized. "Don't preach, don't act in one direction, and then say or do those things in another direction."

I shrank in my chair, because it had been just such a problem that precipitated our quarrel. The reading offered no judgment between us but went quietly on, reinforcing changes Cayce had already begun by his generous reaching out to June and me on our trip. "Be patient with those who are weak. Be kind to those who are even ugly." I felt the hot flush of embarrassment in my face. "Be gentle with those activities wherein there is the necessity that ye live consistently, that ye be consistent with that ye would represent among thy fellow man."

The voice was so low that we had to strain to hear it as it took up the theme of the body as a temple where

the living God would meet us. "For know, the Lord is in
his holy temple. If thou hast, as his child, desecrated thy
temple in word, in act, in deed, know that ye alone may
make those corrections, and that thy body is the temple
of the living God." The counsel was objective and seemed
directed to all of us in the room. But it also became severe as the reading went on. "Act as though it were, and
not as if it were a pigpen or a place of garbage for the
activities of others." Here was scalding rebuke for our
dumping emotions on each other in the office staff. And
it was also a reminder of how difficult it was for Cayce to
call his thoughts and feelings his own when his constant
psychic pickup was at work. "Then keep thy body, thy
mind, wholly in an active service for thy Lord."

Suddenly and without warning there came from
Cayce a tremendous ringing voice, his own, yet full of
stern authority. It was the loudest speaking I had ever
heard, bouncing from the walls. *"Bow thine heads, ye children of men!"* We did. Gladys kept on writing by habit, but
the rest of us froze. *"For I, Michael, Lord of the Way, would
speak with thee. Ye generation of vipers, ye adulterous generation,
be warned! Today there is set before thee good and evil! Choose thou
whom ye will serve! Walk in the way of the Lord! Or else there will
come that sudden reckoning, as ye have seen!"* Nobody doubted
that the recent loss of Cayce's ability was the reference.
Again the voice demanded that we lower our gaze, yield
our pride. *"Bow thine heads, ye who are ungracious, unrepen-
tant! For the glory of the Lord is at hand! The opportunity is before
thee! Accept or reject! But don't be pigs!!"* The last was spat out
with utter disdain, echoing the warning not to wallow in
our emotions.

Then the voice on the couch dropped back to a near
whisper. Instructions were given to speed Cayce's recovery, closing with a quiet admonition: "Do keep the body
in that manner of activity as to eliminate the poisons.
And then keep the body–mind, the body physical, clean
in the sight of thy God." As the counsel ended, all of us
were weeping. I looked around at anguished, pale faces.
Nobody spoke. We each rose quickly to leave. Most of us

scattered out-of-doors in different directions. June and I
went to the ocean only a couple of blocks away, and
pushed along the sand against the mid-March wind.

It did not matter to me exactly who the voice had
been that called itself Michael. Whether a creation of
Cayce's biblically formed mind, a discarnate being dismayed at our behavior, an archetype of wisdom and
purity from the collective unconscious that was briefly
given form, or a genuine angelic presence, it had come
into our midst not to bring blessing or to honor us, but
to express burning rebuke. If this really were an archan-
gel, I never wanted to deal with one again. No special
claims were needed to connect that awesome voice with
our consciences, wounding us to our souls. We were
known. We were seen. We were found wanting.

The ocean waves slammed up beside us, and waves of
understanding began to break within me. I saw my ambition, and I did not like it. Having been a student forever and ever, I wanted to do something in the real world
and had crowded Cayce whenever he got in my way. I
saw my rebelliousness against authority, infusing some
part of my social causes, and knew that it went back to
the imperiousness of my often authoritarian Harmon
clan. I saw my emotional excesses and my critical tongue.
I saw my perfectionism as never before. It had required
Cayce to do things right and never falter as I garbed him
in the idolatry of my understanding of God. Finally I
saw my fear, fear of inadequacy. All my life I had been a
whiz kid, skipping years in school, getting merit scholar-
ships. Now I was into serious, grown-up business for
which I was ill-prepared. It would do me no good to
understand laws of open vision if I stayed frozen in im-
maturity.

As I stared down the miles of deserted beach, I
thought of Cayce's long journey and why there had been
so many failures. If each person who took on his readings with any sustained seriousness ran into the kind of
reality I had just found, it was no wonder things had
gone slowly. The unseen forces that prompted his read-

ings seemed intent on growing souls, not just demon-
strating marvels. But which of us really wanted such
uncompromising growth?

It was already late in the day, and little was said about
the painful reading until two the next afternoon, when
the entire staff gathered around the big library table.
Cayce read aloud of David weeping and prostrating himself as he pleaded with God for the life of his new son,
born from his adulterous and selfish relation with
Bathsheba. Attendants thought the king would be beside himself when the child finally died. But after the
death David arose and cleansed himself and ate, knowing that he could not undo the ending that had occurred.
Cayce closed the big Bible and spoke quietly of the sins
and shortcomings of us all. He took upon himself full
responsibility for the distress we had all been through in
recent weeks. Nobody, he said, had brought more excesses into the work with his readings than he had. But
like David, he could hope to learn from his mistakes, for
David was one of whom it was said that he sinned indeed, but did not repeat the same sins.

As David had done when his child died, we must pick
ourselves up, cleanse, and refresh ourselves, and get on
with helping those who sought our aid. None of us could
claim to be without flaw and sin. None of us was worthy
of the opportunities which God showered on us. Who
could deserve love? And love was what his readings
sought to enact. Who could claim a right to exceptional
knowledge, or trance skill, or guidance from on high? All
fell short, even as King David. But we did not have to
proceed on our merits, which would often be few. We
could throw ourselves on the mercy of the Lord, as David
had done, and expect to find help as he had.

Who was worthy, he asked again? Certainly not Cayce,
he responded, speaking objectively of himself with deep
feeling. Cayce and all of us were part of what we heard
called a wicked and adulterous generation, a generation
of war, bent on its own ends in a time of bitter conflicts.
But if we could help each other keep our best purposes

to the fore, yielding the lead to God, then we would be found helpful even in our weakness. That an awesome voice had come before us, even as Nathan the prophet had called David to account for Bathsheba, was not to exact perfection from us, for who could stand such a test? It was to keep us from getting in the way of ourselves, of one another, and above all of those who needed our aid. Such an unexpected encounter should show us that we did not have to proceed alone, but were always surrounded by a cloud of witnesses, with forces larger and more loving than we, some of whose loving would be stern. He closed with a prayer for forgiveness of us all, asking that the hand of the Lord be on us for the sake of those we sought to aid.

Once More the Riddle of the Body

Edgar never really recovered from his illness, as subsequent trance counseling for him pointed out, though he grew strong enough to give several hundred more readings through the spring and into the summer of 1944. He planned to take a break by going to visit Sugrue in Florida. But warmed by the spring sun, he plunged into his heavy schedule once more, determined to help those who sought his aid for medical problems. By now the Association had enough funds so that he could slow down, yet the spirit of the war effort all around him made that seem irresponsible. At a deeper level (it later seemed to me from comments he had made) he was asking one more question about the riddle of the body, which had engaged him so long in so many ways. He had photographed it from every angle to reveal its mystery and promise as God's dwelling in human flesh and as emblem of individual potential and strength for those who sought his portraits for decades. Back in Egypt he had reportedly set out to make a perfect body by select and careful joining of parents, but instead had fallen into the ways of willful passion. He had focused on healing the

flesh in lifetimes as Ra Ta and Uhjltd and now for forty
years as Cayce. Its secret dignity as carrier of the energies
of creation had tugged at him in ecstatic love affairs during life after life. But now he had a last question to address: how could one lay it down for others? He knew
that young men and women were offering their flesh all
over the world on opposite sides of the searing conflict.
He understood that his Master had done the same, for a
higher purpose. How could he do less? The same restless
hunger for life at its fullest which he felt had drawn him
into the wild explorations of Bainbridge now tugged him
into relentless service day after day. His readings counseled, "Rest, rest, rest," and he had once been told he
could live to be one hundred and four. But it was not his
nature to do things halfway.

The family hoped he might repeat the episodes of re-
juvenation which he had exhibited a few times when ill
in the past. Running a high fever and seriously ill, he
would cover himself in his bed and then turn to that
inner place where he went to give readings. Sweat would
pour from him for two hours, soaking the bed. He would
awaken with the fever gone and his body healed, though
weak. But he had not been able to do this when his system was thrown off by strong drugs, and in his haste to
recover from the current infections, he had taken a sulfa
miracle drug. Now he could not find his way to the inner
connection he wanted.

None of Us Suspected

Soon I received word from my draft board that I must
either take a pastoral post or return to school, and made
plans to leave him. My hope was that his sons would
return before long. None of us suspected how ill he really was. Weighing my alternatives, I decided not to return to the University of Chicago yet, although I was
committed eventually to write my doctoral thesis on
Cayce there. My head was still spinning with all I had

experienced, and I lacked sufficient categories and comparative data to stand my ground with professors who had already pronounced that what Cayce did was impossible. So I persuaded the draft board to let me go to Northfield, Minnesota, where I could serve a Methodist church as director of religious education and, at the same time, be a teaching assistant and continue my studies with a year of graduate work in sacred music at St. Olaf College.

Others might choose, after a year of intimate exposure to Cayce's work, to get training in yoga from a Hindu adept such as Yogananda,[216] or psychological training from Rhine and his colleagues. But for June and me there was only one way to go: straight toward that deeply biblical heritage of faith so crucial for Cayce, in which love and power might find their meeting. This Lutheran college, with its rich but not narrow piety and its world-famed choir, would give us forms to hold the flame of the Spirit that had burned so brightly before us. We could also draw on the prayer training of Glenn Clark[217] at Macalester College in St. Paul, whose widely read books had begun to mean much to us.

As we prepared to leave Virginia Beach, we could see the war beginning to wind down in Europe, and trusted that Hugh Lynn would soon be back from Germany. Volunteers agreed to take on the various publications that had been in my charge, and office people, now more seasoned, were to do the rest. June and I expected to return, though none of us guessed we would be back in a year to spend several months helping the little Association map out a destiny and financing without Cayce[218] (before I went back to campus as a teaching fellow at

---

[216]Yogananda, Paramhansa, *The Autobiography of a Yogi*, 1946. Arthur Ford studied with him after graduating from a Disciple seminary.

[217]Best known in his *I Will Lift Up Mine Eyes*, 1937. Clark was deeply responsive to Cayce's work and thought, as he often told me.

[218]See Bro, Harmon H., in *Venture Inward*, "A Spunky Woman Rescues A Foundering A.R.E.," May/June 1986, p. 25.

Harvard, then to the University of Chicago).

Prior to departing from Virginia Beach, I needed to coordinate the annual Congress held in June. To our surprise, given the wartime travel restrictions and gas rationing, some eighty-five people showed up for most of a week of lectures, a festive dinner with a speaker, and two readings for the entire group. They came from distances spanning the continent, including Portland, Maine, and Spokane, Washington. Cayce was in high spirits as he opened the conference with a rambling, warm talk to those jammed into his library. My mother spoke on a New Testament theme, as a former research assistant in Greek texts to Goodspeed of Chicago. A specialist in ancient Egypt presented material that shed light on the Ra Ta account, while a New York astrologer compared the approach in the readings to more traditional astrology, and a physician reported an his exciting pilot study of treating epilepsy with measures from the readings. When I got up to speak and to read Sugrue's brilliant poetic essay on the destiny of the soul, sent by him from Florida, I found the faces before me sensitive and responsive.

The Choices of the Nations

Toward the end of the event, it was time for the annual reading on a topic from public life. A committee decided to seek a discourse on the spirit and problems of the great nations. D-Day had just occurred in Europe, with Allied troops storming the Normandy beaches at great cost. Eventual victory over Hitler seemed likely, and all of us shared a common hope and yet soberness about the war and its aftermath. Each of us had questions, voiced or unvoiced, about what sort of world might be built upon the millions of deaths and devastated cities, not only of Europe but of Russia, North Africa, the South Pacific, and the Far East.

The reading that followed could have come straight

from a biblical prophet. In the fullness of his years, Cayce crossed, without hesitating, the line that separates a seer serving individuals from a prophet speaking to his people. He took up the character and destiny of nations, beginning and ending with his own, as incisively as medical readings spoke about infected organs and twisted limbs. Warning of selfishness, arrogance, and ignoring the needs of undeveloped peoples, he pointed once again to the principle of responsibility for fellow man being born afresh in Russia, not adequately expressed in Communism but destined to change the world if conducted in friendship with the United States.

He pleaded for a reawakening of faith in the Father God, and for dedication to the service of others, noting that in China we would find a rebirth of applied Christianity for our times. His trance counsel used caricature, observing that the American nation had put on its coin "In God we trust," but adding that we should ask ourselves whether that trust were just for the next dollar. Then the reading turned to other nations, describing the historic weaknesses and challenges of each: British class elitism, French self-indulgence, Italy's efforts to coerce faith, China's tradition-boundness, Russia's isolation, India's absorption in self-development. While the voice on the couch spoke, the guns were exploding shells at the nearby coastal artillery range. Cayce's speech was not as loud as the instruments of violence. But to those of us who heard it, his crisp and vigorous statements, crackling like a banner of the Eternal in the summer breeze, seemed the greater force.

No Cayce Cult

The next day it was time for a reading on Cayce's work and the Association. It was quickly evident from the content and sober tone that a turning point, for better or worse, was directly ahead in our joint efforts. Each member of the board, staff, and Association as a whole, we

were told, was to be asked to offer an earnest prayer
every day that "the work, the power, the might, which
may be that guiding force" would so direct the readings
as to bring to seekers "health, hope, a better understanding of the purpose of life." Then came a totally unexpected challenge to pray daily for Cayce himself, which
chilled me as I listened. "Ask that the life of Edgar Cayce
be spared to serve, to be the greater channel, that the
love of God in Christ-Jesus be manifested in the earth
not to the honor or glory of any individual but to the
glory and honor of God." It was extraordinary to have a
reading indicate that Cayce's life was threatened.

After suggesting how various programs might be
handled after my departure, the reading dealt sternly
with issues of promotion which had occupied me all
through the past year. "As has been indicated, first it must
come to the individual, then to groups, then to masses.
Do not ever attempt to convince, to impress, even to
'expose' the work to those who do not of themselves
seek same." Here the trance counsel departed firmly from
the American ethos which prescribed that anything
good, even the giving of readings, must be advertised
and all possible markets saturated. Instead the spirit of
this work should be a "shadow" or reflection of the patient, unpretentious spirit of the divine. "For God is God
of those who hate Him as well as of those who love Him.
He is patient, He is kind, He is merciful. Thus there
should be the same attitude, in the shadow at least, of
those who conduct the work of the Association." Nothing could be further from the temptations to a Cayce
cult in this public reading, which proved to be the last of
its type. Each of us should act in appreciation for what
we had discovered, and that would be enough. "So conduct thine own life as to show thy appreciation of that
which thou hast received. For he or she who neglects to
be thankful builds that which is condemning in the own
self." The counsel was in the spirit of deep humility which
had marked the study group book: "There is nothing
new here."

How Will You Make Him Follow It?

Then the reading dismayed us by turning directly to Cayce's health. "As to the activities of Edgar Cayce, remember, the physical strength is limited. There should be definite rest periods. *He* did! Are ye greater than he?" Such a comparison was bound to touch a nerve in Cayce. Next a surprising suggestion was given to make certain Cayce's welfare was protected. "Let the board, then, appoint one physically capable of judging according to health as to what the limits may be, guided also by the spirit of the Christ." They should find a "praying physician," though the search might not be easy. "How many will you find? There are such things!" But even as this careful procedure was stipulated, the reading seemed to recognize the proud independence of the man they had often described as a high priest and king. When a question was begun by Gertrude, "Outline a daily routine for Edgar Cayce to follow so that—" the entranced voice copying her interrupted with an abrupt question: "How will you make him follow it?"

Since we all felt the gravity of the counsel, we did not guess that the board, which had been essentially a well-meaning but rubberstamp operation, would fail to appoint such a physician, nor that Cayce would select for himself one who did not follow the counsel of the readings at a time when he grew desperately ill just weeks away. To the board, as to the rest of us, Cayce was a kind of shepherd, a guarantor to his flock. Of course we would pray for him. But he was like a parent to us all, and who really thinks of a parent as mortal? Besides, the readings would surely prevent anything unfortunate from happening to him. It was easy to forget that once he became seriously ill, even readings could not come to his aid.

He Stood Alone

June and I left on the Fourth of July. Gertrude came to

tears, and so did we. Cayce was glum. Soon we received letters and phone calls in Minnesota from Gladys and Gertrude, telling us that he was too ill to give readings. He took a brief trip to Florida to rest and see Sugrue, where he talked about retiring and perhaps giving readings on classes of ailments after all. But his heart was not in the plans. People were his passion, one at a time, and he wanted to help them as long as he could. Besides, with a cruel war still underway, who was he to stop trying? As before, when World War I hounded him in Selma to get out and build a hospital, and when the Depression smashed into his hospital backers, he was profoundly affected by his times, with the passionate love for God's world which came from the heart of his faith.

The events that quickly followed were as much social as personal. The social dimension was lack of supportive and guiding community for this unseasonable seer. His church, which had cut off his teaching service, gave him nothing. The medical profession with which he had so long collaborated did not take his need seriously; Cayce was a way to help others, not one who required aid. Association members were compassionate but busy. His sons were removed by society's war demands, as June and I were. He stood alone, stripped of support and direction, except for the devotion of Gertrude and Gladys, Mae, and his sister Annie.

When Annie first visited in July, just weeks after we left, he was too tired to go with her a few blocks to the sweeping view from the ocean boardwalk, though he did ask for an ice cream cone, such as they had shared in childhood. In mid-August he stopped giving readings for those whose appointments now ran far more than two years ahead of him. By September he was experiencing such trembling in his hands that he could not type letters, which troubled him greatly. He dictated when he could, swiftly as always (including a letter to me, mentioning that he was too ill to give readings, and reminding me that I was to do an extended booklet or book on how best to appreciate his kind of work, considering making it my doctoral thesis as well).

A reading taken on his health told him that his heart was greatly enlarged from poisons and stress, and that he must rest, but that he could still hope to give more readings. He should go away, "Until you are well or dead—one!"; the counsel was just that terse. Treatments were outlined. But whatever was like an old priest in him, weary and proud, wanted to pick his own doctor and did. He went to the mountains of Roanoke, several hundred miles west of Virginia Beach, to stay with Gertrude in a hotel. As Ra Ta had created turmoil which forced many into exile, he seemed now in an exile of his own, far from home and hope. The physician substituted treatments suggested by an English therapist for those stipulated in his readings as best as we could later determine. That he should be treated with well-meant but crippling chemicals provided a final social reflection of an age which put its faith in technology, not open vision. Cayce had a stroke and then another; his left side was paralyzed and he could only whisper. Finally he was brought home, weeping, in an ambulance at Thanksgiving; Edgar Evans was able to get a short military leave after long service overseas and go to him, finding him in misery and Gertrude panicked.

Back at home, he never gave another reading. He was in a coma much of the final two weeks. His lungs filled, and he died on January 3, 1945, of pulmonary edema— dying essentially by drowning, as his readings had told him long before that he had often done in other lifetimes. A few days earlier he had indicated with a weak smile to Mae, as to Gertrude and Gladys and his sister Annie, that his healing had been arranged and would occur on January 5, which proved to be his funeral day. Perhaps his death was indeed a healing, as his readings indicated dying might be for those who had suffered enough.

The final public news about him was simple, yet still freighted with the mystery of his lifework. The *New York Herald Tribune* noted his passing in a piece from Virginia Beach:

Edgar Cayce is Dead;
Mystic Diagnosed Ills

While in Trance, He Advised Patients on Ailments, Did Not Pretend to Heal

Edgar Cayce, widely publicized mystic who claimed the ability to diagnose from a hypnotic trance the ills of any person who communicated with him, died here today at his home . . .

A writer would ask help and Mr. Cayce, in return, would request the patient to inform the mystic where he would be at a given hour. The distance made no difference. At that hour Mr. Cayce would fall into a trance and dictate a diagnosis of the patient's ills, which Mrs. Cayce would take down. She would then ask questions and at the conclusion Mr. Cayce would emerge from his trance.

Did Not Pretend to Heal

He did not pretend to heal or tell the future. On the basis of his diagnosis he would tell the patient by mail to go to a doctor, surgeon, or at times an osteopath, and to advise the healer where the trouble was.

Mr. Sugrue said tonight that Mr. Cayce began to feel the effects of overwork in August of last year, and went into a trance to diagnose his own case. It indicated rest or death, and Mr. Cayce went to Roanoke, Va., for rest. Soon after he again diagnosed himself and dictated a 3,000 word report. Before doctors could begin to treat him, however, he suffered a stroke, and lost the ability to go into his trance. A second stroke brought about his death.

At the time of Mr. Cayce's death, Mr. Sugrue said, he was receiving letters pleading for help at the rate of 400 to 500 a day. Normally capable of two readings daily, he had increased them to eight.[219]

The manner of his end at sixty-seven mirrored his independent spirit. Dying was not essentially frightening for him. He felt he had been in touch with the departed since boyhood, and that as each reading began he passed through planes of consciousness peopled by those who had recently died. When his body wore out, he could walk up to the doorway of death and right through it. The same boldness, the same extravagance and generosity which had enabled him to give up consciousness for a small death into trance twice a day, taking his unique portraits, enabled him to embrace his own dying, when his struggle to serve in his own way, at his own dogged pace, dropped him at last. There was no Camelot of fellow seers to call him to further quests, wrestling with himself and others. He ended his journey as he had lived so much of it: admired by many, sought out for aid by many, but a man finally alone.

In the imagery of his often repeated dream of the golden cloth and the unseen partner, he had climbed an impossible mountain set before him by his strange gift. He had chopped footholds in the cliff and pulled up many behind him, though he had sometimes slipped and hurt himself and others. He had swept out his arm over what he saw as a huge vista of the human pilgrimage through the centuries. He had pointed to the high loveliness in which the human spirit might find its ultimate companionship, and called out formulas to help those in pain. Then he had collapsed, too weary to rise. On the night he died, those who stood beside his bed took note of the soaring flames of color in the sunset, filling the skies over the ocean and around them. They would remember it well when they learned in stunning contrast, only months later, of billowing mushroom

---

[219]*New York Herald Tribune*, January 4, 1945. Reprinted by permission.

clouds climbing mindlessly into the sky, the fruit of the
Manhattan Project.

Hopes Too Deep to Be Quenched

I stood before the St. Olaf Choir the morning after
Cayce's death with the telegram about his dying jammed
in my pocket. My task (as student assistant to the conductor, taking over whenever he was away) was to re-
hearse the tightly knit and disciplined group of fifty
singers for a coming trip to perform at the Mayo Clinic,
only miles from us across the frozen and snow-laden
Minnesota farmlands. There we would find, we were told,
not only the usual audience for our concerts, but aisles
crowded with wheelchairs and bandaged patients, most
of them severely wounded and amputated military personnel. For me, going to the clinic was to be an event of
wonder and hope, for I would see at last the kind of
hospital Cayce had envisioned, with specialists gathered
for all sorts of baffling ailments, working cooperatively.

I had the choir, with June among the first altos, pull
out from their folders the unaccompanied Russian anthem with the stately text: "Salvation is created in midst
of the earth." Haltingly I reminded the disciplined singers, planted upright and alert in their chairs, that salvation was not just a pious after-death state. It was health
and wholeness and creative freedom in holiness, both
personal and social right here among us. We ought to
sing at the clinic of a way prepared for each individual,
transmuting all our weaknesses and suffering with incredible patience. We ought to sing of a just Kingdom,
beyond the deliberate maiming and tearing of the flesh
still going on in battle arenas around the globe that
morning, filling up clinics and hospitals.

The choir could see that I meant deeply what I said,
and the room was very still. But then I could speak no
more. There was too much to say. Instead I lifted my
arms to conduct the second part of the anthem, where

the entire work was restated with just one word of praise and thanksgiving, "Alleluia," repeated again and again in song. The ancient cry in a single word carried more than any explanation or proclamation, telling of hopes too deep to be quenched, and mysteries of goodness let loose in the human family which we could not name. The rich, low tugging of resonant male voices began. The women's voices picked up the same subdued figure and then leaped to a high note like a tongue of fire, affirming with the ringing tones of the entire choir that something of moment still goes on in the earth, and that the glory from ancient times has not departed from our midst. Something, Someone, the song seemed to promise as its full-voiced chords dropped to a hushed murmur, has to do with each of us and will not give up.

CHRONOLOGY OF THE LIFE
OF EDGAR CAYCE

Year	Edgar Cayce's Age	
1877	Birth	Edgar Cayce born on farm near Hopkinsville, Ky., March 18.
1887	10	Starts as a country church sexton, Old Liberty Church.
1890	13	Vision, followed by incident of spelling book clairvoyance next evening.
1892	15	Baseball injury incident: dictates strange items while in state of shock. Quits school at end of eighth grade, goes to work on relative's farm.
1893	16	Family moves to Hopkinsville from country. Edgar Cayce works in Hopper's Bookstore and then in Richard's Dry Goods Store, shoe department.
1895	18	Meets Dwight L. Moody, finally gives up plans to become a minister.
1897	20	Proposes to Gertrude Evans.
1898	21	Moves to Louisville, Ky., works in J.P. Morton Bookstore.
1900	23	Starts out from Hopkinsville in new job as traveling salesman and insurance agent for father; becomes ill, loses voice and returns to Hopkinsville.
1901	24	First psychic reading, March 31: recovers voice. Gives readings for patients of Al C. Layne. Works as photographer's apprentice to Mr. Bowles, Hopkinsville.
1902	25	Moves to Bowling Green, Ky., with job in Potter's Bookstore, May. Gives readings in dramatic Dietrich case at home.

Year	Edgar Cayce's Age	
1903	26	Marries Gertrude Evans, June 17, settling in Bowling Green.
1906	29	Has acquired through a partnership two photographic studios which burn down in November and December, leaving him in debt. Incident with physicians harming him, and giving of readings on races, ends experimental and entertainment readings.
1907	30	Son Hugh Lynn born, March 16.
1909	32	Pays off studio debts in Bowling Green. Goes alone to Alabama, works as traveling photographer for H.P. Tressler Co.
1910	33	*N.Y. Times* article on Edgar Cayce, October 9, followed by much publicity. He moves home to Hopkinsville, in partnership there with Dr. Ketchum and Mr. Noe to give readings daily for first time, as Psychic Diagnostician.
1911	34	Ten day trip to Chicago to give readings for *Chicago Examiner*. Second child born and dies. Wife ill with tuberculosis and readings save her from apparent death, convincing Edgar Cayce of their value. Investigation by Dr. Hugo Münsterberg of Harvard Univ.
1912	35	Quits Ketchum and Noe partnership, moving to Selma, Ala., to give up readings and open photography studio for Tressler Co. Soon buys out studio.
1913	36	Wife and son come to Selma in spring.
1914	37	Six–year–old son injures eyes, January, but readings achieve recovery and

Year	Edgar Cayce's Age	
		prove their value. Edgar Cayce has appendectomy.
1915	38	Edgar Cayce meets David Kahn in Lexington, Ky., in August.
1918	41	Son Edgar Evans born, February 9.
1920	43	First trip to N.Y. and Texas with Kahn on oil well hopes; start of Cayce Petroleum Company.
1922	45	Oil boring fails, leases sold. Cayce goes to Columbus to see Mohr about hospital, then to Denver, then to Birmingham, Ala., Oct. 4, for lectures and readings.
1923	46	After trips from Birmingham to Texas, New York, Pittsburgh, Chicago, Kansas City, and Dayton, gets family from Hopkinsville and decides to return to Selma to give readings as life work. Secures Gladys Davis as secretary, September 10. Gives up thriving Selma studio to move family to Dayton, Ohio, with Arthur Lammers, and to give readings on the mind and soul as well as on illness. First life readings, information on reincarnation. First dream readings.
1924	47	Interest shown by Tim Brown, M.B. Wyrick, Morton Blumenthal.
1925	48	Blumenthal arranges for family to move, September 16, to Virginia Beach, where readings say hospital can be built.
1926	49	Mrs. Leslie Cayce, Edgar Cayce's mother, dies on October 26. Son Hugh Lynn starts in college.

Year	Edgar Cayce's Age	
1927	50	Association of National Investigators is incorporated on May 6. Leslie Cayce, Edgar Cayce's father, comes to Virginia Beach.
1928	51	Dr. Wm. M. Brown, psychology professor at Washington & Lee University, visits first time. Dr. and Mrs. House come to run hospital. Cayce Hospital opened, November 11.
1929	52	Dr. House dies, October.
1930	53	Dr. Lydic, osteopath, comes to head hospital staff, January; also Miss Annie Cayce, sister of Edgar Cayce, as housekeeper. Magazine, *The New Tomorrow*, is begun in April. Atlantic University opens, Dr. Brown as president, autumn. Hospital returned to Blumenthal, September 16.
1931	54	Association discontinued, hospital closed, February. Meeting to found new association, June 6; incorporation of Association for Research and Enlightenment, July. Cayces move to house across from closed hospital. Trip to New York, October, with Edgar Cayce arrested, November 7. First study group begun, September 14, with lessons which develop into *A Search for God*.
1932	55	Atlantic University closed at mid-year. Cayces move to Shore Drive in March, then to house on Arctic Crescent in May. Bulletin started, September. First Congress, June.

Year	Edgar Cayce's Age	
1935	58	Edgar Evans goes to Duke University. Mrs. Evans, mother of Gertrude Cayce, dies. Health Home Remedies Co. is started to handle products of readings; fails. Detroit arrest.
1936	59	Contacts with parapsychologists: Dr. Rhine, Dr. Murphy. Dr. Lucien Warner visits Virginia Beach.
1937	60	Leslie Cayce dies, April 11, on trip away from Virginia Beach.
1939	62	Thomas Sugrue comes to live with Cayces, ill; writes *Such Is the Kingdom* and works on biography of Edgar Cayce; stays until 1941.
1940	63	Office unit added to Cayce residence, September 29.
1942	65	*A Search for God* published by No. 1 Study Group of Norfolk, VA., after eleven years of work.
1943	66	*There Is a River*, biography of Edgar Cayce, published in March. Hugh Lynn enters Army, April, 1943. *Coronet* article, "Miracle Man of Virginia Beach," published in September
1944	67	*This Week's Readings*, weekly sheet of extracts, started on January 5. Last reading given by Edgar Cayce, September 17; far more than 14,500 readings had been given in his lifetime. Stroke and final illness of Edgar Cayce.
1945	67	Death of Edgar Cayce, January 3. Death of Gertrude Cayce, April 1.

Selected Bibliography
Primary Sources and Firsthand Accounts

Association for Research and Enlightenment. *Edgar Cayce Library Series.* Vols. 1, *Life and Death,* 1973; 2, *Meditation,* Part I, 1974; 3, *Meditation,* Part II, 1975; 4, *Dreams and Dreaming,* Part I, 1976; 5, *Dreams and Dreaming,* Part II, 1976; 6, *Early Christian Epoch,* 1976; 7, *The Study Group Readings,* 1977; 8, *Psychic Development,* 1978; 9, *Psychic Awareness,* 1979; 10, *Jesus, the Pattern,* 1980; 11, *Christ Consciousness,* 1980; 12, *Daily Living,* 1981; 13, *Attitudes and Emotions,* Part I, 1981; 14, *Attitudes and Emotions,* Part 11, 1982; 15, *Attitudes and Emotions,* Part III, 1982; 16, *Expanded Search for God,* Part 1, 1983; 17, *Expanded Search for God,* Part II, 1983; 18, *Astrology,* Part 1,1985; 19, *Astrology,* Part II, 1985; 20, *Mind,* 1986; 21, *Soul Development,* 1986; 22, *Atlantis,* 1987. Virginia Beach, Va.: A.R.E. Press.

Bro, Harmon H. *The Charisma of the Seer: A Study in the Phenomenology of Religious Leadership.* University of Chicago Libraries, unpublished doctoral dissertation, 1955.

Bro, Harmon H. *Edgar Cayce on Religion and Psychic Experience. New York: Constellation, 1970.*

Bro, Harmon H. with June Avis Bro, *Growing through Personal Crisis.* San Francisco: Harper and Row, 1988.

Carter, Mary Ellen, with Gladys Davis Turner. *My Years with Edgar Cayce.* New York: Harper and Row, 1971.

Cayce, Edgar. *Edgar Cayce: His Life and Work.* Virginia Beach, Va.: Association for Research and Enlightenment, 1943.

Cayce, Edgar. *What I Believe.* Virginia Beach, Va.: ARE Press, 1976 ed.

Cayce, Edgar Evans, and Hugh Lynn Cayce. *The Outer Limits of Edgar Cayce's Power.* New York: Harper and Row, 1971.

Cayce, Hugh Lynn. *Venture Inward.* New York: Harper and Row, 1964.

Kahn, David. *My Life with Edgar Cayce.* New York: Doubleday, 1970.

Ketchum, Wesley H. *The Discovery of Edgar Cayce.* Virginia Beach, Va.: A.R.E. Press, 1964.

Leary, David M. *Edgar Cayce's Photographic Legacy.* New York: Doubleday, 1978.

Sugrue, Thomas. *Stranger in the Earth.* New York: Paperback Library, 1971.

Sugrue, Thomas. *There Is a River: The Story of Edgar Cayce.* New York: Henry Holt, 1942.

Secondary Sources

Venture Inward, now published quarterly for members only, by the Association for Research and Enlightenment, Inc., Virginia Beach, Va., starting with vol. I, no. 1, September/October 1984. (Predecessors to this periodical were *The New Tomorrow,* starting in April 1930, and then the *Bulletin,* starting in September 1932, which became the *Searchlight,* beginning in November 1950, and the quarterly *A.R.E. Journal,* beginning in January 1966.)

A.R.E. Readings Research Dept. *A Closer Walk.* Virginia Beach, Va.: A.R.E. Press, 1974.

Anonymous. *A Search for God,* Books I, II. Virginia Beach, Va.: A.R.E. Press, 1942, 1946.

Bro, Harmon H. *Begin a New Life.* New York: Harper and Row, 1971.

Bro, Harmon H. *Dreams in the Life of Prayer.* New York: Harper and Row, 1970. (Revised as *Dreams in the Life of Prayer and Meditation.* Virginia Beach, Va.: Inner Vision, 1985.)

Bro, Harmon H. *Edgar Cayce on Dreams.* New York: Warner, 1970.

Bro, Harmon H. *High Play.* New York: Coward McCann Geoghegan, 1970.

Cayce, Edgar and Thomas Sugrue. *Auras*. Virginia Beach, Va.: A.R.E. Press, 1945.

Cayce, Edgar Evans. *Edgar Cayce on Atlantis*. New York: Paperback Library, 1971.

Cayce, Hugh Lynn and Thomas Sugrue. *Times of Crisis* (formerly *Am I My Brother's Keeper?*). Virginia Beach, Va.: A.R.E. Press, 1945.

Cayce, Hugh Lynn. *Faces of Fear*. New York: Harper & Row, 1980.

Cayce, Hugh Lynn. *The Jesus I Remember*. Virginia Beach, Va.: A.R.E. Press, 1984.

Cerminara, Gina. *Many Lives, Many Loves*. Marina del Rey, Cal.: DeVorss, 1981.

Cerminara, Gina. *Many Mansions*. New York: New American Library, 1967.

Cerminara, Gina. *The World Within*. Virginia Beach, Va.: A.R.E. Press, 1985 ed.

Church, W.H. *Many Happy Returns*. San Francisco: Harper & Row, 1984.

Drummond, Richard. *Unto the Churches*. Virginia Beach, Va.: A.R.E. Press, 1978.

Eddy, Sherwood. *You Will Survive after Death*. New York: Rinehart, 1950.

Karp, Reba Ann. *Edgar Cayce Encyclopedia of Healing*. New York: Warner, 1986.

Kittler, Glen D. *Edgar Cayce on the Dead Sea Scrolls*. New York: Paperback Library, 1970.

LaCroix, Mary. *Sons of Darkness, Sons of Light*. Virginia Beach, Va.: A.R.E. Press, 1987.

LaCroix, Mary. *The Remnant*. New York: Avon, 1981.

Lehner, Mark. *The Egyptian Heritage*. Virginia Beach, Va.: ARE Press, 1984.

McGarey, William. *The Edgar Cayce Remedies*. New York: Bantam, 1983.

McGarey, William and Gladys McGarey. *There Will Your Heart Be Also*. New York: Warner, 1976.

McGarey, William. *Edgar Cayce's Medicine for Today*. San Francisco: Harper and Row, 1988.

McGarey, William. *Edgar Cayce and the Palma Christi*. Virginia Beach, Va.: A.R.E. Press, 1970.

Millard, Joseph. *Edgar Cayce: Man of Miracles*. London: Neville Spearman, 1961.

Puryear, Herbert B. and Mark A. Thurston. *Meditation and the Mind of Man*. Virginia Beach, Va.: A.R.E. Press, 1978.

Puryear, Herbert B. *The Edgar Cayce Primer*. New York: Bantam, 1982.

Puryear, Meredith Ann. *Healing Through Meditation and Prayer*. Virginia Beach, Va.: A.R.E. Press, 1978.

Redd, Ry. *Toward a New Astrology*. Virginia Beach, Va.: Inner Vision, 1985.

Reed, Henry. *Awakening Your Psychic Powers*. San Francisco: Harper & Row, 1988.

Reilly, Harold. *The Edgar Cayce Handbook for Health through Drugless Therapy*. New York: Berkley, 1985.

Runnels, Rachel. *Marriage and the Home*. Virginia Beach, Va.: A.R.E. Press, 1973.

Sechrist, Elsie. *Dreams, Your Magic Mirror*. New York: Cowles, 1968.

Stearn, Jess. *A Prophet in His Own Country*. New York: Ballantine, 1974.

Stearn, Jess. *Edgar Cayce, The Sleeping Prophet*. New York: Doubleday, 1967.

Thurston, Mark A. *Discovering Your Soul's Purpose*. Virginia Beach, Va.: A.R.E. Press, 1984.

Thurston, Mark A. *Dreams: Tonight's Answers for Tomorrow's Questions*. San Francisco: Harper & Row, 1988.

Thurston, Mark A. *Experiments in Practical Spirituality*. *Virginia Beach, Va.: A.R.E. Press, 1980.*

Thurston, Mark A. *Experiments in a Search for God.* Virginia Beach, Va.: A.R.E. Press, 1976.

Thurston, Mark A. *How to Interpret Your Dreams.* Virginia Beach, Va.: A.R.E. Press, 1978.

Thurston, Mark A. *Paradox of Power.* Virginia Beach, Va.: A.R.E. Press, 1987.

Thurston, Mark A. *The Inner Power of Silence.* Virginia Beach, Va.: Inner Vision, 1987.

Thurston, Mark A. *Understand and Develop Your ESP.* Virginia Beach, Va.: A.R.E. Press, 1981.

Thurston, Mark A. *Visions and Prophecies for a New Age.* Virginia Beach, Va.: A.R.E. Press, 1981.

Index

of, 214; in dreams, 217–222; of the soul, 214

There Is a River: The Story of Edgar Cayce, 1, 122

Trance process, Edgar Cayce's: absent from body, 73; accuracy, 143; answering unposed questions, 7–58; asides, 45, 58; Bible study and, 204; birth details, 58; bonus material, 197; like Cayce awake, 64; Cayce's health and, 204; daily variations in form and content, 197; dangers to Cayce, 42, 65; developed in past lives, 262; discarnates, 67; 'dying' daily, 42; end of trance, 70; entry into, 67; errors, 6, 66, 121, 382, 420; evaluation of, 122; fatigue, 65; first reading on self, 316; following light, 67; foreign languages, 78, 366; headaches in, 65; humor in, 201; hypnotic state, 42, 62; individualized counsel, 74–78; length of, 60; locator ability, 57–58, 65, 118; manner of speech, 63, 68–71; meeting of love and power, 74–80; peripheral awareness, 60; prayer and, 67, 200–204; predictions, 407–409, 448–452; price of, 5; procedures, 66–67; questions in, 55; range of targets, 56; reference to prior readings, 144; relationship with God in, 64; responses of recipients, 79; selectivity, 77; service and, 76; shortest reading, 61; simplicity of, 44; spelling corrected, 59; studio description, 138; successors to, 43, 180; suggestions and directions in, 42, 58, 68, 249; values in, 59; variables affecting trance, 198; "the information," 61; theories and models, 75; what not said, 77; why trance, 202

Transylvania University, 15

Tschesnokoff, 24

U

Uhjltd, 278–279

University of Chicago, 1, 9–13, 480

University of Chicago Divinity School, 12

V

Vatican, Second Council of, 459

Verhoeven, Mae (St. Clair), 262, 436, 440; past lives, 274, 440

Virginia Beach, VA, in wartime, 25

Vows, 88

W

Wach, Joachim, 130

Walgreen, Myrtle, 13

Wallace, Henry, 453

War and peace (see World I, II), 7

Warner, Lucien, 10, 136, 447

Wesley, John

White House, 129, 367

Will, 97, 238

Wilson, Woodrow, and Edith, 367

Windsor, Duke and Duchess of, 180

Wisdom, 53, 74, 233

Woodmen of the World, 361

World Religions, study of, 8, 124

World War I, 367–368

World War II: deaths in, 17, 25;

EDGAR CAYCE'S A.R.E.

What Is A.R.E.?

The Association for Research and Enlightenment, Inc., (A.R.E.®) was founded in 1931 to research and make available information on psychic development, dreams, holistic health, meditation, and life after death. As an open-membership research organization, the A.R.E. continues to study and publish such information, to initiate research, and to promote conferences, distance learning, and regional events. Edgar Cayce, the most documented psychic of our time, was the moving force in the establishment of A.R.E.

Who Was Edgar Cayce?

Edgar Cayce (1877-1945) was born on a farm near Hopkinsville, Ky. He was an average individual in most respects. Yet, throughout his life, he manifested one of the most remarkable psychic talents of all time. As a young man, he found that he was able to enter into a self-induced trance state, which enabled him to place his mind in contact with an unlimited source of information. While asleep, he could answer questions or give accurate discourses on any topic. These discourses, more than 14,000 in number, were transcribed as he spoke and are called "readings."

Given the name and location of an individual anywhere in the world, he could correctly describe a person's condition and outline a regimen of treatment. The consistent accuracy of his diagnoses and the effectiveness of the treatments he prescribed made him a medical phenomenon, and he came to be called the "father of holistic medicine."

Eventually, the scope of Cayce's readings expanded to include such subjects as world religions, philosophy, psychology, parapsychology, dreams, history, the missing years of Jesus, ancient civilizations, soul growth, psychic development, prophecy, and reincarnation.

A.R.E. Membership

People from all walks of life have discovered meaningful and life-transforming insights through membership in A.R.E. To learn more about Edgar Cayce's A.R.E. and how membership in the A.R.E. can enhance your life, visit our Web site at EdgarCayce.org, or call us toll-free at 800-333-4499.

Edgar Cayce's A.R.E.
215 67th Street
Virginia Beach, VA 23451-2061

EDGARCAYCE.ORG